S EATER

12

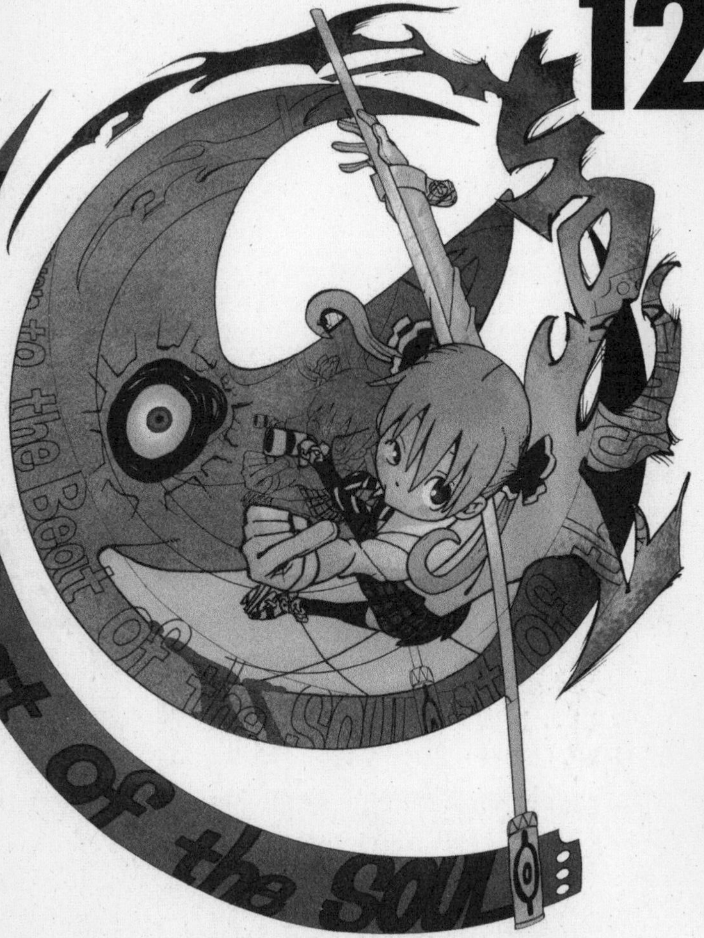
to the Beat of the Soul

ATSUSHI OHKUBO

Mask : Disguise : Visor

SOUL EATER

vol. 12

by ATSUSHI OHKUBO

SOULS, yet hidden, quite obscure.

SOUL EATER 12

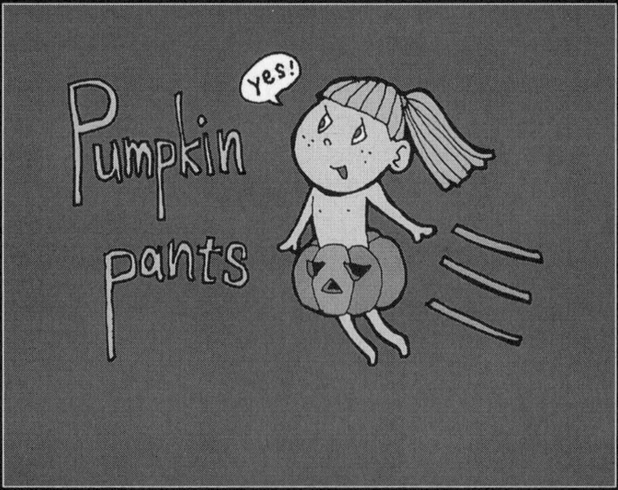
Pumpkin pants
yes!

CONTENTS

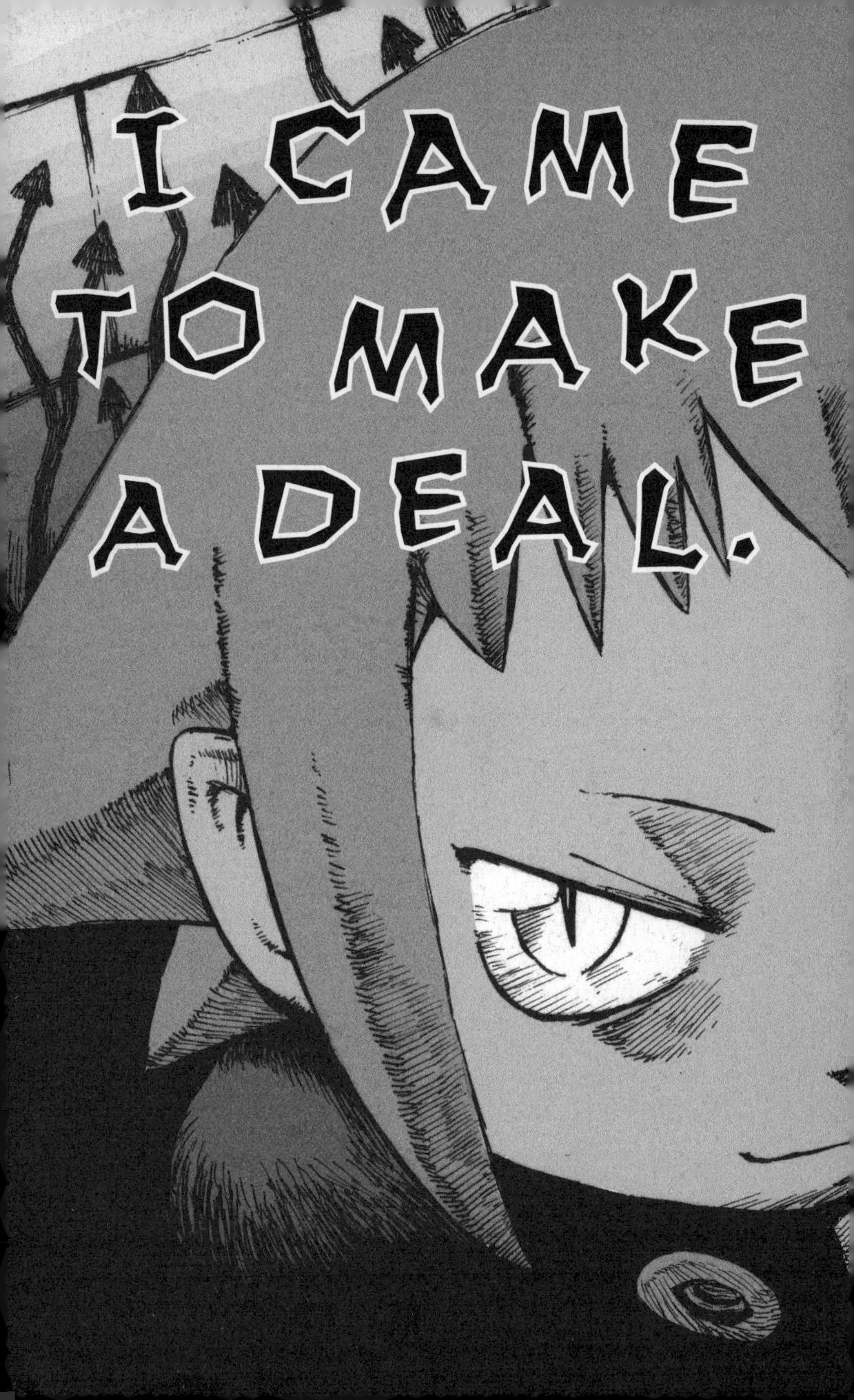
I CAME TO MAKE A DEAL.

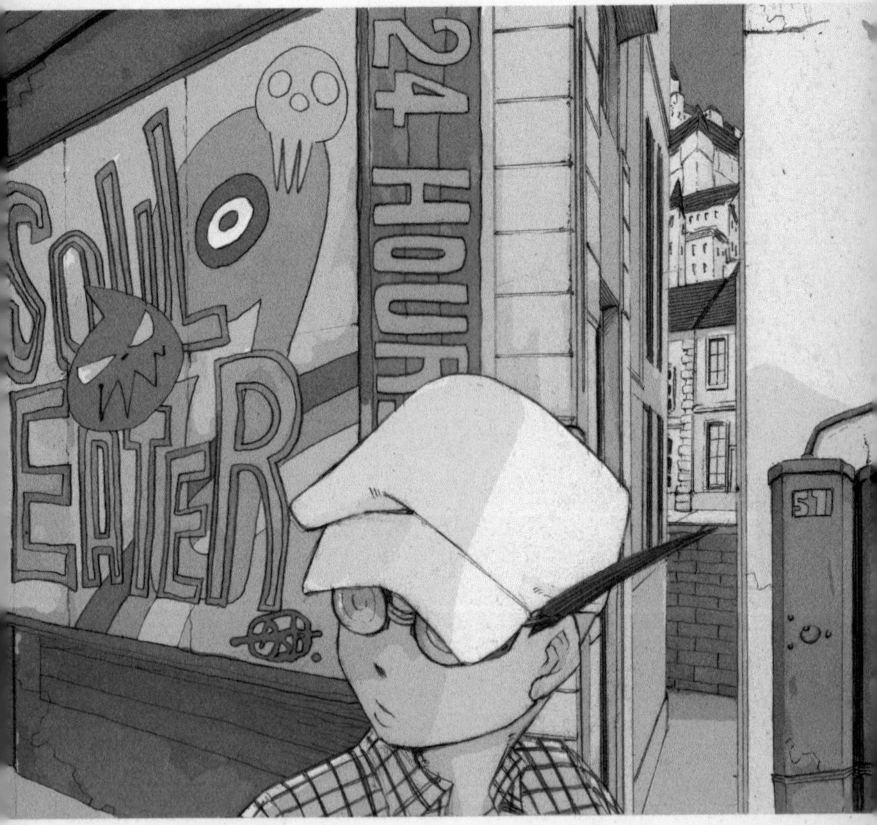
SOUL EATER
24 HOUR
51

SOUL EATER

CHAPTER 45: THE DEAL

SIGN: LIVE OR DIE?

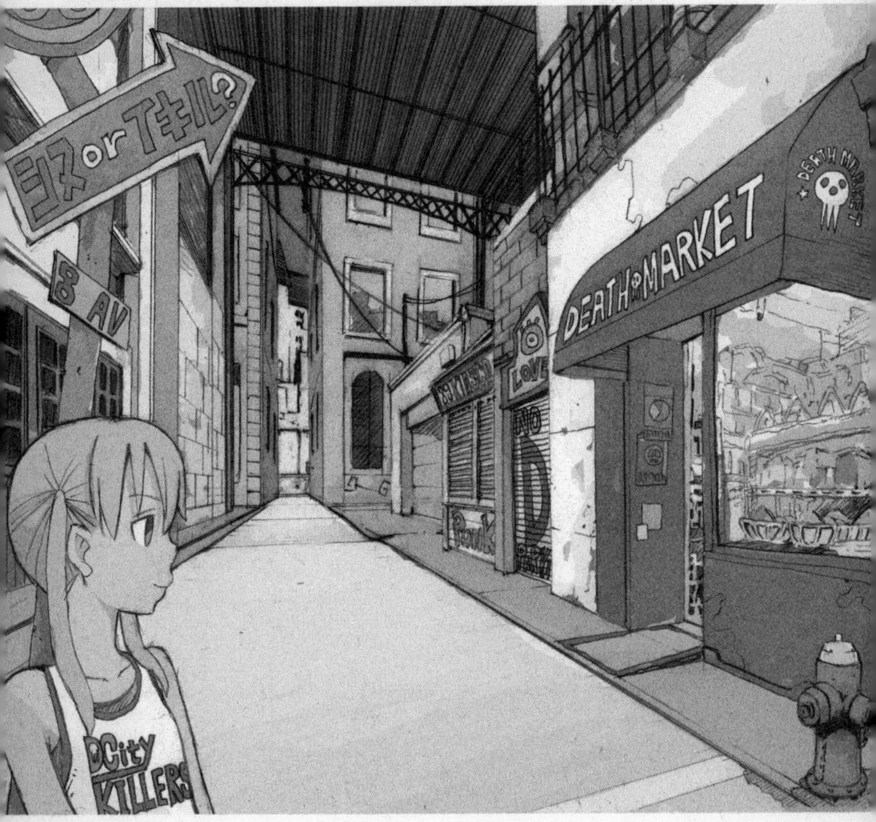
8 AV
DEATH MARKET
DEATH MARKET
LOVE
DCity KILLERS

SOUL EATER

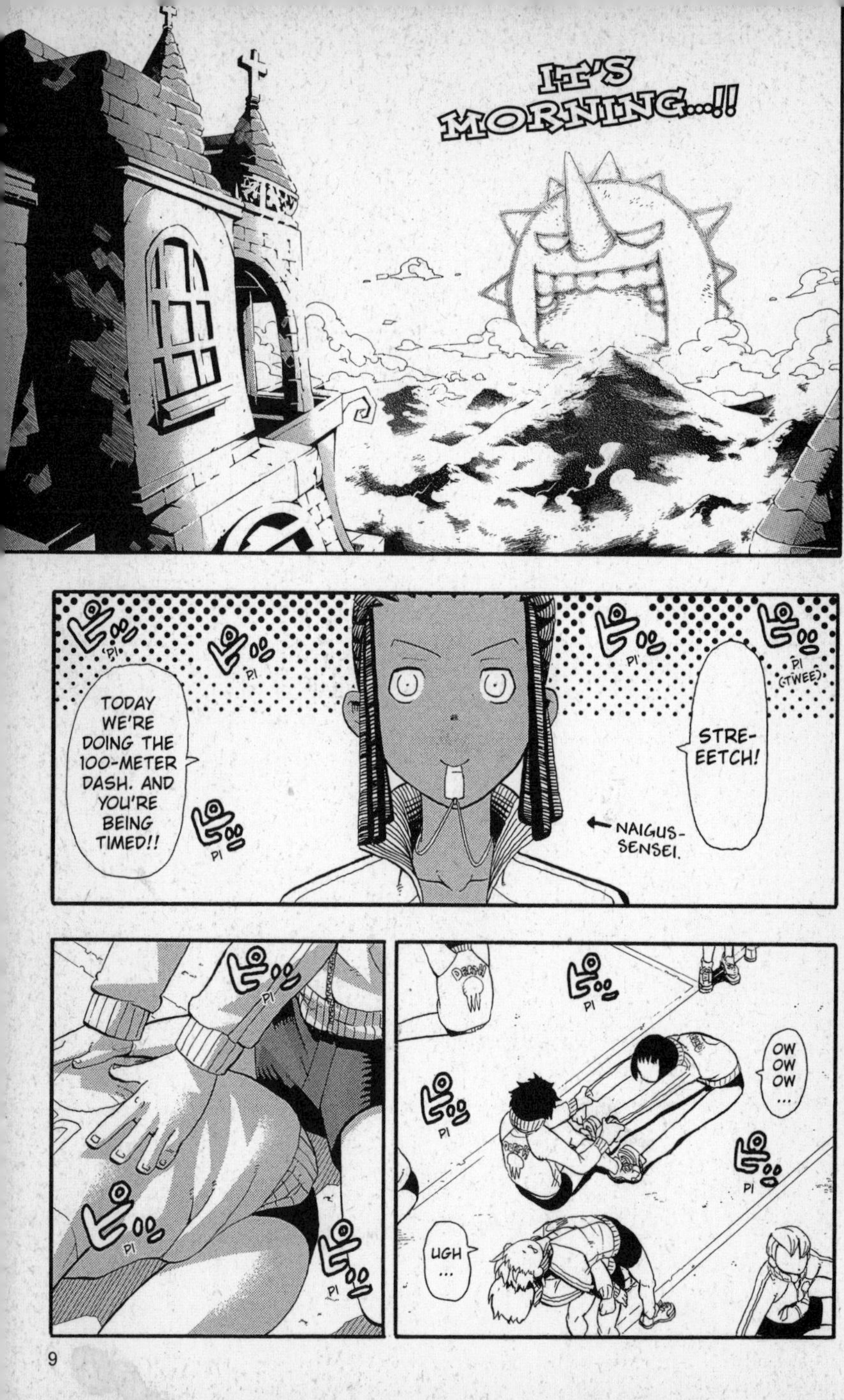
IT'S MORNING...!!
PI (TWEE)
STREE-EETCH!
PI
PI
PI
NAIGUS-SENSEI.
TODAY WE'RE DOING THE 100-METER DASH. AND YOU'RE BEING TIMED!!
PI
PI
OW OW OW ...
PI
PI
UGH ...
PI
PI
PI

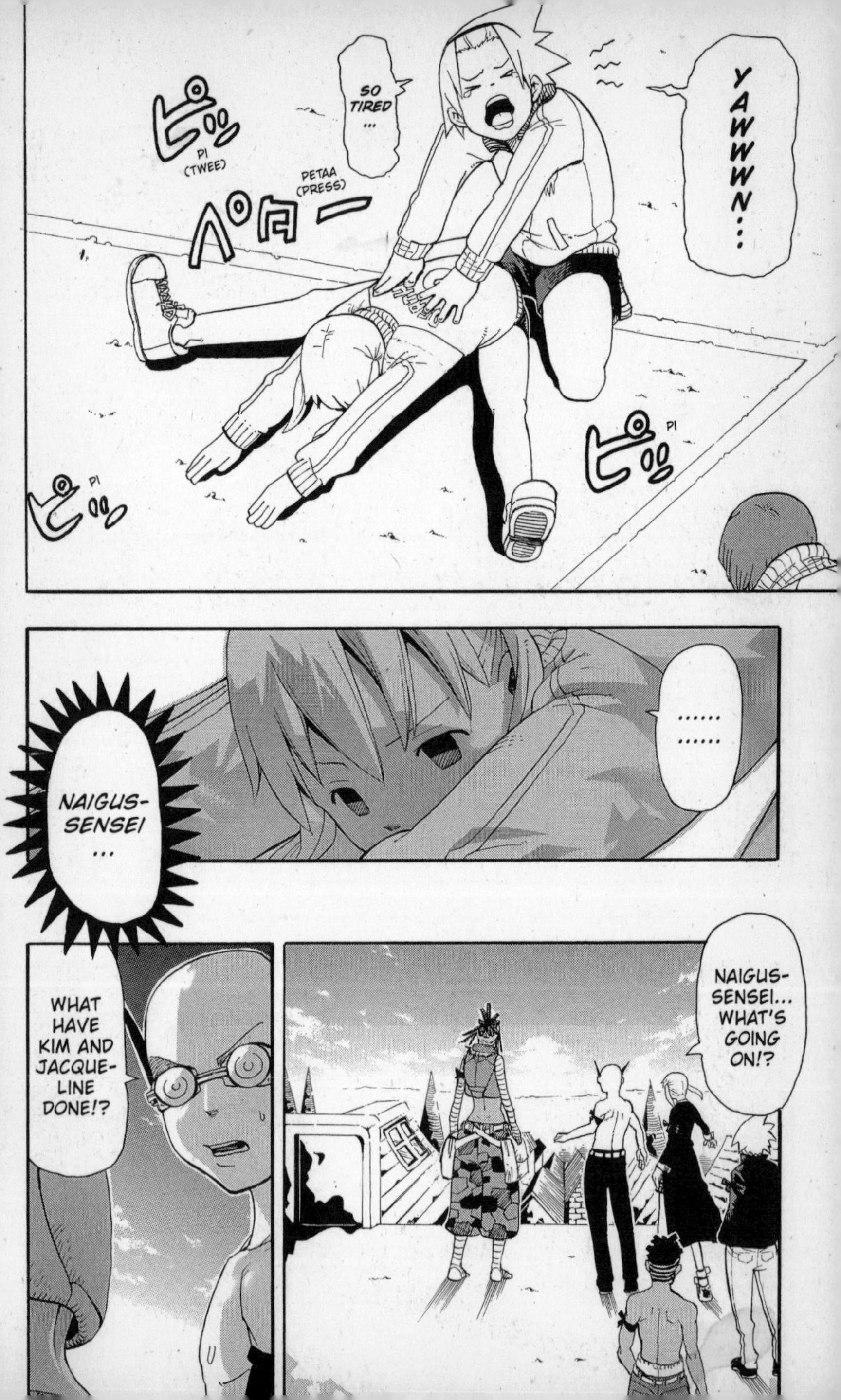
YAWWWN...
SO TIRED...
PI (TWEE)
PETAA (PRESS)
PI
PI
......
......
NAIGUS-SENSEI...
NAIGUS-SENSEI... WHAT'S GOING ON!?
WHAT HAVE KIM AND JACQUELINE DONE!?

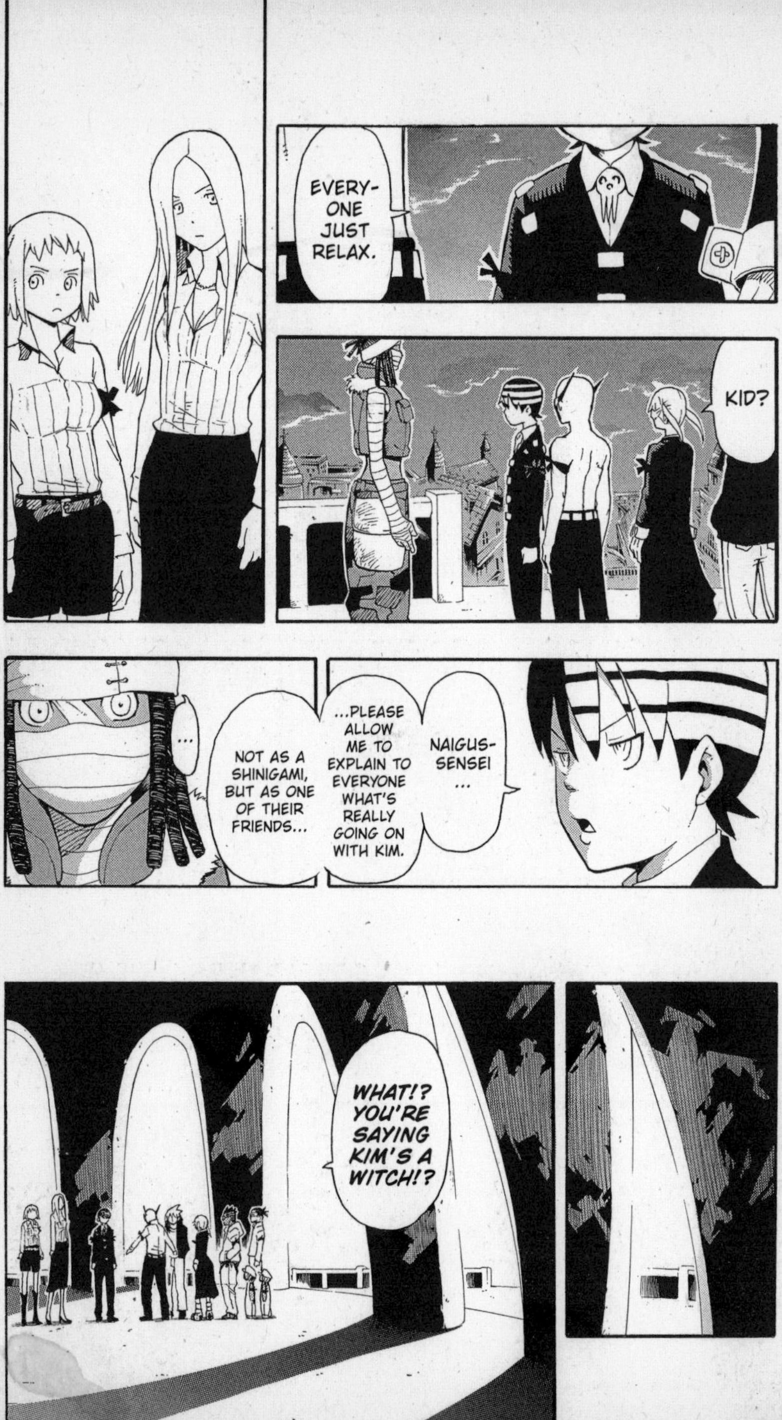
EVERY-ONE JUST RELAX.
KID?
NAIGUS-SENSEI ...
...PLEASE ALLOW ME TO EXPLAIN TO EVERYONE WHAT'S REALLY GOING ON WITH KIM.
NOT AS A SHINIGAMI, BUT AS ONE OF THEIR FRIENDS...
...
WHAT!? YOU'RE SAYING KIM'S A WITCH!?

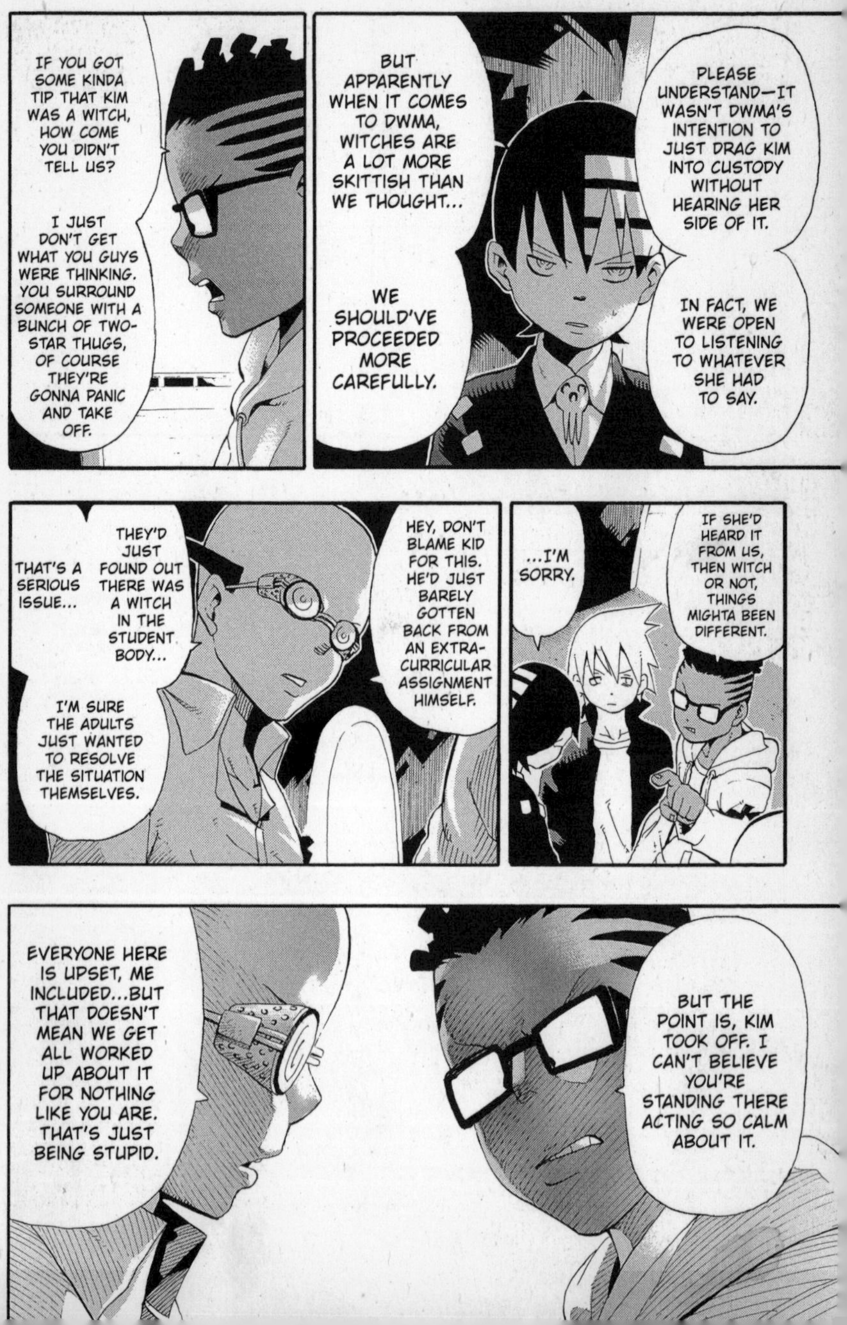
PLEASE UNDERSTAND—IT WASN'T DWMA'S INTENTION TO JUST DRAG KIM INTO CUSTODY WITHOUT HEARING HER SIDE OF IT.
IN FACT, WE WERE OPEN TO LISTENING TO WHATEVER SHE HAD TO SAY.
BUT APPARENTLY WHEN IT COMES TO DWMA, WITCHES ARE A LOT MORE SKITTISH THAN WE THOUGHT...
WE SHOULD'VE PROCEEDED MORE CAREFULLY.
IF YOU GOT SOME KINDA TIP THAT KIM WAS A WITCH, HOW COME YOU DIDN'T TELL US?
I JUST DON'T GET WHAT YOU GUYS WERE THINKING. YOU SURROUND SOMEONE WITH A BUNCH OF TWO-STAR THUGS, OF COURSE THEY'RE GONNA PANIC AND TAKE OFF.
IF SHE'D HEARD IT FROM US, THEN WITCH OR NOT, THINGS MIGHTA BEEN DIFFERENT.
...I'M SORRY.
HEY, DON'T BLAME KID FOR THIS. HE'D JUST BARELY GOTTEN BACK FROM AN EXTRA-CURRICULAR ASSIGNMENT HIMSELF.
THEY'D JUST FOUND OUT THERE WAS A WITCH IN THE STUDENT BODY...
THAT'S A SERIOUS ISSUE...
I'M SURE THE ADULTS JUST WANTED TO RESOLVE THE SITUATION THEMSELVES.
BUT THE POINT IS, KIM TOOK OFF. I CAN'T BELIEVE YOU'RE STANDING THERE ACTING SO CALM ABOUT IT.
EVERYONE HERE IS UPSET, ME INCLUDED...BUT THAT DOESN'T MEAN WE GET ALL WORKED UP ABOUT IT FOR NOTHING LIKE YOU ARE. THAT'S JUST BEING STUPID.

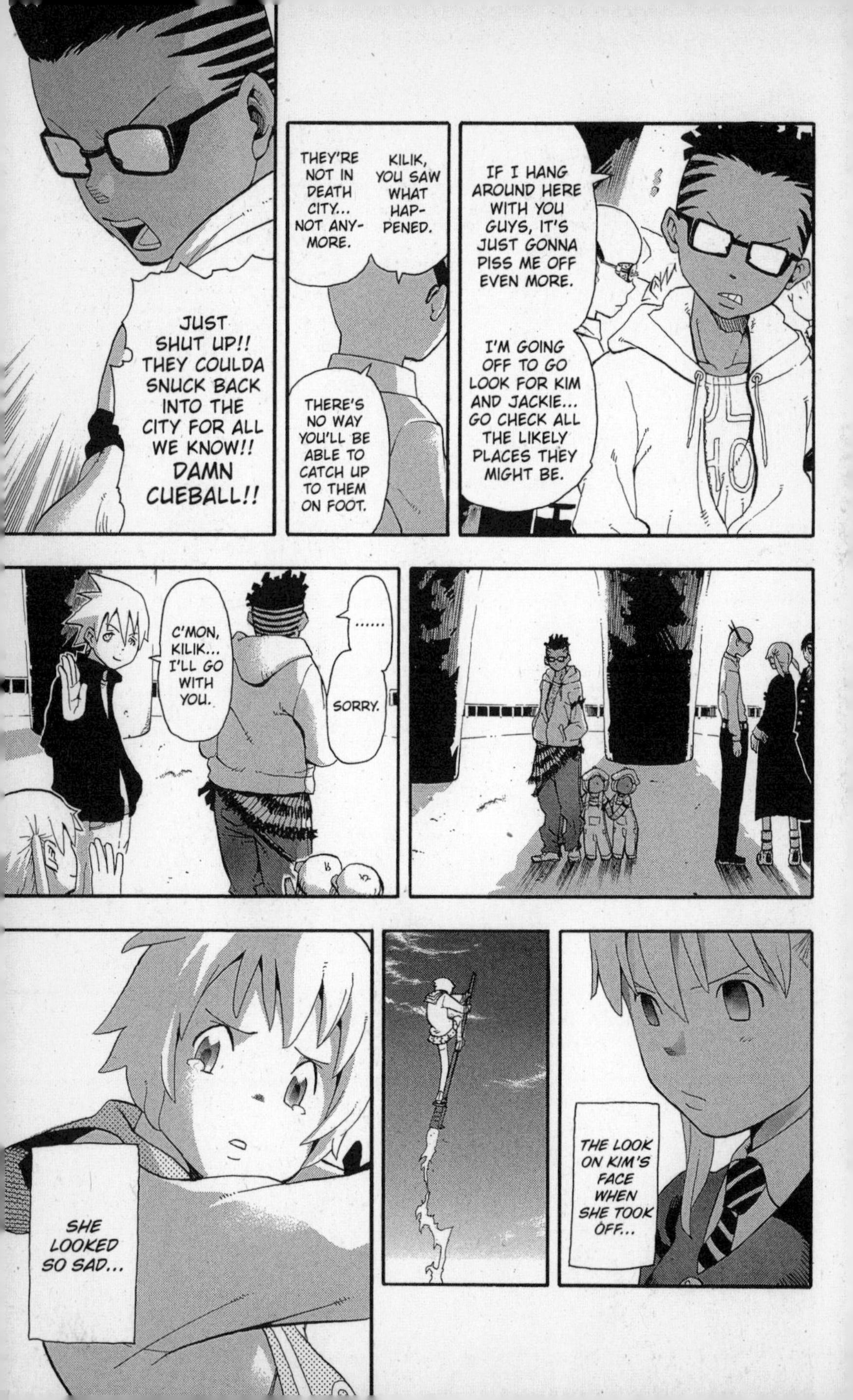
IF I HANG AROUND HERE WITH YOU GUYS, IT'S JUST GONNA PISS ME OFF EVEN MORE.
I'M GOING OFF TO GO LOOK FOR KIM AND JACKIE... GO CHECK ALL THE LIKELY PLACES THEY MIGHT BE.
KILIK, YOU SAW WHAT HAP-PENED.
THEY'RE NOT IN DEATH CITY... NOT ANY-MORE.
THERE'S NO WAY YOU'LL BE ABLE TO CATCH UP TO THEM ON FOOT.
JUST SHUT UP!! THEY COULDA SNUCK BACK INTO THE CITY FOR ALL WE KNOW!! DAMN CUEBALL!!
...... SORRY.
C'MON, KILIK... I'LL GO WITH YOU.
THE LOOK ON KIM'S FACE WHEN SHE TOOK OFF...
SHE LOOKED SO SAD...

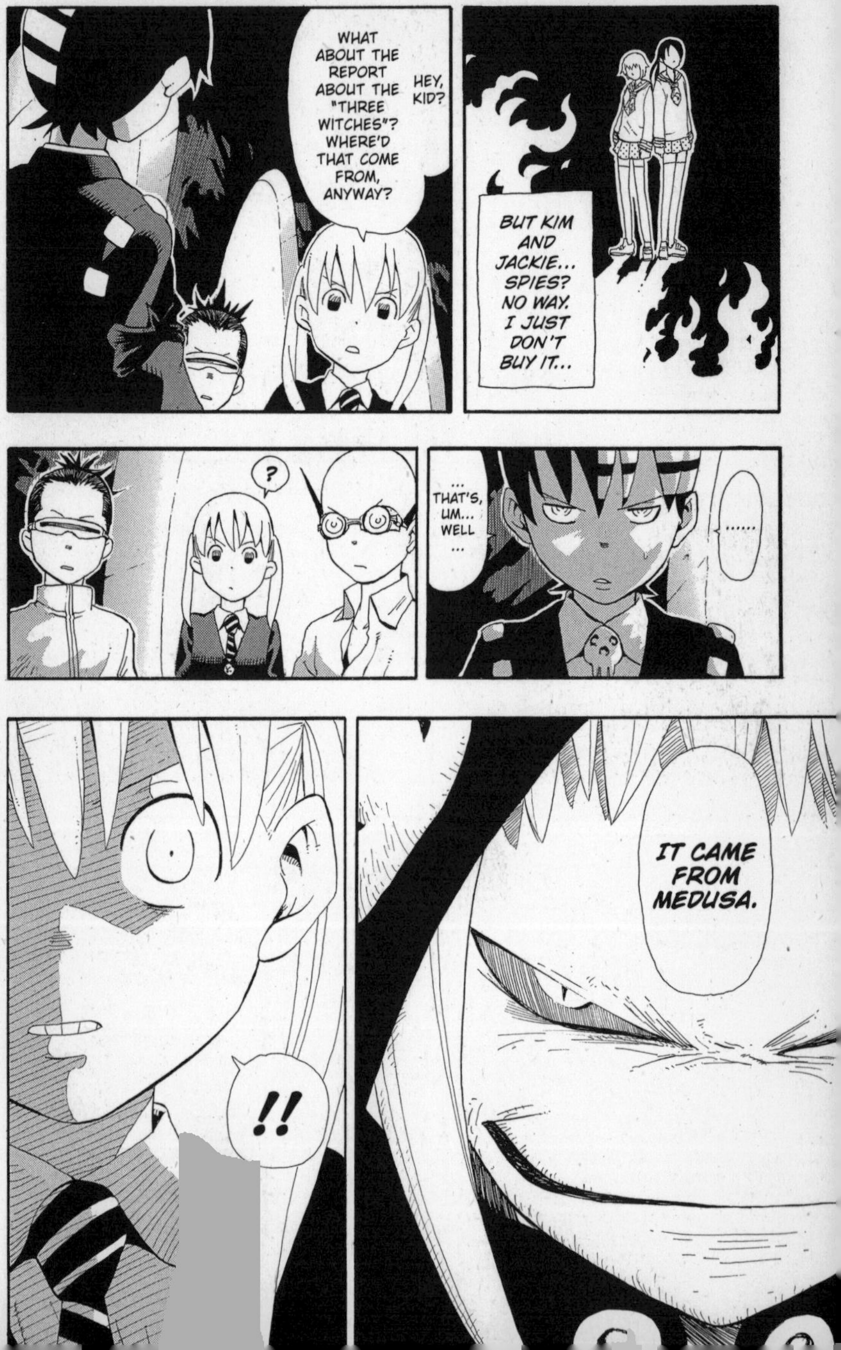
BUT KIM AND JACKIE... SPIES? NO WAY. I JUST DON'T BUY IT...
HEY, KID?
WHAT ABOUT THE REPORT ABOUT THE "THREE WITCHES"? WHERE'D THAT COME FROM, ANYWAY?
......
... THAT'S, UM... WELL ...
?
IT CAME FROM MEDUSA.
!!

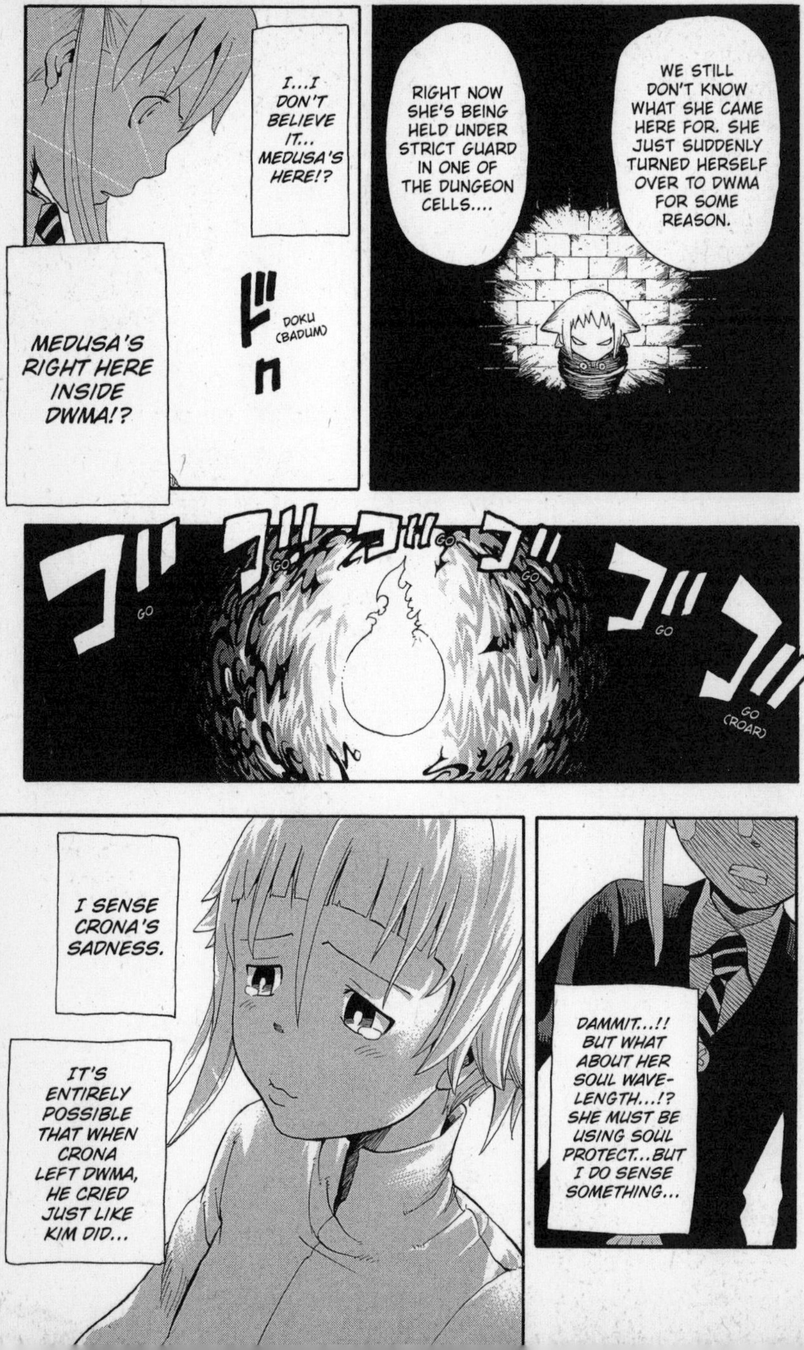
WE STILL DON'T KNOW WHAT SHE CAME HERE FOR. SHE JUST SUDDENLY TURNED HERSELF OVER TO DWMA FOR SOME REASON.
RIGHT NOW SHE'S BEING HELD UNDER STRICT GUARD IN ONE OF THE DUNGEON CELLS....
I...I DON'T BELIEVE IT... MEDUSA'S HERE!?
DOKU (BADUM)
MEDUSA'S RIGHT HERE INSIDE DWMA!?
GO
GO
GO
GO
GO
GO (ROAR)
DAMMIT...!! BUT WHAT ABOUT HER SOUL WAVE-LENGTH...!? SHE MUST BE USING SOUL PROTECT...BUT I DO SENSE SOMETHING...
I SENSE CRONA'S SADNESS.
IT'S ENTIRELY POSSIBLE THAT WHEN CRONA LEFT DWMA, HE CRIED JUST LIKE KIM DID...

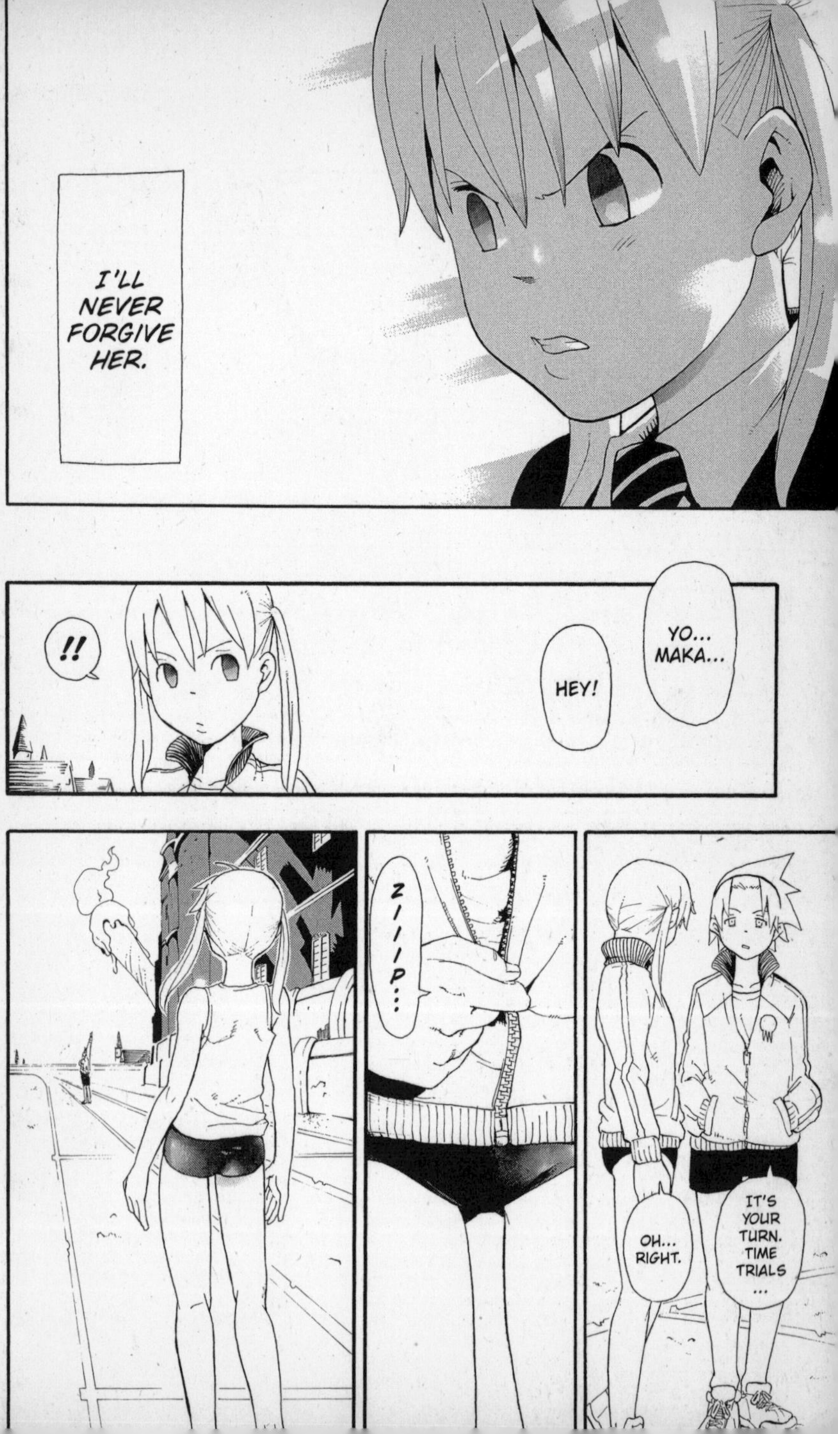
I'LL NEVER FORGIVE HER.
YO... MAKA...
HEY!
!!
IT'S YOUR TURN. TIME TRIALS ...
OH... RIGHT.
ZIIIP...

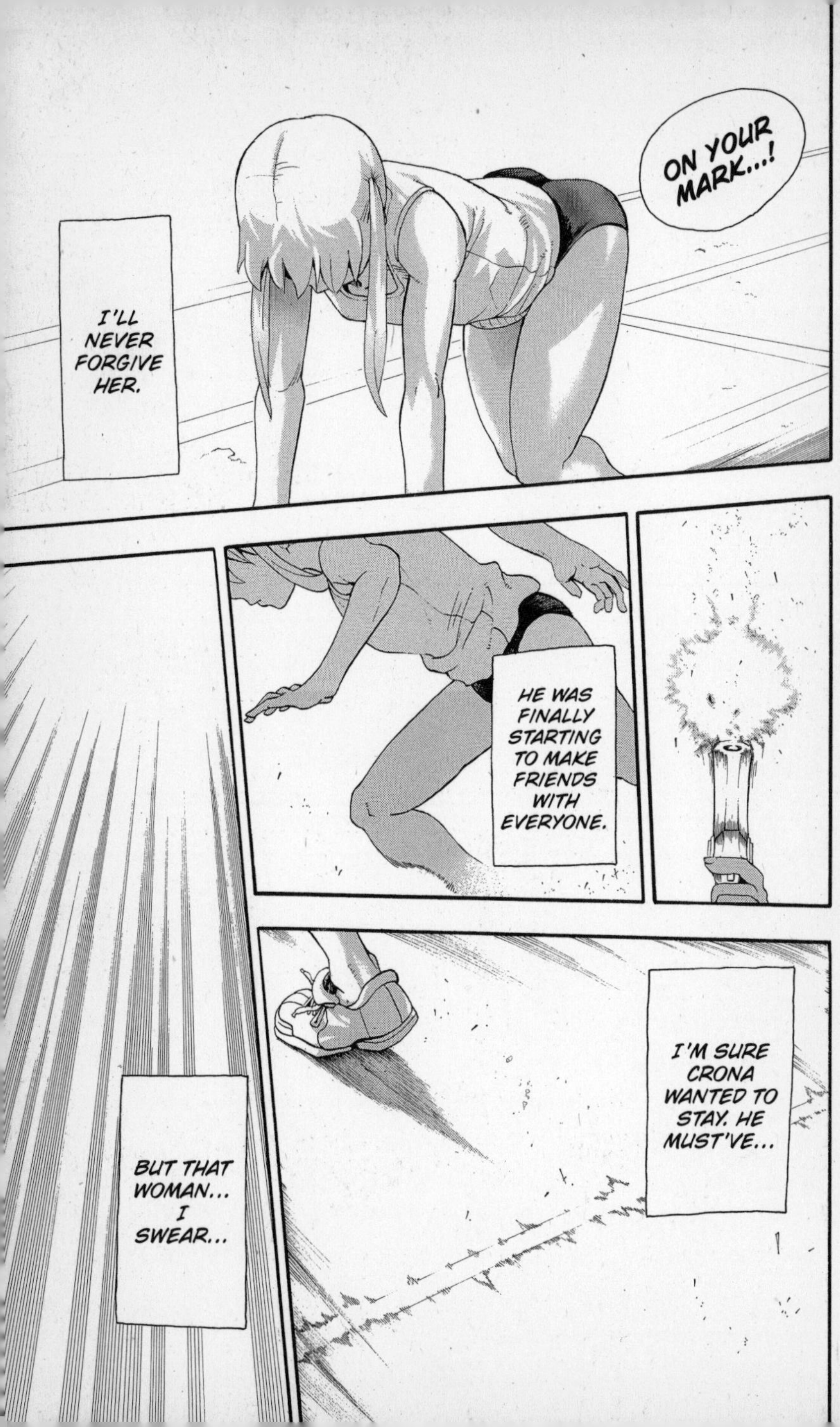
ON YOUR MARK...!
I'LL NEVER FORGIVE HER.
HE WAS FINALLY STARTING TO MAKE FRIENDS WITH EVERYONE.
I'M SURE CRONA WANTED TO STAY. HE MUST'VE...
BUT THAT WOMAN... I SWEAR...

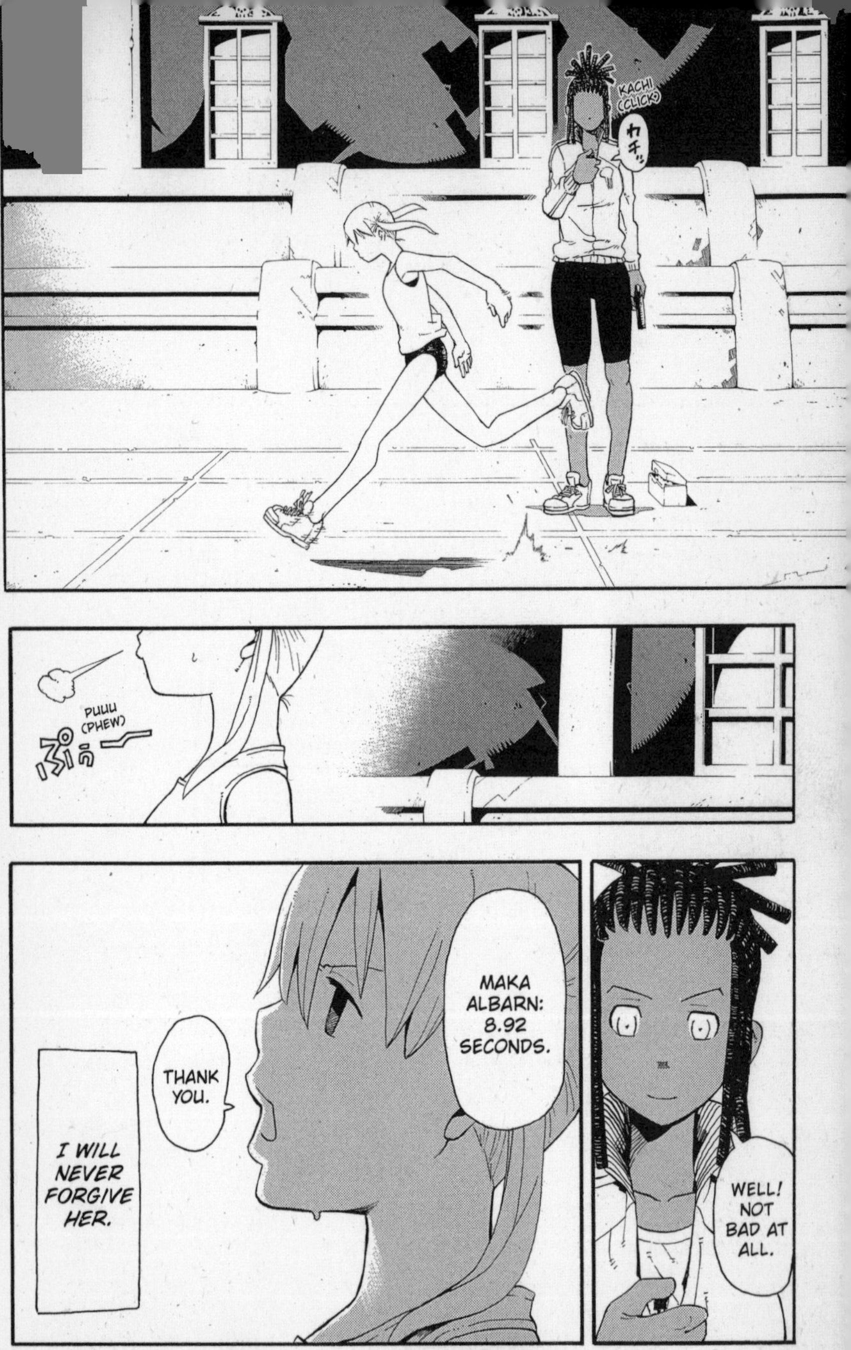
KACHI (CLICK)
カチッ
PUUU (PHEW)
ぷぅ〜
WELL! NOT BAD AT ALL.
MAKA ALBARN: 8.92 SECONDS.
THANK YOU.
I WILL NEVER FORGIVE HER.

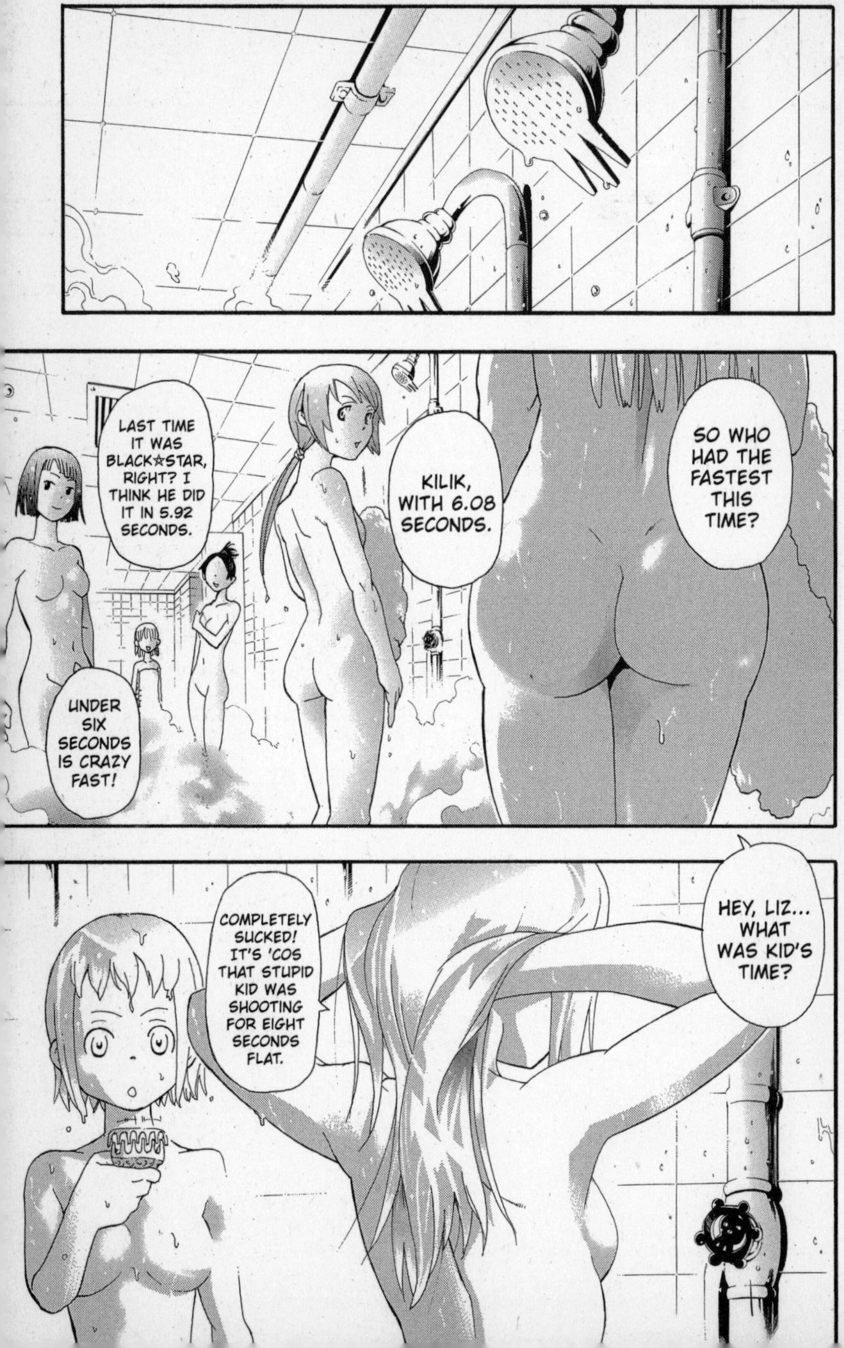
SO WHO HAD THE FASTEST THIS TIME?
KILIK, WITH 6.08 SECONDS.
LAST TIME IT WAS BLACK☆STAR, RIGHT? I THINK HE DID IT IN 5.92 SECONDS.
UNDER SIX SECONDS IS CRAZY FAST!
HEY, LIZ... WHAT WAS KID'S TIME?
COMPLETELY SUCKED! IT'S 'COS THAT STUPID KID WAS SHOOTING FOR EIGHT SECONDS FLAT.

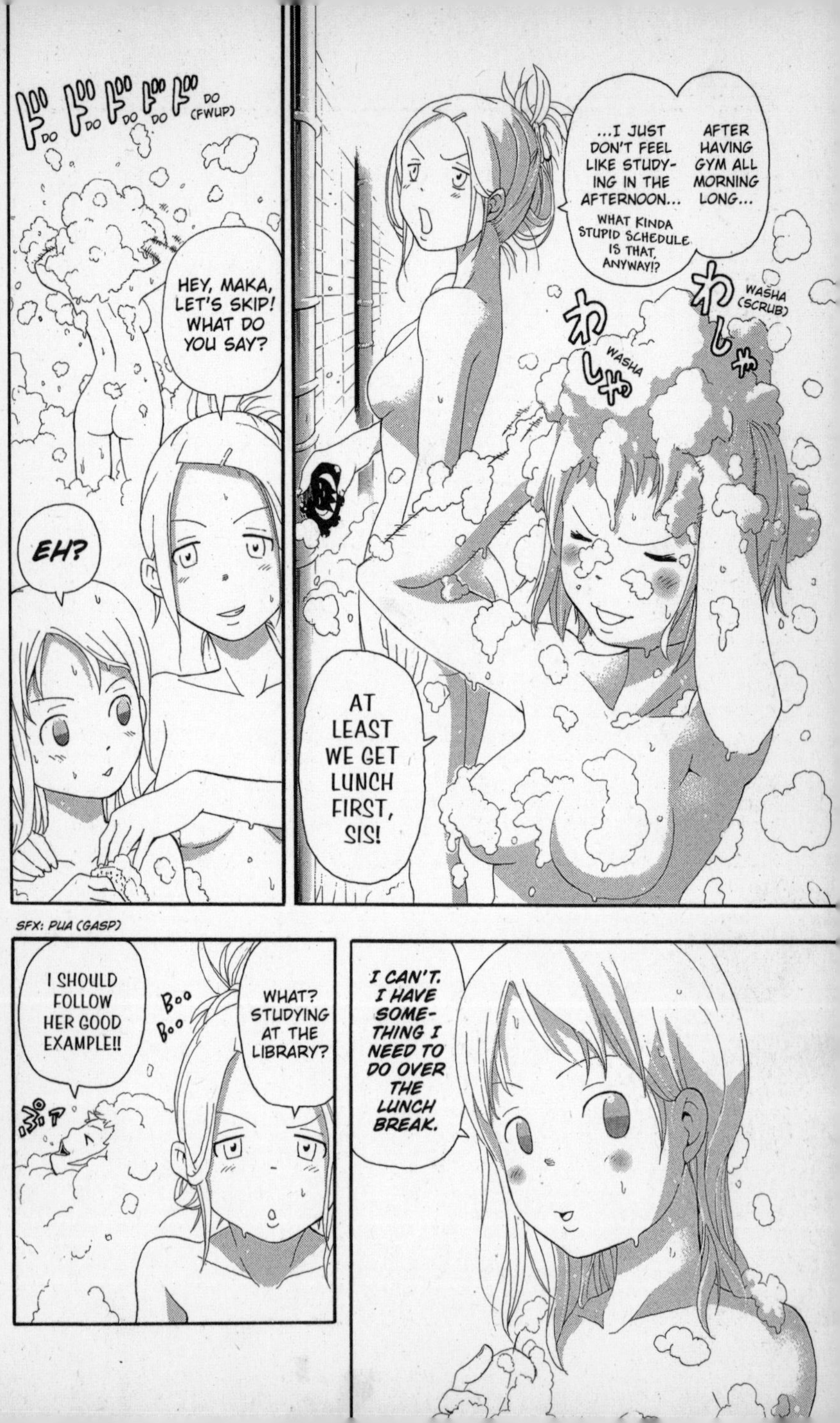

AFTER HAVING GYM ALL MORNING LONG...
...I JUST DON'T FEEL LIKE STUDY-ING IN THE AFTERNOON...
WHAT KINDA STUPID SCHEDULE IS THAT, ANYWAY!?
わしゃ WASHA (SCRUB)
わしゃ WASHA
AT LEAST WE GET LUNCH FIRST, SIS!
ドドドドド DO DO DO DO DO DO (FWUP)
HEY, MAKA, LET'S SKIP! WHAT DO YOU SAY?
EH?
SFX: PUA (GASP)
I CAN'T. I HAVE SOME-THING I NEED TO DO OVER THE LUNCH BREAK.
WHAT? STUDYING AT THE LIBRARY?
BOO BOO
I SHOULD FOLLOW HER GOOD EXAMPLE!!

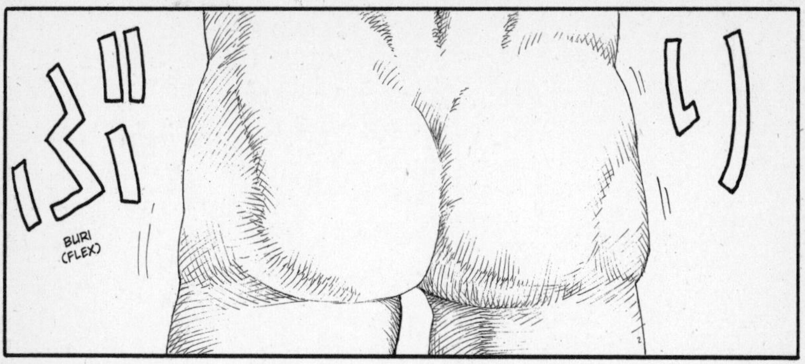
BURI (FLEX)

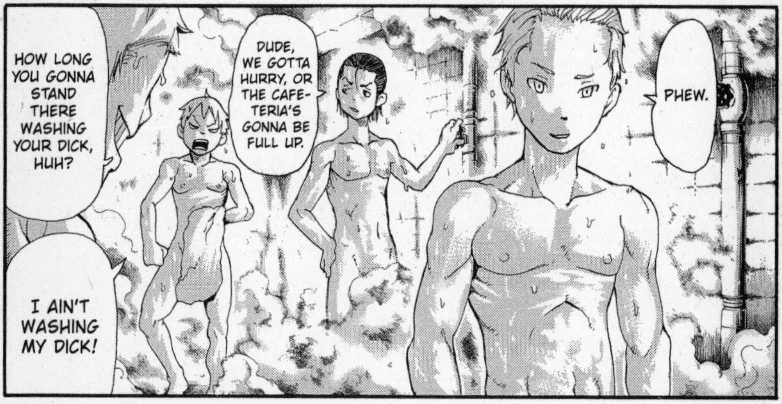
PHEW.
DUDE, WE GOTTA HURRY, OR THE CAFE-TERIA'S GONNA BE FULL UP.
HOW LONG YOU GONNA STAND THERE WASHING YOUR DICK, HUH?
I AIN'T WASHING MY DICK!

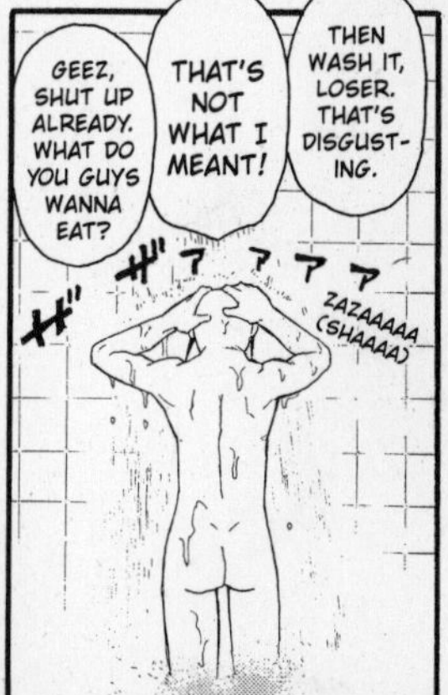
THEN WASH IT, LOSER. THAT'S DISGUST-ING.
THAT'S NOT WHAT I MEANT!
GEEZ, SHUT UP ALREADY. WHAT DO YOU GUYS WANNA EAT?
ザザァァァァ
ZAZAAAAA (SHAAAA)

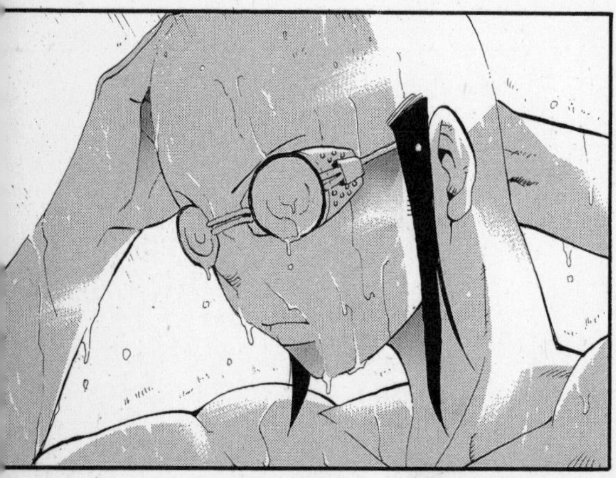

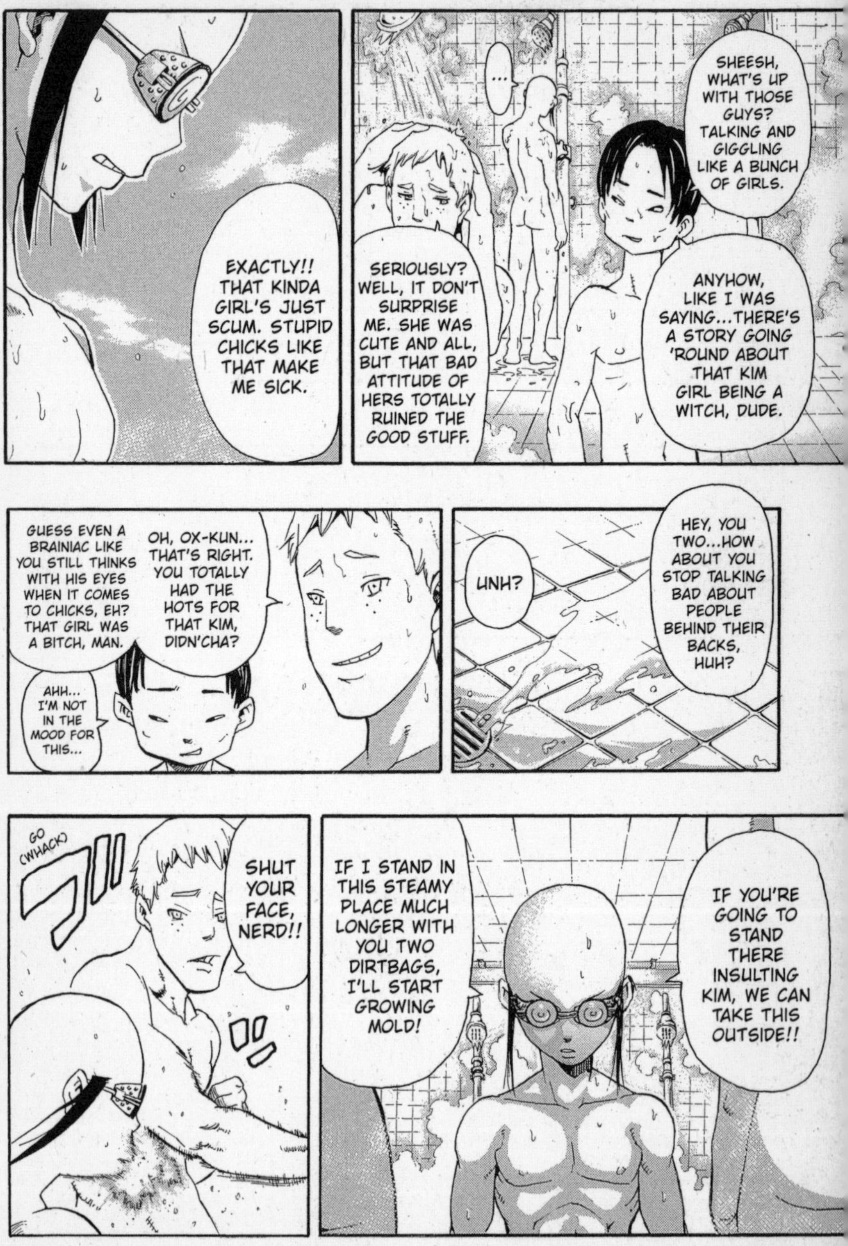
SHEESH, WHAT'S UP WITH THOSE GUYS? TALKING AND GIGGLING LIKE A BUNCH OF GIRLS.
...
ANYHOW, LIKE I WAS SAYING...THERE'S A STORY GOING 'ROUND ABOUT THAT KIM GIRL BEING A WITCH, DUDE.
SERIOUSLY? WELL, IT DON'T SURPRISE ME. SHE WAS CUTE AND ALL, BUT THAT BAD ATTITUDE OF HERS TOTALLY RUINED THE GOOD STUFF.
EXACTLY!! THAT KINDA GIRL'S JUST SCUM. STUPID CHICKS LIKE THAT MAKE ME SICK.
HEY, YOU TWO...HOW ABOUT YOU STOP TALKING BAD ABOUT PEOPLE BEHIND THEIR BACKS, HUH?
UNH?
OH, OX-KUN... THAT'S RIGHT. YOU TOTALLY HAD THE HOTS FOR THAT KIM, DIDN'CHA?
GUESS EVEN A BRAINIAC LIKE YOU STILL THINKS WITH HIS EYES WHEN IT COMES TO CHICKS, EH? THAT GIRL WAS A BITCH, MAN.
AHH... I'M NOT IN THE MOOD FOR THIS...
IF YOU'RE GOING TO STAND THERE INSULTING KIM, WE CAN TAKE THIS OUTSIDE!!
IF I STAND IN THIS STEAMY PLACE MUCH LONGER WITH YOU TWO DIRTBAGS, I'LL START GROWING MOLD!
SHUT YOUR FACE, NERD!!
GO (WHACK)

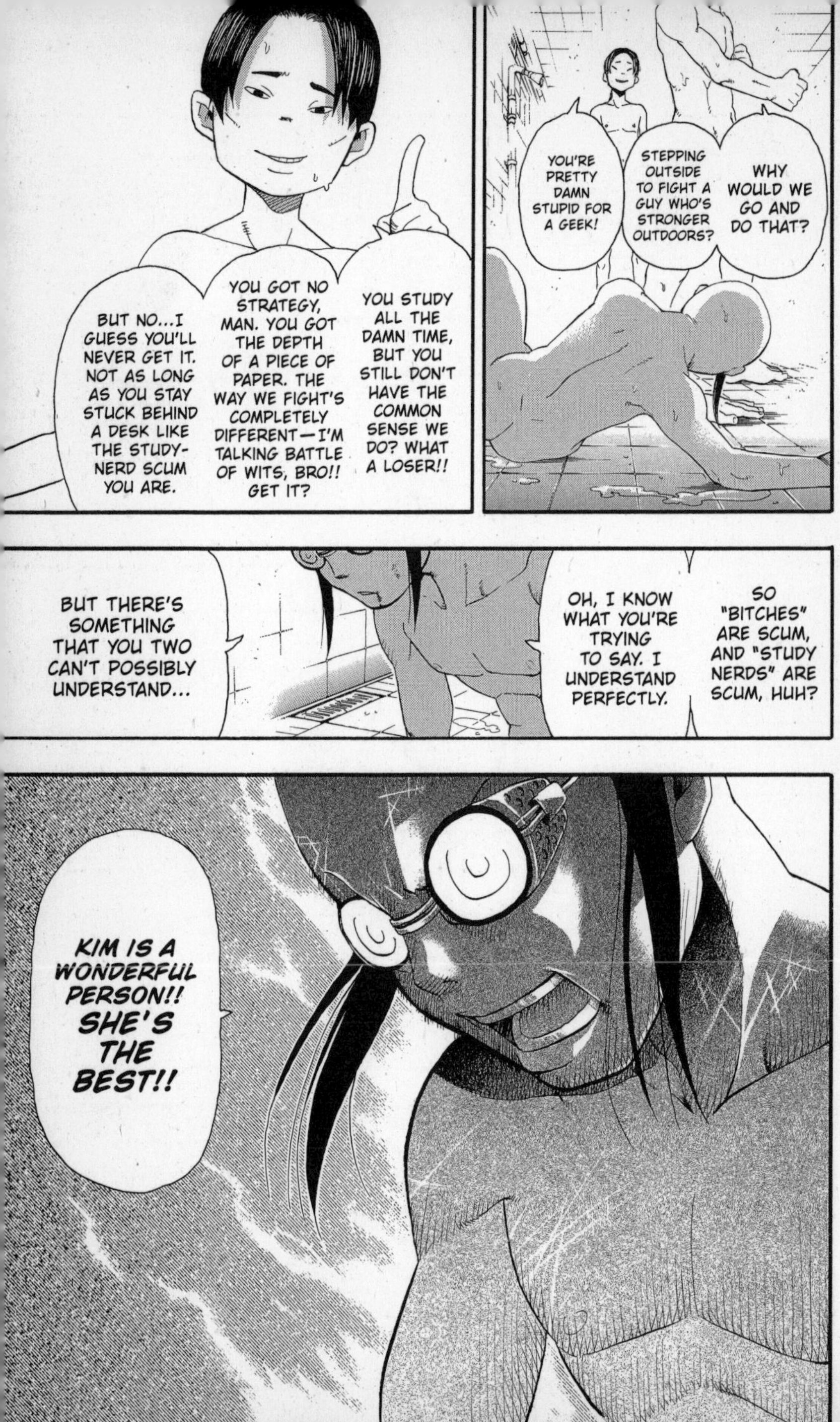
WHY WOULD WE GO AND DO THAT?
STEPPING OUTSIDE TO FIGHT A GUY WHO'S STRONGER OUTDOORS?
YOU'RE PRETTY DAMN STUPID FOR A GEEK!
YOU STUDY ALL THE DAMN TIME, BUT YOU STILL DON'T HAVE THE COMMON SENSE WE DO? WHAT A LOSER!!
YOU GOT NO STRATEGY, MAN. YOU GOT THE DEPTH OF A PIECE OF PAPER. THE WAY WE FIGHT'S COMPLETELY DIFFERENT—I'M TALKING BATTLE OF WITS, BRO!! GET IT?
BUT NO...I GUESS YOU'LL NEVER GET IT. NOT AS LONG AS YOU STAY STUCK BEHIND A DESK LIKE THE STUDY-NERD SCUM YOU ARE.
SO "BITCHES" ARE SCUM, AND "STUDY NERDS" ARE SCUM, HUH?
OH, I KNOW WHAT YOU'RE TRYING TO SAY. I UNDERSTAND PERFECTLY.
BUT THERE'S SOMETHING THAT YOU TWO CAN'T POSSIBLY UNDERSTAND...
KIM IS A WONDERFUL PERSON!! SHE'S THE BEST!!

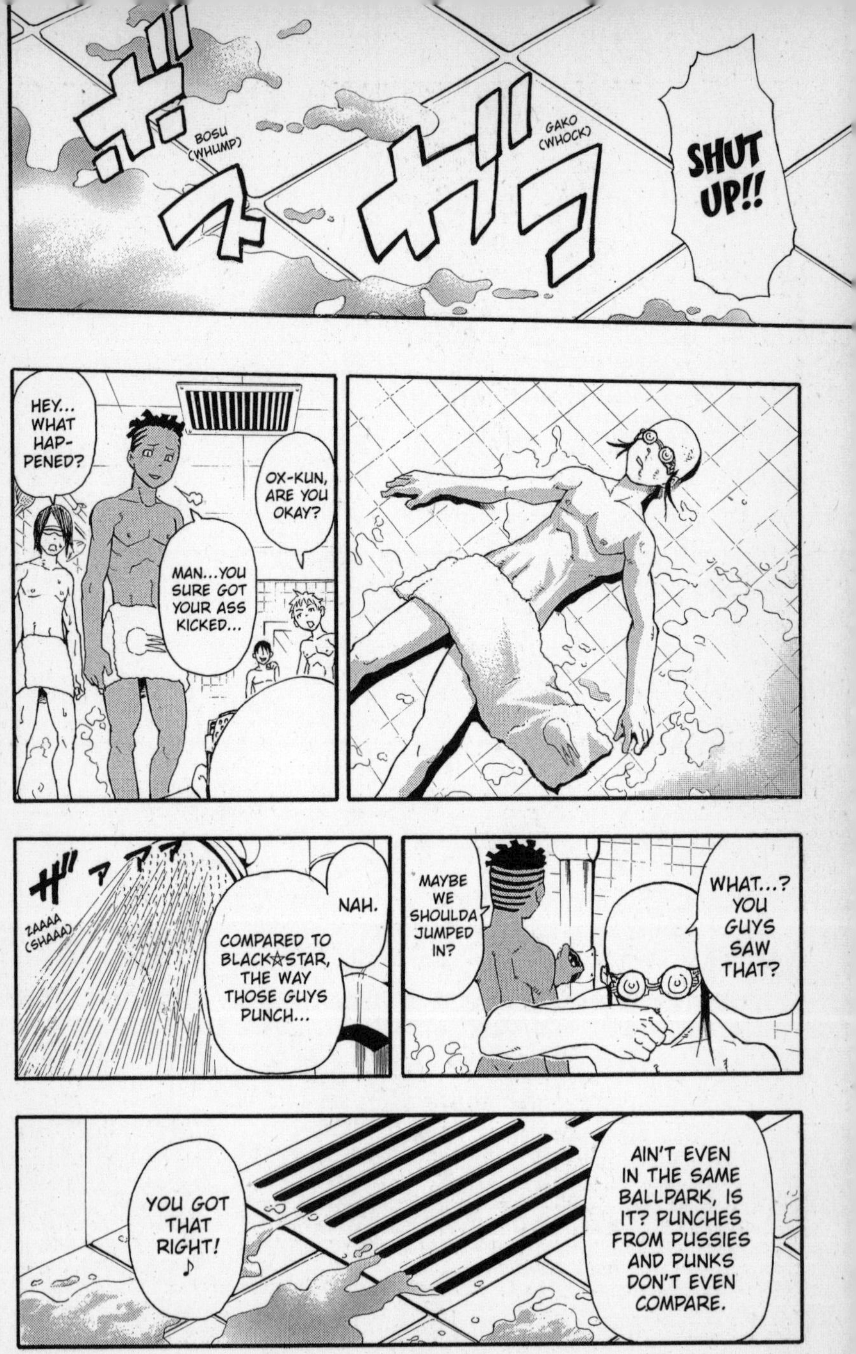
SHUT UP!!
GAKO (WHOCK)
BOSU (WHUMP)
OX-KUN, ARE YOU OKAY?
HEY... WHAT HAP-PENED?
MAN...YOU SURE GOT YOUR ASS KICKED...
WHAT...? YOU GUYS SAW THAT?
MAYBE WE SHOULDA JUMPED IN?
NAH.
COMPARED TO BLACK☆STAR, THE WAY THOSE GUYS PUNCH...
ZAAAA (SHAAA)
AIN'T EVEN IN THE SAME BALLPARK, IS IT? PUNCHES FROM PUSSIES AND PUNKS DON'T EVEN COMPARE.
YOU GOT THAT RIGHT! ♪

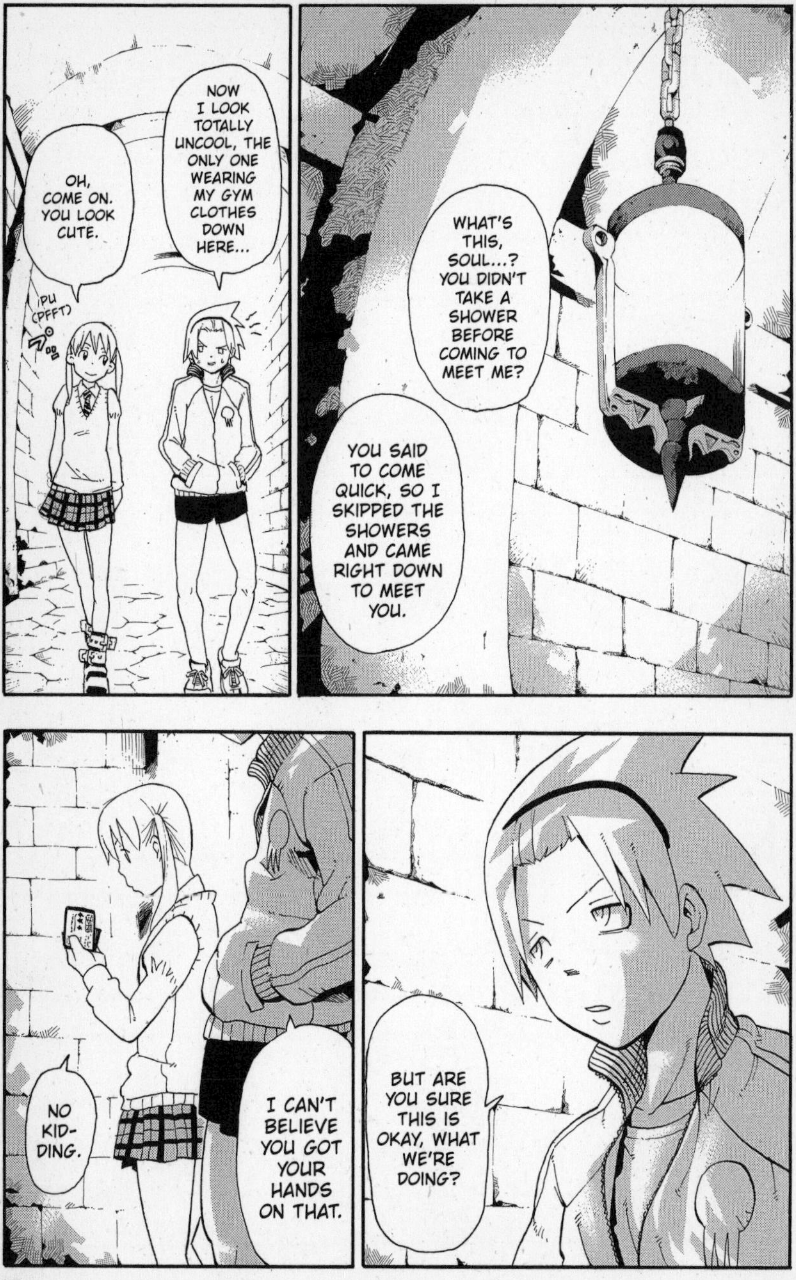
WHAT'S THIS, SOUL...? YOU DIDN'T TAKE A SHOWER BEFORE COMING TO MEET ME?
YOU SAID TO COME QUICK, SO I SKIPPED THE SHOWERS AND CAME RIGHT DOWN TO MEET YOU.
NOW I LOOK TOTALLY UNCOOL, THE ONLY ONE WEARING MY GYM CLOTHES DOWN HERE...
OH, COME ON. YOU LOOK CUTE.
PU (PFFT)
BUT ARE YOU SURE THIS IS OKAY, WHAT WE'RE DOING?
I CAN'T BELIEVE YOU GOT YOUR HANDS ON THAT.
NO KID-DING.

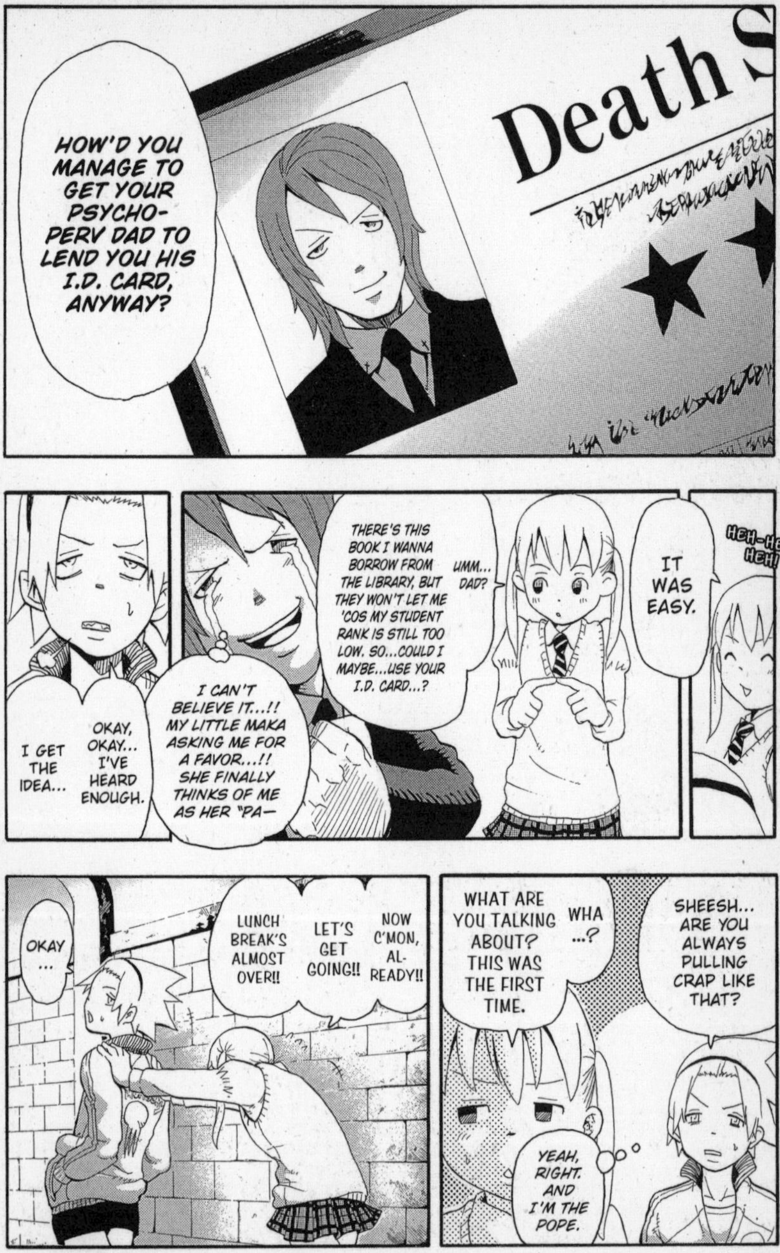
HOW'D YOU MANAGE TO GET YOUR PSYCHO-PERV DAD TO LEND YOU HIS I.D. CARD, ANYWAY?
Death S
HEH-HEH-HEH!
IT WAS EASY.
UMM... DAD?
THERE'S THIS BOOK I WANNA BORROW FROM THE LIBRARY, BUT THEY WON'T LET ME 'COS MY STUDENT RANK IS STILL TOO LOW. SO...COULD I MAYBE...USE YOUR I.D. CARD...?
I CAN'T BELIEVE IT...!! MY LITTLE MAKA ASKING ME FOR A FAVOR...!! SHE FINALLY THINKS OF ME AS HER "PA—
OKAY, OKAY... I'VE HEARD ENOUGH.
I GET THE IDEA...
SHEESH... ARE YOU ALWAYS PULLING CRAP LIKE THAT?
WHA ...?
WHAT ARE YOU TALKING ABOUT? THIS WAS THE FIRST TIME.
YEAH, RIGHT. AND I'M THE POPE.
NOW C'MON, AL-READY!!
LET'S GET GOING!!
LUNCH BREAK'S ALMOST OVER!!
OKAY ...

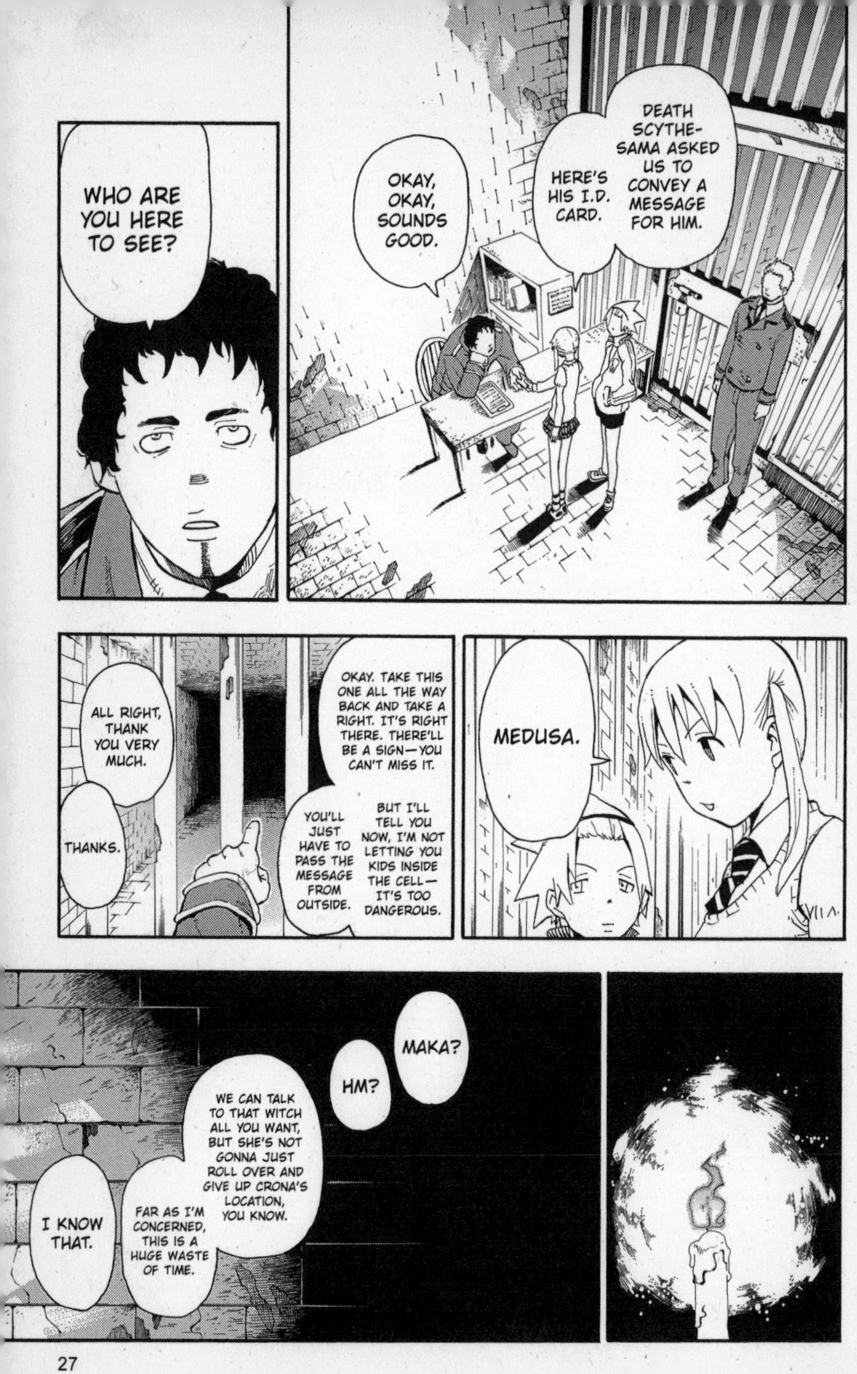
DEATH SCYTHE-SAMA ASKED US TO CONVEY A MESSAGE FOR HIM.
HERE'S HIS I.D. CARD.
OKAY, OKAY, SOUNDS GOOD.
WHO ARE YOU HERE TO SEE?
MEDUSA.
OKAY. TAKE THIS ONE ALL THE WAY BACK AND TAKE A RIGHT. IT'S RIGHT THERE. THERE'LL BE A SIGN—YOU CAN'T MISS IT.
BUT I'LL TELL YOU NOW, I'M NOT LETTING YOU KIDS INSIDE THE CELL—IT'S TOO DANGEROUS.
YOU'LL JUST HAVE TO PASS THE MESSAGE FROM OUTSIDE.
ALL RIGHT, THANK YOU VERY MUCH.
THANKS.
MAKA?
HM?
WE CAN TALK TO THAT WITCH ALL YOU WANT, BUT SHE'S NOT GONNA JUST ROLL OVER AND GIVE UP CRONA'S LOCATION, YOU KNOW.
FAR AS I'M CONCERNED, THIS IS A HUGE WASTE OF TIME.
I KNOW THAT.

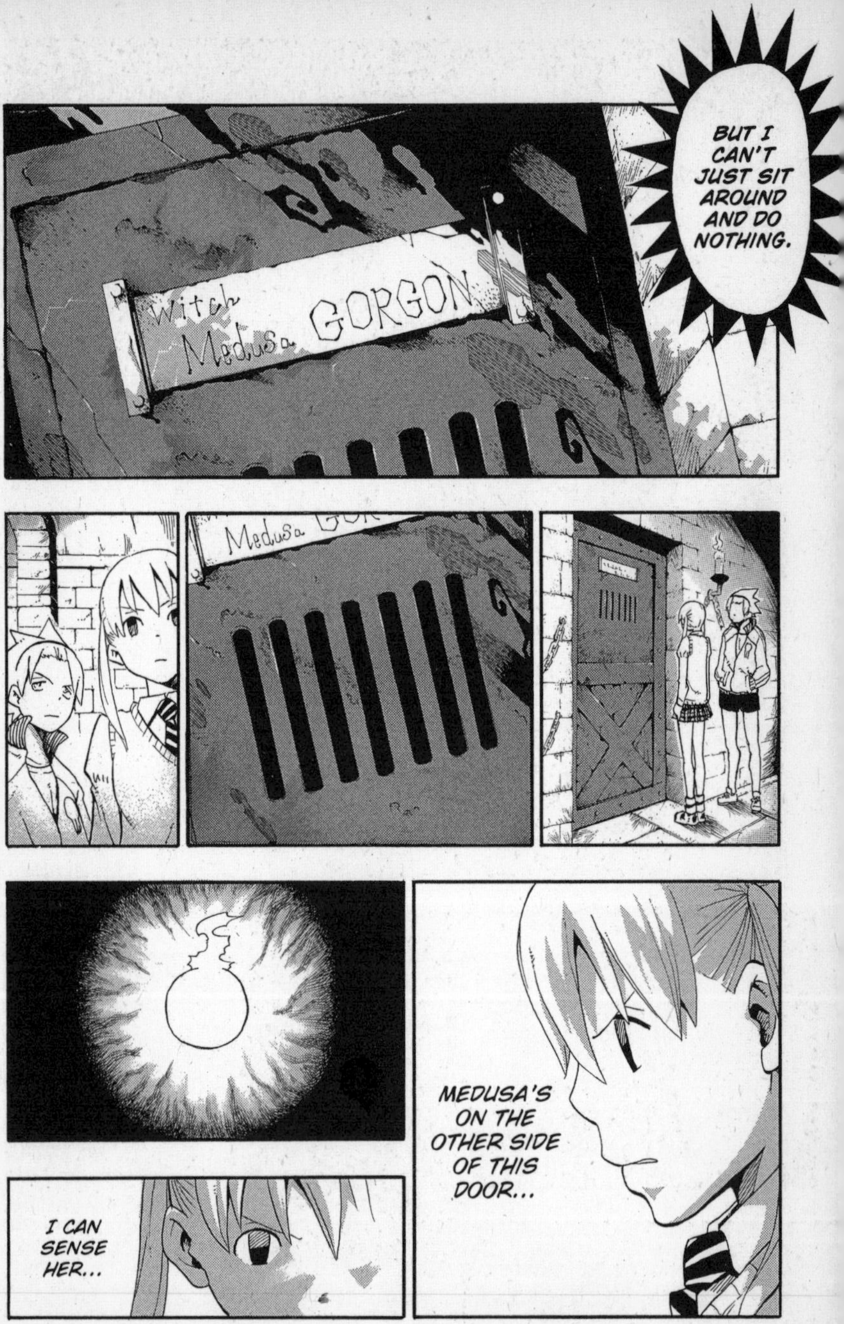
BUT I CAN'T JUST SIT AROUND AND DO NOTHING.
witch Medusa GORGON
Medusa
MEDUSA'S ON THE OTHER SIDE OF THIS DOOR...
I CAN SENSE HER...

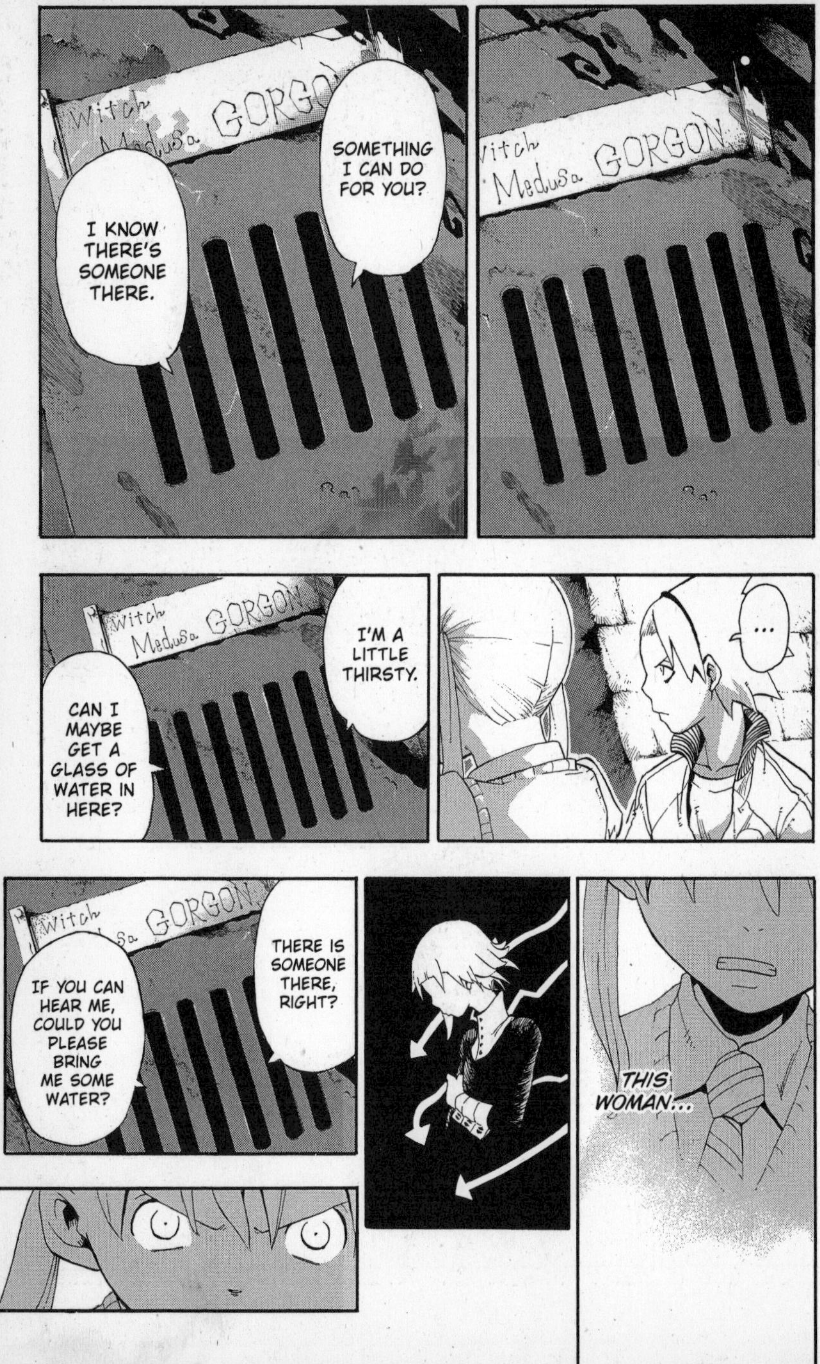
Witch Medusa GORGON
SOMETHING I CAN DO FOR YOU?
I KNOW THERE'S SOMEONE THERE.
...
I'M A LITTLE THIRSTY.
CAN I MAYBE GET A GLASS OF WATER IN HERE?
THIS WOMAN...
THERE IS SOMEONE THERE, RIGHT?
IF YOU CAN HEAR ME, COULD YOU PLEASE BRING ME SOME WATER?

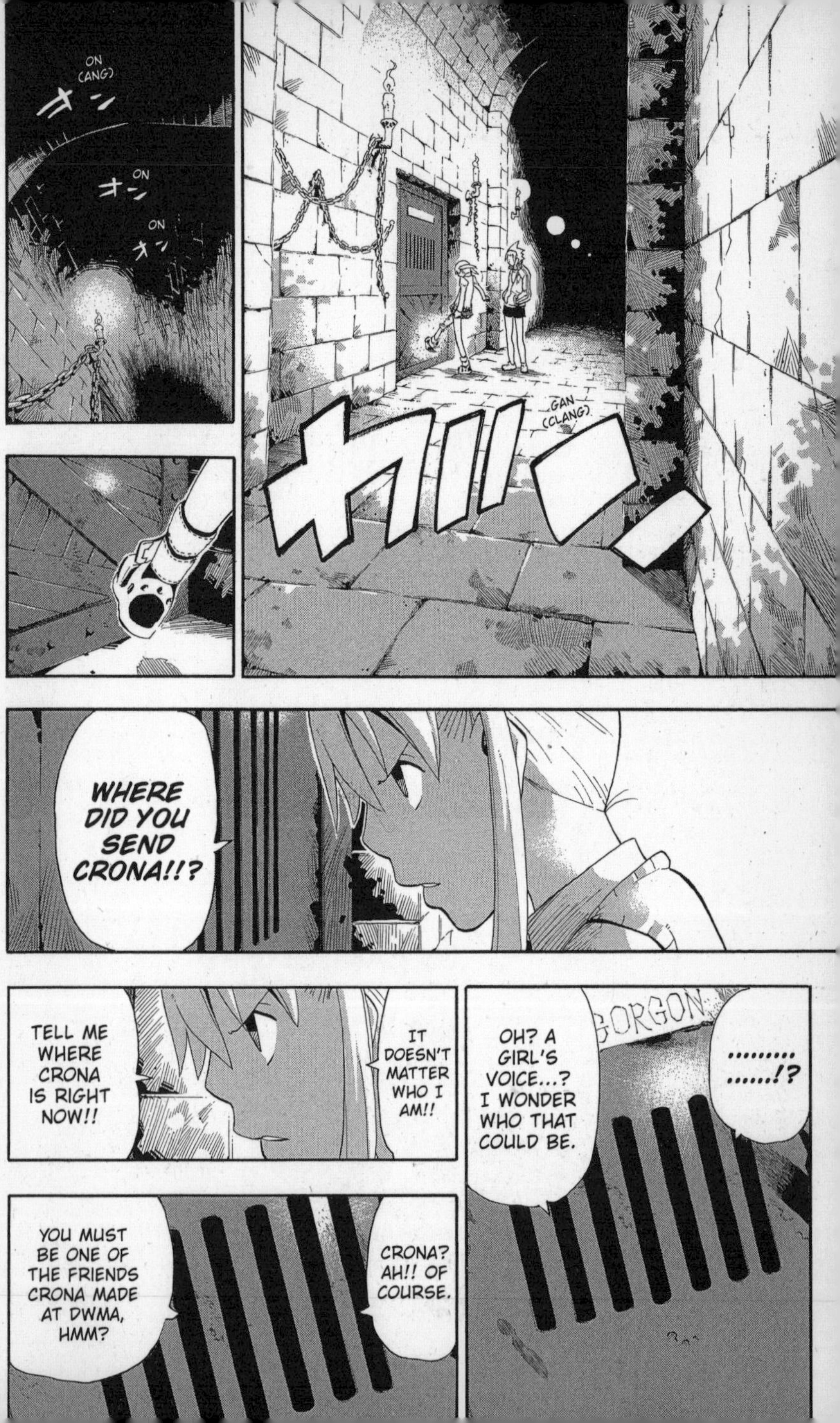
GAN (CLANG)
ON (ANG)
オン
ON
オン
ON
オン
WHERE DID YOU SEND CRONA!!?
GORGON
..............!?
OH? A GIRL'S VOICE...? I WONDER WHO THAT COULD BE.
IT DOESN'T MATTER WHO I AM!!
TELL ME WHERE CRONA IS RIGHT NOW!!
CRONA? AH!! OF COURSE.
YOU MUST BE ONE OF THE FRIENDS CRONA MADE AT DWMA, HMM?

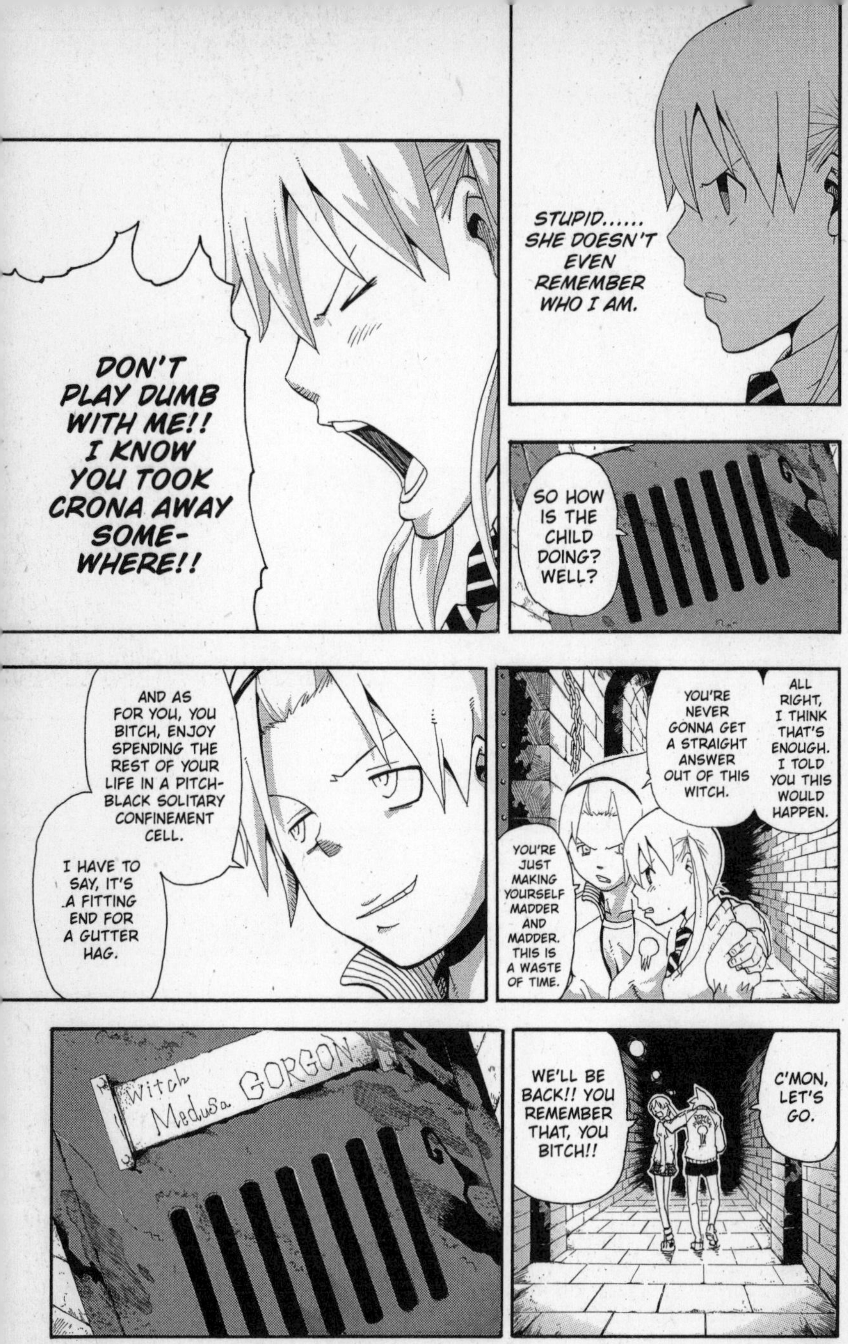
STUPID...... SHE DOESN'T EVEN REMEMBER WHO I AM.
SO HOW IS THE CHILD DOING? WELL?
DON'T PLAY DUMB WITH ME!! I KNOW YOU TOOK CRONA AWAY SOME-WHERE!!
ALL RIGHT, I THINK THAT'S ENOUGH. I TOLD YOU THIS WOULD HAPPEN.
YOU'RE NEVER GONNA GET A STRAIGHT ANSWER OUT OF THIS WITCH.
YOU'RE JUST MAKING YOURSELF MADDER AND MADDER. THIS IS A WASTE OF TIME.
AND AS FOR YOU, YOU BITCH, ENJOY SPENDING THE REST OF YOUR LIFE IN A PITCH-BLACK SOLITARY CONFINEMENT CELL.
I HAVE TO SAY, IT'S A FITTING END FOR A GUTTER HAG.
C'MON, LET'S GO.
WE'LL BE BACK!! YOU REMEMBER THAT, YOU BITCH!!
Witch Medusa GORGON

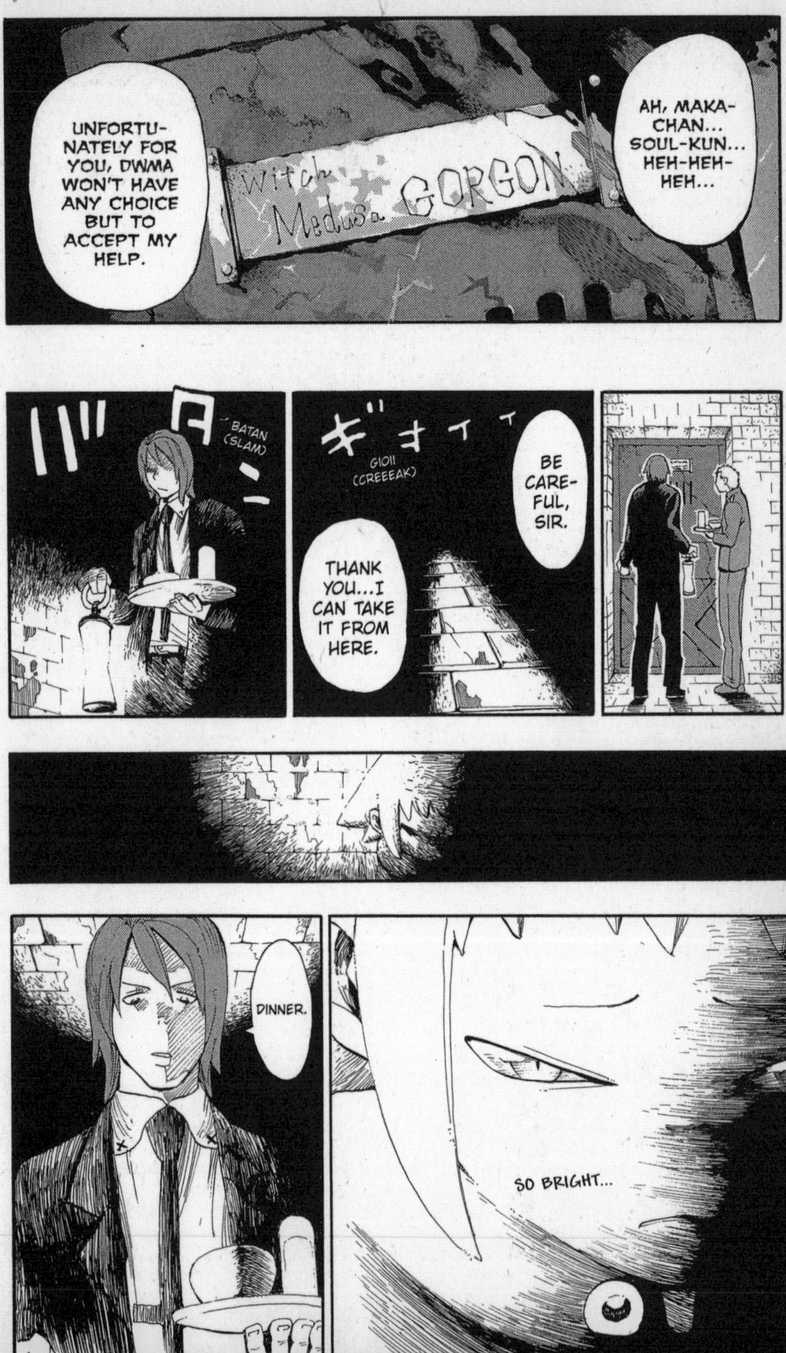
AH, MAKA-CHAN... SOUL-KUN... HEH-HEH-HEH...
witch Medusa GORGON
UNFORTUNATELY FOR YOU, DWMA WON'T HAVE ANY CHOICE BUT TO ACCEPT MY HELP.
BE CAREFUL, SIR.
GIOII (CREEEAK)
THANK YOU...I CAN TAKE IT FROM HERE.
BATAN (SLAM)
SO BRIGHT...
DINNER.

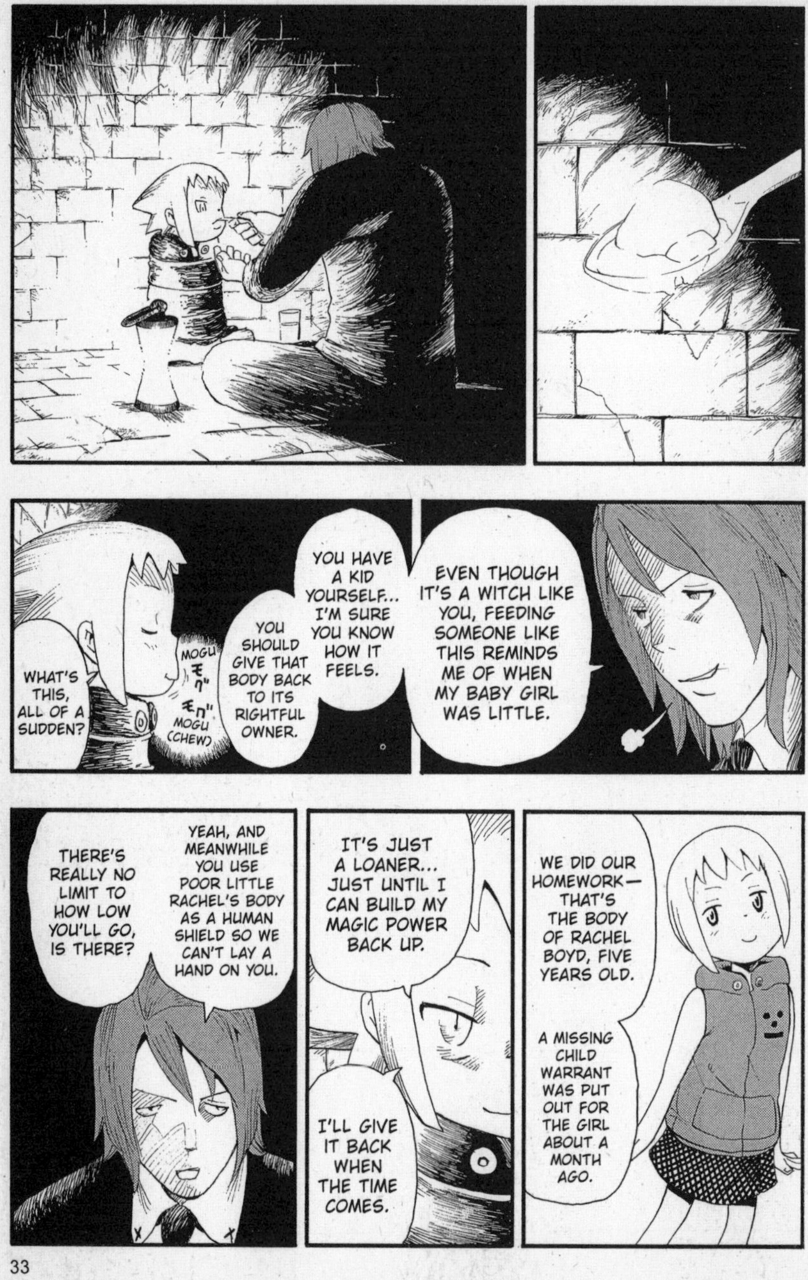
EVEN THOUGH IT'S A WITCH LIKE YOU, FEEDING SOMEONE LIKE THIS REMINDS ME OF WHEN MY BABY GIRL WAS LITTLE.
YOU HAVE A KID YOURSELF... I'M SURE YOU KNOW HOW IT FEELS.
YOU SHOULD GIVE THAT BODY BACK TO ITS RIGHTFUL OWNER.
MOGU
モグ
MOGU (CHEW)
WHAT'S THIS, ALL OF A SUDDEN?
WE DID OUR HOMEWORK— THAT'S THE BODY OF RACHEL BOYD, FIVE YEARS OLD.
A MISSING CHILD WARRANT WAS PUT OUT FOR THE GIRL ABOUT A MONTH AGO.
IT'S JUST A LOANER... JUST UNTIL I CAN BUILD MY MAGIC POWER BACK UP.
I'LL GIVE IT BACK WHEN THE TIME COMES.
YEAH, AND MEANWHILE YOU USE POOR LITTLE RACHEL'S BODY AS A HUMAN SHIELD SO WE CAN'T LAY A HAND ON YOU.
THERE'S REALLY NO LIMIT TO HOW LOW YOU'LL GO, IS THERE?

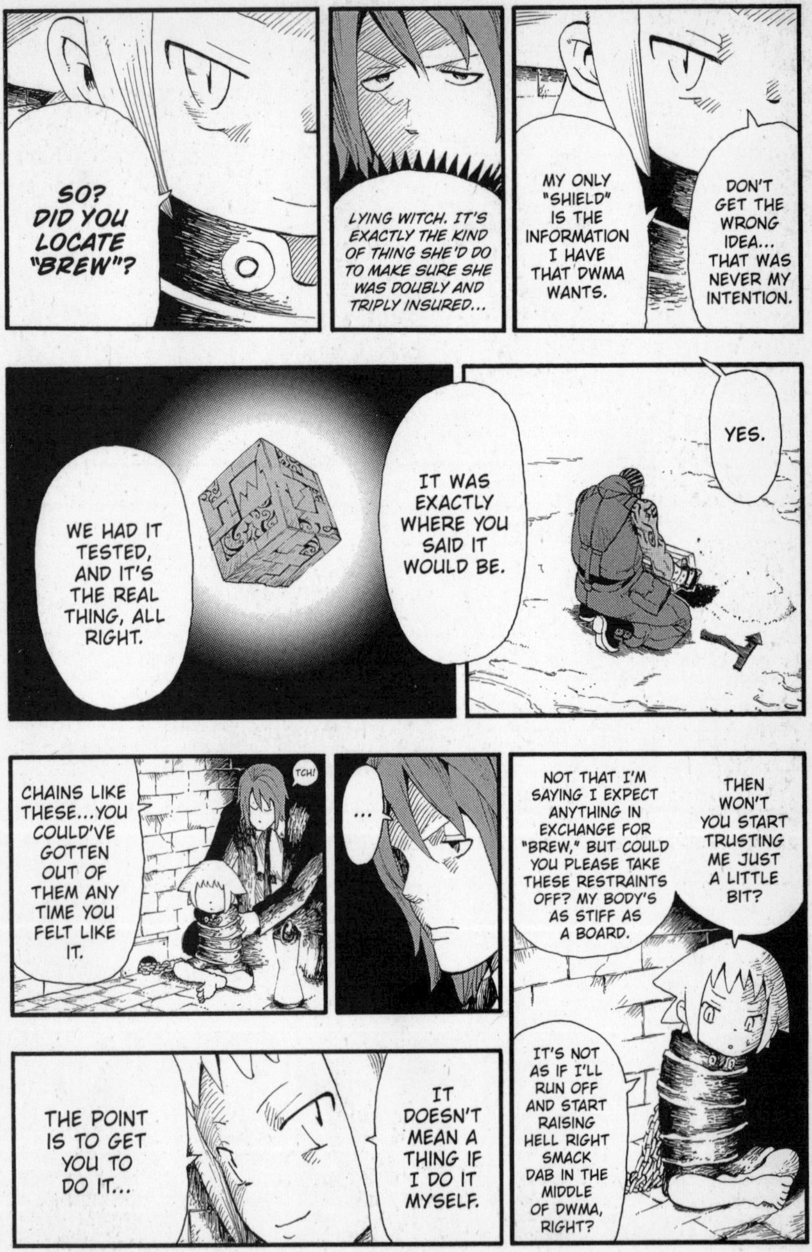

DON'T GET THE WRONG IDEA... THAT WAS NEVER MY INTENTION.
MY ONLY "SHIELD" IS THE INFORMATION I HAVE THAT DWMA WANTS.
LYING WITCH. IT'S EXACTLY THE KIND OF THING SHE'D DO TO MAKE SURE SHE WAS DOUBLY AND TRIPLY INSURED...
SO? DID YOU LOCATE "BREW"?
YES.
IT WAS EXACTLY WHERE YOU SAID IT WOULD BE.
WE HAD IT TESTED, AND IT'S THE REAL THING, ALL RIGHT.
THEN WON'T YOU START TRUSTING ME JUST A LITTLE BIT?
NOT THAT I'M SAYING I EXPECT ANYTHING IN EXCHANGE FOR "BREW," BUT COULD YOU PLEASE TAKE THESE RESTRAINTS OFF? MY BODY'S AS STIFF AS A BOARD.
IT'S NOT AS IF I'LL RUN OFF AND START RAISING HELL RIGHT SMACK DAB IN THE MIDDLE OF DWMA, RIGHT?
...
TCH!
CHAINS LIKE THESE...YOU COULD'VE GOTTEN OUT OF THEM ANY TIME YOU FELT LIKE IT.
IT DOESN'T MEAN A THING IF I DO IT MYSELF.
THE POINT IS TO GET YOU TO DO IT...

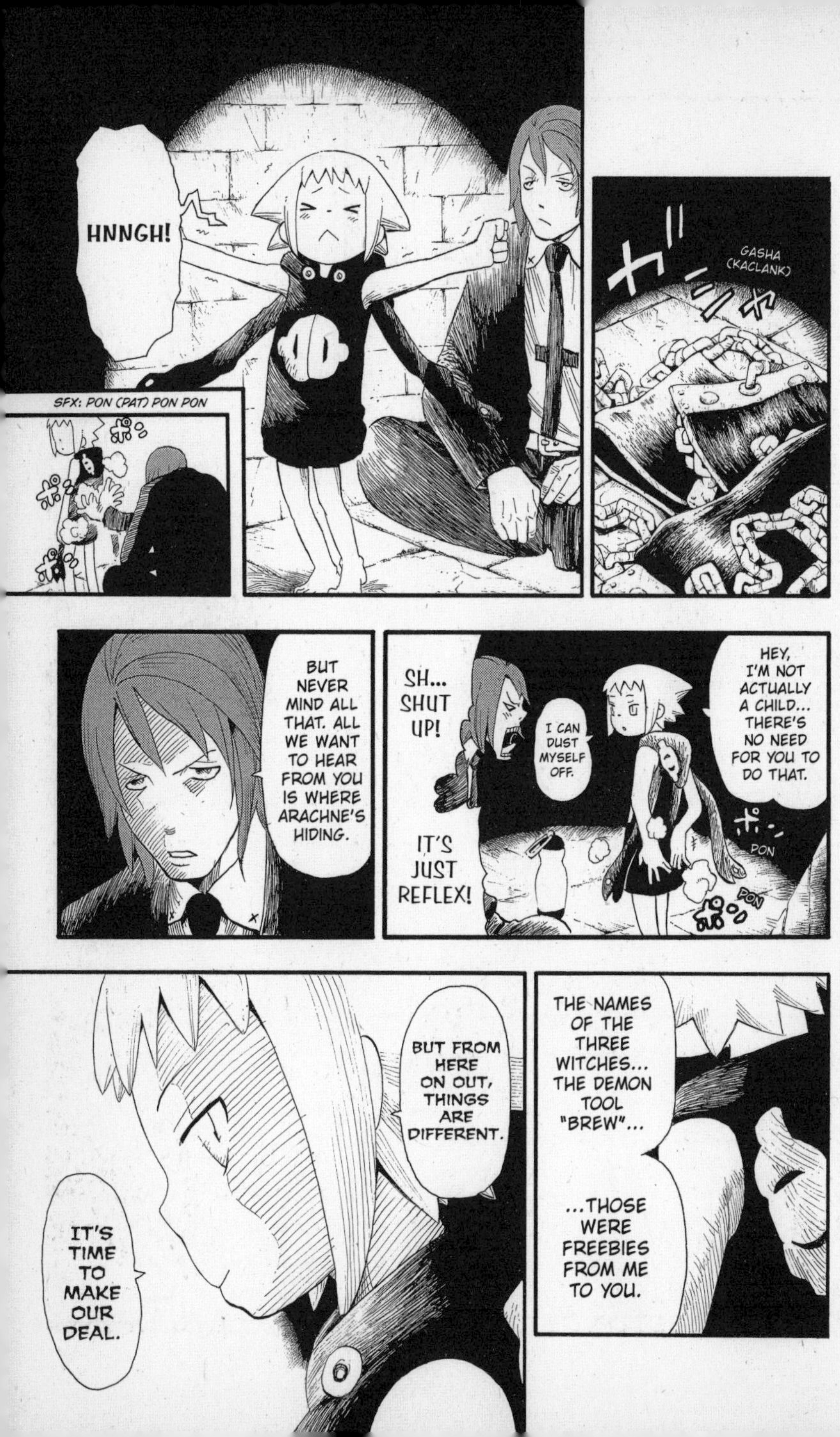
GASHA (KACLANK)
HNNGH!
SFX: PON (PAT) PON PON
HEY, I'M NOT ACTUALLY A CHILD... THERE'S NO NEED FOR YOU TO DO THAT.
PON
PON
I CAN DUST MYSELF OFF.
SH... SHUT UP!
IT'S JUST REFLEX!
BUT NEVER MIND ALL THAT. ALL WE WANT TO HEAR FROM YOU IS WHERE ARACHNE'S HIDING.
THE NAMES OF THE THREE WITCHES... THE DEMON TOOL "BREW"...
...THOSE WERE FREEBIES FROM ME TO YOU.
BUT FROM HERE ON OUT, THINGS ARE DIFFERENT.
IT'S TIME TO MAKE OUR DEAL.

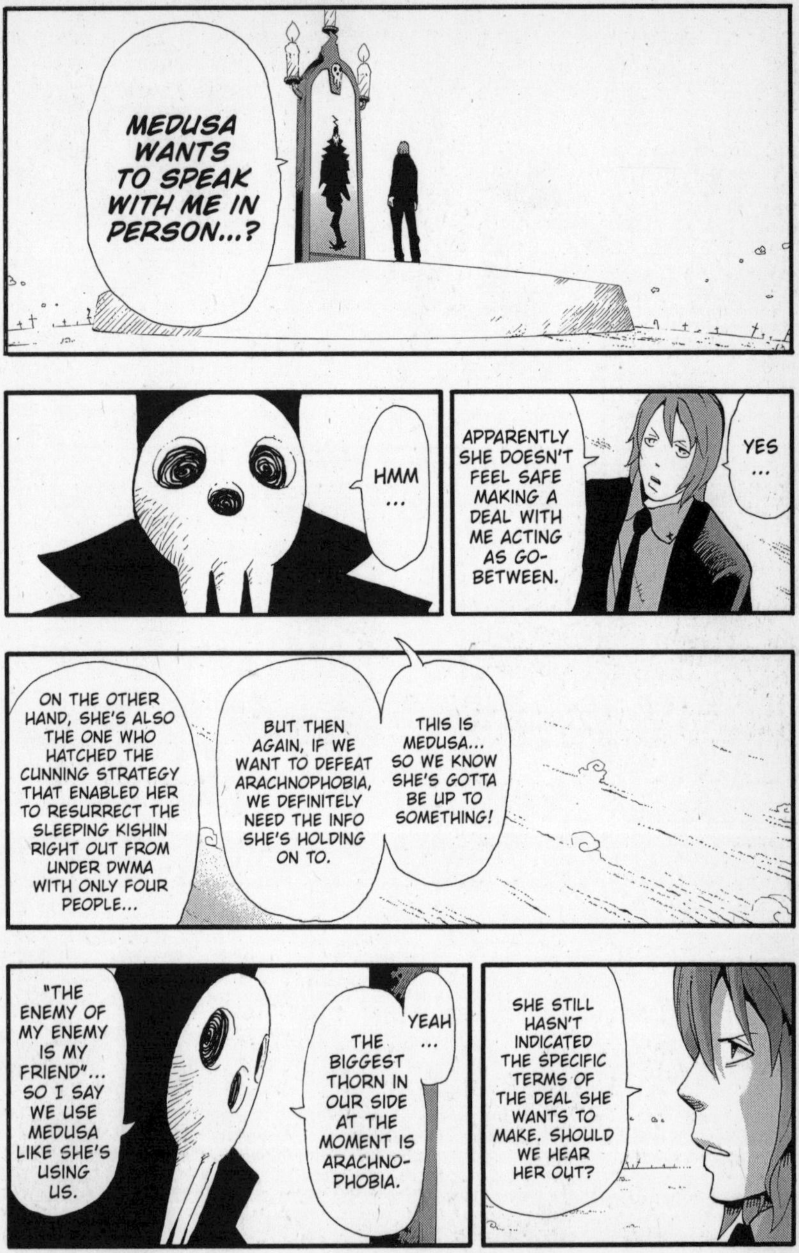
MEDUSA WANTS TO SPEAK WITH ME IN PERSON...?
YES ...
APPARENTLY SHE DOESN'T FEEL SAFE MAKING A DEAL WITH ME ACTING AS GO-BETWEEN.
HMM ...
THIS IS MEDUSA... SO WE KNOW SHE'S GOTTA BE UP TO SOMETHING!
BUT THEN AGAIN, IF WE WANT TO DEFEAT ARACHNOPHOBIA, WE DEFINITELY NEED THE INFO SHE'S HOLDING ON TO.
ON THE OTHER HAND, SHE'S ALSO THE ONE WHO HATCHED THE CUNNING STRATEGY THAT ENABLED HER TO RESURRECT THE SLEEPING KISHIN RIGHT OUT FROM UNDER DWMA WITH ONLY FOUR PEOPLE...
SHE STILL HASN'T INDICATED THE SPECIFIC TERMS OF THE DEAL SHE WANTS TO MAKE. SHOULD WE HEAR HER OUT?
YEAH ...
THE BIGGEST THORN IN OUR SIDE AT THE MOMENT IS ARACHNO-PHOBIA.
"THE ENEMY OF MY ENEMY IS MY FRIEND"... SO I SAY WE USE MEDUSA LIKE SHE'S USING US.

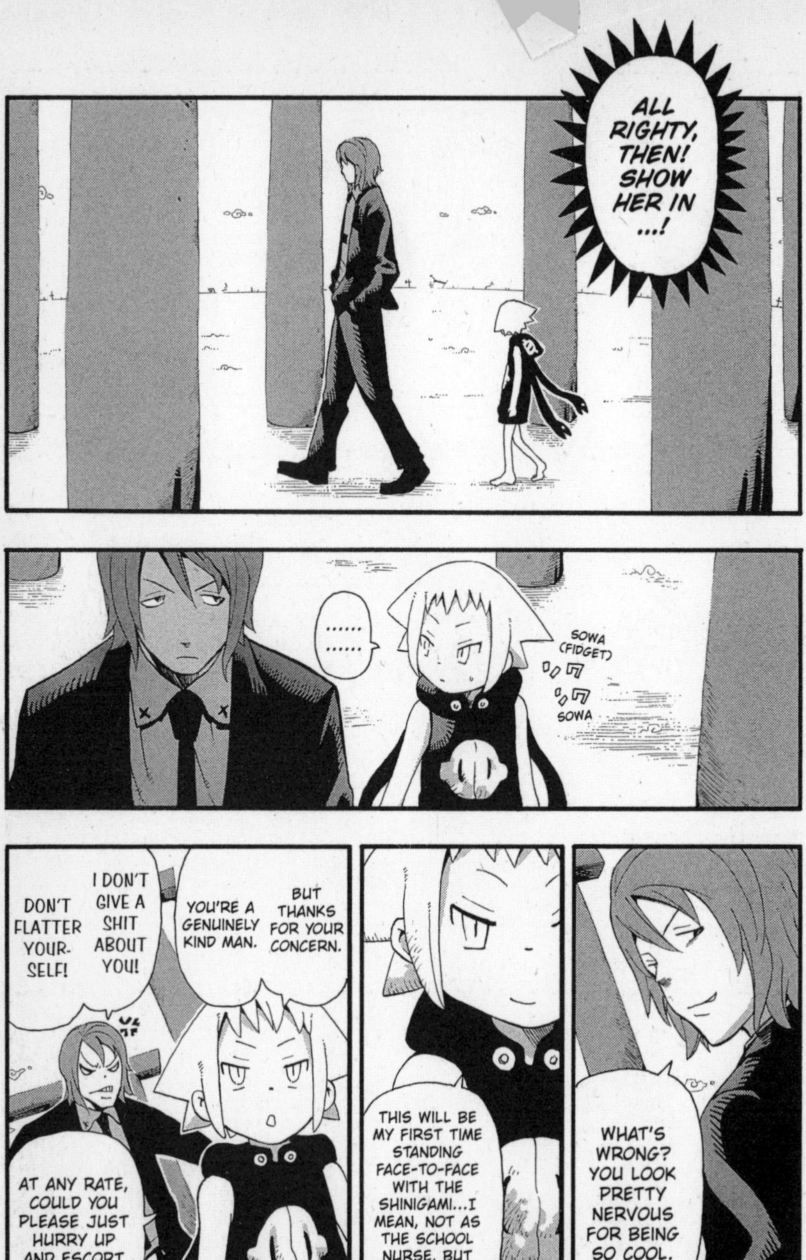
ALL RIGHTY, THEN! SHOW HER IN ...!
SOWA (FIDGET)
SOWA
......
......
WHAT'S WRONG? YOU LOOK PRETTY NERVOUS FOR BEING SO COOL.
THIS WILL BE MY FIRST TIME STANDING FACE-TO-FACE WITH THE SHINIGAMI...I MEAN, NOT AS THE SCHOOL NURSE, BUT AS AN ACTUAL WITCH.
BUT THANKS FOR YOUR CONCERN.
YOU'RE A GENUINELY KIND MAN.
I DON'T GIVE A SHIT ABOUT YOU!
DON'T FLATTER YOUR-SELF!
AT ANY RATE, COULD YOU PLEASE JUST HURRY UP AND ESCORT ME IN?

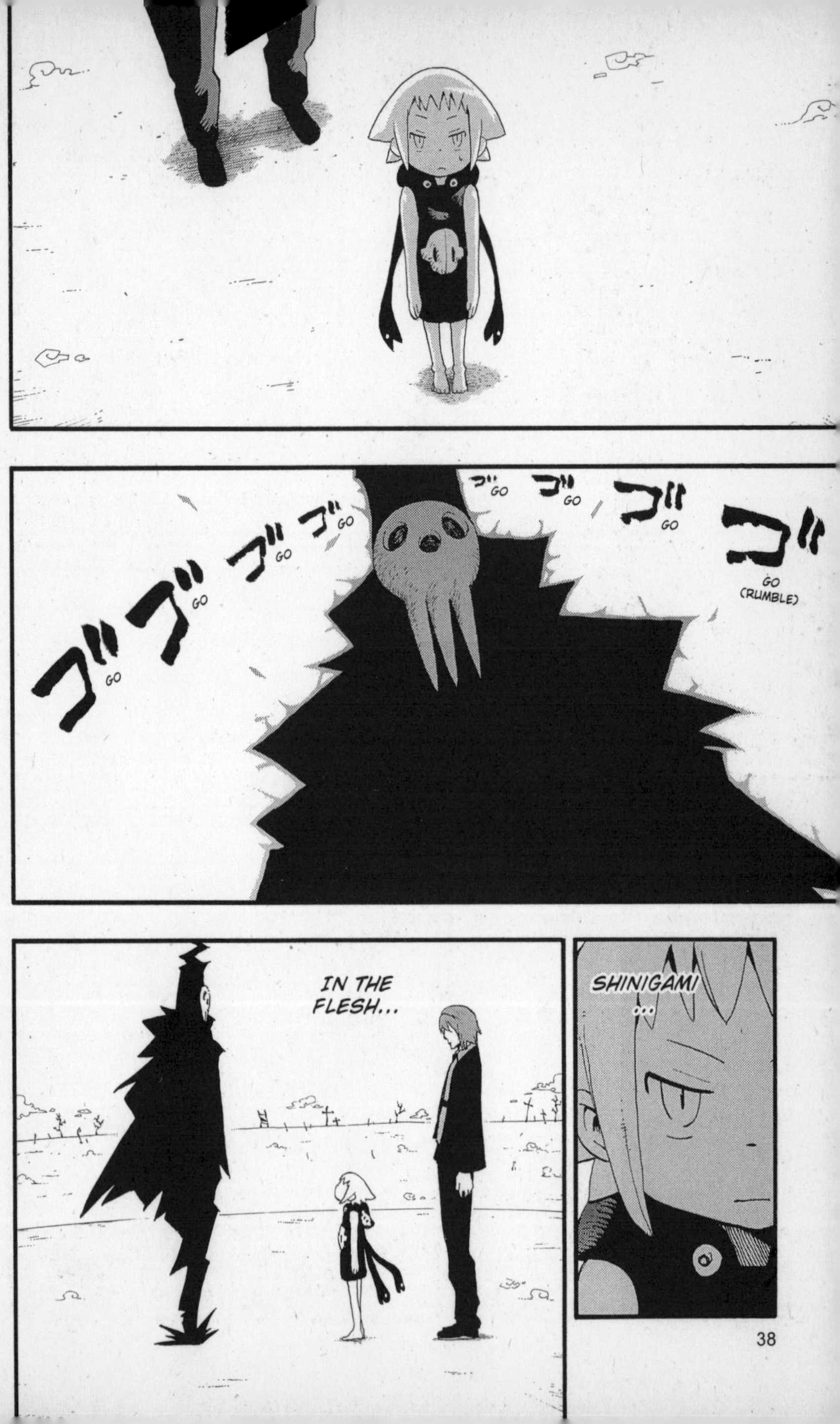
ゴ GO (RUMBLE)
ゴ GO
ゴ GO
ゴ GO
ゴ GO
ゴ GO
ゴ GO
SHINIGAMI...
IN THE FLESH...

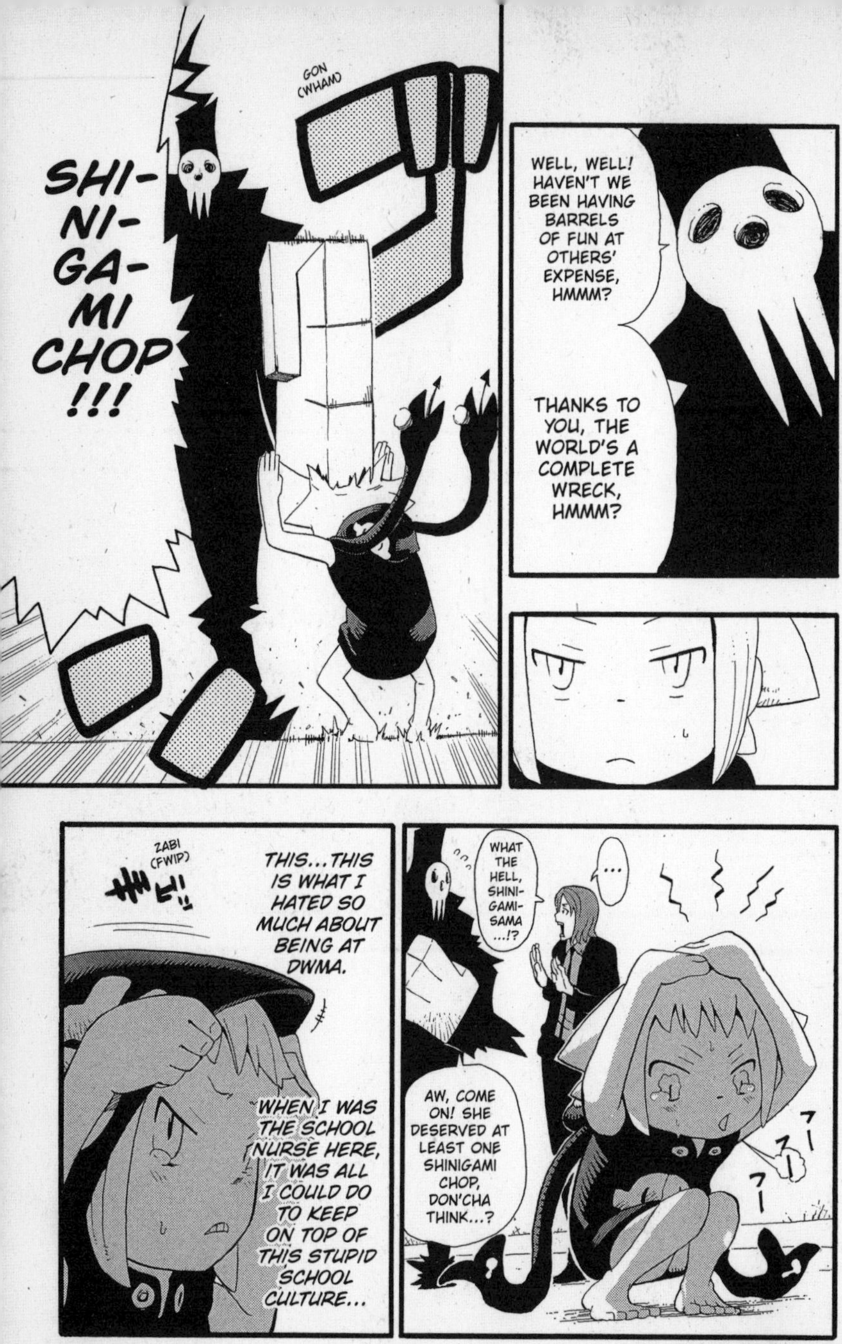

WELL, WELL! HAVEN'T WE BEEN HAVING BARRELS OF FUN AT OTHERS' EXPENSE, HMMM?
THANKS TO YOU, THE WORLD'S A COMPLETE WRECK, HMMM?
GON (WHAM)
SHI-NI-GA-MI CHOP!!!
WHAT THE HELL, SHINIGAMI-SAMA...!?
...
AW, COME ON! SHE DESERVED AT LEAST ONE SHINIGAMI CHOP, DON'CHA THINK...?
ZABI (FWIP)
THIS...THIS IS WHAT I HATED SO MUCH ABOUT BEING AT DWMA.
WHEN I WAS THE SCHOOL NURSE HERE, IT WAS ALL I COULD DO TO KEEP ON TOP OF THIS STUPID SCHOOL CULTURE...

SFX: FUU (PANT) FUU FUU

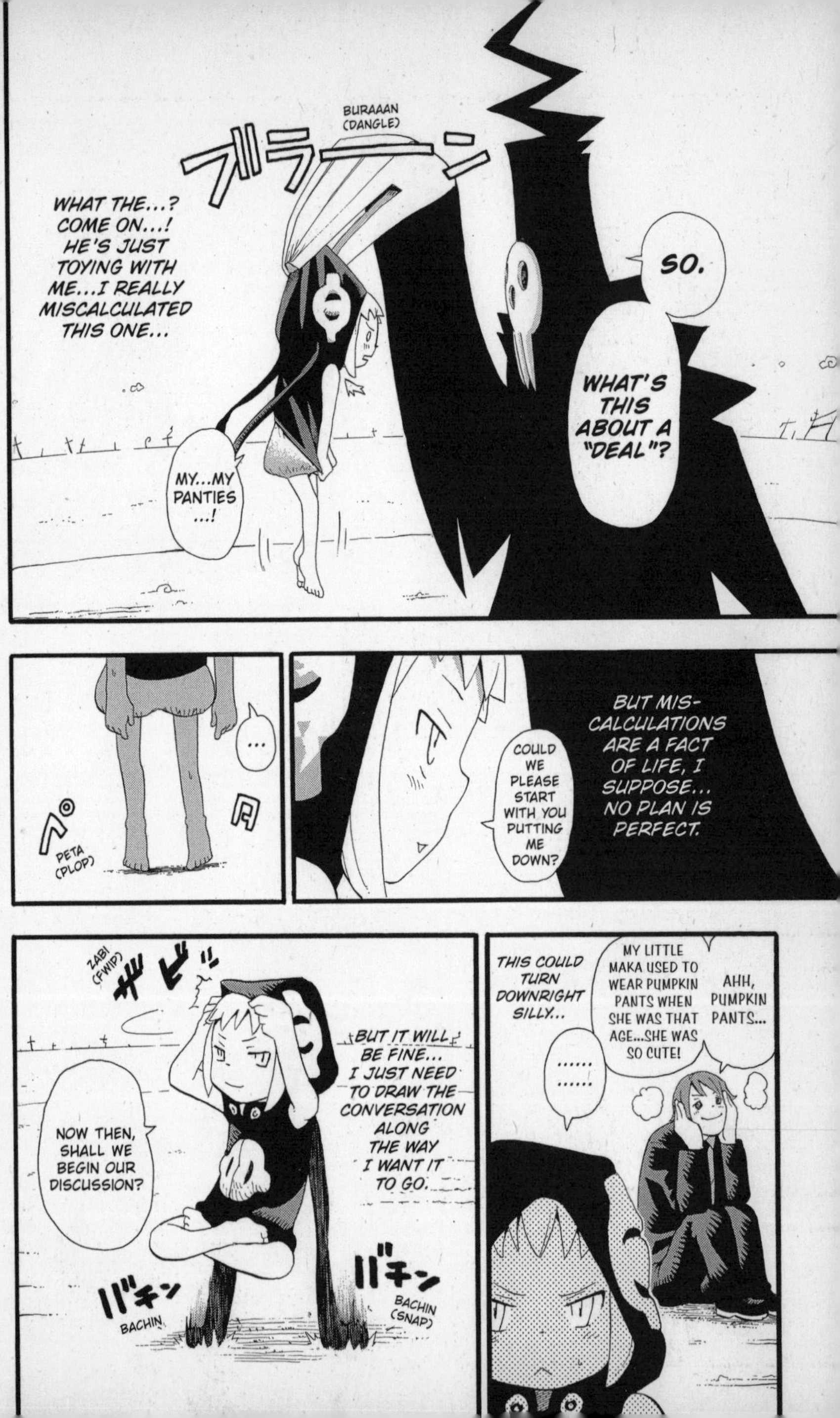
SO.
WHAT'S THIS ABOUT A "DEAL"?
BURAAAN (DANGLE)
WHAT THE...? COME ON...! HE'S JUST TOYING WITH ME...I REALLY MISCALCULATED THIS ONE...
MY...MY PANTIES...!
BUT MIS-CALCULATIONS ARE A FACT OF LIFE, I SUPPOSE... NO PLAN IS PERFECT.
COULD WE PLEASE START WITH YOU PUTTING ME DOWN?
...
PETA (PLOP)
AHH, PUMPKIN PANTS...
MY LITTLE MAKA USED TO WEAR PUMPKIN PANTS WHEN SHE WAS THAT AGE...SHE WAS SO CUTE!
THIS COULD TURN DOWNRIGHT SILLY...
....
ZABI (FWIP)
BUT IT WILL BE FINE... I JUST NEED TO DRAW THE CONVERSATION ALONG THE WAY I WANT IT TO GO.
NOW THEN, SHALL WE BEGIN OUR DISCUSSION?
BACHIN (SNAP)
BACHIN

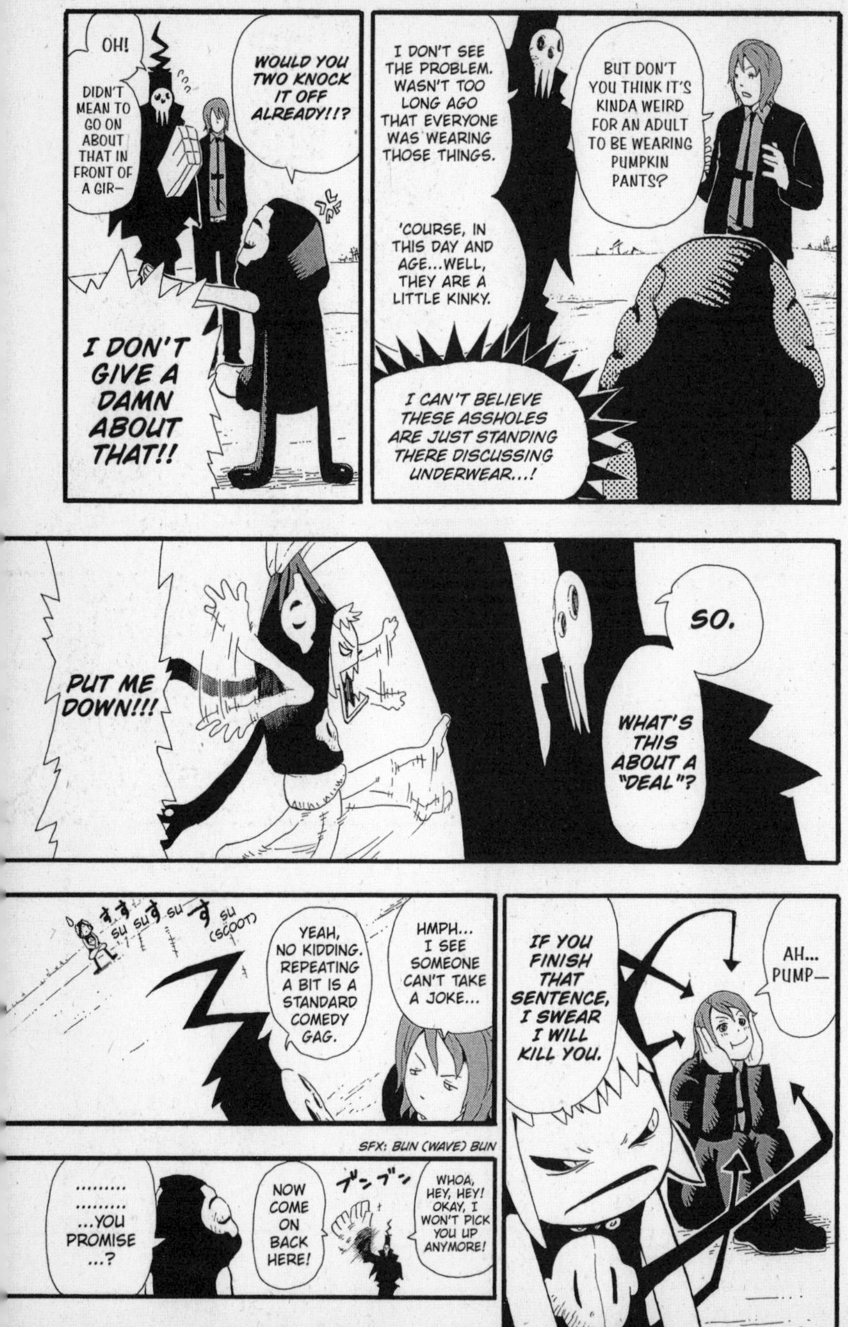
BUT DON'T YOU THINK IT'S KINDA WEIRD FOR AN ADULT TO BE WEARING PUMPKIN PANTS?
I DON'T SEE THE PROBLEM. WASN'T TOO LONG AGO THAT EVERYONE WAS WEARING THOSE THINGS.
'COURSE, IN THIS DAY AND AGE...WELL, THEY ARE A LITTLE KINKY.
I CAN'T BELIEVE THESE ASSHOLES ARE JUST STANDING THERE DISCUSSING UNDERWEAR...!
WOULD YOU TWO KNOCK IT OFF ALREADY!!?
OH!
DIDN'T MEAN TO GO ON ABOUT THAT IN FRONT OF A GIR—
I DON'T GIVE A DAMN ABOUT THAT!!
SO.
WHAT'S THIS ABOUT A "DEAL"?
PUT ME DOWN!!!
AH... PUMP—
IF YOU FINISH THAT SENTENCE, I SWEAR I WILL KILL YOU.
HMPH... I SEE SOMEONE CAN'T TAKE A JOKE...
YEAH, NO KIDDING. REPEATING A BIT IS A STANDARD COMEDY GAG.
すす SU SU す SU す SU (SCOOT)
SFX: BUN (WAVE) BUN
ブンブン
WHOA, HEY, HEY! OKAY, I WON'T PICK YOU UP ANYMORE!
NOW COME ON BACK HERE!
....YOU PROMISE ...?

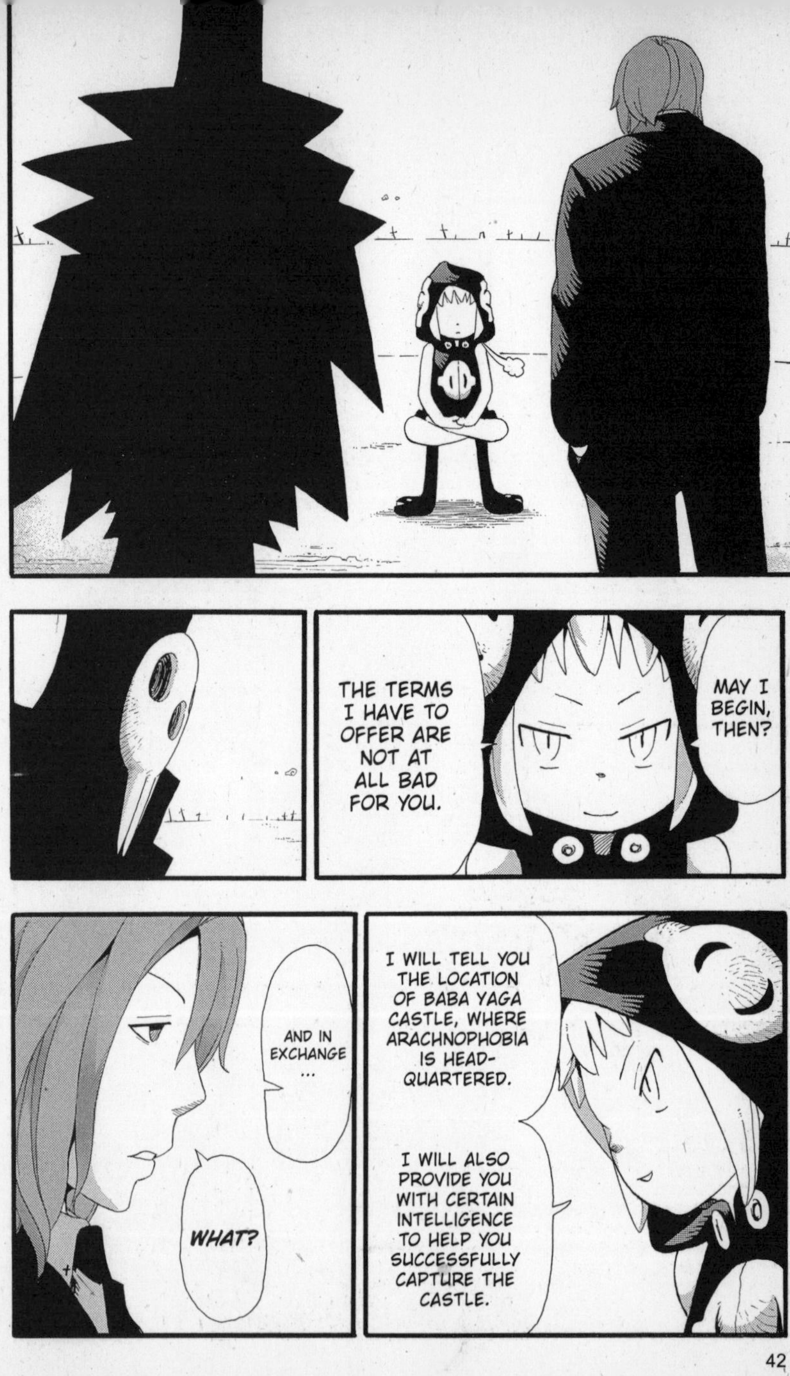
MAY I BEGIN, THEN?
THE TERMS I HAVE TO OFFER ARE NOT AT ALL BAD FOR YOU.
I WILL TELL YOU THE LOCATION OF BABA YAGA CASTLE, WHERE ARACHNOPHOBIA IS HEAD-QUARTERED.
I WILL ALSO PROVIDE YOU WITH CERTAIN INTELLIGENCE TO HELP YOU SUCCESSFULLY CAPTURE THE CASTLE.
AND IN EXCHANGE ...
WHAT?

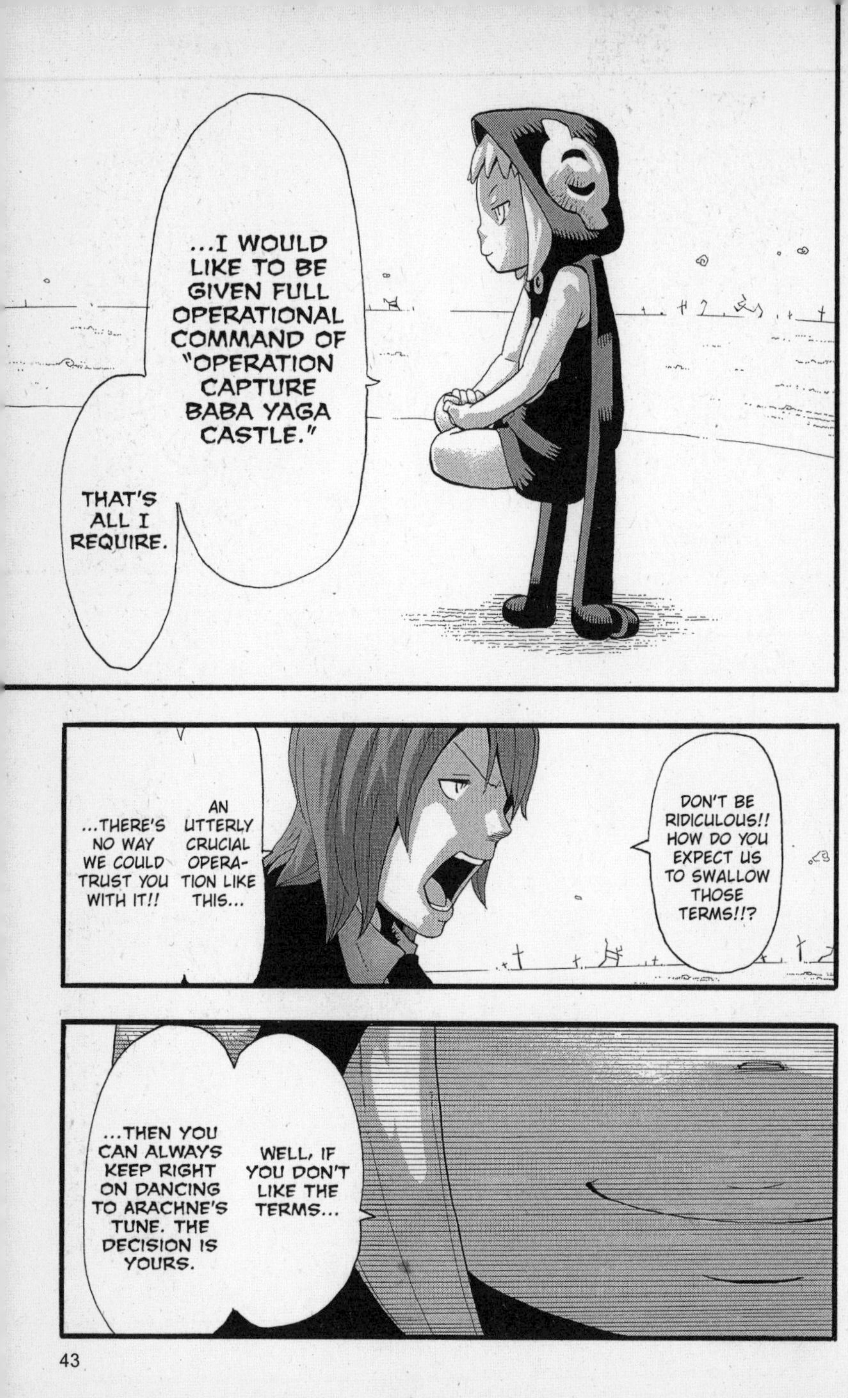
...I WOULD LIKE TO BE GIVEN FULL OPERATIONAL COMMAND OF "OPERATION CAPTURE BABA YAGA CASTLE."
THAT'S ALL I REQUIRE.
DON'T BE RIDICULOUS!! HOW DO YOU EXPECT US TO SWALLOW THOSE TERMS!!?
AN UTTERLY CRUCIAL OPERATION LIKE THIS...
...THERE'S NO WAY WE COULD TRUST YOU WITH IT!!
WELL, IF YOU DON'T LIKE THE TERMS...
...THEN YOU CAN ALWAYS KEEP RIGHT ON DANCING TO ARACHNE'S TUNE. THE DECISION IS YOURS.

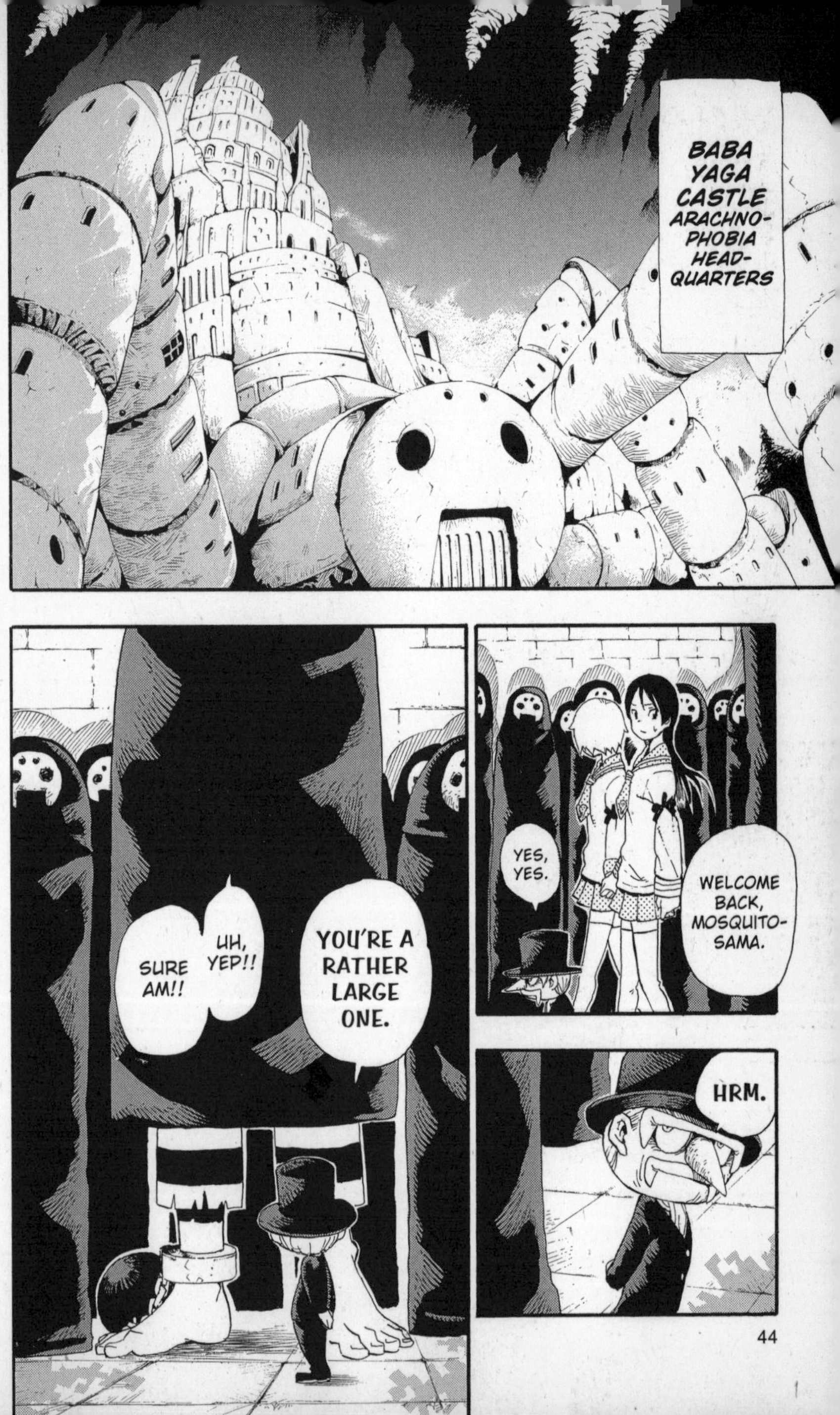
BABA YAGA CASTLE ARACHNOPHOBIA HEADQUARTERS
WELCOME BACK, MOSQUITO-SAMA.
YES, YES.
HRM.
YOU'RE A RATHER LARGE ONE.
UH, YEP!!
SURE AM!!

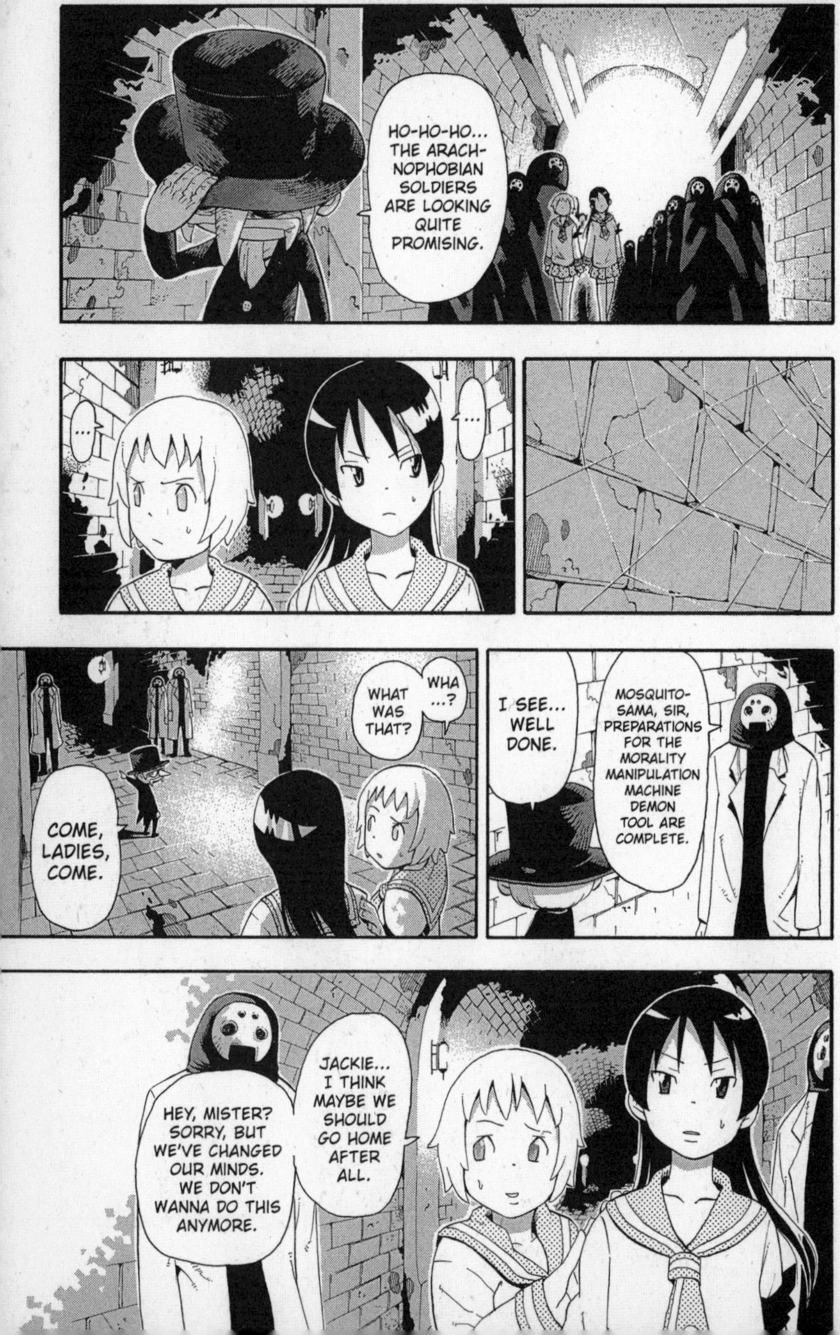
HO-HO-HO... THE ARACH-NOPHOBIAN SOLDIERS ARE LOOKING QUITE PROMISING.
...
...
MOSQUITO-SAMA, SIR, PREPARATIONS FOR THE MORALITY MANIPULATION MACHINE DEMON TOOL ARE COMPLETE.
I SEE... WELL DONE.
WHA ...?
WHAT WAS THAT?
COME, LADIES, COME.
JACKIE... I THINK MAYBE WE SHOULD GO HOME AFTER ALL.
HEY, MISTER? SORRY, BUT WE'VE CHANGED OUR MINDS. WE DON'T WANNA DO THIS ANYMORE.

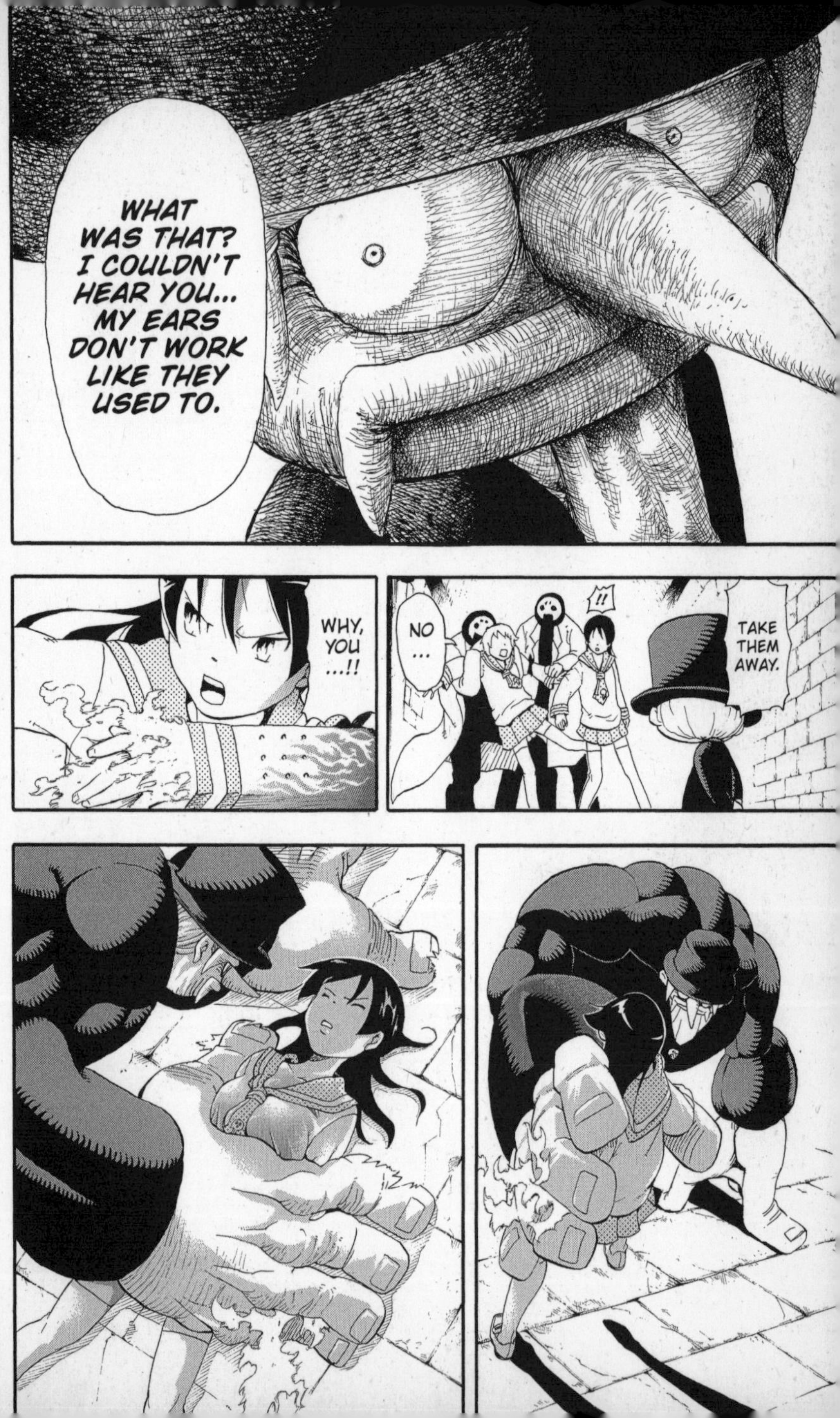
WHAT WAS THAT? I COULDN'T HEAR YOU... MY EARS DON'T WORK LIKE THEY USED TO.
TAKE THEM AWAY.
!!
NO ...
WHY, YOU ...!!

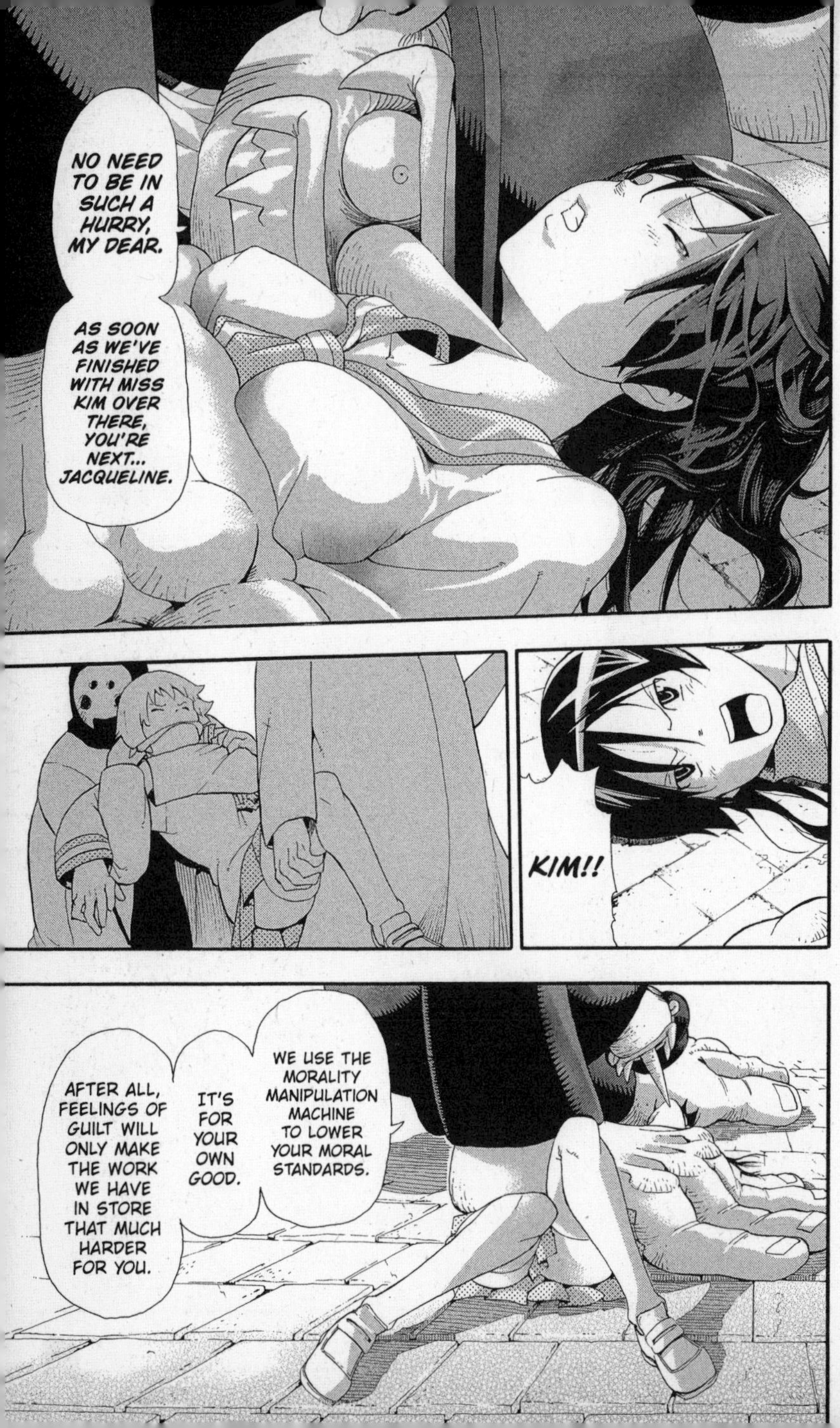
NO NEED TO BE IN SUCH A HURRY, MY DEAR.
AS SOON AS WE'VE FINISHED WITH MISS KIM OVER THERE, YOU'RE NEXT... JACQUELINE.
KIM!!
WE USE THE MORALITY MANIPULATION MACHINE TO LOWER YOUR MORAL STANDARDS.
IT'S FOR YOUR OWN GOOD.
AFTER ALL, FEELINGS OF GUILT WILL ONLY MAKE THE WORK WE HAVE IN STORE THAT MUCH HARDER FOR YOU.

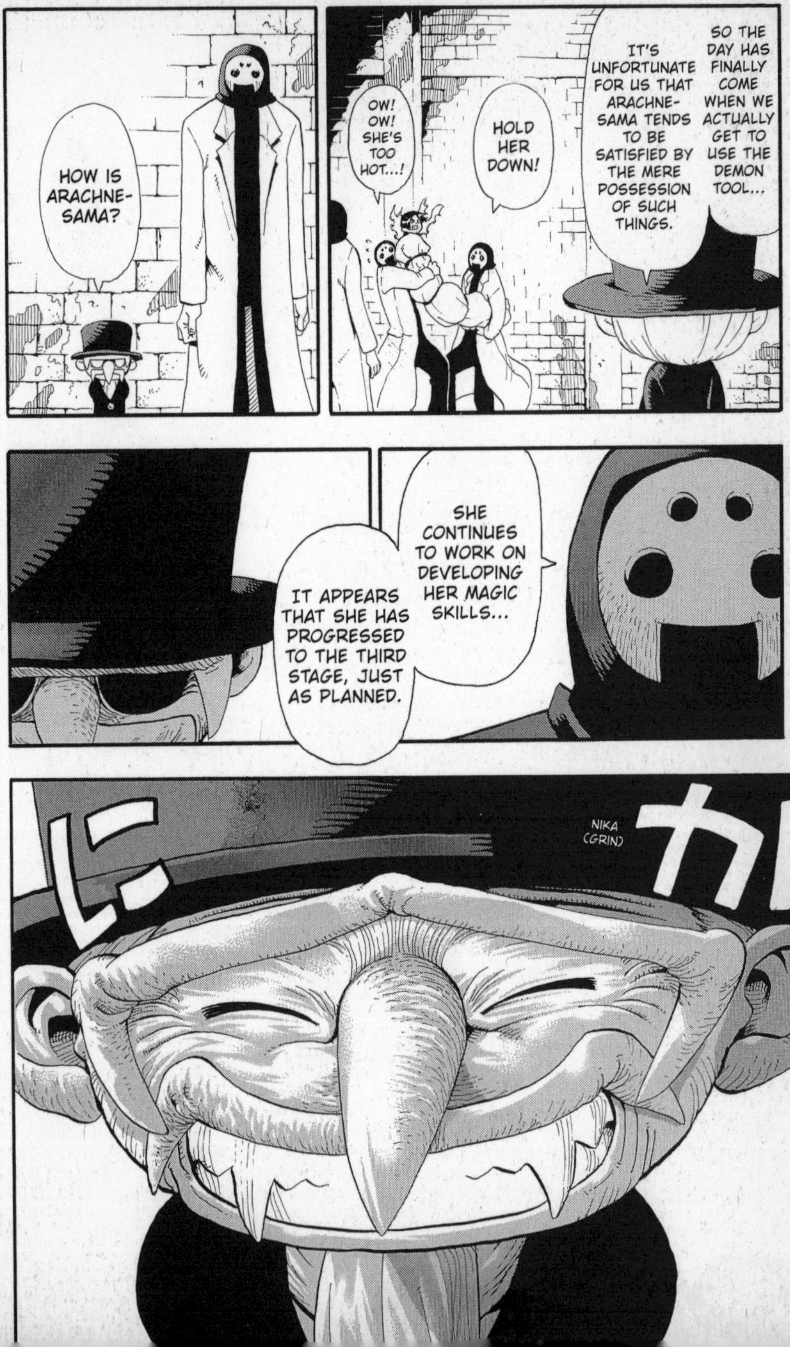
SO THE DAY HAS FINALLY COME WHEN WE ACTUALLY GET TO USE THE DEMON TOOL...
IT'S UNFORTUNATE FOR US THAT ARACHNE-SAMA TENDS TO BE SATISFIED BY THE MERE POSSESSION OF SUCH THINGS.
HOLD HER DOWN!
OW! OW! SHE'S TOO HOT...!
HOW IS ARACHNE-SAMA?
SHE CONTINUES TO WORK ON DEVELOPING HER MAGIC SKILLS...
IT APPEARS THAT SHE HAS PROGRESSED TO THE THIRD STAGE, JUST AS PLANNED.
ニカ
NIKA (GRIN)

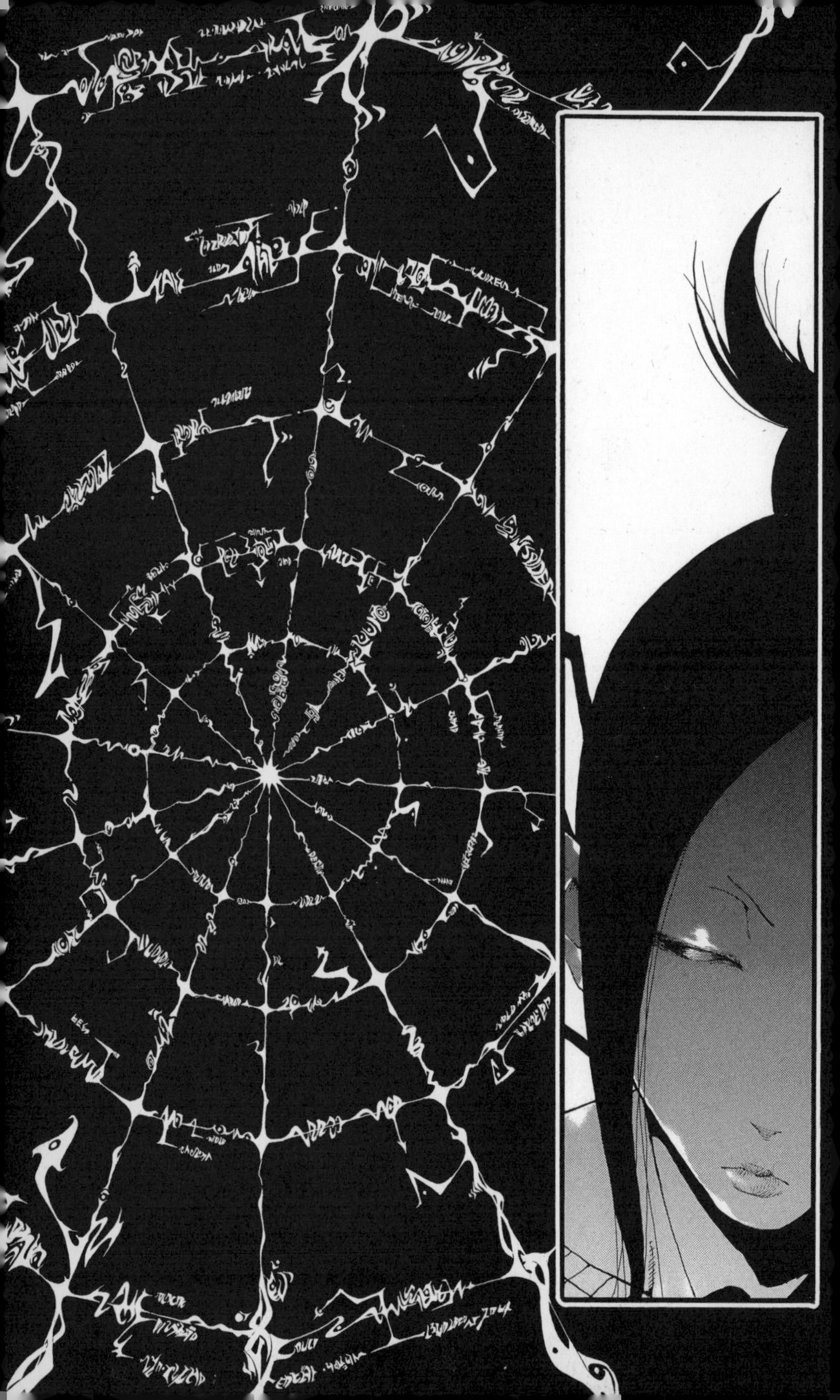

SOUL EATER

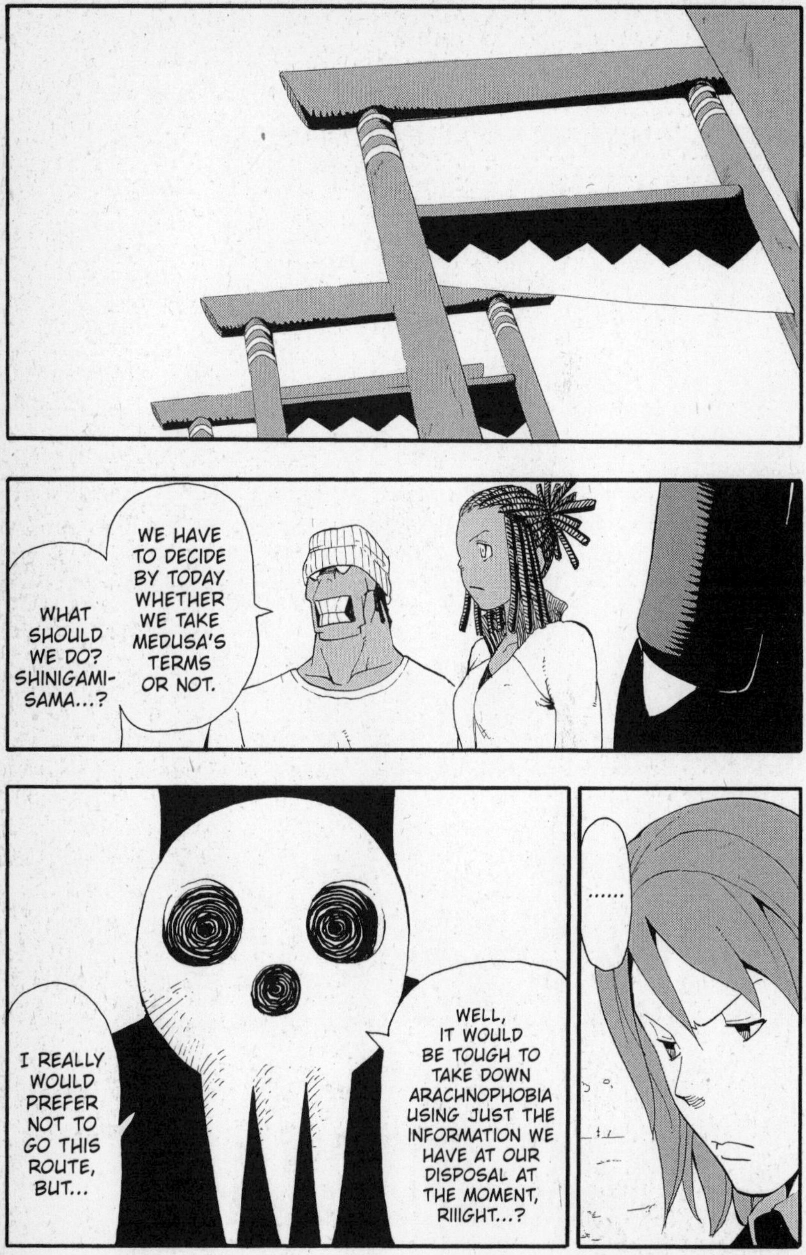
WE HAVE TO DECIDE BY TODAY WHETHER WE TAKE MEDUSA'S TERMS OR NOT.
WHAT SHOULD WE DO? SHINIGAMI-SAMA...?
......
WELL, IT WOULD BE TOUGH TO TAKE DOWN ARACHNOPHOBIA USING JUST THE INFORMATION WE HAVE AT OUR DISPOSAL AT THE MOMENT, RIIIGHT...?
I REALLY WOULD PREFER NOT TO GO THIS ROUTE, BUT...

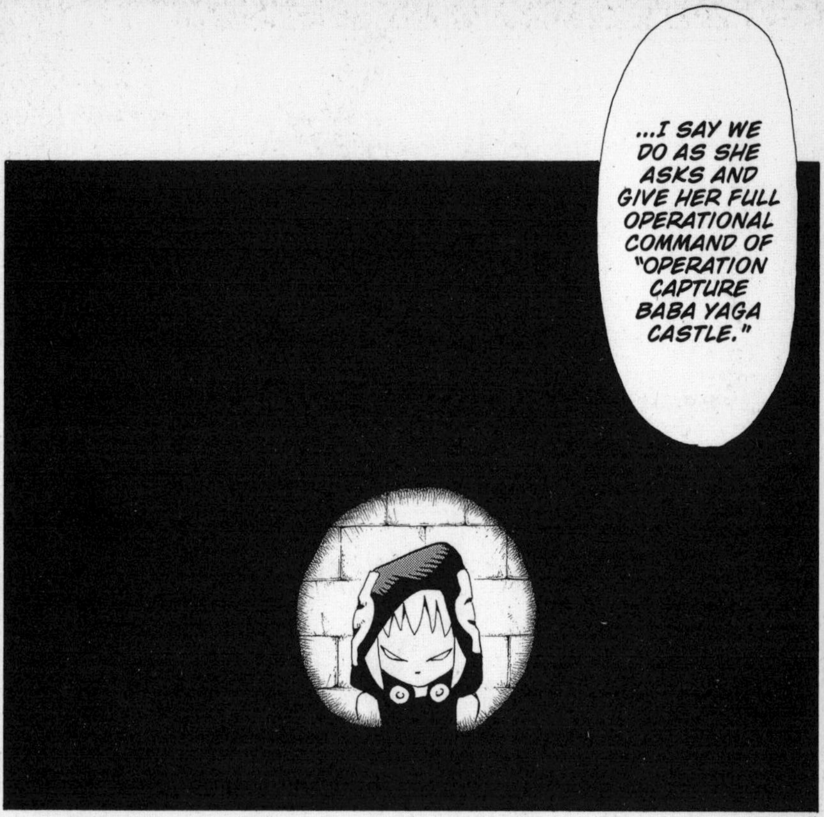
...I SAY WE DO AS SHE ASKS AND GIVE HER FULL OPERATIONAL COMMAND OF "OPERATION CAPTURE BABA YAGA CASTLE."

SOUL EATER

CHAPTER 46: OPERATION CAPTURE BABA YAGA CASTLE (PART 1)

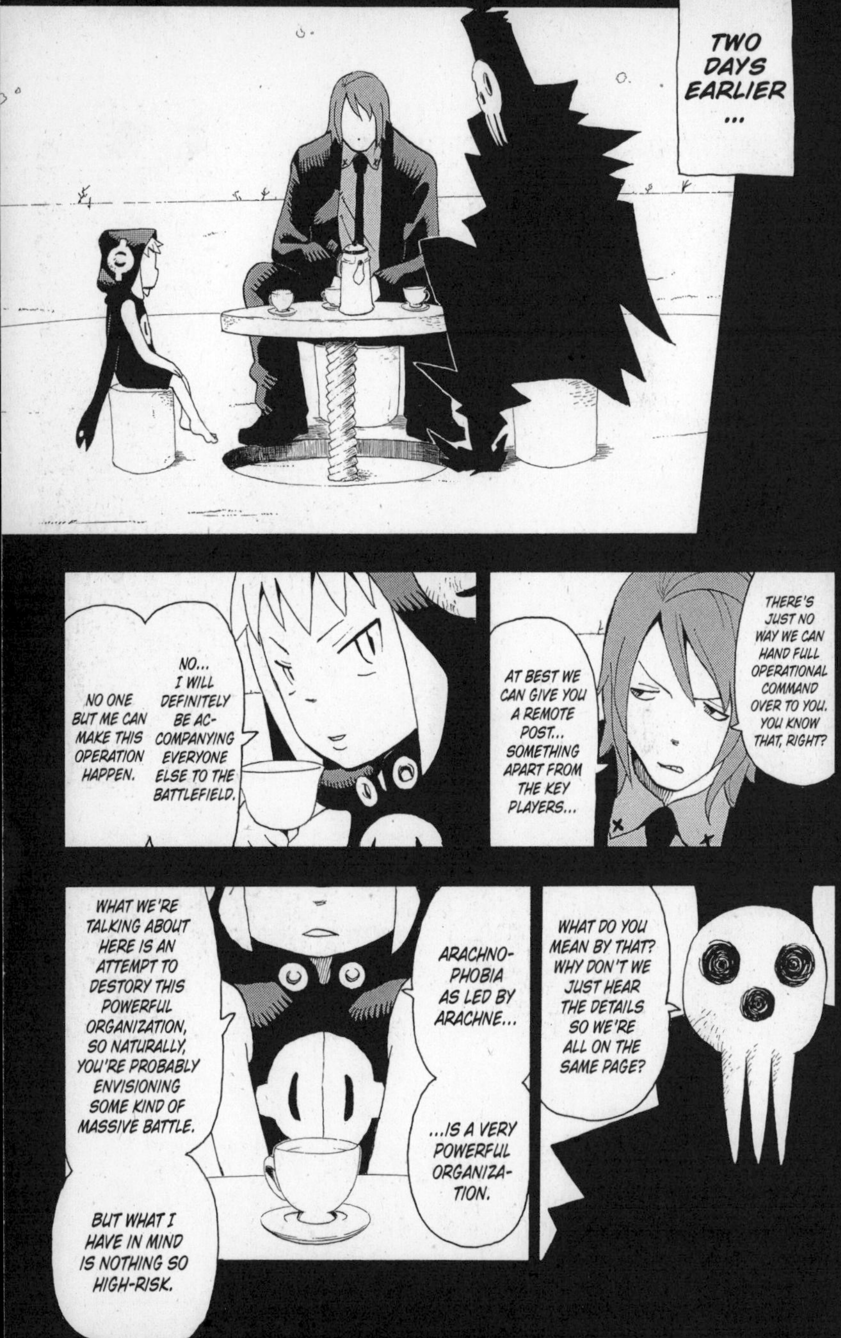
TWO DAYS EARLIER ...
THERE'S JUST NO WAY WE CAN HAND FULL OPERATIONAL COMMAND OVER TO YOU. YOU KNOW THAT, RIGHT?
AT BEST WE CAN GIVE YOU A REMOTE POST... SOMETHING APART FROM THE KEY PLAYERS...
NO... I WILL DEFINITELY BE AC-COMPANYING EVERYONE ELSE TO THE BATTLEFIELD.
NO ONE BUT ME CAN MAKE THIS OPERATION HAPPEN.
WHAT DO YOU MEAN BY THAT? WHY DON'T WE JUST HEAR THE DETAILS SO WE'RE ALL ON THE SAME PAGE?
ARACHNO-PHOBIA AS LED BY ARACHNE...
...IS A VERY POWERFUL ORGANIZA-TION.
WHAT WE'RE TALKING ABOUT HERE IS AN ATTEMPT TO DESTORY THIS POWERFUL ORGANIZATION, SO NATURALLY, YOU'RE PROBABLY ENVISIONING SOME KIND OF MASSIVE BATTLE.
BUT WHAT I HAVE IN MIND IS NOTHING SO HIGH-RISK.

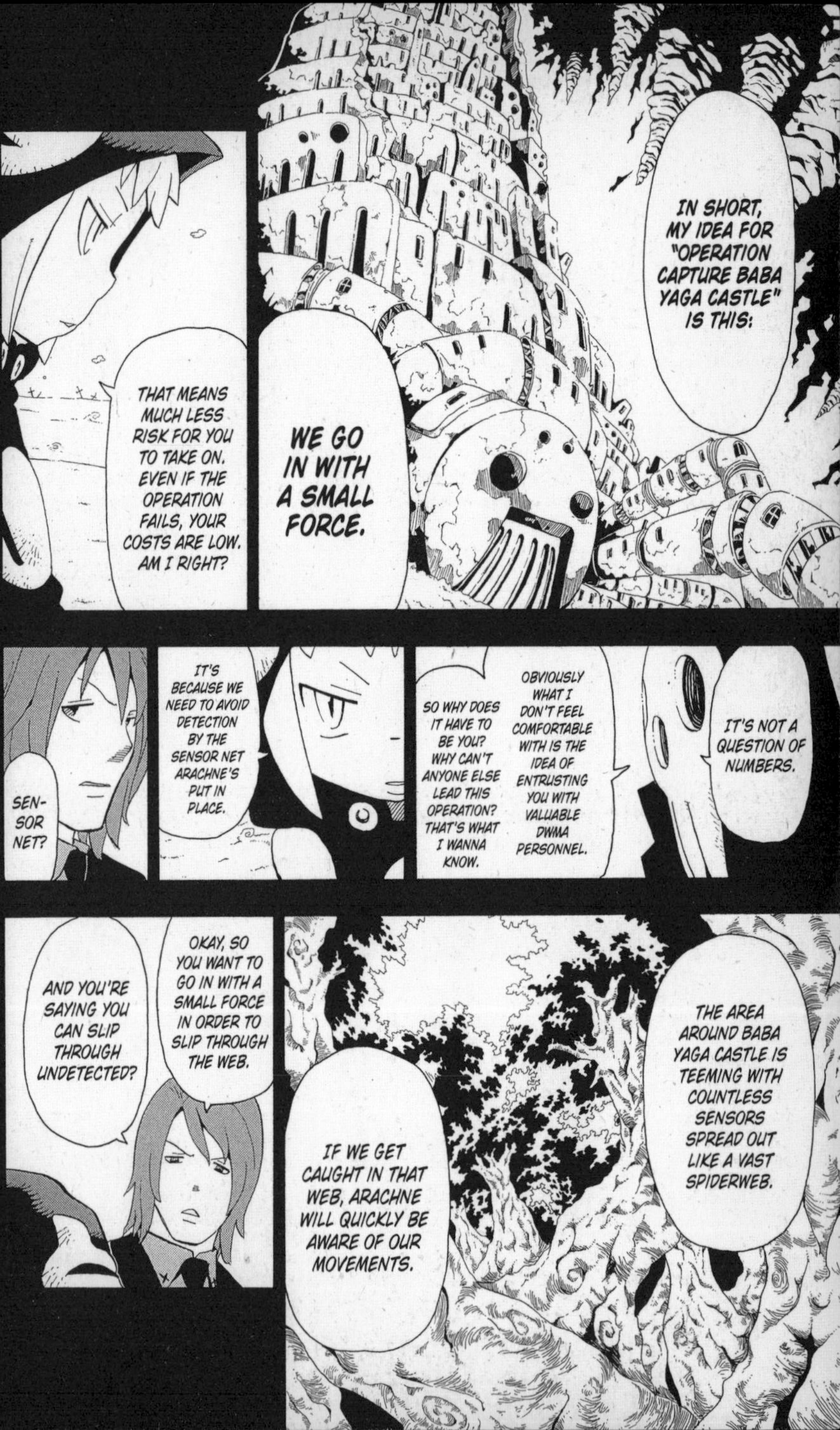
IN SHORT, MY IDEA FOR "OPERATION CAPTURE BABA YAGA CASTLE" IS THIS:
WE GO IN WITH A SMALL FORCE.
THAT MEANS MUCH LESS RISK FOR YOU TO TAKE ON. EVEN IF THE OPERATION FAILS, YOUR COSTS ARE LOW. AM I RIGHT?
IT'S NOT A QUESTION OF NUMBERS.
OBVIOUSLY WHAT I DON'T FEEL COMFORTABLE WITH IS THE IDEA OF ENTRUSTING YOU WITH VALUABLE DWMA PERSONNEL.
SO WHY DOES IT HAVE TO BE YOU? WHY CAN'T ANYONE ELSE LEAD THIS OPERATION? THAT'S WHAT I WANNA KNOW.
IT'S BECAUSE WE NEED TO AVOID DETECTION BY THE SENSOR NET ARACHNE'S PUT IN PLACE.
SEN-SOR NET?
THE AREA AROUND BABA YAGA CASTLE IS TEEMING WITH COUNTLESS SENSORS SPREAD OUT LIKE A VAST SPIDERWEB.
IF WE GET CAUGHT IN THAT WEB, ARACHNE WILL QUICKLY BE AWARE OF OUR MOVEMENTS.
OKAY, SO YOU WANT TO GO IN WITH A SMALL FORCE IN ORDER TO SLIP THROUGH THE WEB.
AND YOU'RE SAYING YOU CAN SLIP THROUGH UNDETECTED?

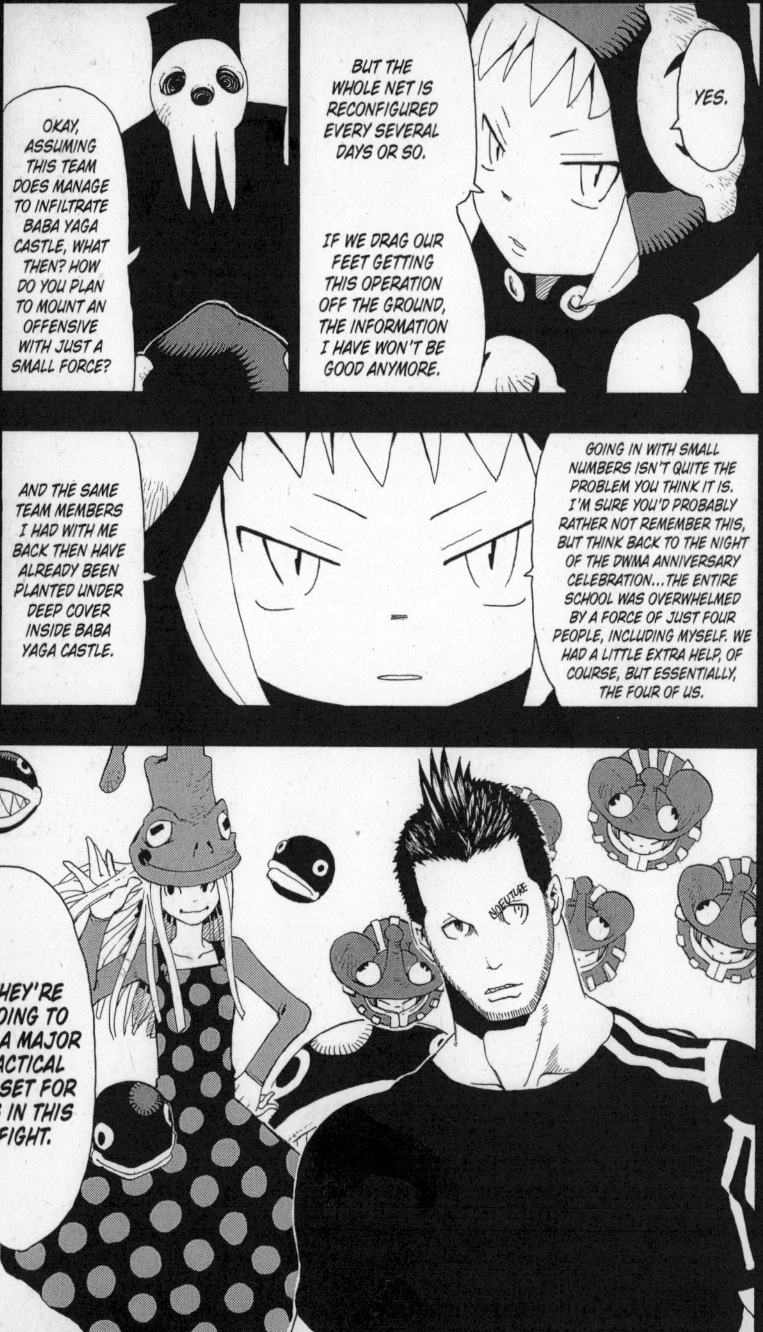
YES.
BUT THE WHOLE NET IS RECONFIGURED EVERY SEVERAL DAYS OR SO.
IF WE DRAG OUR FEET GETTING THIS OPERATION OFF THE GROUND, THE INFORMATION I HAVE WON'T BE GOOD ANYMORE.
OKAY, ASSUMING THIS TEAM DOES MANAGE TO INFILTRATE BABA YAGA CASTLE, WHAT THEN? HOW DO YOU PLAN TO MOUNT AN OFFENSIVE WITH JUST A SMALL FORCE?
GOING IN WITH SMALL NUMBERS ISN'T QUITE THE PROBLEM YOU THINK IT IS. I'M SURE YOU'D PROBABLY RATHER NOT REMEMBER THIS, BUT THINK BACK TO THE NIGHT OF THE DWMA ANNIVERSARY CELEBRATION...THE ENTIRE SCHOOL WAS OVERWHELMED BY A FORCE OF JUST FOUR PEOPLE, INCLUDING MYSELF. WE HAD A LITTLE EXTRA HELP, OF COURSE, BUT ESSENTIALLY, THE FOUR OF US.
AND THE SAME TEAM MEMBERS I HAD WITH ME BACK THEN HAVE ALREADY BEEN PLANTED UNDER DEEP COVER INSIDE BABA YAGA CASTLE.
THEY'RE GOING TO BE A MAJOR TACTICAL ASSET FOR US IN THIS FIGHT.

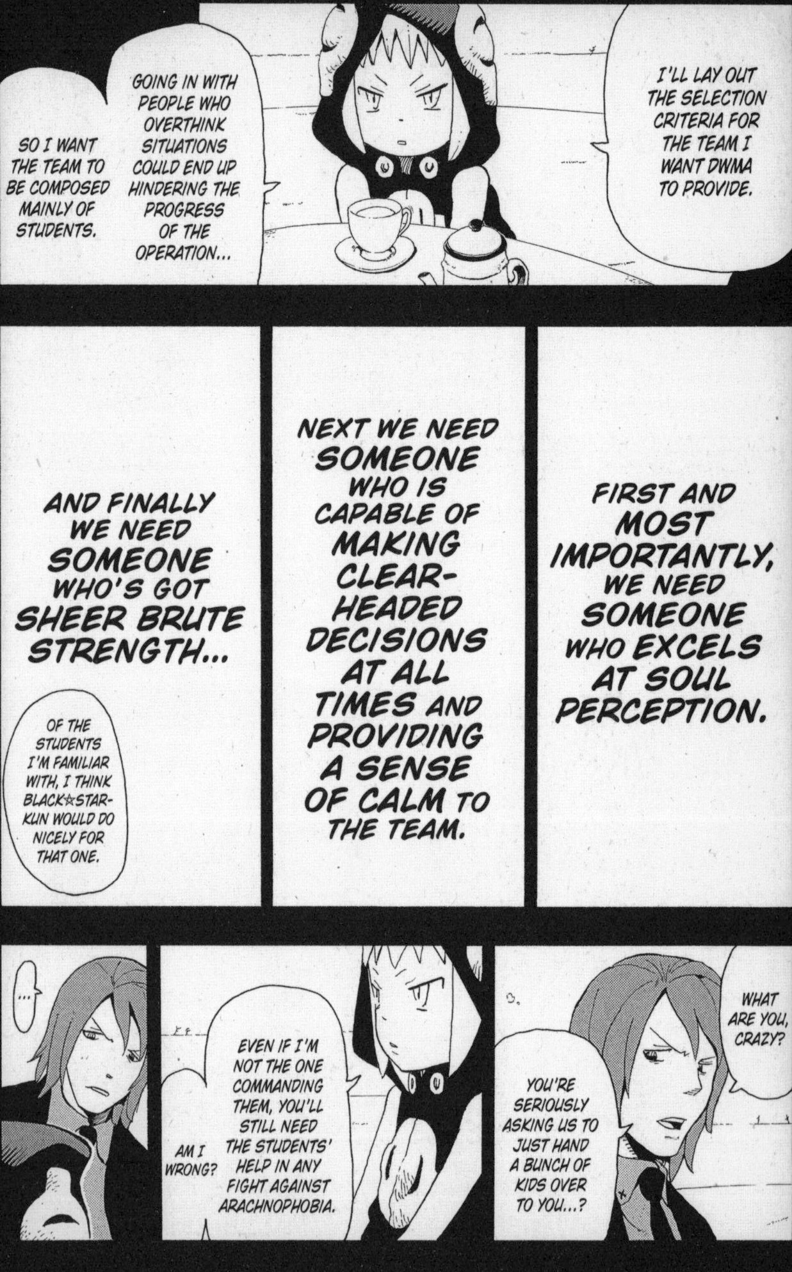
I'LL LAY OUT THE SELECTION CRITERIA FOR THE TEAM I WANT DWMA TO PROVIDE.
GOING IN WITH PEOPLE WHO OVERTHINK SITUATIONS COULD END UP HINDERING THE PROGRESS OF THE OPERATION...
SO I WANT THE TEAM TO BE COMPOSED MAINLY OF STUDENTS.
FIRST AND MOST IMPORTANTLY, WE NEED SOMEONE WHO EXCELS AT SOUL PERCEPTION.
NEXT WE NEED SOMEONE WHO IS CAPABLE OF MAKING CLEAR-HEADED DECISIONS AT ALL TIMES AND PROVIDING A SENSE OF CALM TO THE TEAM.
AND FINALLY WE NEED SOMEONE WHO'S GOT SHEER BRUTE STRENGTH...
OF THE STUDENTS I'M FAMILIAR WITH, I THINK BLACK☆STAR-KUN WOULD DO NICELY FOR THAT ONE.
WHAT ARE YOU, CRAZY?
YOU'RE SERIOUSLY ASKING US TO JUST HAND A BUNCH OF KIDS OVER TO YOU...?
EVEN IF I'M NOT THE ONE COMMANDING THEM, YOU'LL STILL NEED THE STUDENTS' HELP IN ANY FIGHT AGAINST ARACHNOPHOBIA.
AM I WRONG?
...

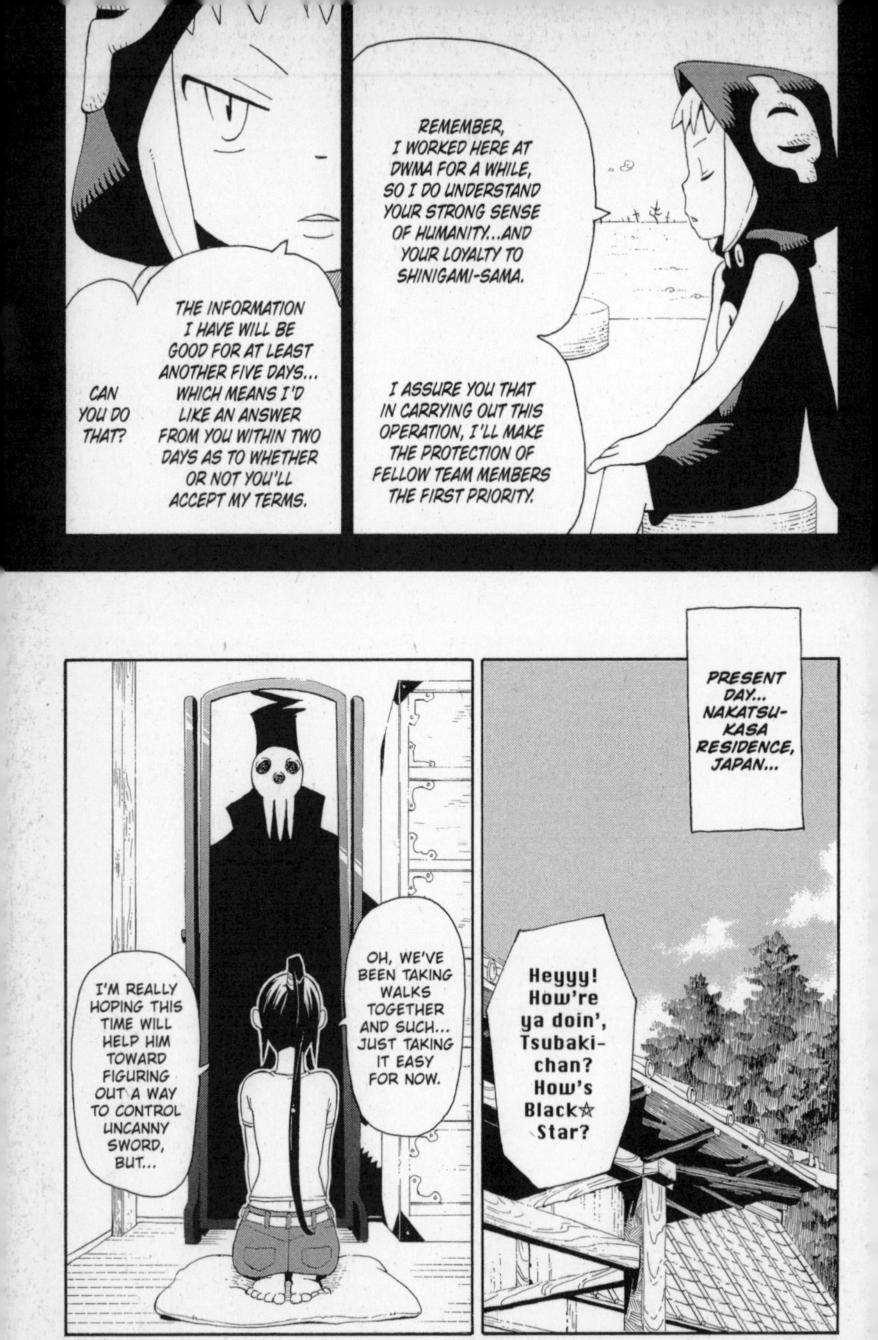
REMEMBER, I WORKED HERE AT DWMA FOR A WHILE, SO I DO UNDERSTAND YOUR STRONG SENSE OF HUMANITY...AND YOUR LOYALTY TO SHINIGAMI-SAMA.
I ASSURE YOU THAT IN CARRYING OUT THIS OPERATION, I'LL MAKE THE PROTECTION OF FELLOW TEAM MEMBERS THE FIRST PRIORITY.
THE INFORMATION I HAVE WILL BE GOOD FOR AT LEAST ANOTHER FIVE DAYS... WHICH MEANS I'D LIKE AN ANSWER FROM YOU WITHIN TWO DAYS AS TO WHETHER OR NOT YOU'LL ACCEPT MY TERMS.
CAN YOU DO THAT?
PRESENT DAY... NAKATSUKASA RESIDENCE, JAPAN...
Heyyy! How're ya doin', Tsubaki-chan? How's Black☆Star?
OH, WE'VE BEEN TAKING WALKS TOGETHER AND SUCH... JUST TAKING IT EASY FOR NOW.
I'M REALLY HOPING THIS TIME WILL HELP HIM TOWARD FIGURING OUT A WAY TO CONTROL UNCANNY SWORD, BUT...

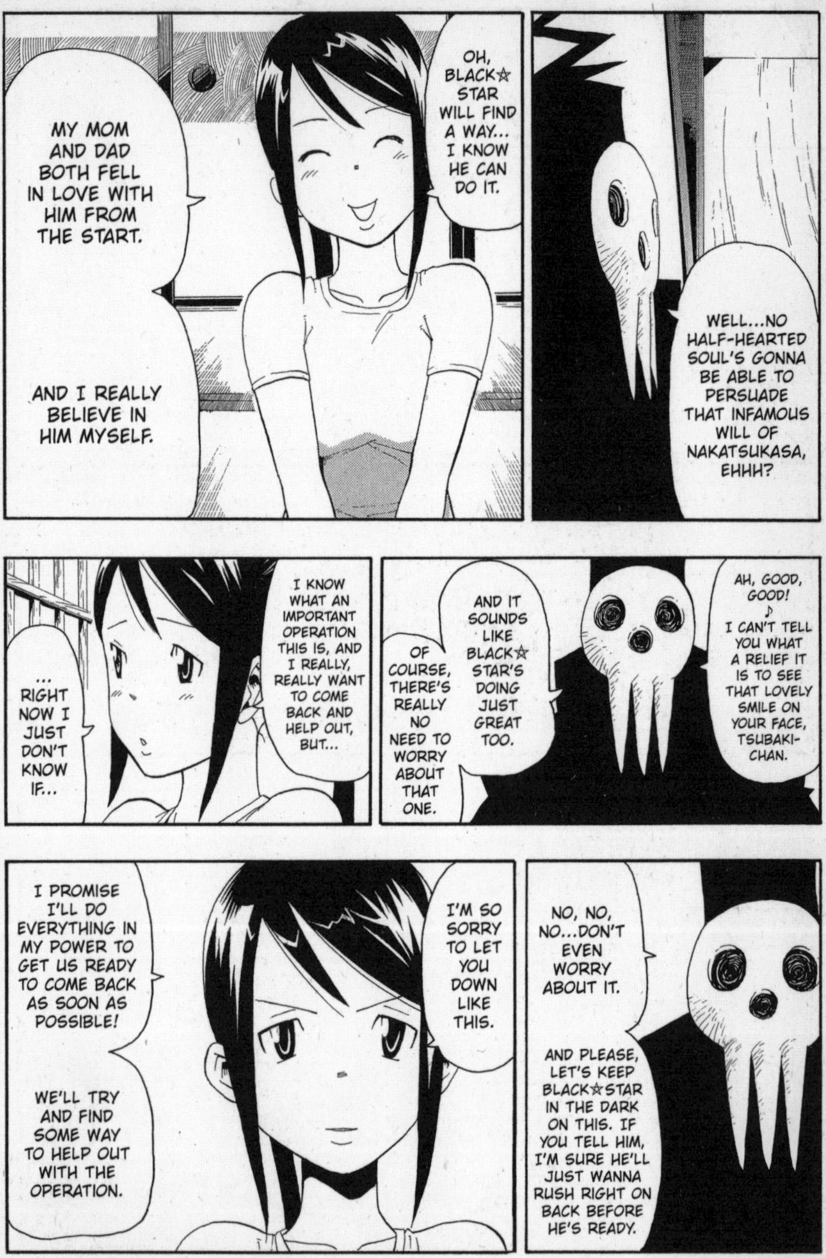
WELL...NO HALF-HEARTED SOUL'S GONNA BE ABLE TO PERSUADE THAT INFAMOUS WILL OF NAKATSUKASA, EHHH?
OH, BLACK☆ STAR WILL FIND A WAY... I KNOW HE CAN DO IT.
MY MOM AND DAD BOTH FELL IN LOVE WITH HIM FROM THE START.
AND I REALLY BELIEVE IN HIM MYSELF.
AH, GOOD, GOOD! ♪ I CAN'T TELL YOU WHAT A RELIEF IT IS TO SEE THAT LOVELY SMILE ON YOUR FACE, TSUBAKI-CHAN.
AND IT SOUNDS LIKE BLACK☆STAR'S DOING JUST GREAT TOO.
OF COURSE, THERE'S REALLY NO NEED TO WORRY ABOUT THAT ONE.
I KNOW WHAT AN IMPORTANT OPERATION THIS IS, AND I REALLY, REALLY WANT TO COME BACK AND HELP OUT, BUT...
...RIGHT NOW I JUST DON'T KNOW IF...
NO, NO, NO...DON'T EVEN WORRY ABOUT IT.
AND PLEASE, LET'S KEEP BLACK☆STAR IN THE DARK ON THIS. IF YOU TELL HIM, I'M SURE HE'LL JUST WANNA RUSH RIGHT ON BACK BEFORE HE'S READY.
I'M SO SORRY TO LET YOU DOWN LIKE THIS.
I PROMISE I'LL DO EVERYTHING IN MY POWER TO GET US READY TO COME BACK AS SOON AS POSSIBLE!
WE'LL TRY AND FIND SOME WAY TO HELP OUT WITH THE OPERATION.

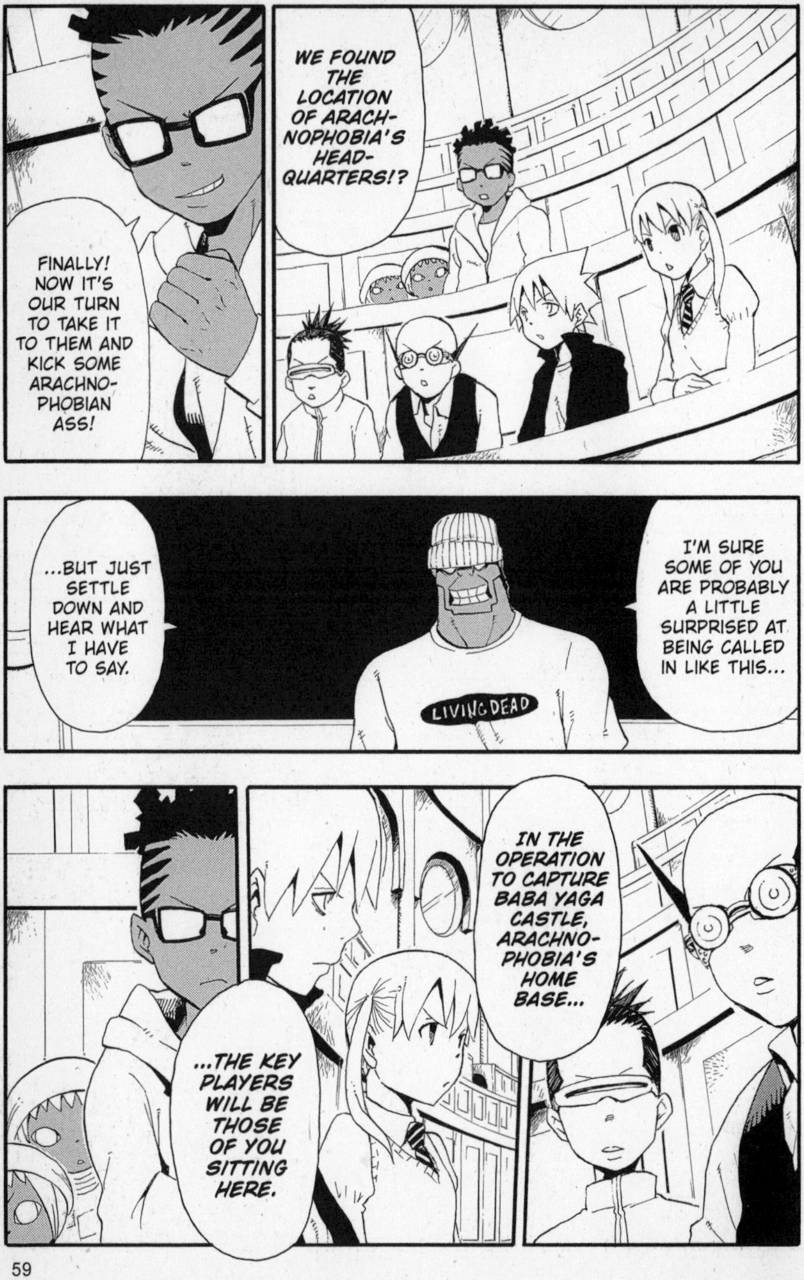
WE FOUND THE LOCATION OF ARACHNOPHOBIA'S HEADQUARTERS!?
FINALLY! NOW IT'S OUR TURN TO TAKE IT TO THEM AND KICK SOME ARACHNOPHOBIAN ASS!
I'M SURE SOME OF YOU ARE PROBABLY A LITTLE SURPRISED AT BEING CALLED IN LIKE THIS...
LIVING DEAD
...BUT JUST SETTLE DOWN AND HEAR WHAT I HAVE TO SAY.
IN THE OPERATION TO CAPTURE BABA YAGA CASTLE, ARACHNOPHOBIA'S HOME BASE...
...THE KEY PLAYERS WILL BE THOSE OF YOU SITTING HERE.

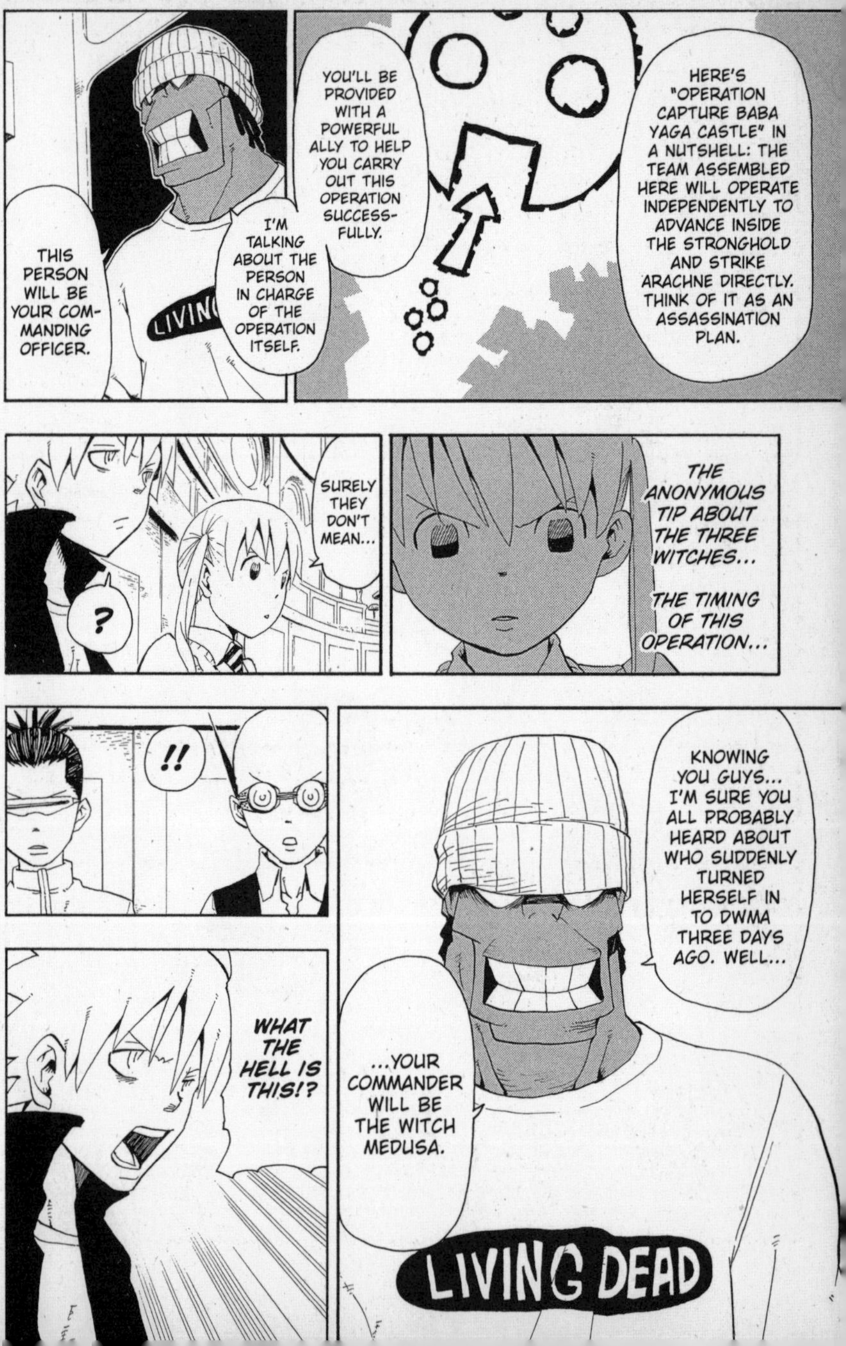
HERE'S "OPERATION CAPTURE BABA YAGA CASTLE" IN A NUTSHELL: THE TEAM ASSEMBLED HERE WILL OPERATE INDEPENDENTLY TO ADVANCE INSIDE THE STRONGHOLD AND STRIKE ARACHNE DIRECTLY. THINK OF IT AS AN ASSASSINATION PLAN.
YOU'LL BE PROVIDED WITH A POWERFUL ALLY TO HELP YOU CARRY OUT THIS OPERATION SUCCESS-FULLY.
I'M TALKING ABOUT THE PERSON IN CHARGE OF THE OPERATION ITSELF.
THIS PERSON WILL BE YOUR COM-MANDING OFFICER.
THE ANONYMOUS TIP ABOUT THE THREE WITCHES...
THE TIMING OF THIS OPERATION...
SURELY THEY DON'T MEAN...
?
KNOWING YOU GUYS... I'M SURE YOU ALL PROBABLY HEARD ABOUT WHO SUDDENLY TURNED HERSELF IN TO DWMA THREE DAYS AGO. WELL...
...YOUR COMMANDER WILL BE THE WITCH MEDUSA.
LIVING DEAD
!!
WHAT THE HELL IS THIS!?

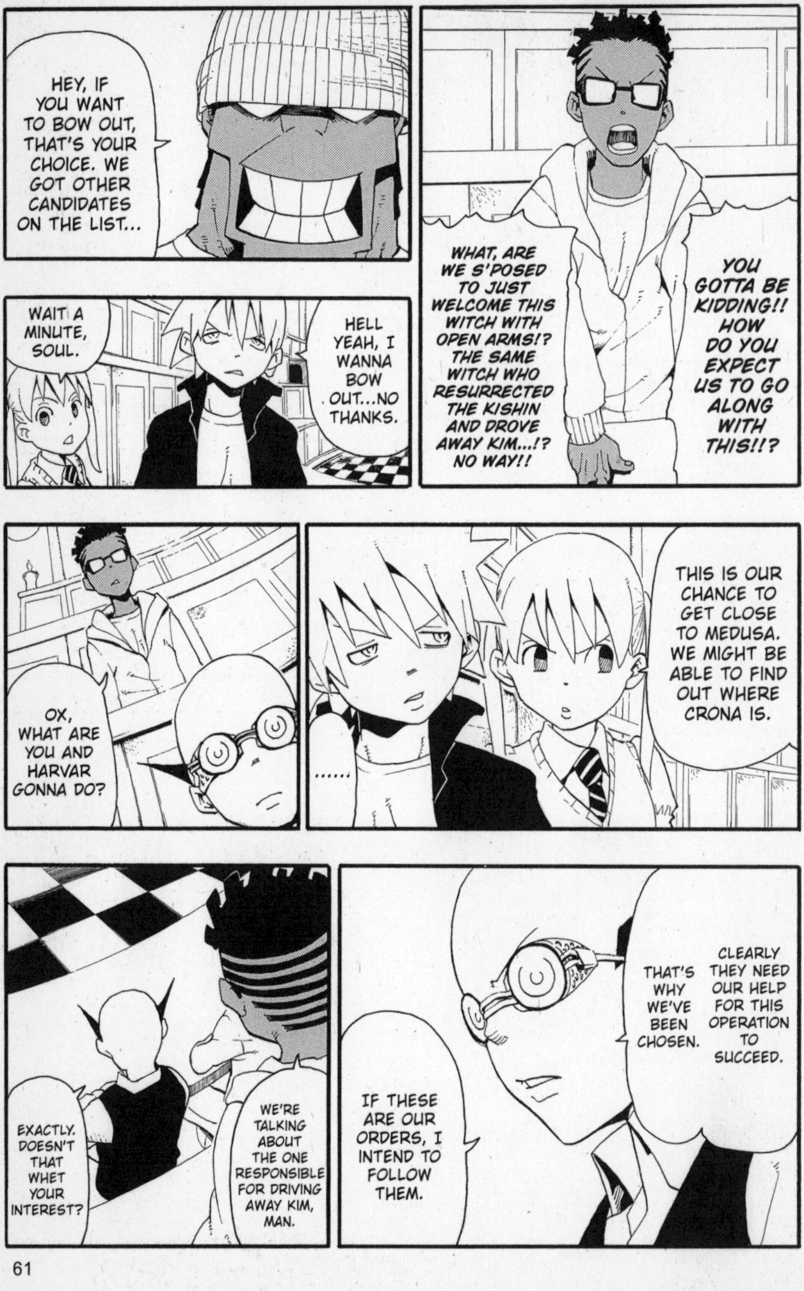
YOU GOTTA BE KIDDING!! HOW DO YOU EXPECT US TO GO ALONG WITH THIS!!?
WHAT, ARE WE S'POSED TO JUST WELCOME THIS WITCH WITH OPEN ARMS!? THE SAME WITCH WHO RESURRECTED THE KISHIN AND DROVE AWAY KIM...!? NO WAY!!
HEY, IF YOU WANT TO BOW OUT, THAT'S YOUR CHOICE. WE GOT OTHER CANDIDATES ON THE LIST...
HELL YEAH, I WANNA BOW OUT...NO THANKS.
WAIT A MINUTE, SOUL.
THIS IS OUR CHANCE TO GET CLOSE TO MEDUSA. WE MIGHT BE ABLE TO FIND OUT WHERE CRONA IS.
......
OX, WHAT ARE YOU AND HARVAR GONNA DO?
CLEARLY THEY NEED OUR HELP FOR THIS OPERATION TO SUCCEED.
THAT'S WHY WE'VE BEEN CHOSEN.
IF THESE ARE OUR ORDERS, I INTEND TO FOLLOW THEM.
WE'RE TALKING ABOUT THE ONE RESPONSIBLE FOR DRIVING AWAY KIM, MAN.
EXACTLY. DOESN'T THAT WHET YOUR INTEREST?

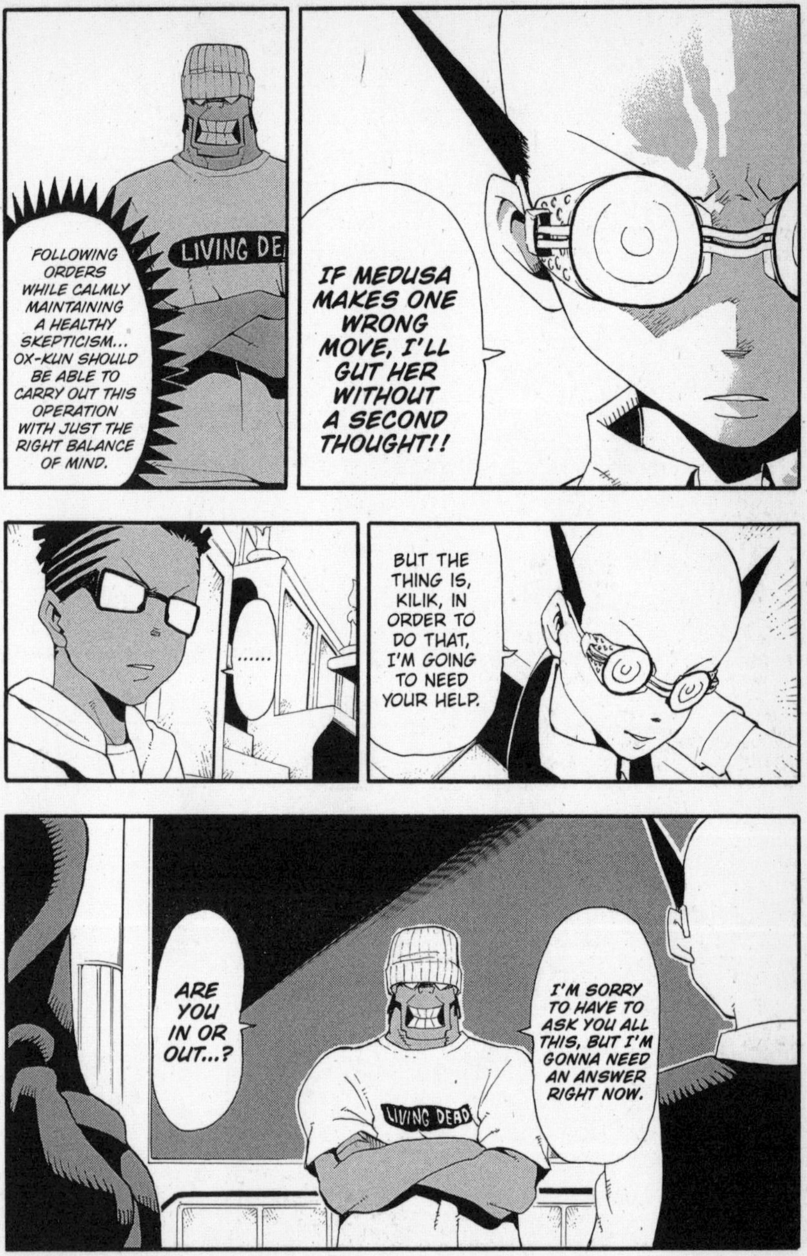
IF MEDUSA MAKES ONE WRONG MOVE, I'LL GUT HER WITHOUT A SECOND THOUGHT!!
LIVING DE
FOLLOWING ORDERS WHILE CALMLY MAINTAINING A HEALTHY SKEPTICISM... OX-KUN SHOULD BE ABLE TO CARRY OUT THIS OPERATION WITH JUST THE RIGHT BALANCE OF MIND.
BUT THE THING IS, KILIK, IN ORDER TO DO THAT, I'M GOING TO NEED YOUR HELP.
......
I'M SORRY TO HAVE TO ASK YOU ALL THIS, BUT I'M GONNA NEED AN ANSWER RIGHT NOW.
LIVING DEAD
ARE YOU IN OR OUT...?

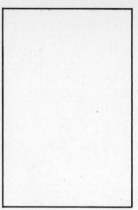

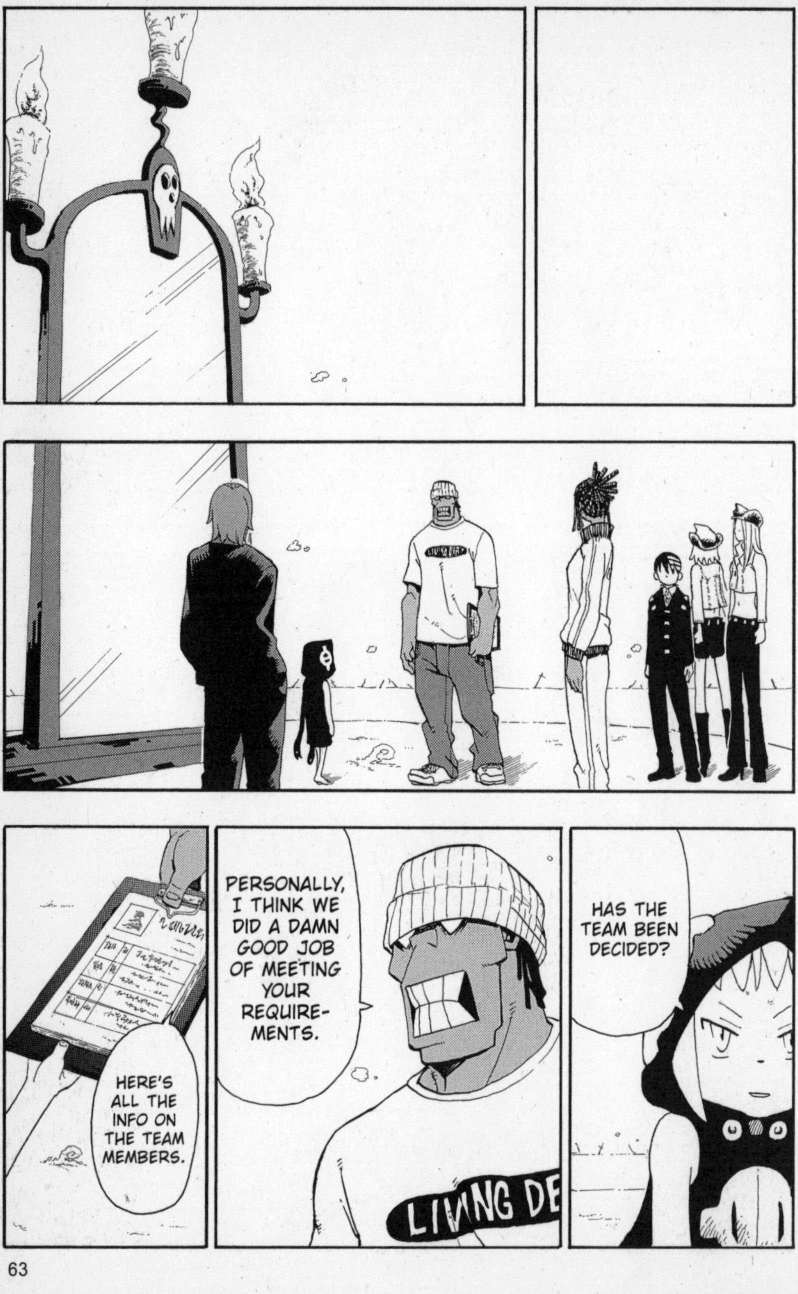
HAS THE TEAM BEEN DECIDED?
PERSONALLY, I THINK WE DID A DAMN GOOD JOB OF MEETING YOUR REQUIRE-MENTS.
HERE'S ALL THE INFO ON THE TEAM MEMBERS.

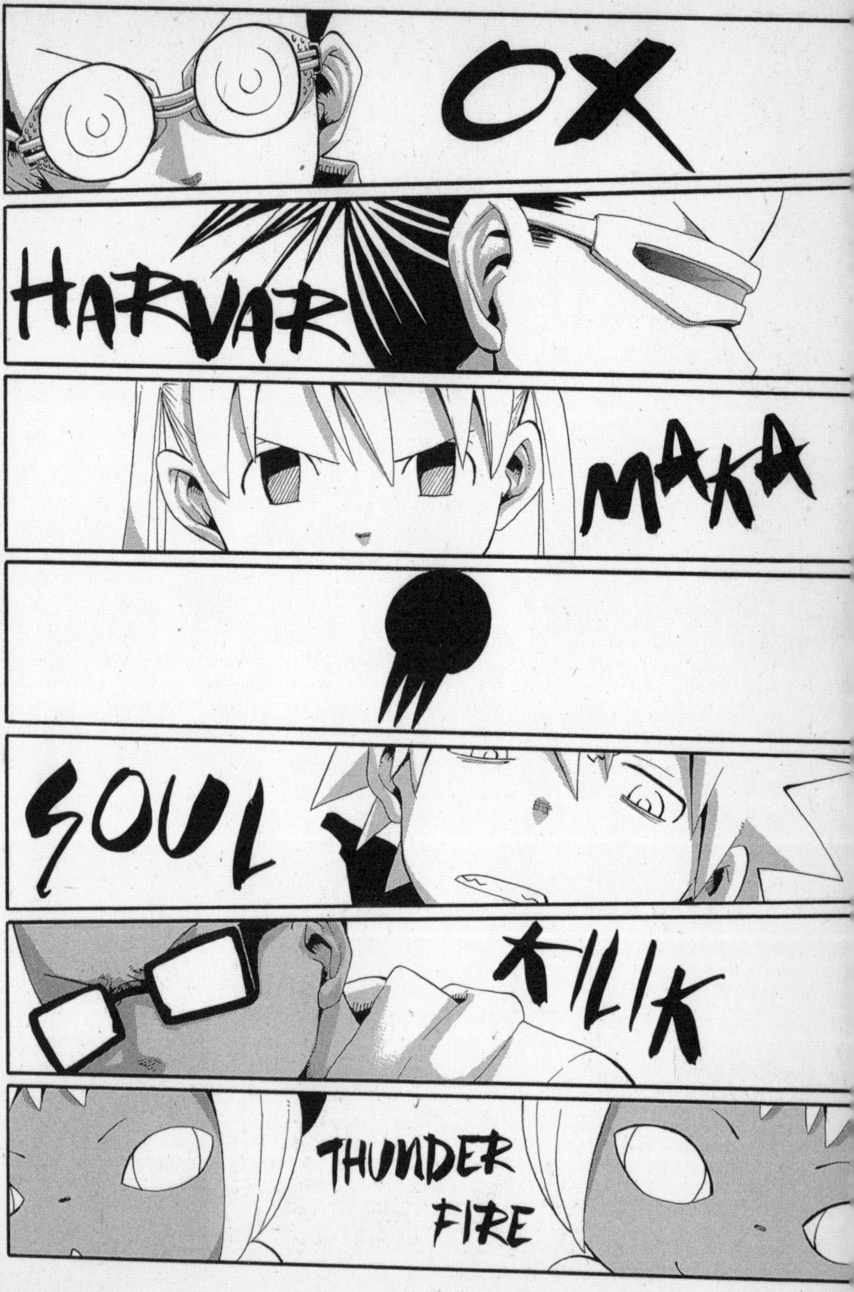
OX
HARVAR
MAKA
SOUL
KILIK
THUNDER
FIRE

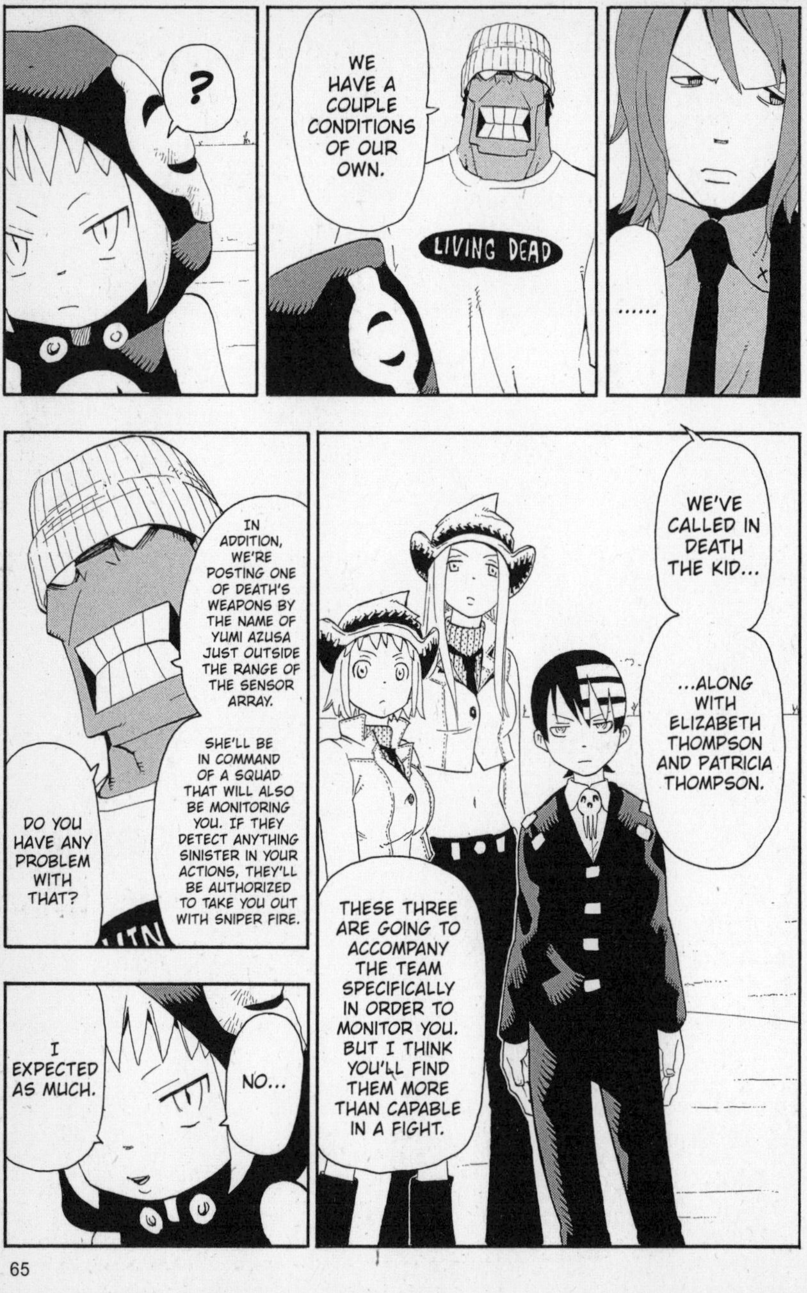
......
WE HAVE A COUPLE CONDITIONS OF OUR OWN.
LIVING DEAD
?
WE'VE CALLED IN DEATH THE KID...
...ALONG WITH ELIZABETH THOMPSON AND PATRICIA THOMPSON.
THESE THREE ARE GOING TO ACCOMPANY THE TEAM SPECIFICALLY IN ORDER TO MONITOR YOU. BUT I THINK YOU'LL FIND THEM MORE THAN CAPABLE IN A FIGHT.
IN ADDITION, WE'RE POSTING ONE OF DEATH'S WEAPONS BY THE NAME OF YUMI AZUSA JUST OUTSIDE THE RANGE OF THE SENSOR ARRAY.
SHE'LL BE IN COMMAND OF A SQUAD THAT WILL ALSO BE MONITORING YOU. IF THEY DETECT ANYTHING SINISTER IN YOUR ACTIONS, THEY'LL BE AUTHORIZED TO TAKE YOU OUT WITH SNIPER FIRE.
DO YOU HAVE ANY PROBLEM WITH THAT?
NO...
I EXPECTED AS MUCH.

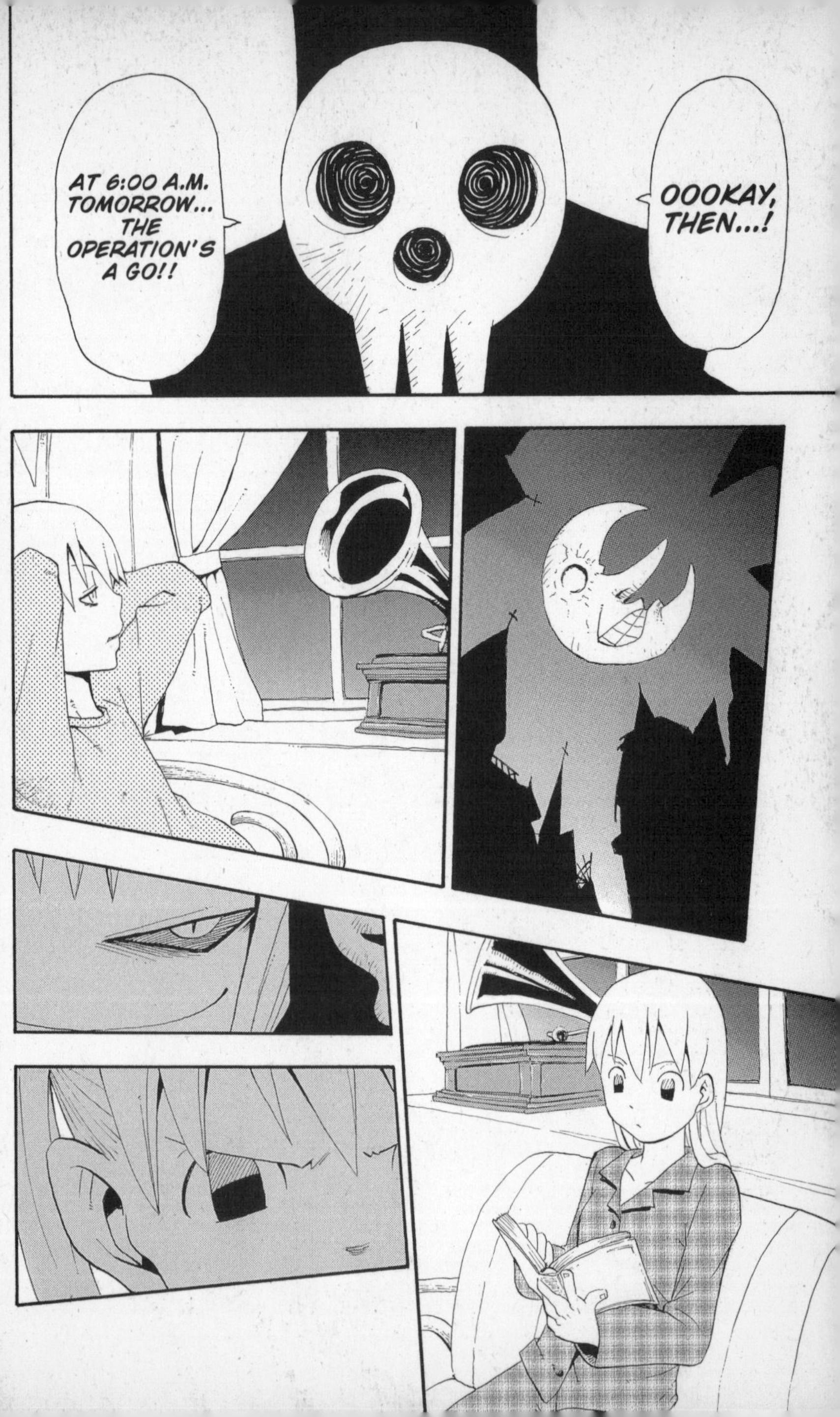
OOOKAY, THEN...!
AT 6:00 A.M. TOMORROW... THE OPERATION'S A GO!!

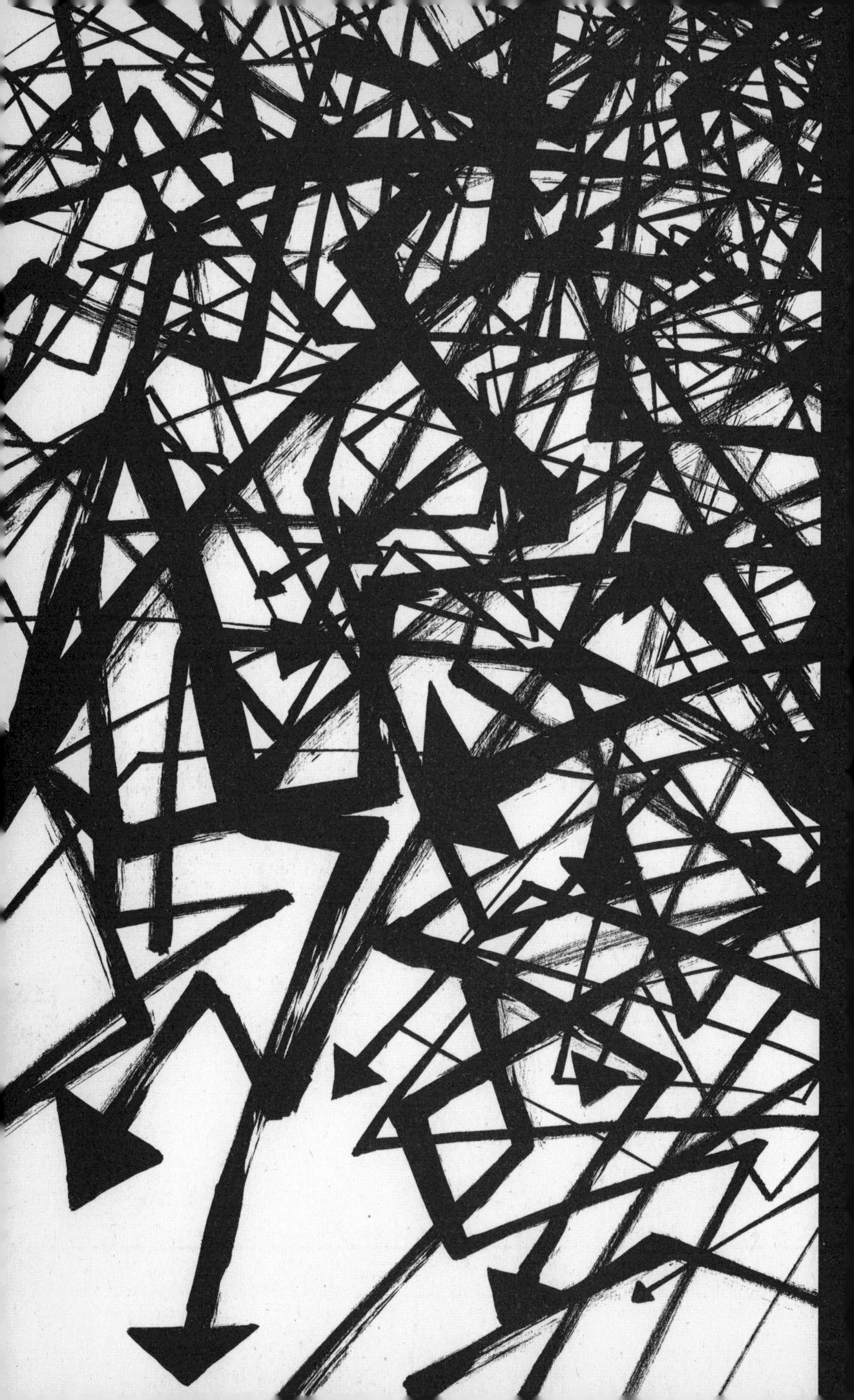

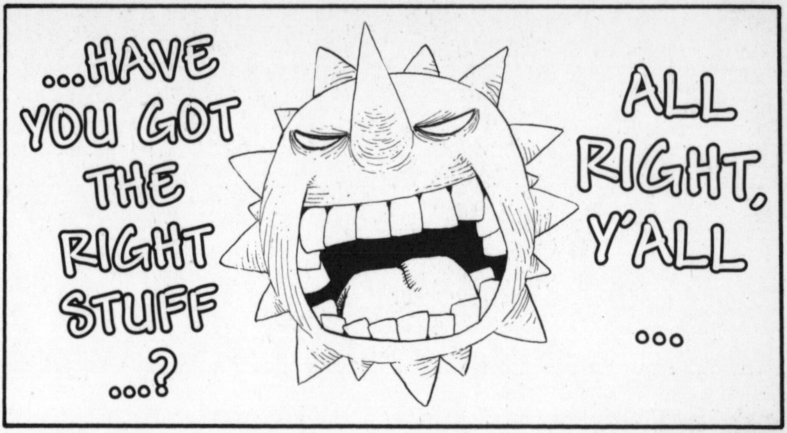
ALL RIGHT, Y'ALL ...
...HAVE YOU GOT THE RIGHT STUFF ...?

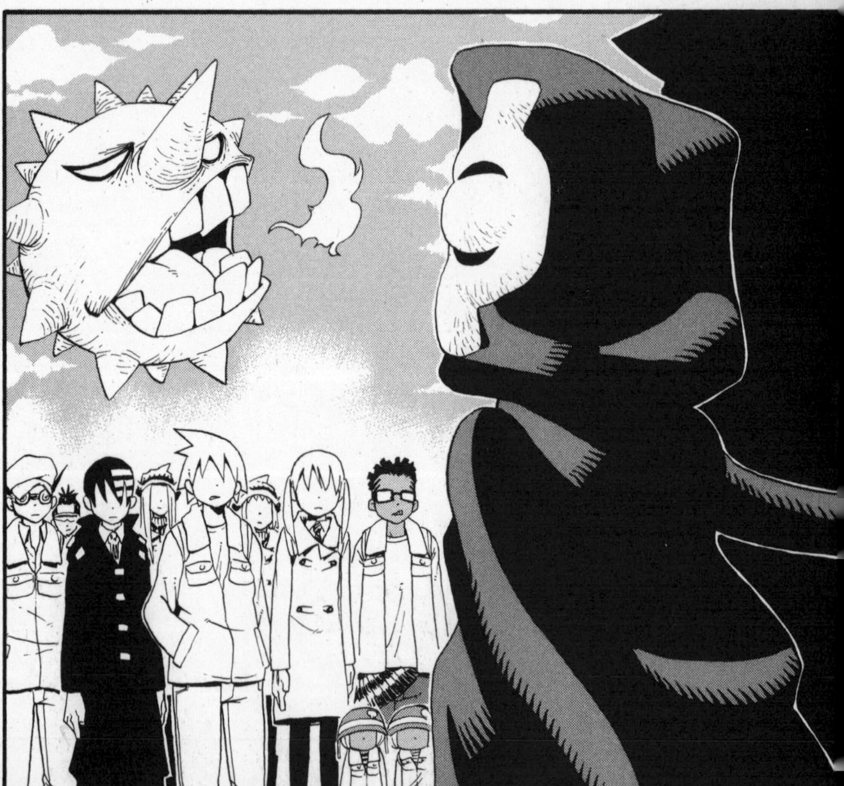

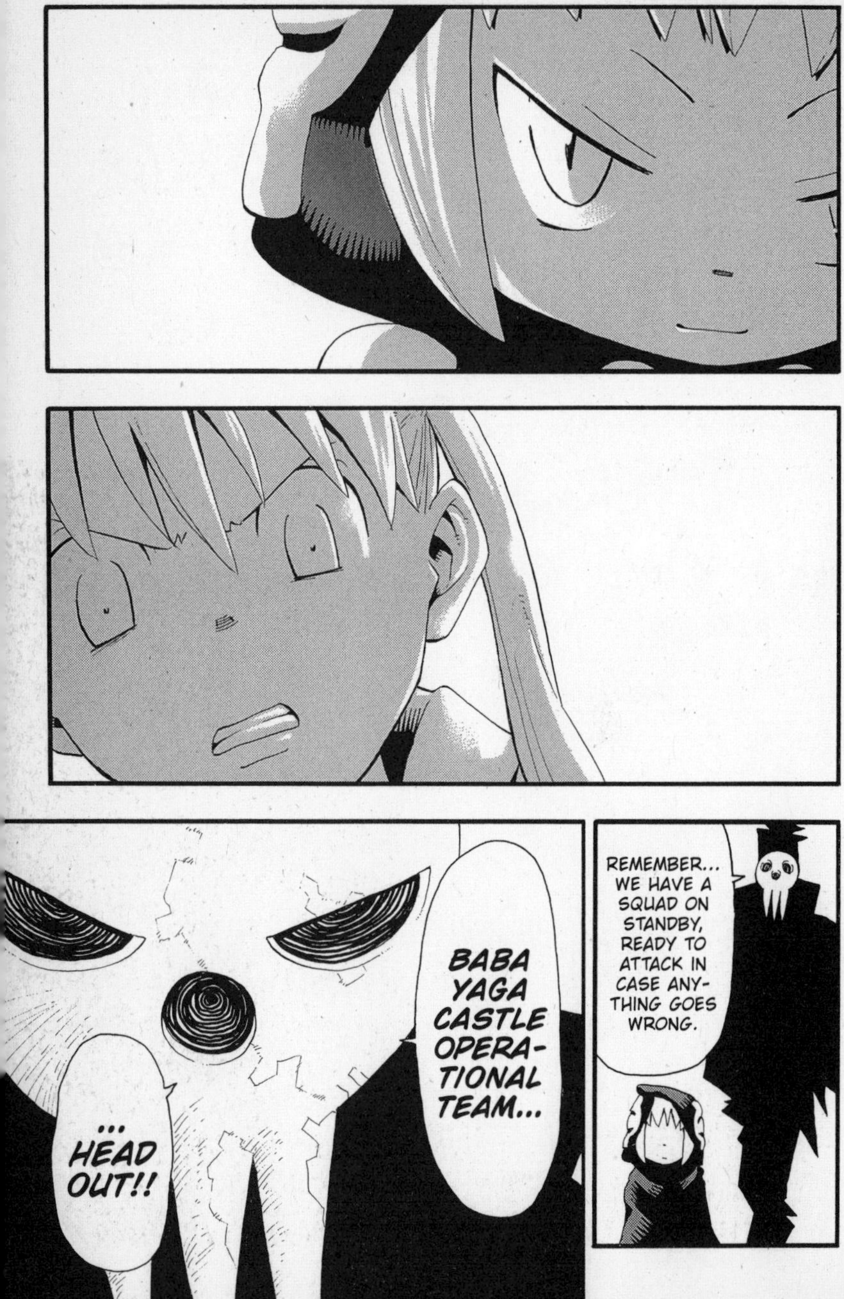

REMEMBER... WE HAVE A SQUAD ON STANDBY, READY TO ATTACK IN CASE ANY-THING GOES WRONG.
BABA YAGA CASTLE OPERA-TIONAL TEAM...
...HEAD OUT!!

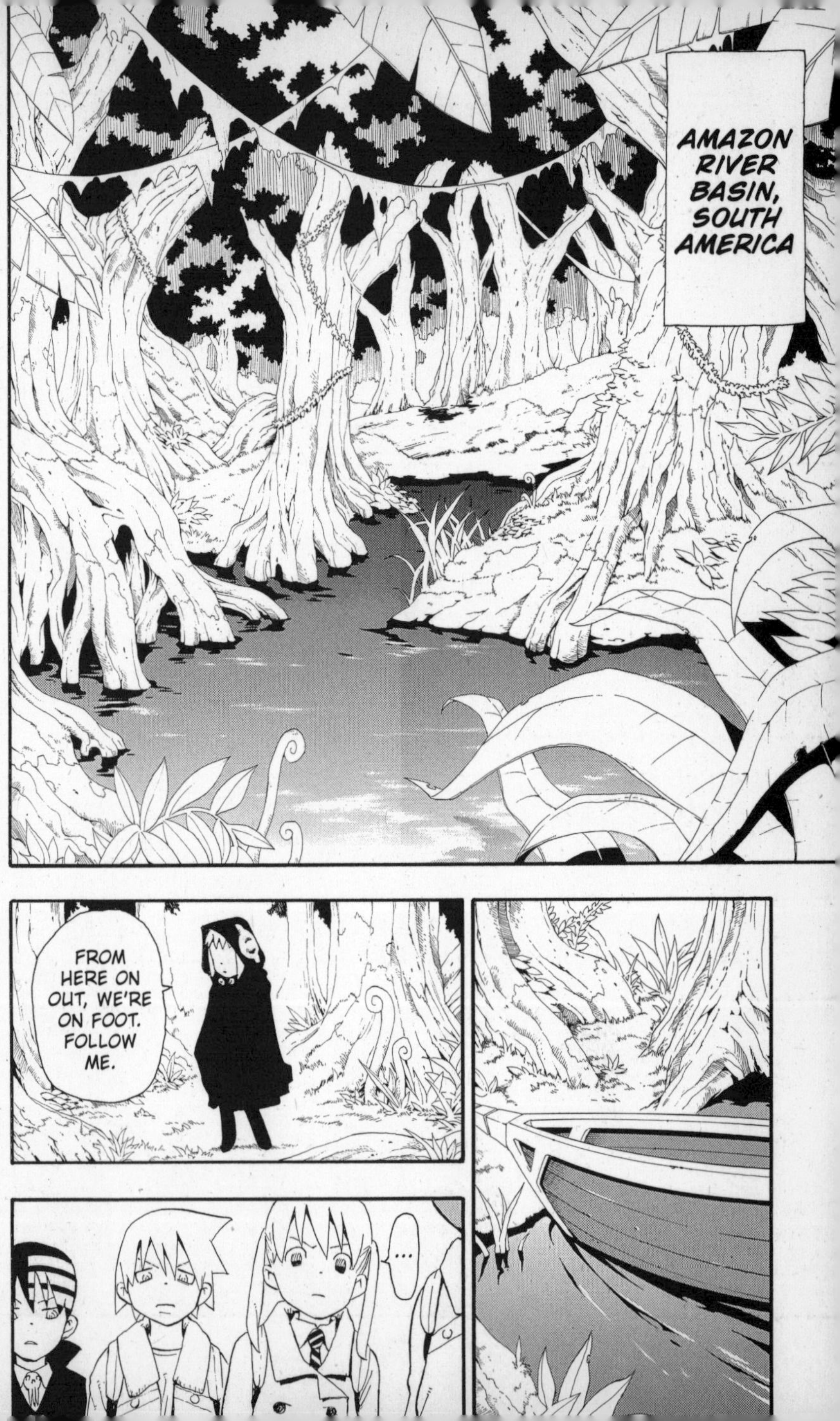
AMAZON RIVER BASIN, SOUTH AMERICA
FROM HERE ON OUT, WE'RE ON FOOT. FOLLOW ME.
...

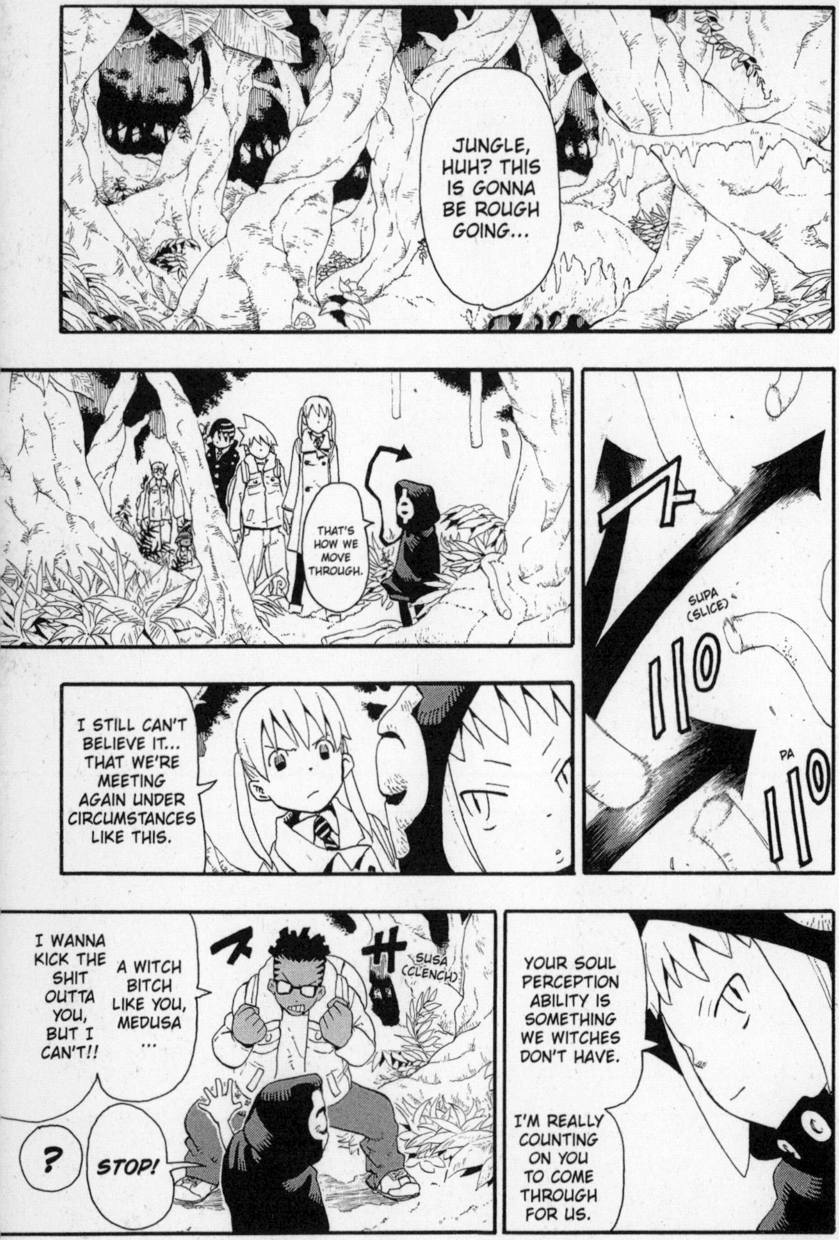

JUNGLE, HUH? THIS IS GONNA BE ROUGH GOING...
SUPA (SLICE)
PA
THAT'S HOW WE MOVE THROUGH.
I STILL CAN'T BELIEVE IT... THAT WE'RE MEETING AGAIN UNDER CIRCUMSTANCES LIKE THIS.
YOUR SOUL PERCEPTION ABILITY IS SOMETHING WE WITCHES DON'T HAVE.
I'M REALLY COUNTING ON YOU TO COME THROUGH FOR US.
SUSA (CLENCH)
A WITCH BITCH LIKE YOU, MEDUSA ...
I WANNA KICK THE SHIT OUTTA YOU, BUT I CAN'T!!
STOP!
?

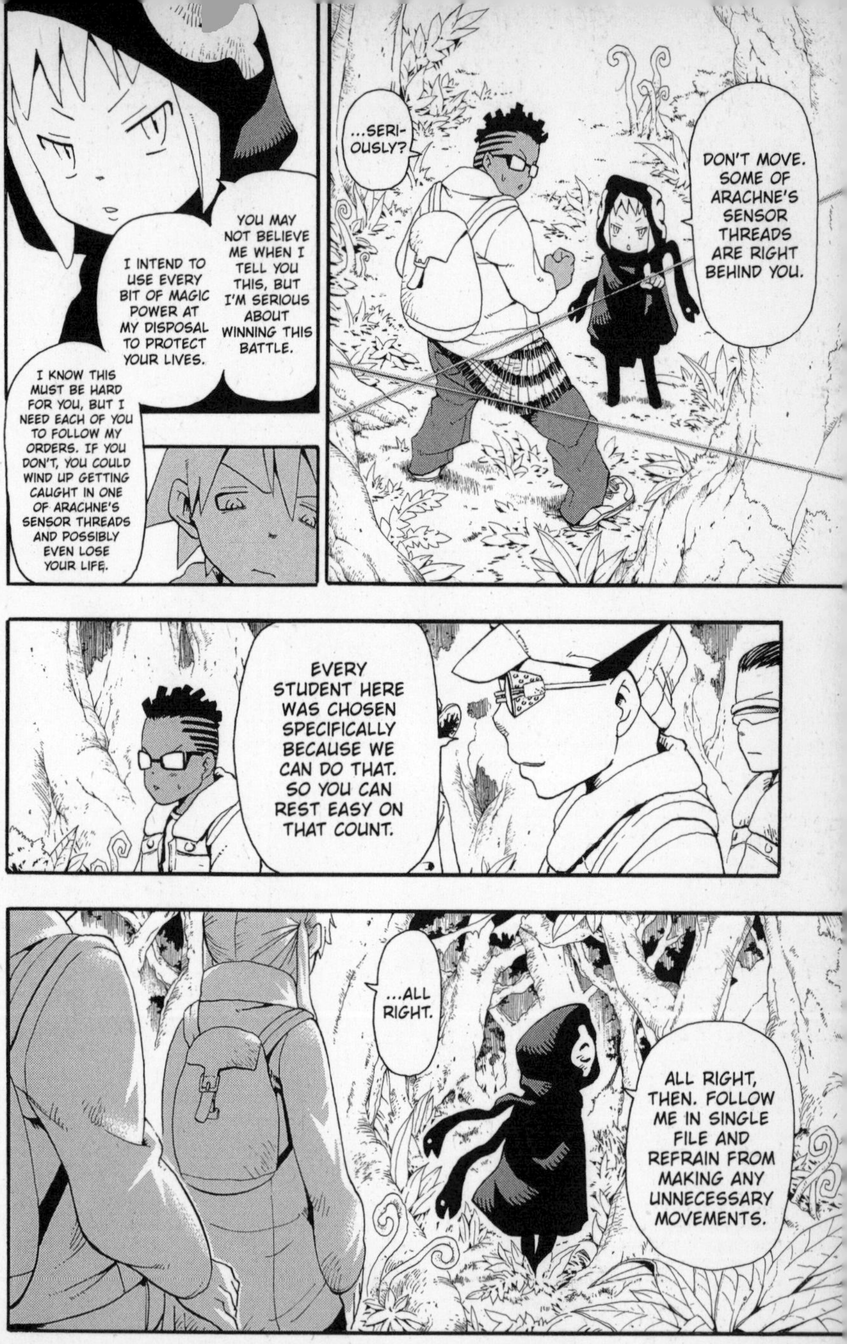
DON'T MOVE. SOME OF ARACHNE'S SENSOR THREADS ARE RIGHT BEHIND YOU.
...SERI-OUSLY?
YOU MAY NOT BELIEVE ME WHEN I TELL YOU THIS, BUT I'M SERIOUS ABOUT WINNING THIS BATTLE.
I INTEND TO USE EVERY BIT OF MAGIC POWER AT MY DISPOSAL TO PROTECT YOUR LIVES.
I KNOW THIS MUST BE HARD FOR YOU, BUT I NEED EACH OF YOU TO FOLLOW MY ORDERS. IF YOU DON'T, YOU COULD WIND UP GETTING CAUGHT IN ONE OF ARACHNE'S SENSOR THREADS AND POSSIBLY EVEN LOSE YOUR LIFE.
EVERY STUDENT HERE WAS CHOSEN SPECIFICALLY BECAUSE WE CAN DO THAT. SO YOU CAN REST EASY ON THAT COUNT.
ALL RIGHT, THEN. FOLLOW ME IN SINGLE FILE AND REFRAIN FROM MAKING ANY UNNECESSARY MOVEMENTS.
...ALL RIGHT.

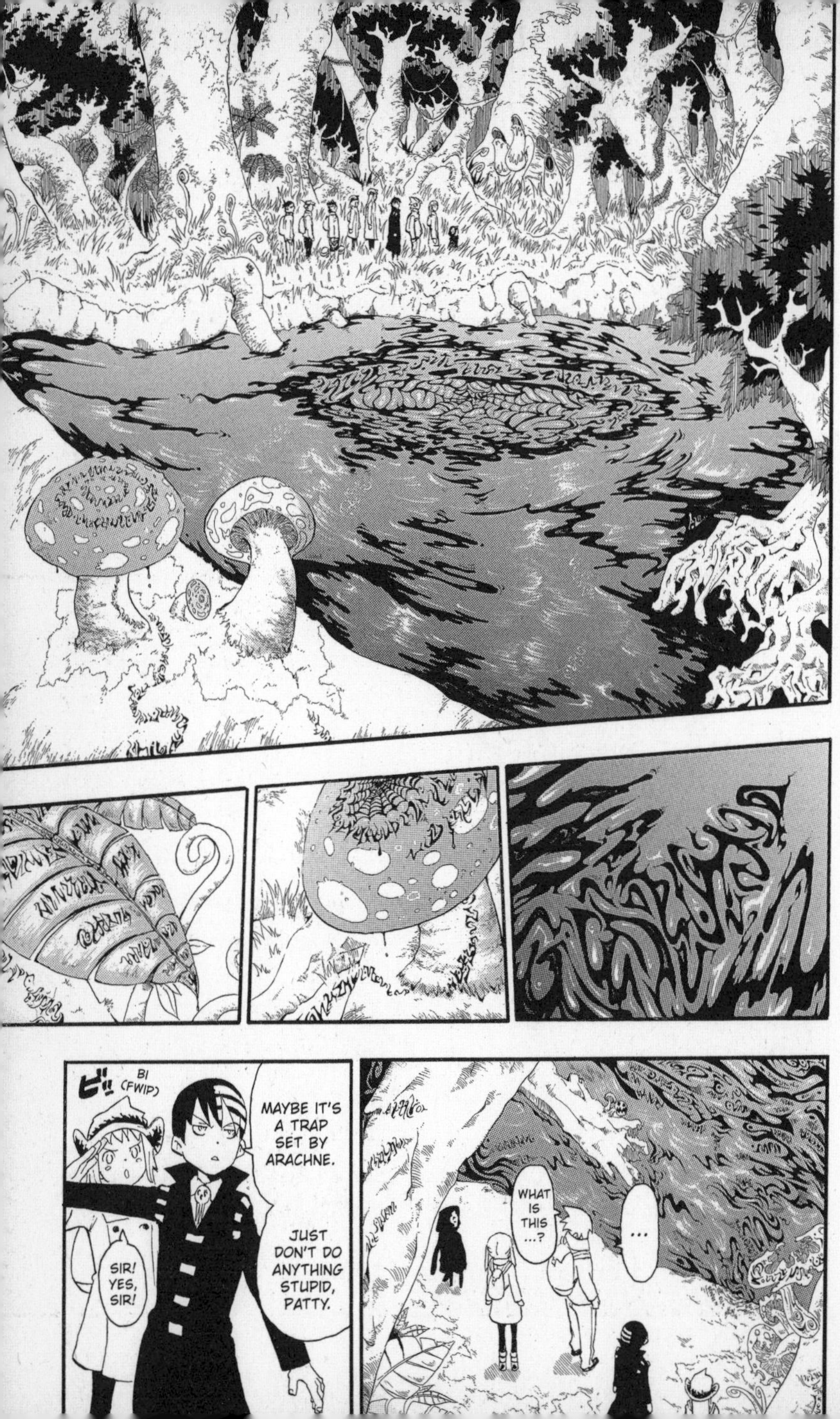
...
WHAT IS THIS ...?
MAYBE IT'S A TRAP SET BY ARACHNE.
JUST DON'T DO ANYTHING STUPID, PATTY.
ビ!! BI (FWIP)
SIR! YES, SIR!

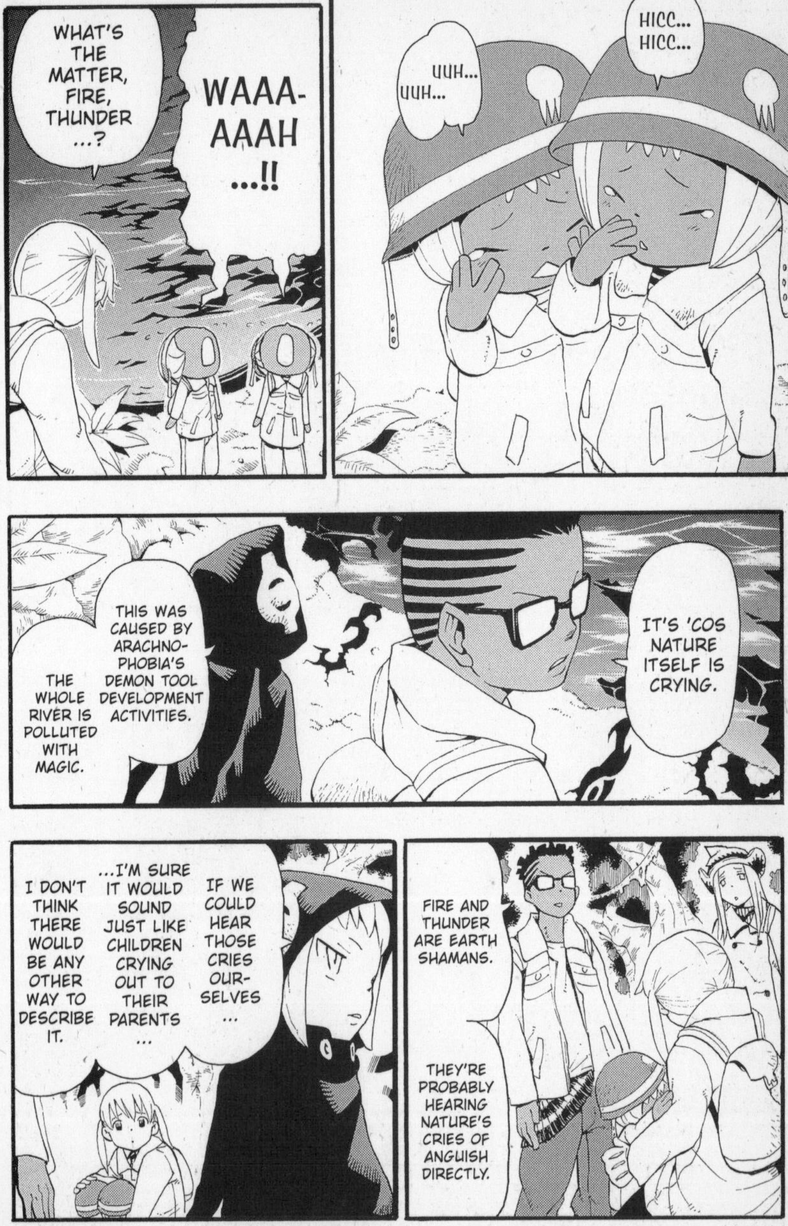
HICC... HICC...
UUH... UUH...
WAAA-AAAH ...!!
WHAT'S THE MATTER, FIRE, THUNDER ...?
IT'S 'COS NATURE ITSELF IS CRYING.
THE WHOLE RIVER IS POLLUTED WITH MAGIC.
THIS WAS CAUSED BY ARACHNO-PHOBIA'S DEMON TOOL DEVELOPMENT ACTIVITIES.
FIRE AND THUNDER ARE EARTH SHAMANS.
THEY'RE PROBABLY HEARING NATURE'S CRIES OF ANGUISH DIRECTLY.
IF WE COULD HEAR THOSE CRIES OUR-SELVES ...
...I'M SURE IT WOULD SOUND JUST LIKE CHILDREN CRYING OUT TO THEIR PARENTS ...
I DON'T THINK THERE WOULD BE ANY OTHER WAY TO DESCRIBE IT.

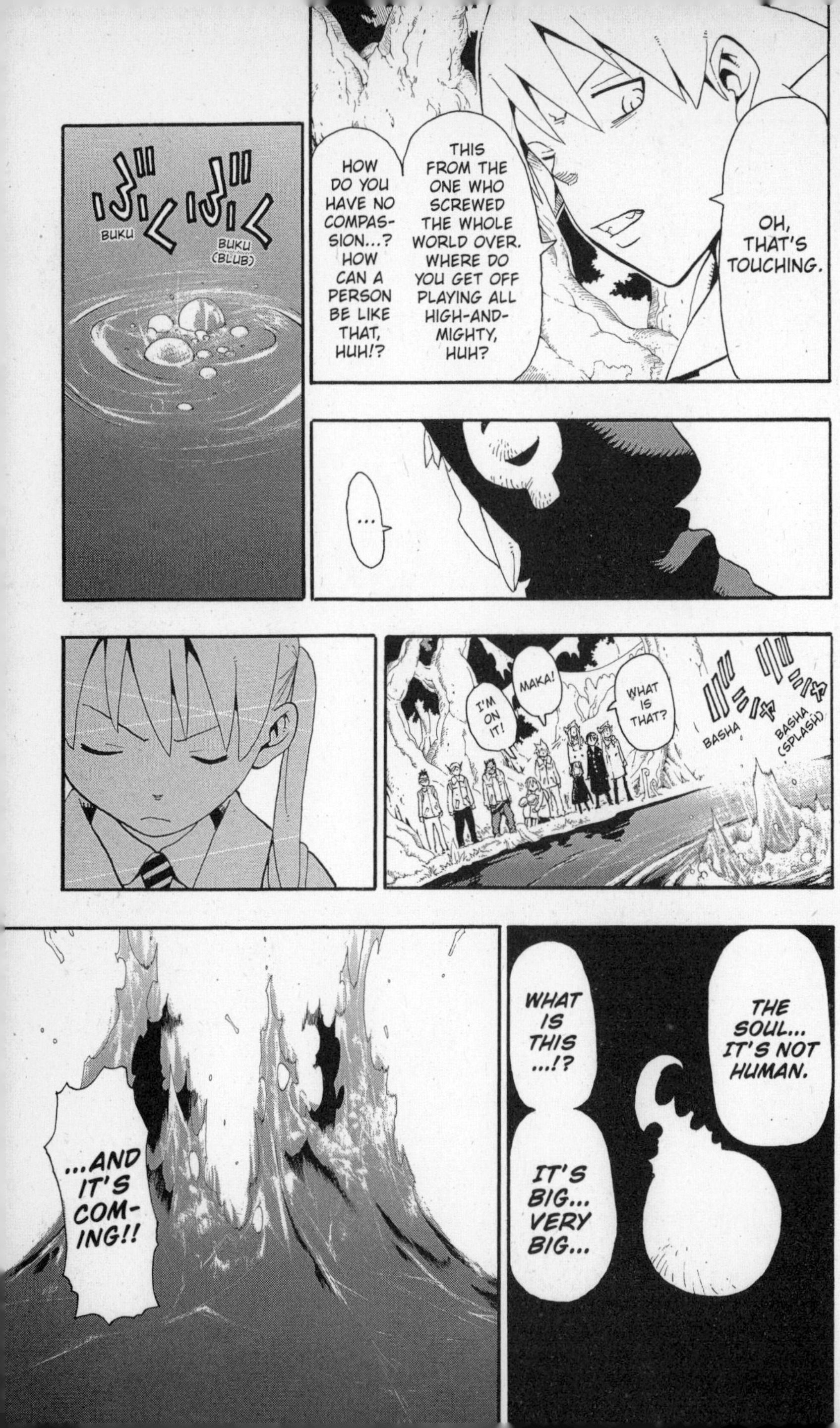
OH, THAT'S TOUCHING.
THIS FROM THE ONE WHO SCREWED THE WHOLE WORLD OVER. WHERE DO YOU GET OFF PLAYING ALL HIGH-AND-MIGHTY, HUH?
HOW DO YOU HAVE NO COMPASSION...? HOW CAN A PERSON BE LIKE THAT, HUH!?
...
BUKU
BUKU (BLUB)
BASHA
BASHA (SPLASH)
WHAT IS THAT?
MAKA!
I'M ON IT!
THE SOUL... IT'S NOT HUMAN.
WHAT IS THIS ...!?
IT'S BIG... VERY BIG...
...AND IT'S COMING!!

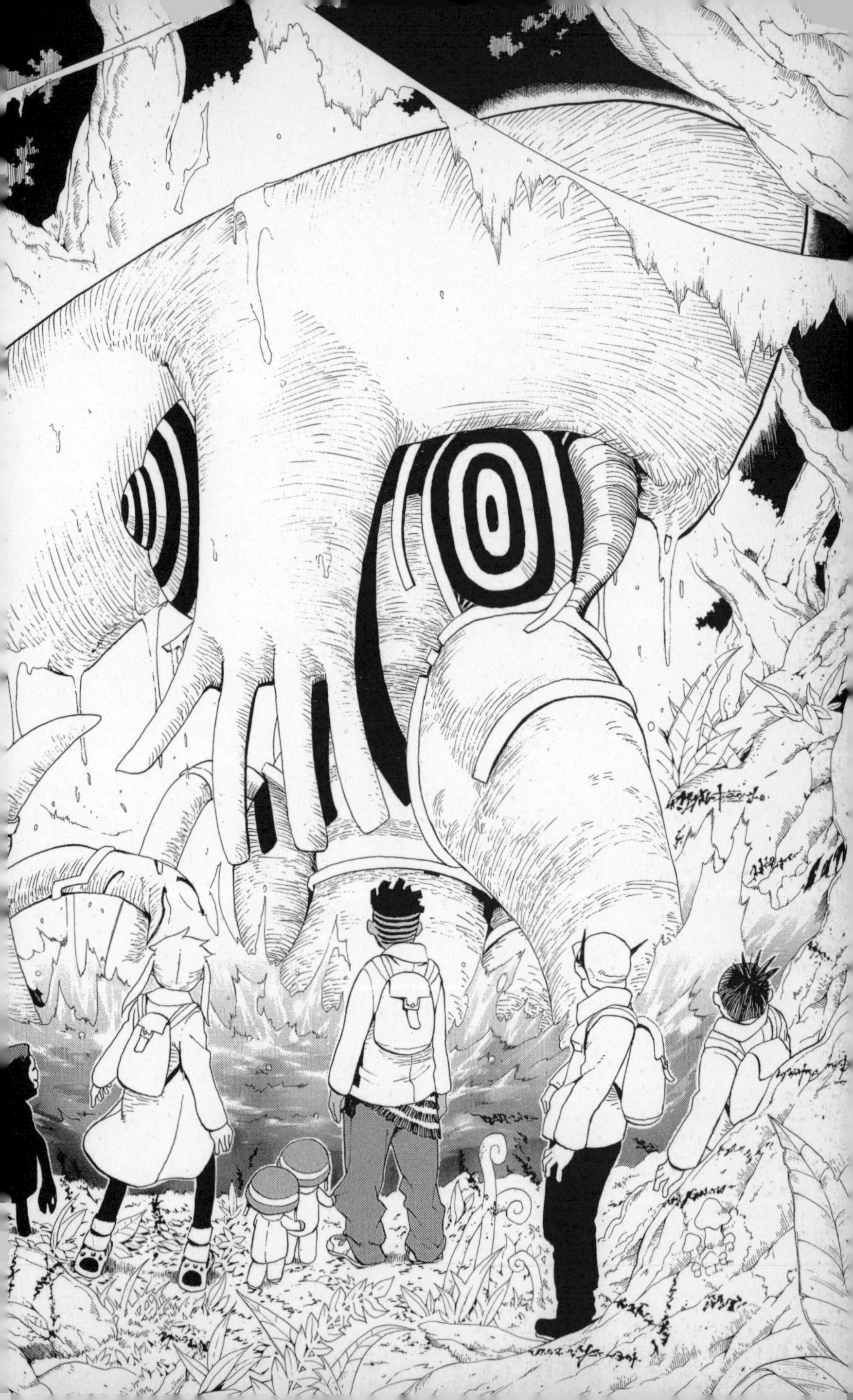

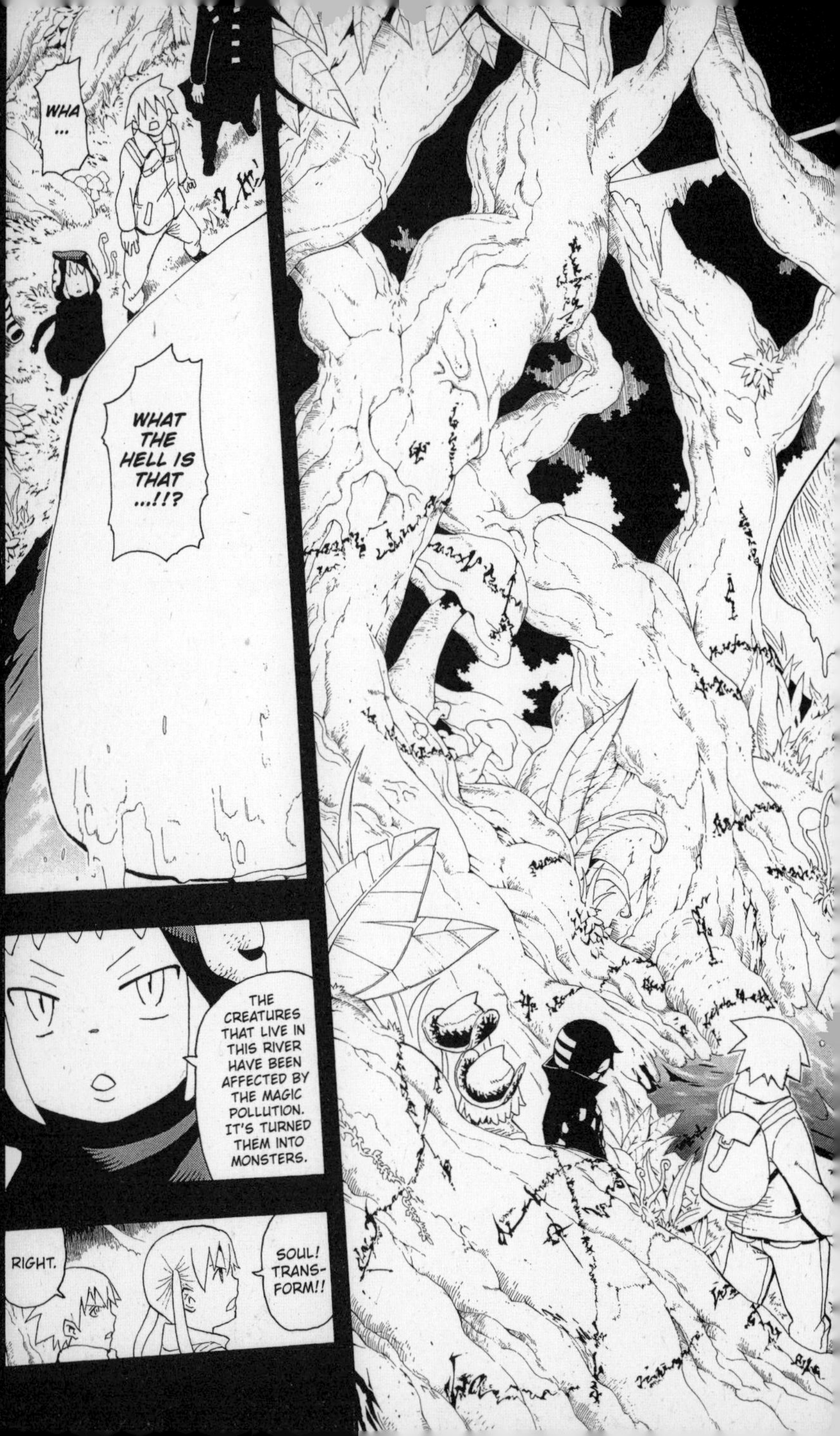
WHA ...
WHAT THE HELL IS THAT ...!!?
THE CREATURES THAT LIVE IN THIS RIVER HAVE BEEN AFFECTED BY THE MAGIC POLLUTION. IT'S TURNED THEM INTO MONSTERS.
SOUL! TRANS-FORM!!
RIGHT.

TA
(LEAP)

SPREAD
OUT!!

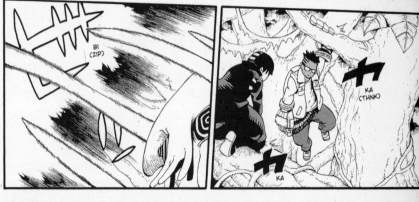

BI
(ZIP)

KA
(THNK)

KA

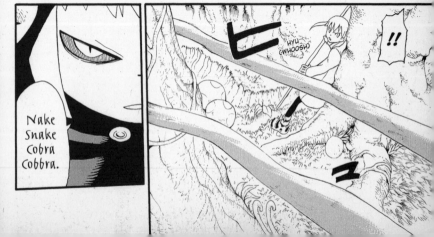

Nake
Snake
Cobra
Cobbra.

HYU
(WHOOSH)

!!

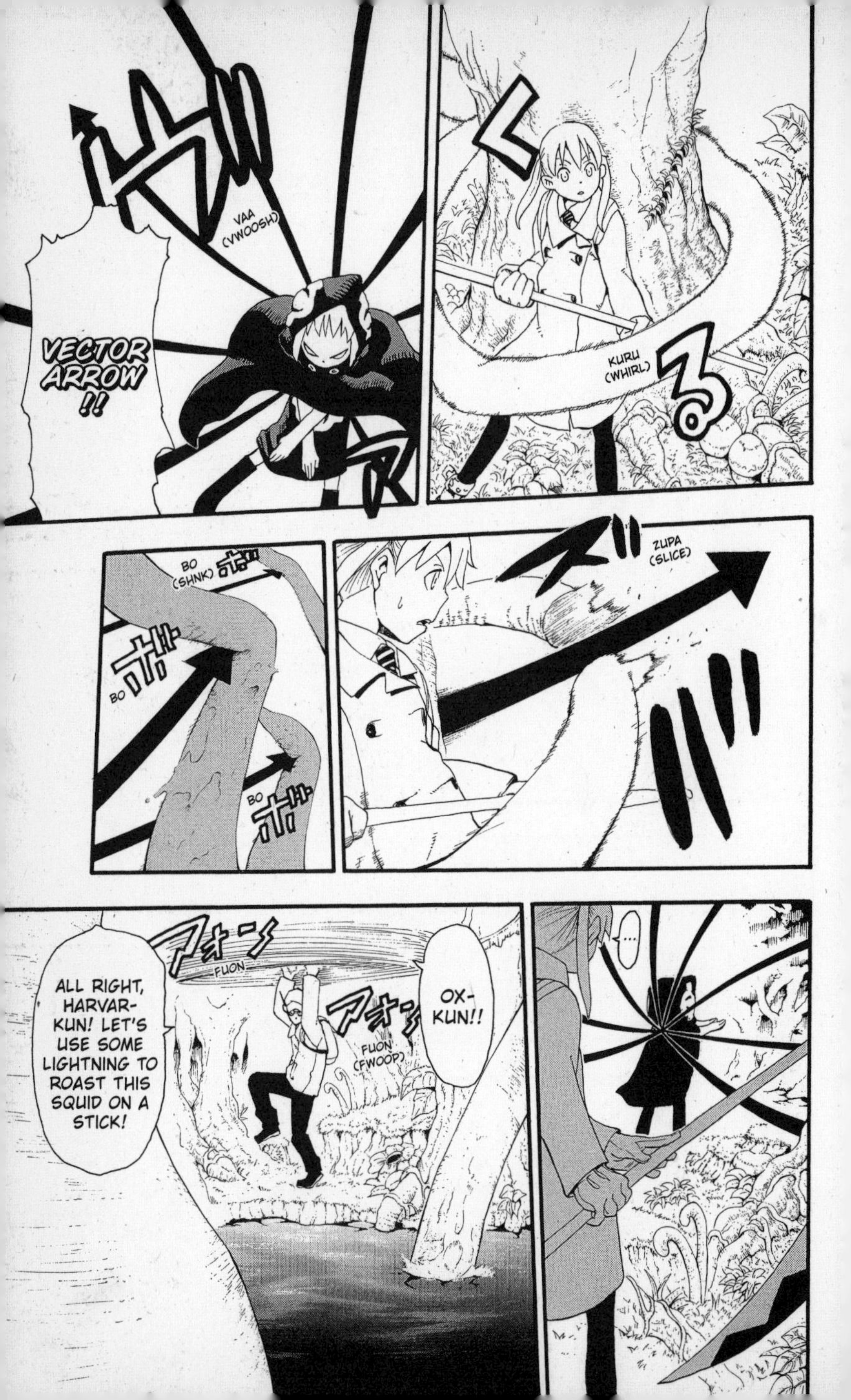
KURU (WHIRL)
VAA (VWOOSH)
VECTOR ARROW!!
ZUPA (SLICE)
BO (SHNK)
BO
BO
...
OX-KUN!!
FUON
FUON (FWOOP)
ALL RIGHT, HARVAR-KUN! LET'S USE SOME LIGHTNING TO ROAST THIS SQUID ON A STICK!

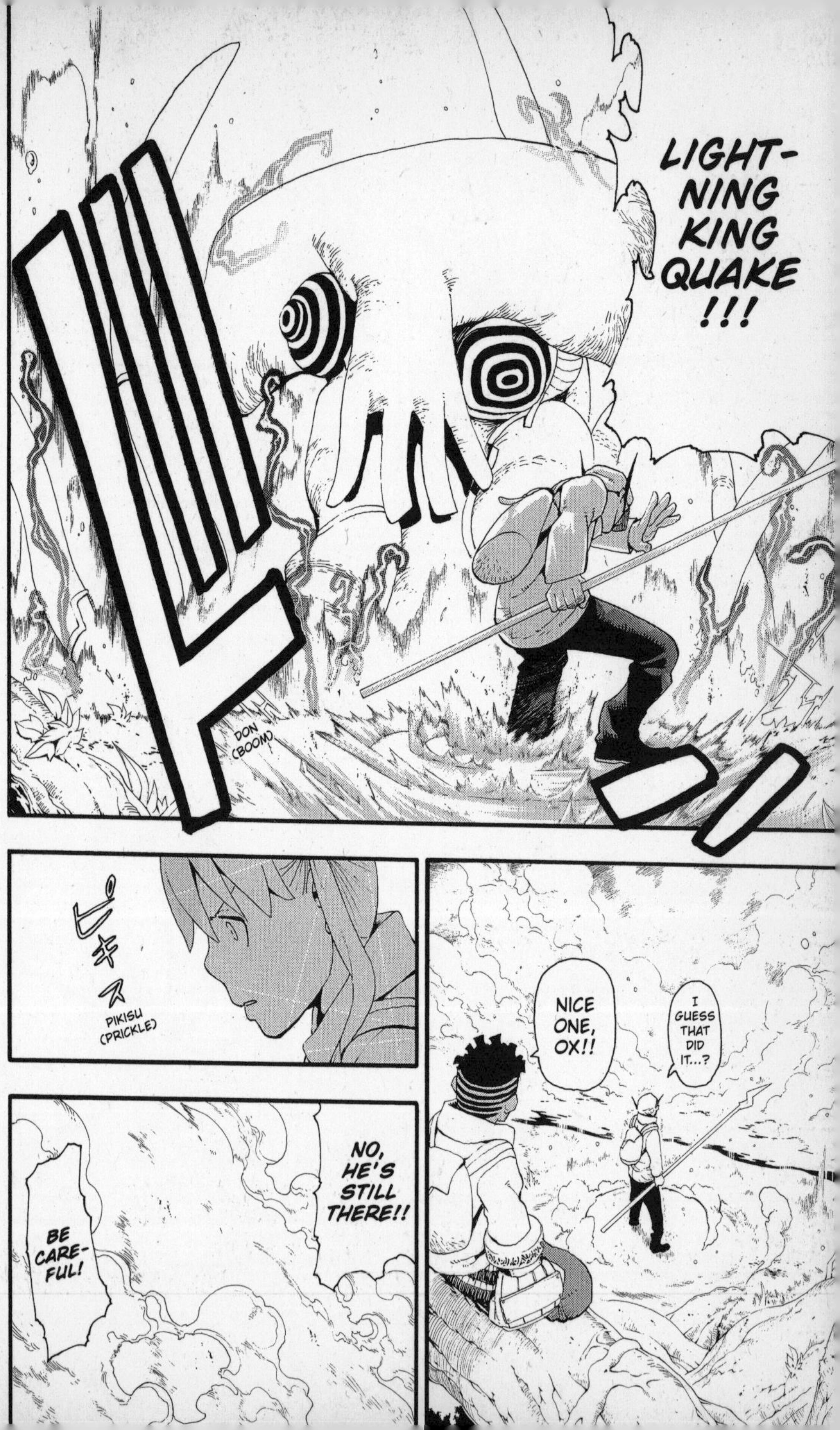
LIGHT-NING KING QUAKE!!!
DON (BOOM)
I GUESS THAT DID IT...?
NICE ONE, OX!!
ピキス
PIKISU (PRICKLE)
NO, HE'S STILL THERE!!
BE CARE-FUL!

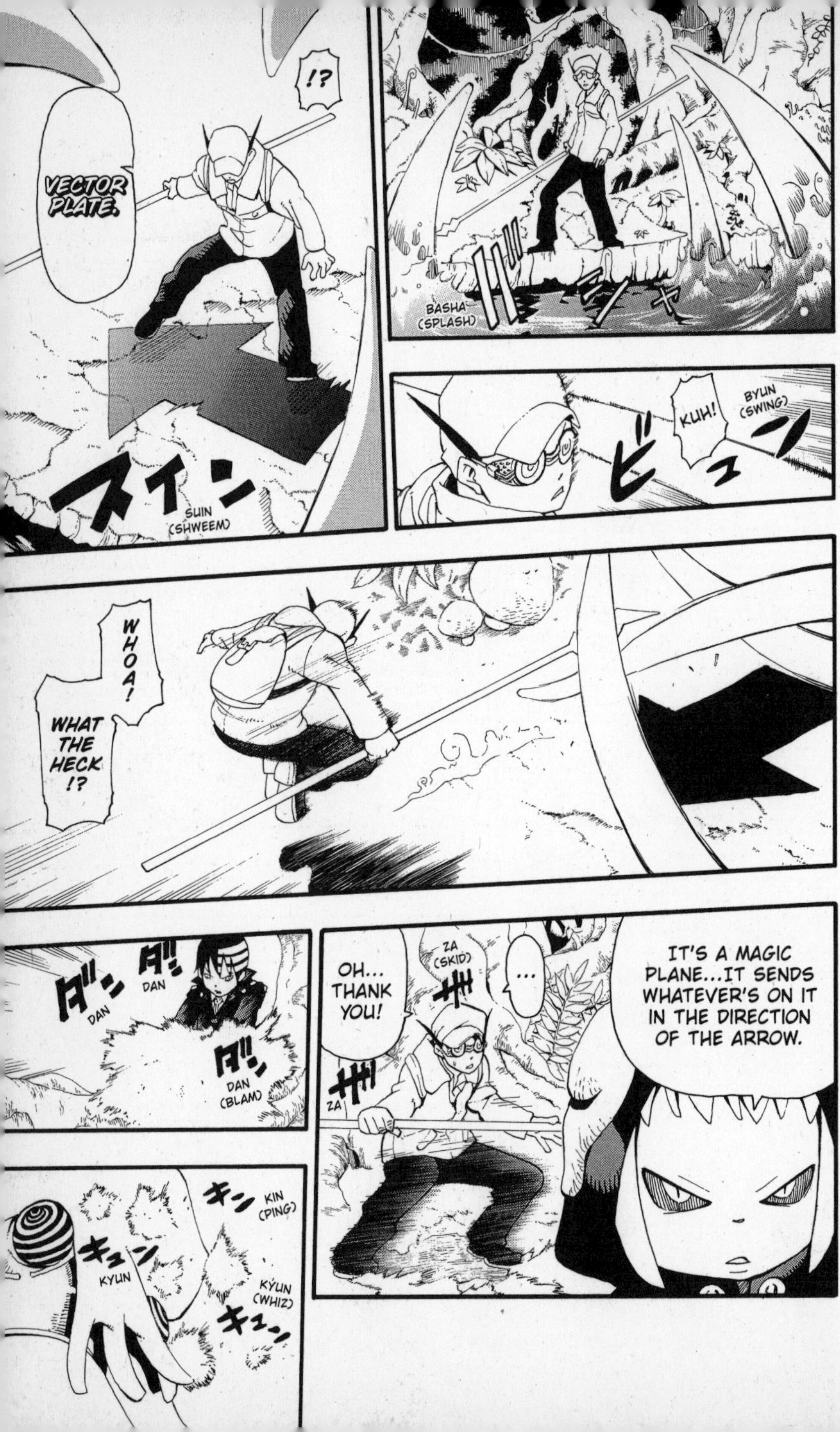
BASHA (SPLASH)
KUH!
BYUN (SWING)
!?
VECTOR PLATE.
SUIN (SHWEEM)
WHOA!
WHAT THE HECK!?
IT'S A MAGIC PLANE...IT SENDS WHATEVER'S ON IT IN THE DIRECTION OF THE ARROW.
...
ZA (SKID)
OH... THANK YOU!
ZA
DAN
DAN
DAN (BLAM)
KIN (PING)
KYUN
KYUN (WHIZ)

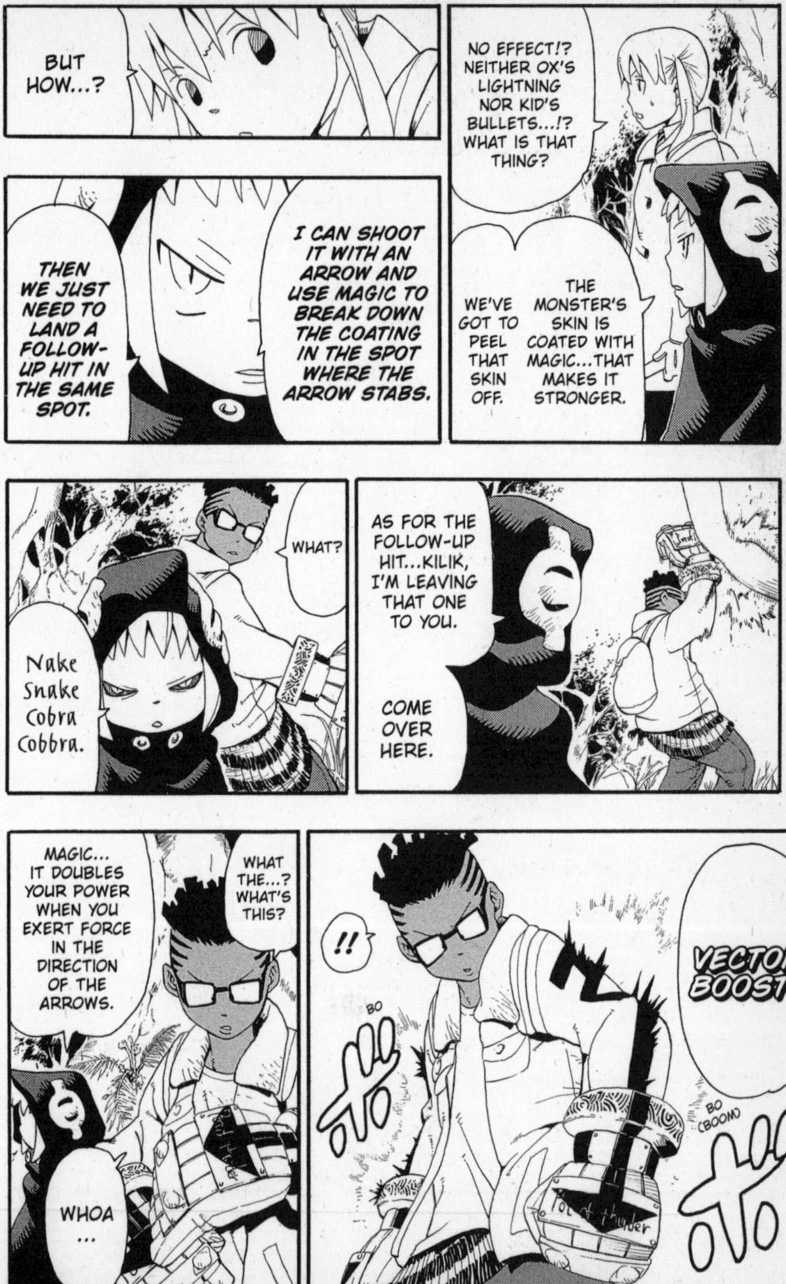
NO EFFECT!? NEITHER OX'S LIGHTNING NOR KID'S BULLETS...!? WHAT IS THAT THING?
THE MONSTER'S SKIN IS COATED WITH MAGIC...THAT MAKES IT STRONGER.
WE'VE GOT TO PEEL THAT SKIN OFF.
BUT HOW...?
I CAN SHOOT IT WITH AN ARROW AND USE MAGIC TO BREAK DOWN THE COATING IN THE SPOT WHERE THE ARROW STABS.
THEN WE JUST NEED TO LAND A FOLLOW-UP HIT IN THE SAME SPOT.
AS FOR THE FOLLOW-UP HIT...KILIK, I'M LEAVING THAT ONE TO YOU.
COME OVER HERE.
WHAT?
Nake Snake Cobra Cobbra.
VECTOR BOOST!
BO (BOOM)
!!
BO
WHAT THE...? WHAT'S THIS?
MAGIC... IT DOUBLES YOUR POWER WHEN YOU EXERT FORCE IN THE DIRECTION OF THE ARROWS.
WHOA ...

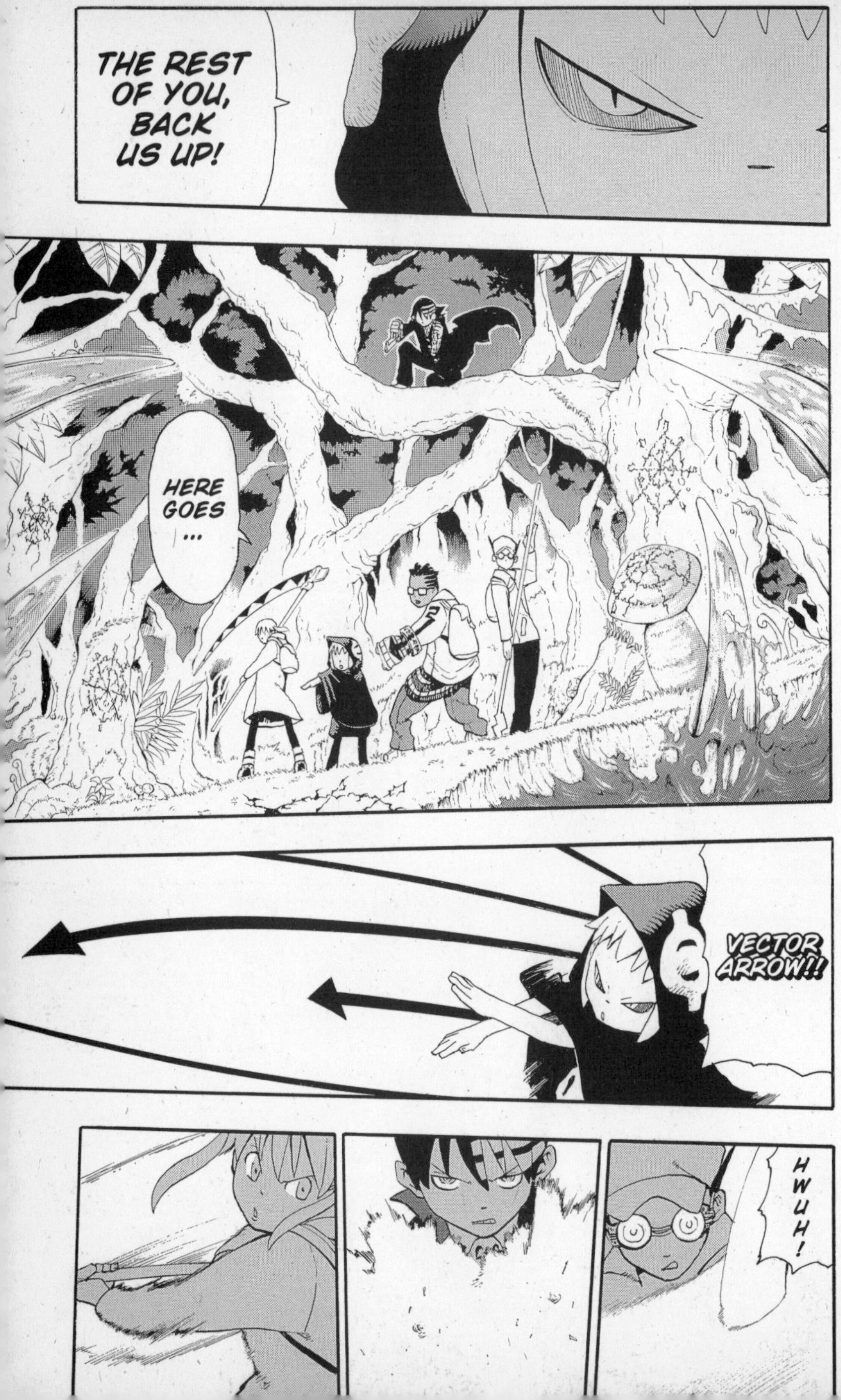
THE REST OF YOU, BACK US UP!
HERE GOES ...
VECTOR ARROW!!
HWUH!

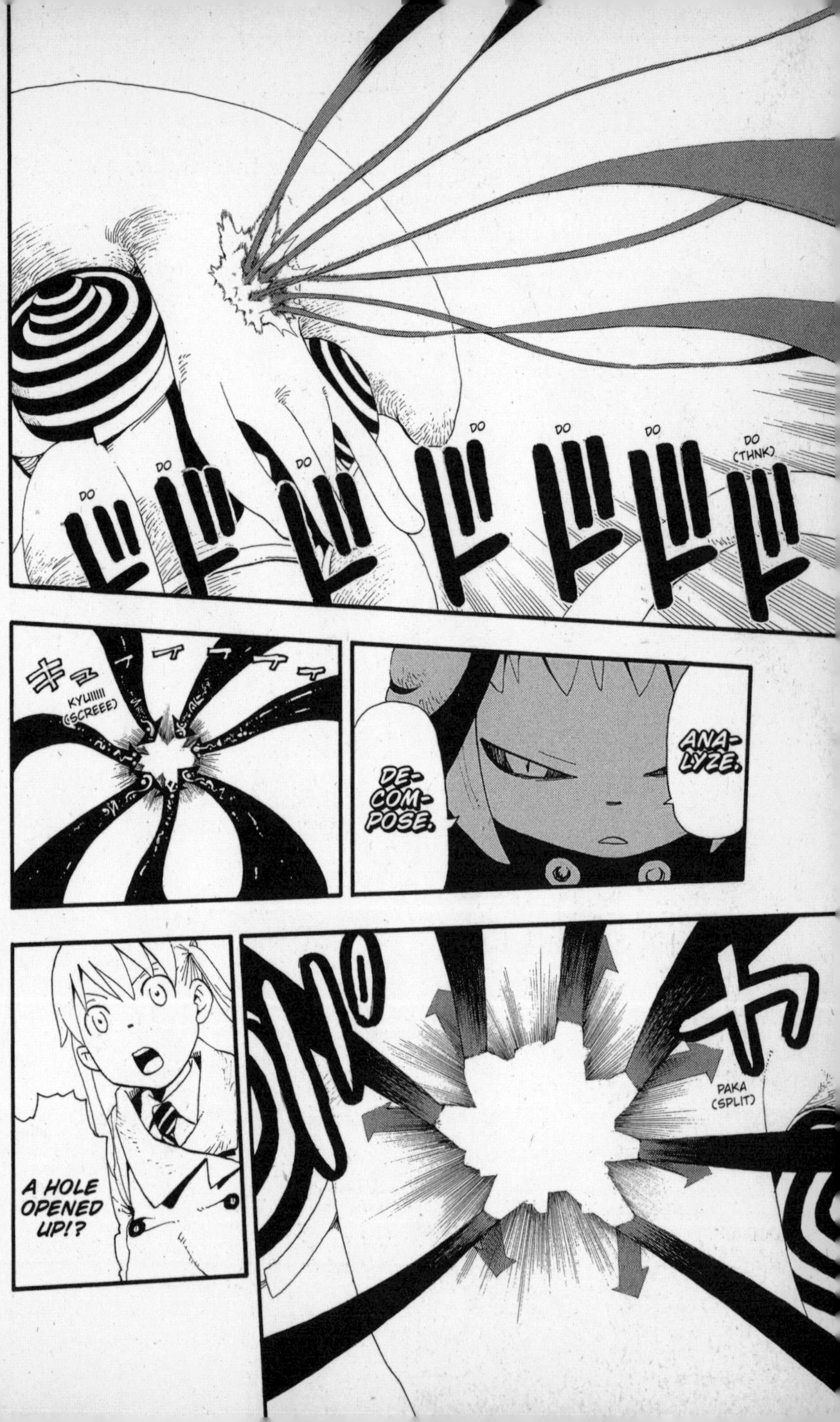
ドドドドドドドド
DO (THNK)
DO
DO
DO
DO
DO
DO
DO
ANA-LYZE.
DE-COM-POSE.
キュイイイイ
KYUIIIII (SCREEE)
パカ
PAKA (SPLIT)
A HOLE OPENED UP!?

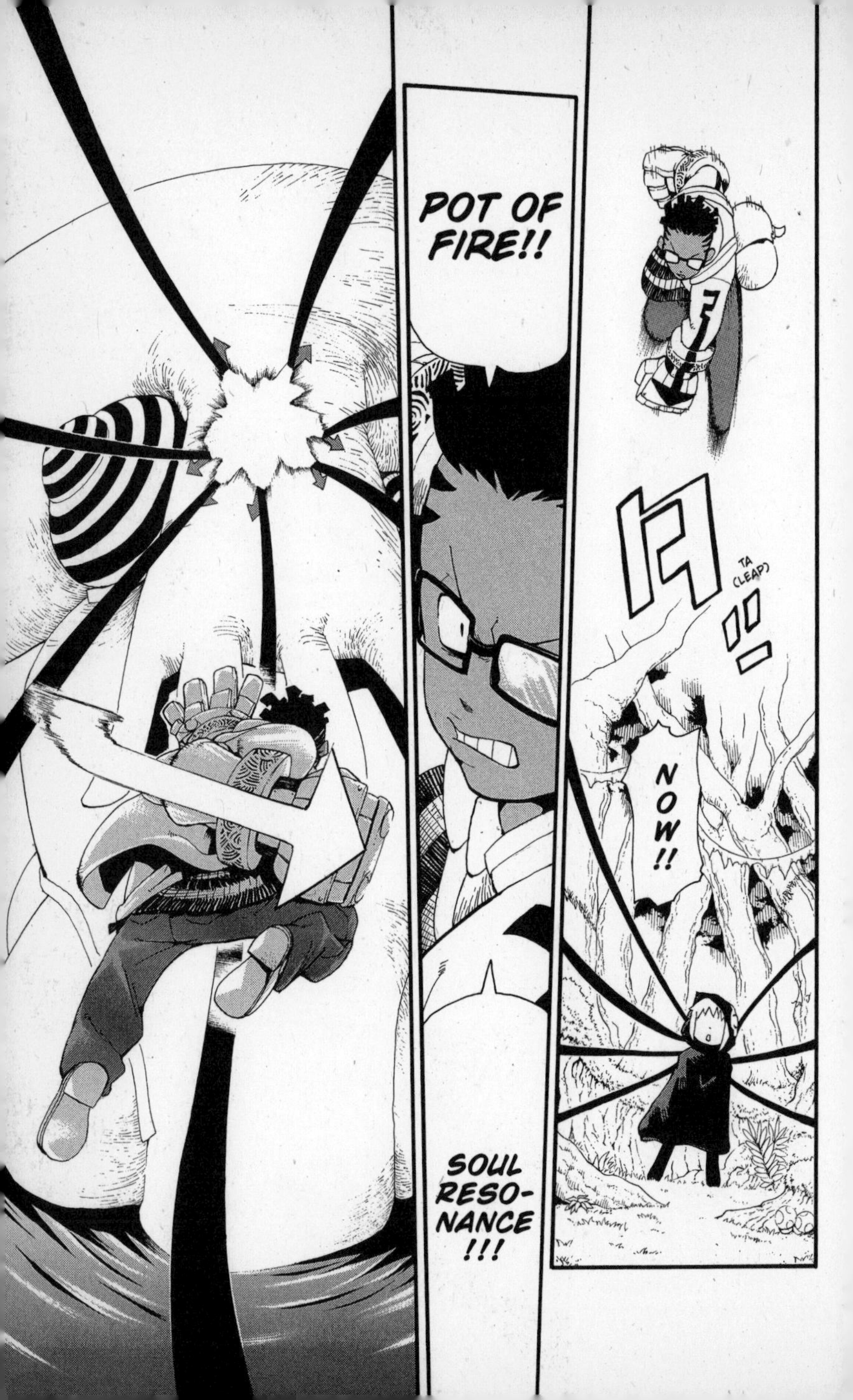
TA (LEAP)
NOW!!
POT OF FIRE!!
SOUL RESONANCE!!!

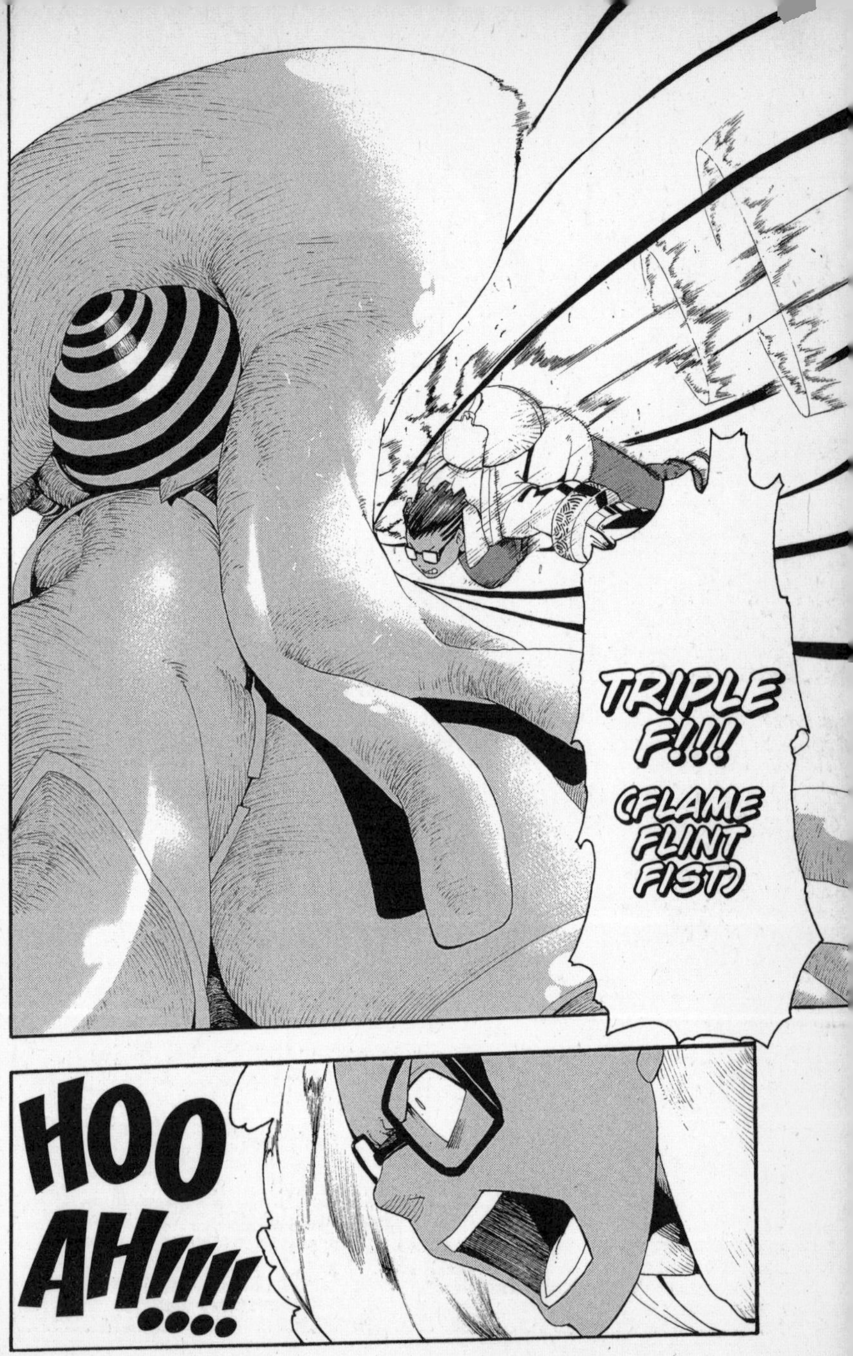
TRIPLE F!!! (FLAME FLINT FIST)
HOO AH!!!...

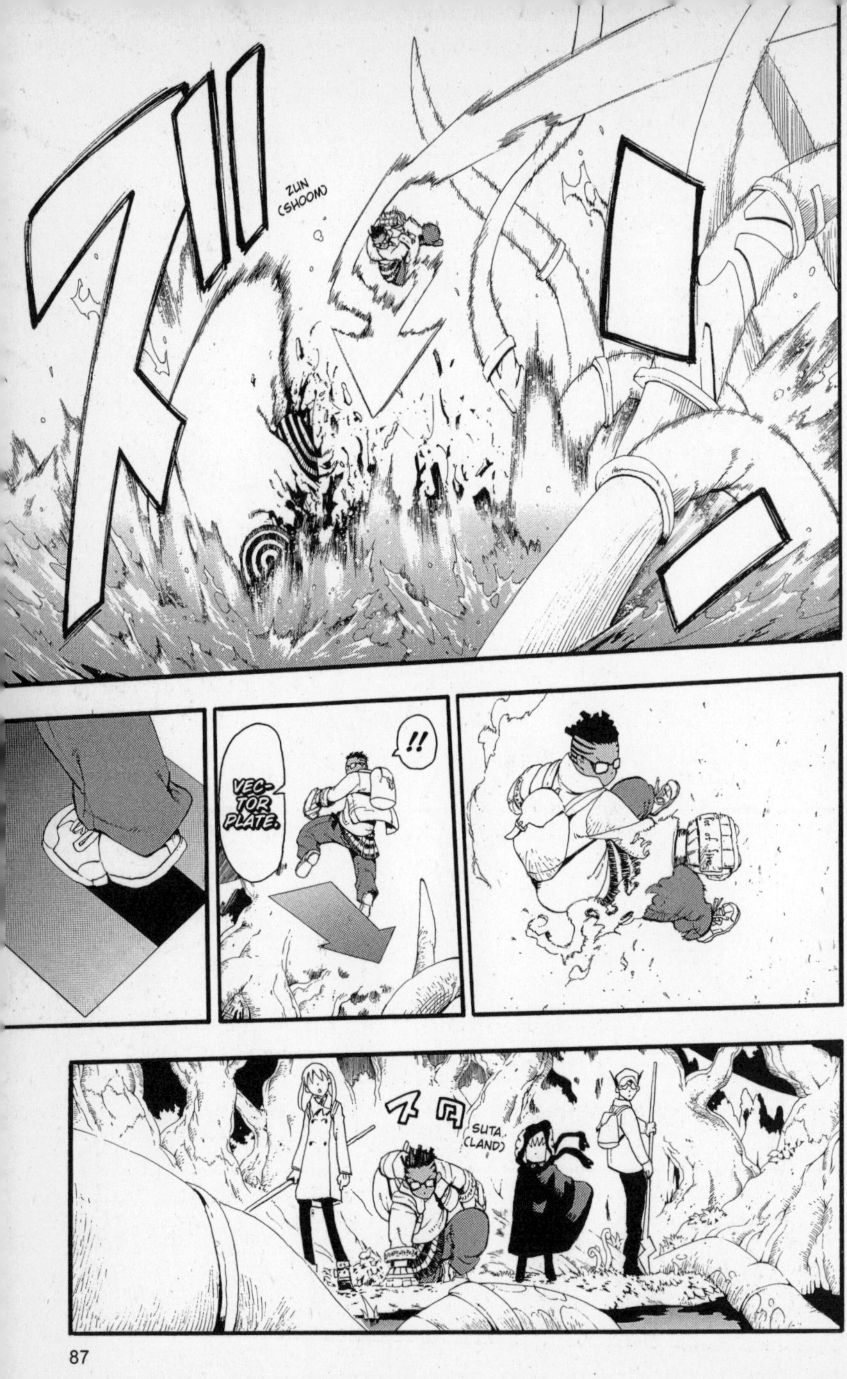
ZUN (SHOOM)
!!
VEC-TOR PLATE.
SUTA (LAND)

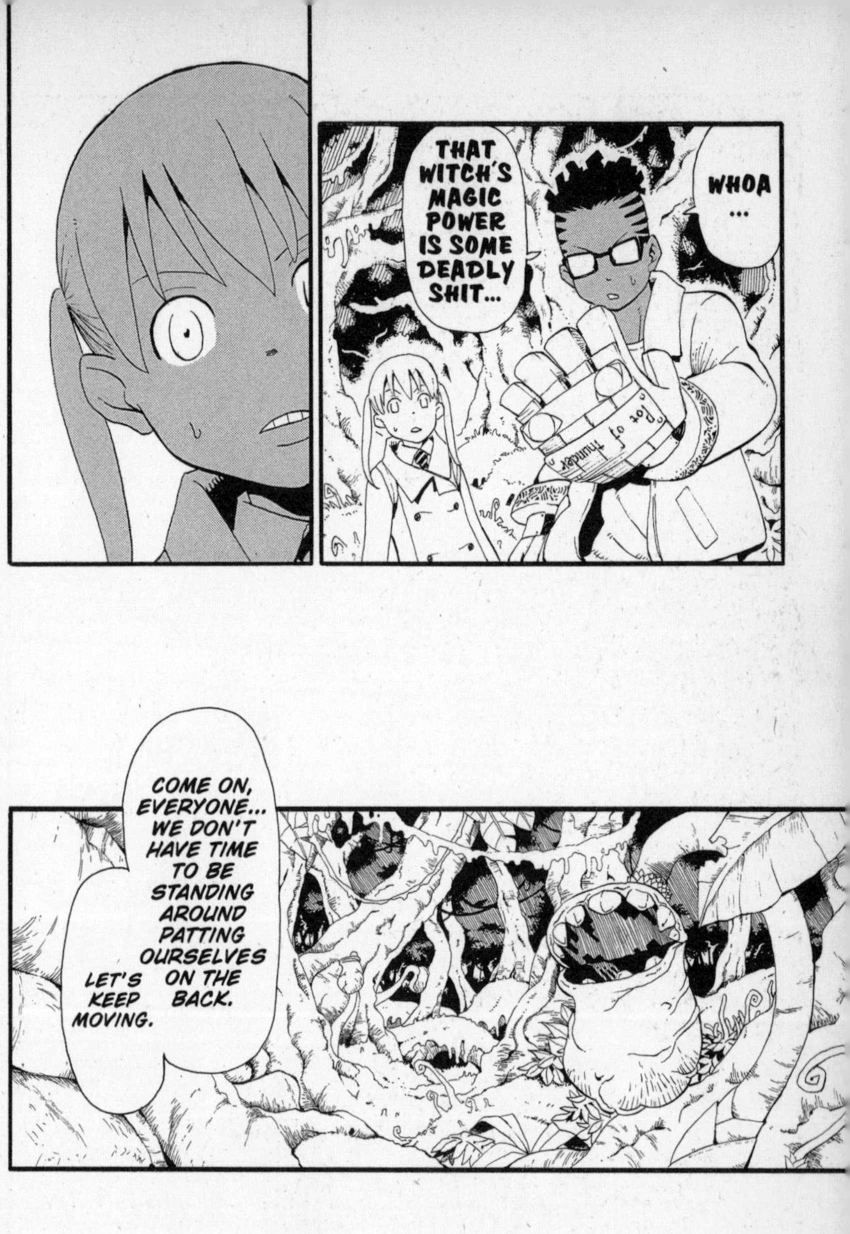
WHOA ...
THAT WITCH'S MAGIC POWER IS SOME DEADLY SHIT...
Pot of thunder
COME ON, EVERYONE... WE DON'T HAVE TIME TO BE STANDING AROUND PATTING OURSELVES ON THE BACK.
LET'S KEEP MOVING.

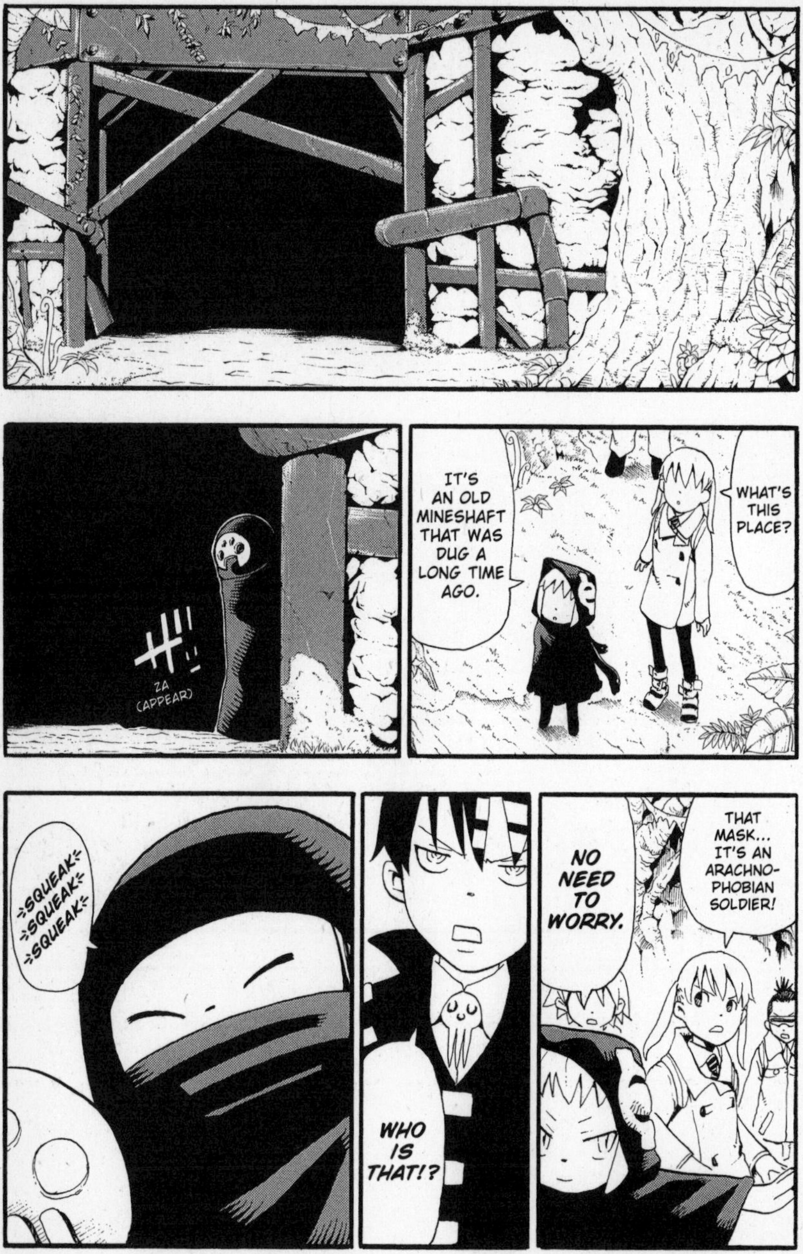
WHAT'S THIS PLACE?
IT'S AN OLD MINESHAFT THAT WAS DUG A LONG TIME AGO.
ZA (APPEAR)
THAT MASK... IT'S AN ARACHNO-PHOBIAN SOLDIER!
NO NEED TO WORRY.
WHO IS THAT!?
SQUEAK SQUEAK SQUEAK

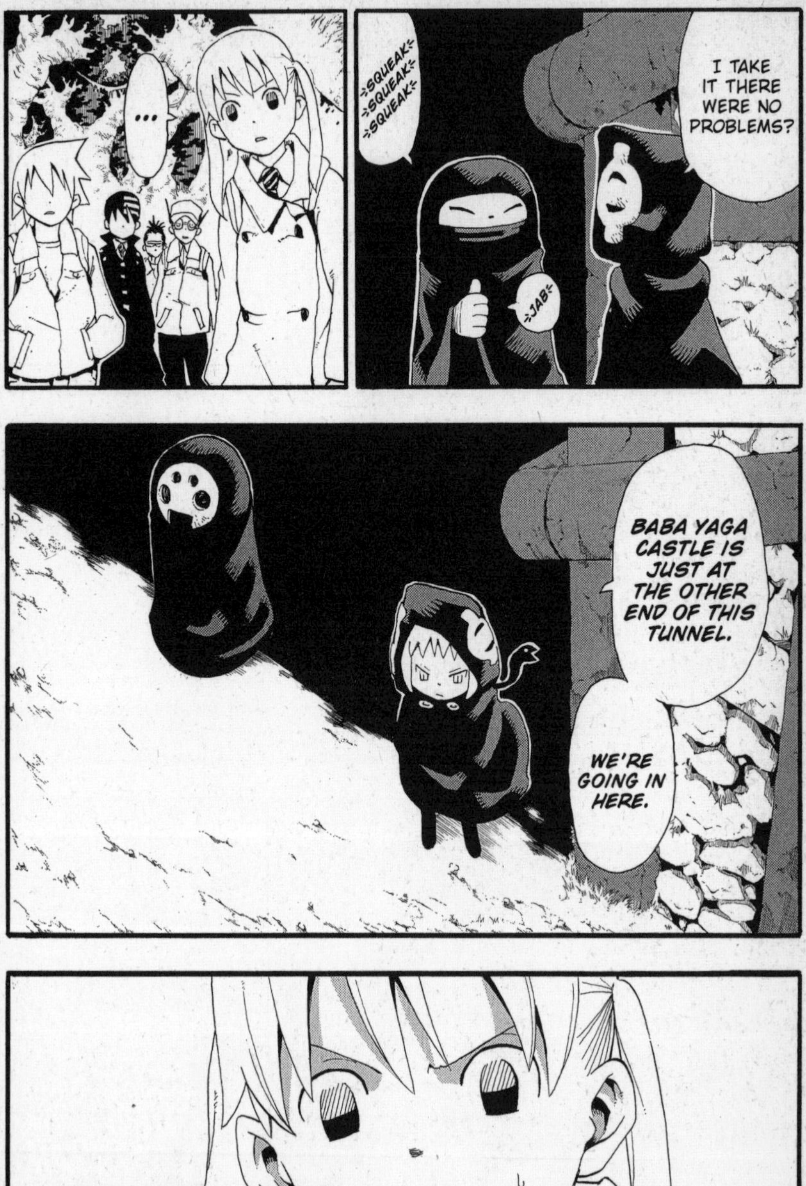
I TAKE IT THERE WERE NO PROBLEMS?
SQUEAK SQUEAK SQUEAK
JAB
...
BABA YAGA CASTLE IS JUST AT THE OTHER END OF THIS TUNNEL.
WE'RE GOING IN HERE.

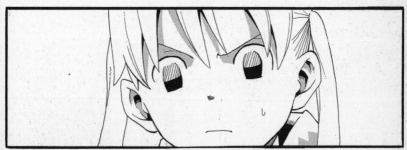

SOUL EATER

CHAPTER 47: OPERATION CAPTURE BABA YAGA CASTLE (PART 2)

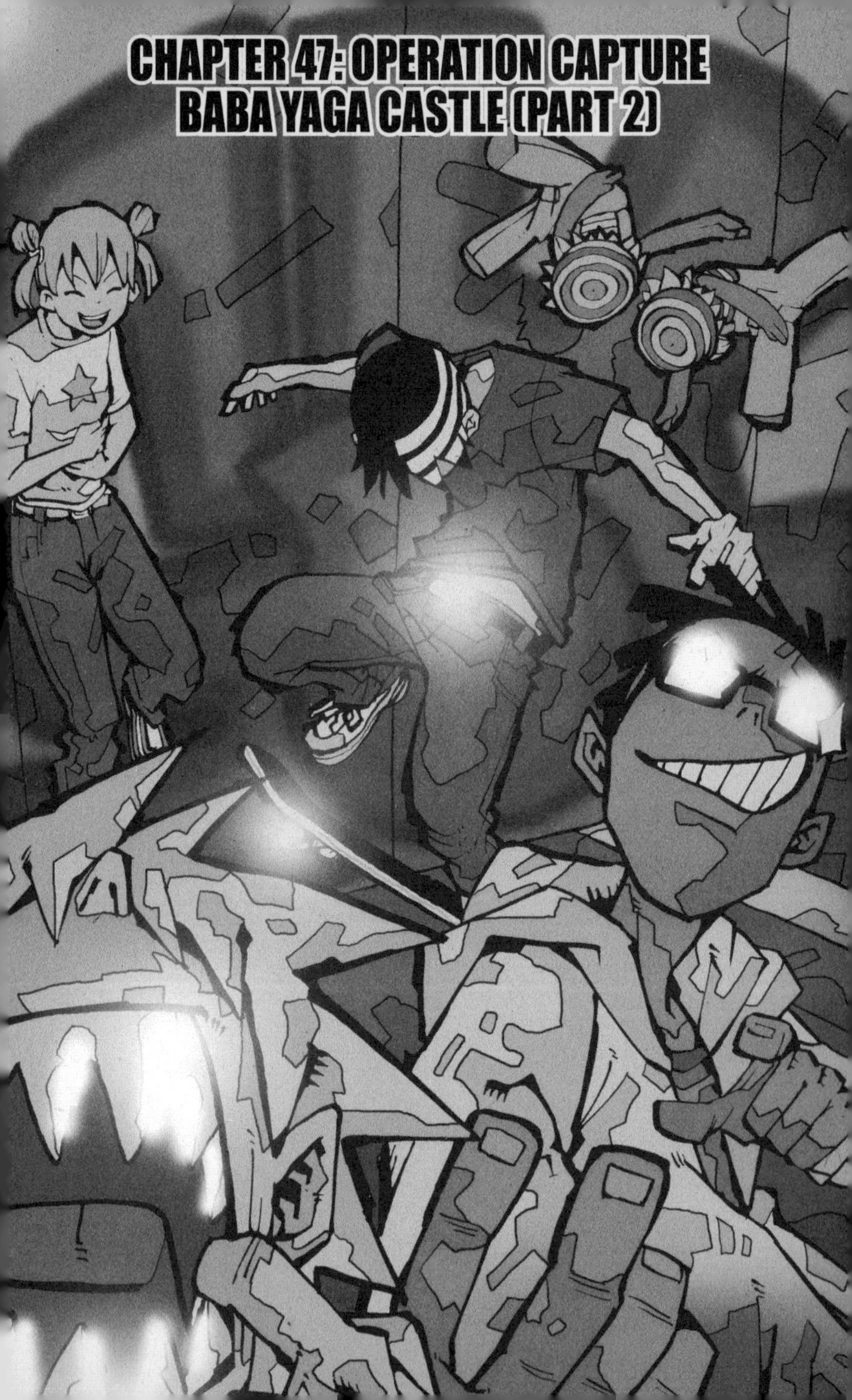

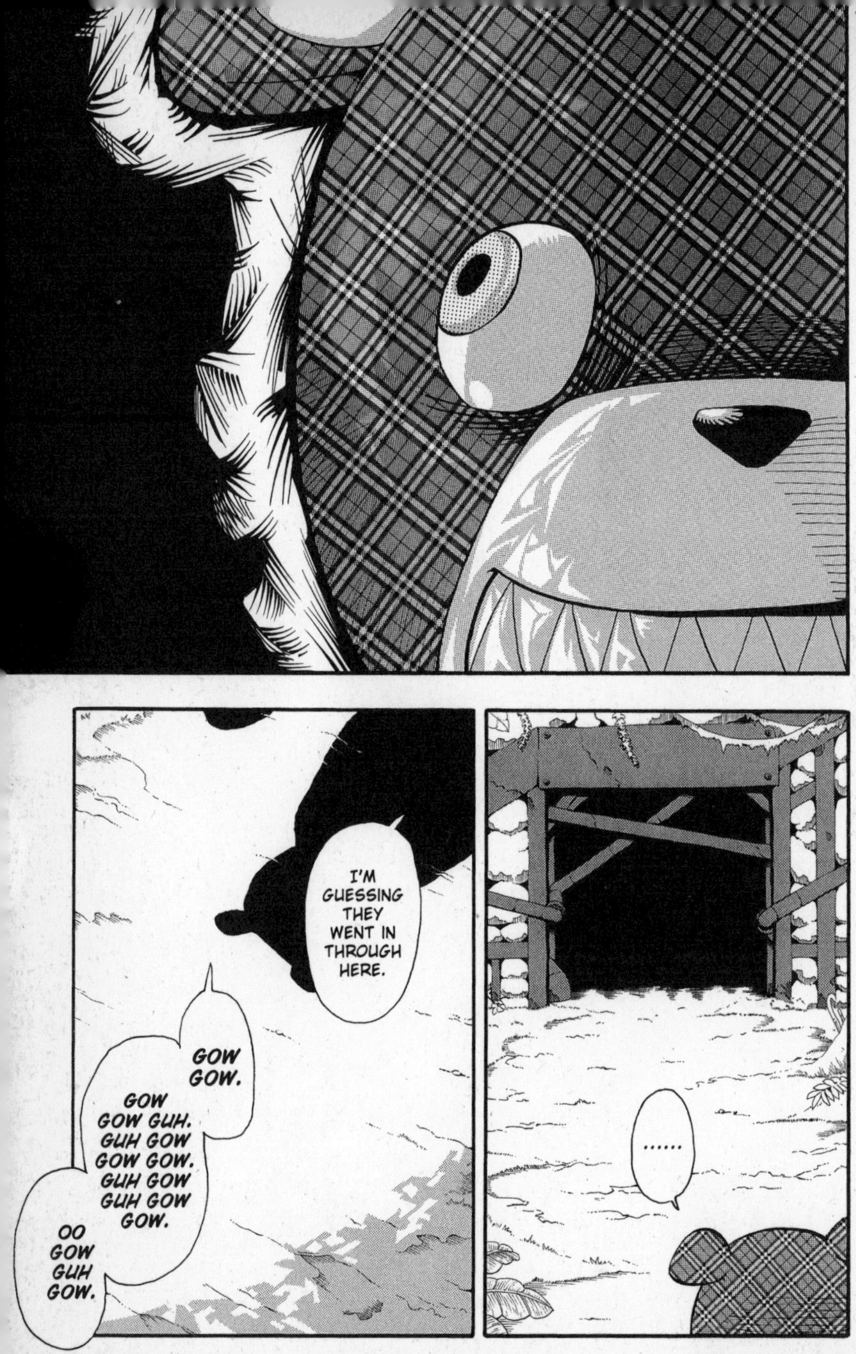
……
I'M GUESSING THEY WENT IN THROUGH HERE.
GOW GOW.
GOW GOW GUH. GUH GOW GOW GOW. GUH GOW GUH GOW GOW.
OO GOW GUH GOW.

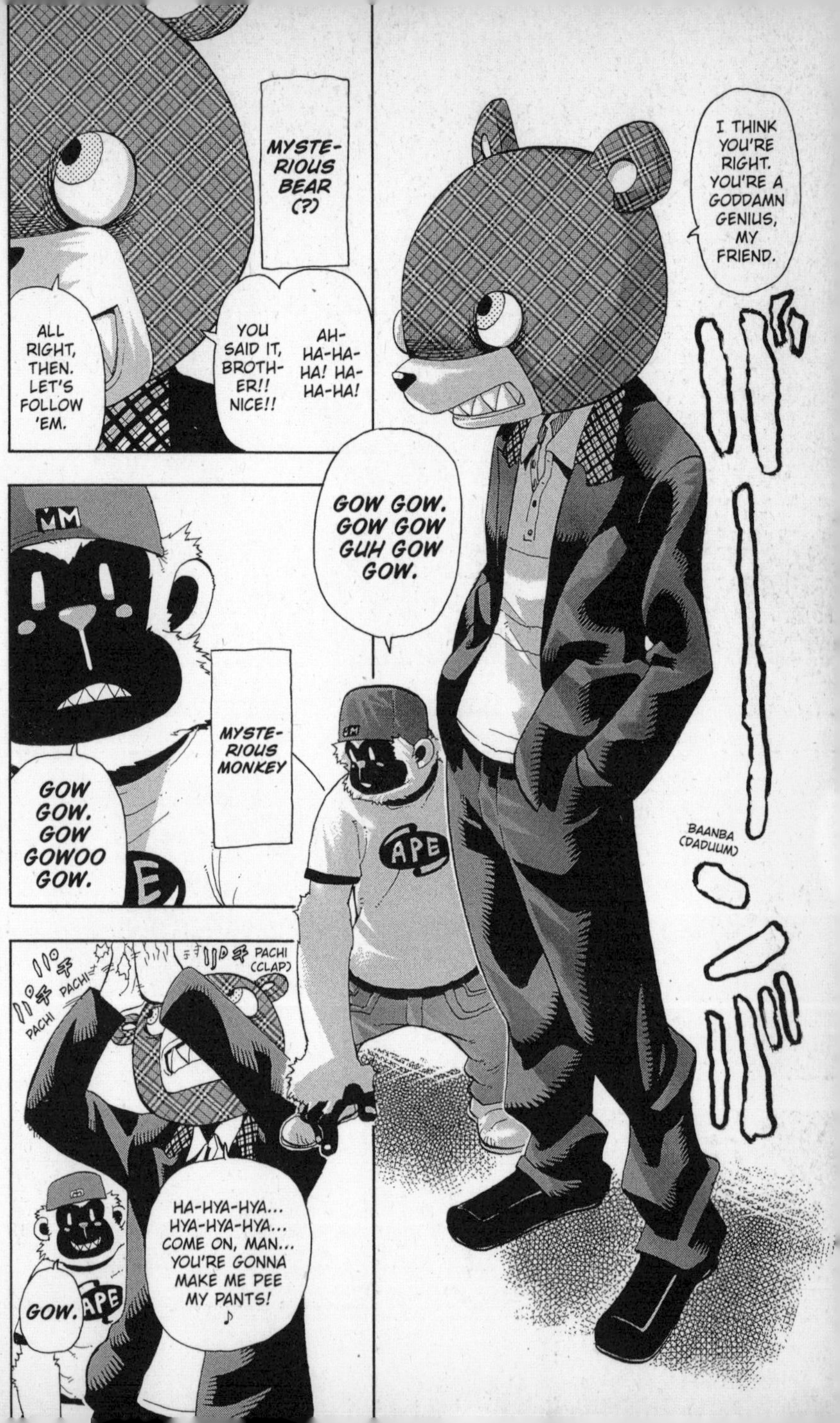
I THINK YOU'RE RIGHT. YOU'RE A GODDAMN GENIUS, MY FRIEND.
GOW GOW. GOW GOW GUH GOW GOW.
BAANBA (DADUUM)
MYSTE-RIOUS BEAR (?)
AH-HA-HA-HA! HA-HA-HA!
YOU SAID IT, BROTH-ER!! NICE!!
ALL RIGHT, THEN. LET'S FOLLOW 'EM.
MYSTE-RIOUS MONKEY
GOW GOW. GOW GOWOO GOW.
PACHI (CLAP)
PACHI
PACHI
HA-HYA-HYA... HYA-HYA-HYA... COME ON, MAN... YOU'RE GONNA MAKE ME PEE MY PANTS! ♪
GOW.

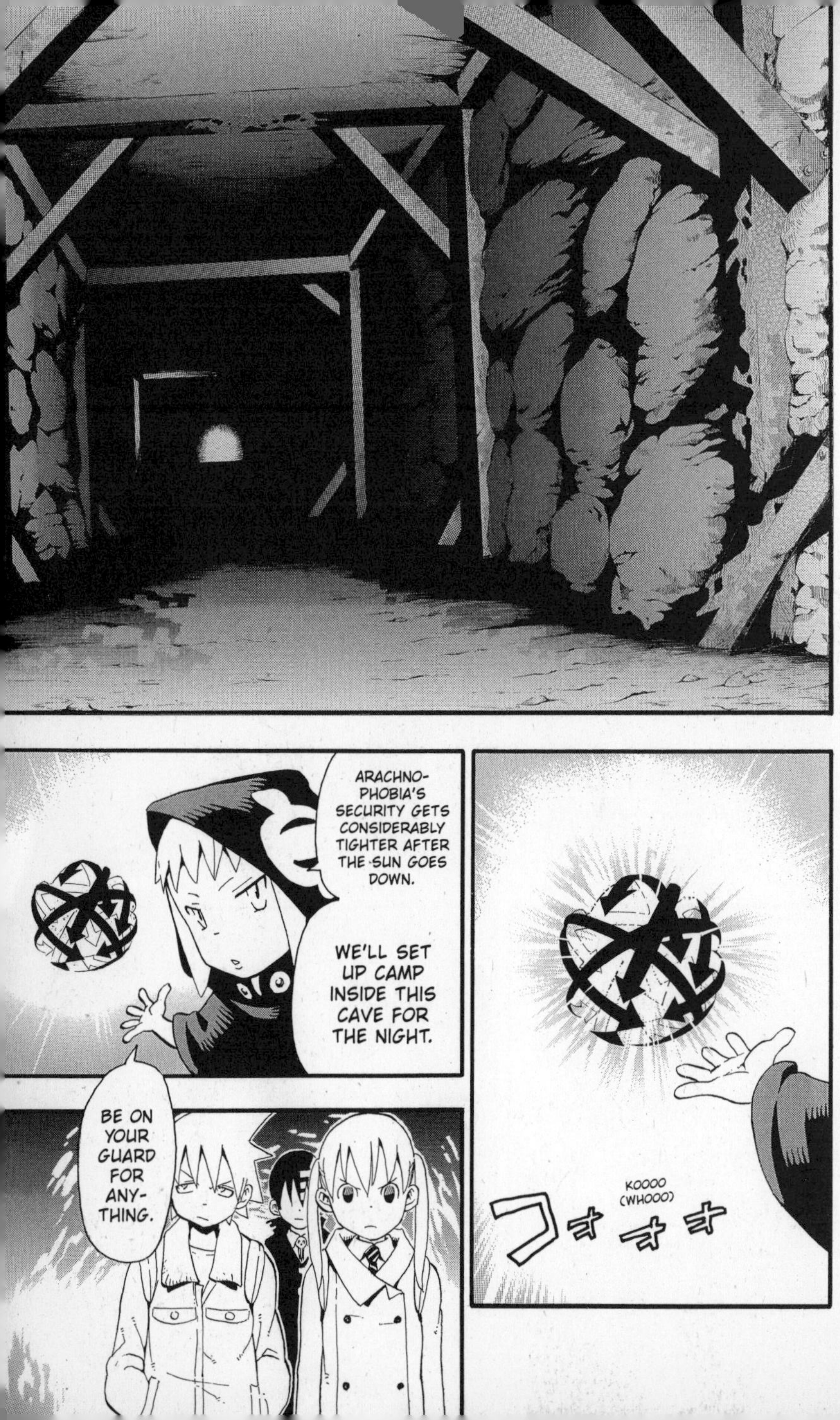
KOOOO (WHOOO)
フォォォ
ARACHNO-PHOBIA'S SECURITY GETS CONSIDERABLY TIGHTER AFTER THE SUN GOES DOWN.
WE'LL SET UP CAMP INSIDE THIS CAVE FOR THE NIGHT.
BE ON YOUR GUARD FOR ANY-THING.

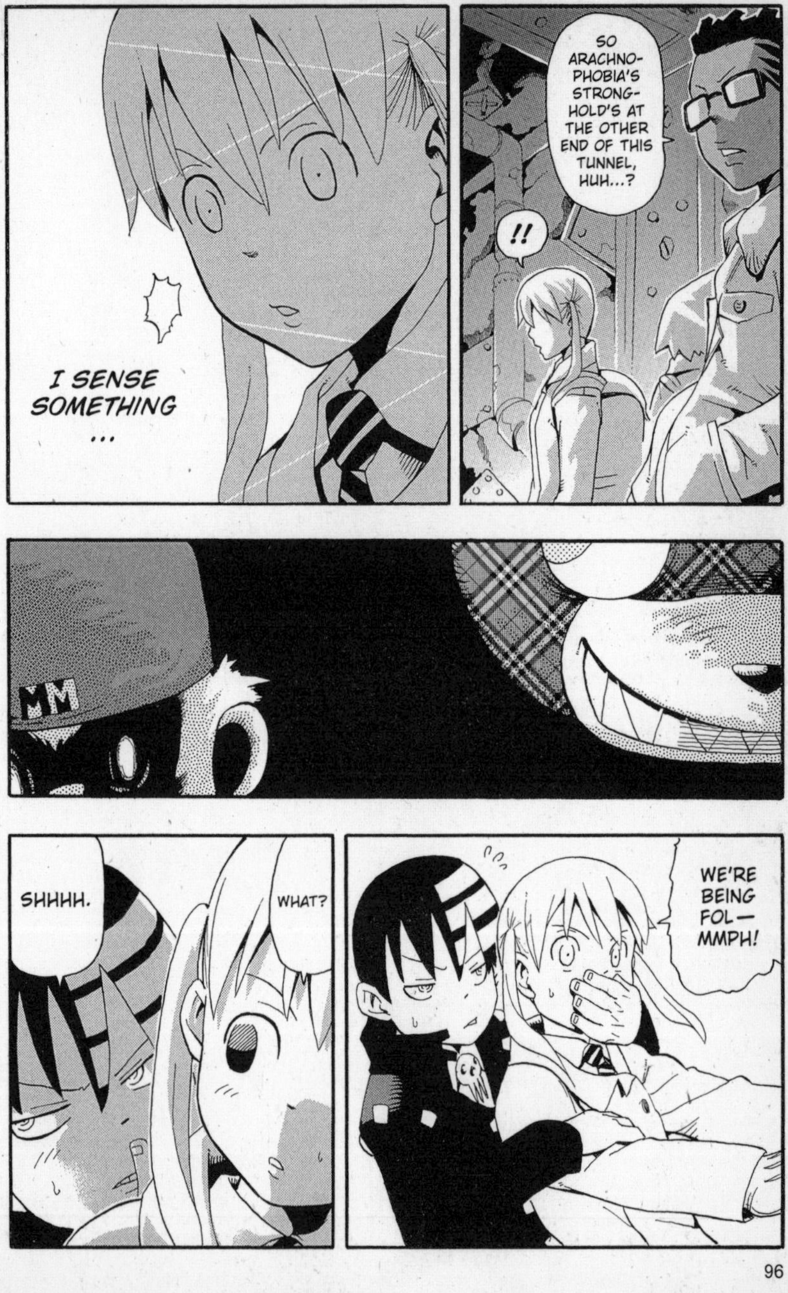
SO ARACHNOPHOBIA'S STRONGHOLD'S AT THE OTHER END OF THIS TUNNEL, HUH...?
!!
I SENSE SOMETHING ...
WE'RE BEING FOL— MMPH!
WHAT?
SHHHH.

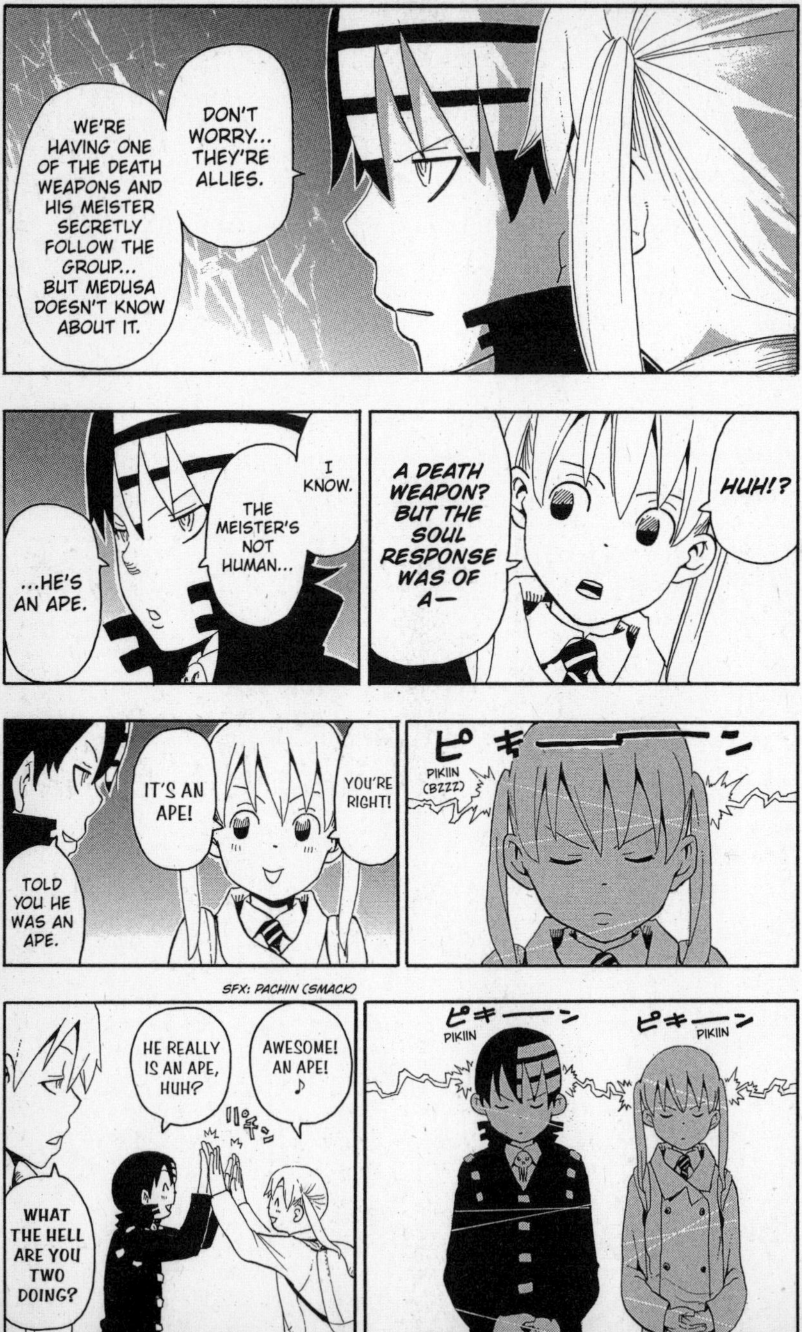
DON'T WORRY... THEY'RE ALLIES.
WE'RE HAVING ONE OF THE DEATH WEAPONS AND HIS MEISTER SECRETLY FOLLOW THE GROUP... BUT MEDUSA DOESN'T KNOW ABOUT IT.
HUH!?
A DEATH WEAPON? BUT THE SOUL RESPONSE WAS OF A—
I KNOW.
THE MEISTER'S NOT HUMAN...
...HE'S AN APE.
ピキーーーン
PIKIIN (BZZZ)
YOU'RE RIGHT!
IT'S AN APE!
TOLD YOU HE WAS AN APE.
SFX: PACHIN (SMACK)
ピキーン
PIKIIN
ピキーン
PIKIIN
AWESOME! AN APE! ♪
HE REALLY IS AN APE, HUH?
パチン
WHAT THE HELL ARE YOU TWO DOING?

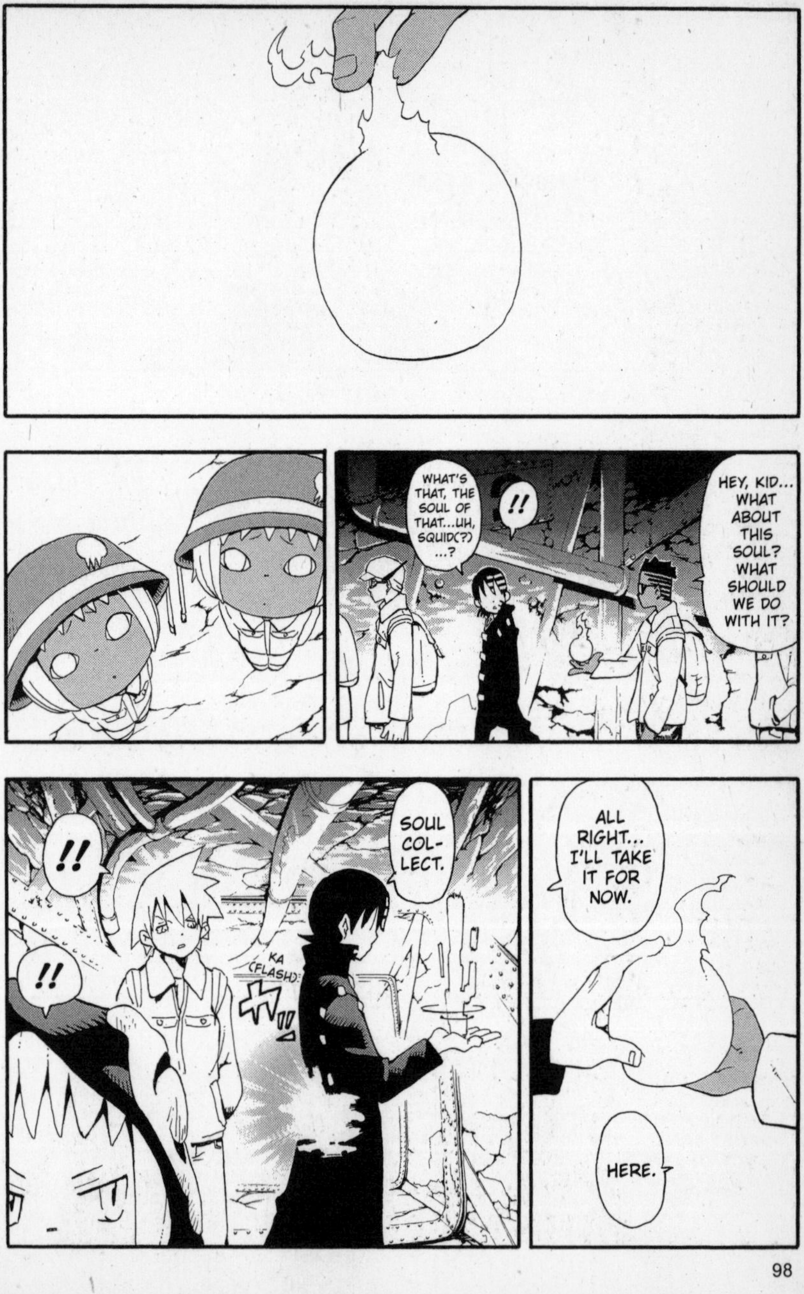
HEY, KID... WHAT ABOUT THIS SOUL? WHAT SHOULD WE DO WITH IT?
!!
WHAT'S THAT, THE SOUL OF THAT...UH, SQUID(?) ...?
ALL RIGHT... I'LL TAKE IT FOR NOW.
HERE.
SOUL COL-LECT.
!!
KA (FLASH)
!!

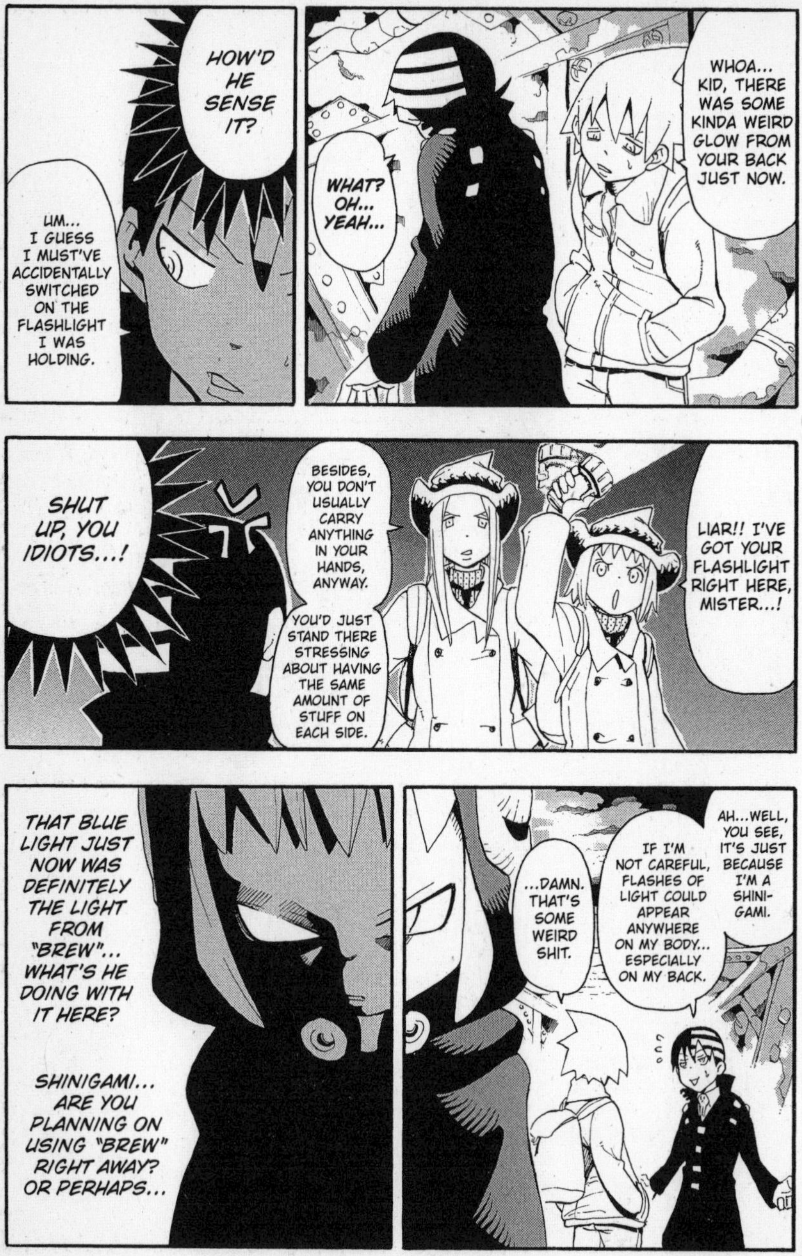
WHOA... KID, THERE WAS SOME KINDA WEIRD GLOW FROM YOUR BACK JUST NOW.
WHAT? OH... YEAH...
HOW'D HE SENSE IT?
UM... I GUESS I MUST'VE ACCIDENTALLY SWITCHED ON THE FLASHLIGHT I WAS HOLDING.
LIAR!! I'VE GOT YOUR FLASHLIGHT RIGHT HERE, MISTER...!
BESIDES, YOU DON'T USUALLY CARRY ANYTHING IN YOUR HANDS, ANYWAY.
YOU'D JUST STAND THERE STRESSING ABOUT HAVING THE SAME AMOUNT OF STUFF ON EACH SIDE.
SHUT UP, YOU IDIOTS...!
AH...WELL, YOU SEE, IT'S JUST BECAUSE I'M A SHINI-GAMI.
IF I'M NOT CAREFUL, FLASHES OF LIGHT COULD APPEAR ANYWHERE ON MY BODY... ESPECIALLY ON MY BACK.
...DAMN. THAT'S SOME WEIRD SHIT.
THAT BLUE LIGHT JUST NOW WAS DEFINITELY THE LIGHT FROM "BREW"... WHAT'S HE DOING WITH IT HERE?
SHINIGAMI... ARE YOU PLANNING ON USING "BREW" RIGHT AWAY? OR PERHAPS...

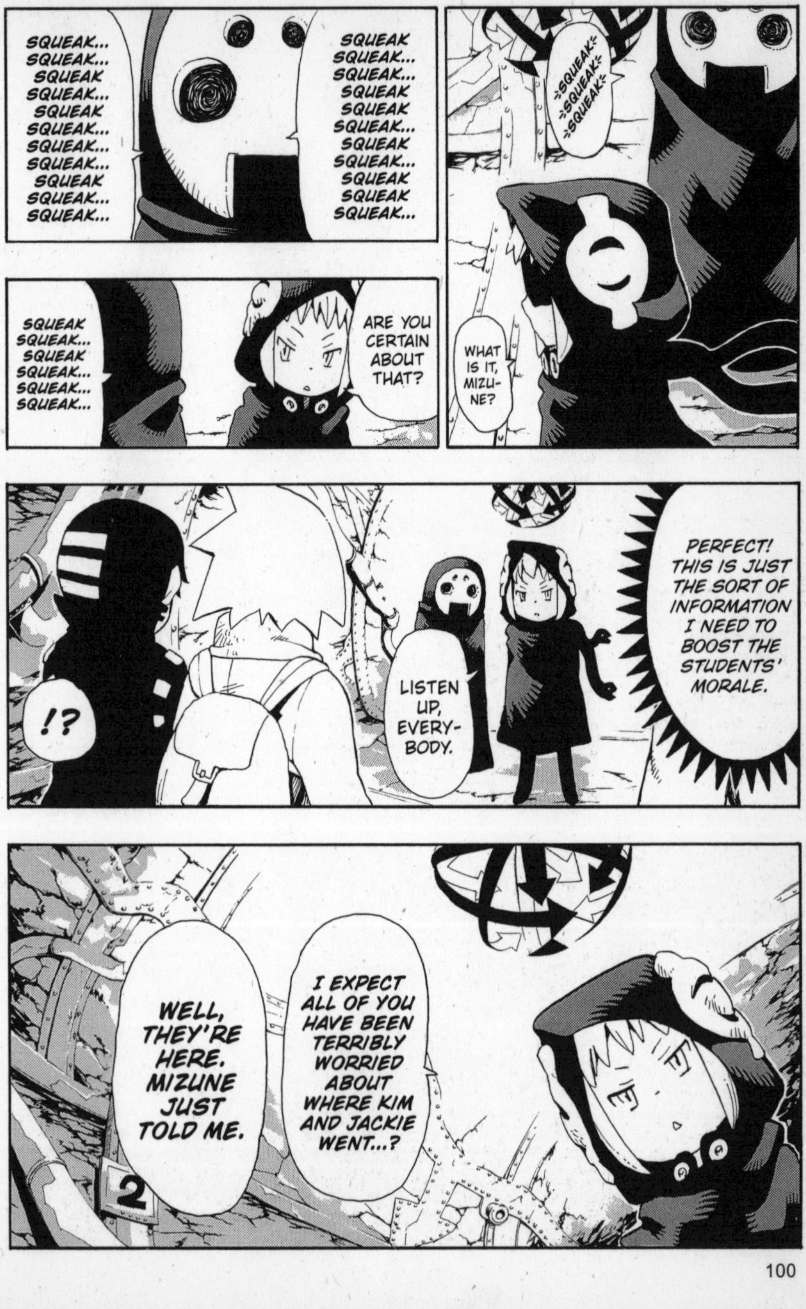
SQUEAK SQUEAK SQUEAK
WHAT IS IT, MIZUNE?
SQUEAK SQUEAK... SQUEAK... SQUEAK SQUEAK SQUEAK... SQUEAK SQUEAK... SQUEAK SQUEAK SQUEAK...
SQUEAK... SQUEAK... SQUEAK SQUEAK... SQUEAK SQUEAK... SQUEAK... SQUEAK... SQUEAK SQUEAK... SQUEAK...
ARE YOU CERTAIN ABOUT THAT?
SQUEAK SQUEAK... SQUEAK SQUEAK... SQUEAK... SQUEAK...
PERFECT! THIS IS JUST THE SORT OF INFORMATION I NEED TO BOOST THE STUDENTS' MORALE.
LISTEN UP, EVERYBODY.
!?
I EXPECT ALL OF YOU HAVE BEEN TERRIBLY WORRIED ABOUT WHERE KIM AND JACKIE WENT...?
WELL, THEY'RE HERE. MIZUNE JUST TOLD ME.
2

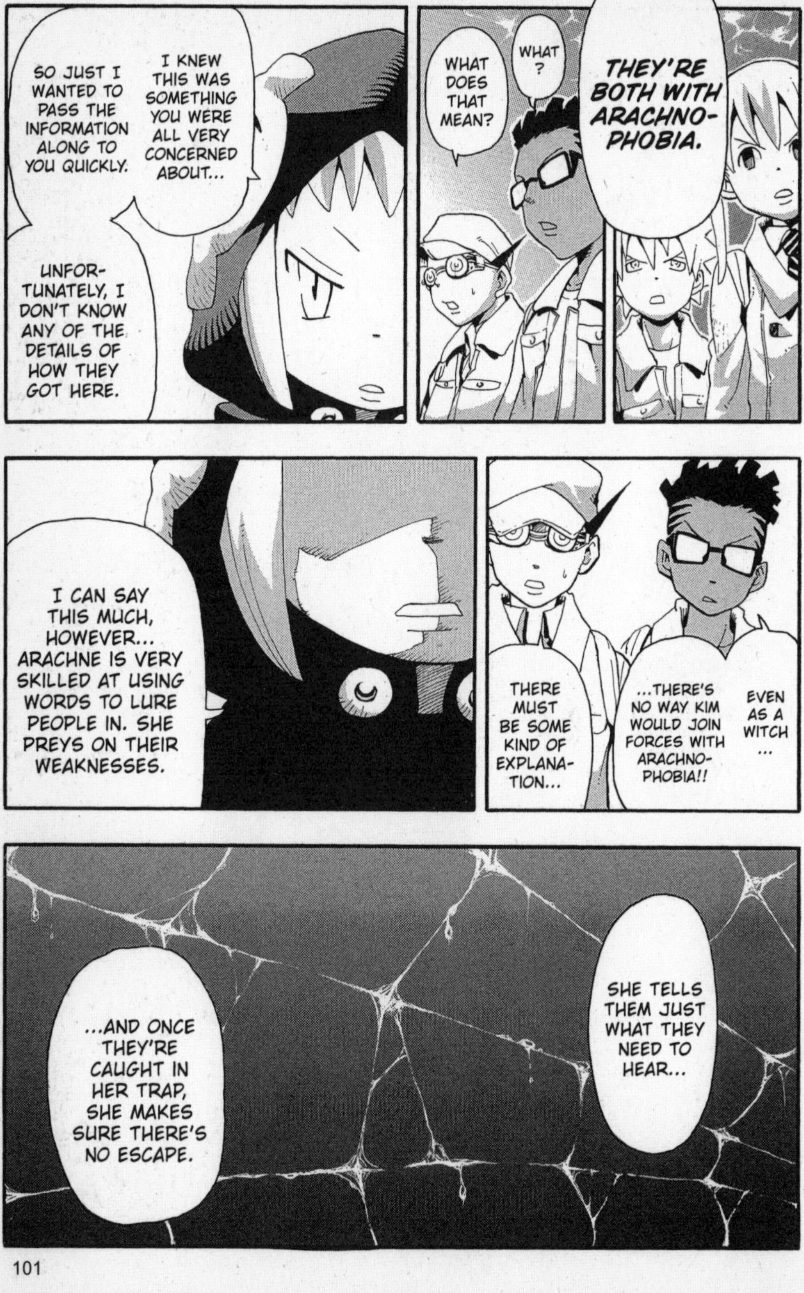
THEY'RE BOTH WITH ARACHNOPHOBIA.
WHAT?
WHAT DOES THAT MEAN?
I KNEW THIS WAS SOMETHING YOU WERE ALL VERY CONCERNED ABOUT...
SO JUST I WANTED TO PASS THE INFORMATION ALONG TO YOU QUICKLY.
UNFORTUNATELY, I DON'T KNOW ANY OF THE DETAILS OF HOW THEY GOT HERE.
EVEN AS A WITCH...
...THERE'S NO WAY KIM WOULD JOIN FORCES WITH ARACHNOPHOBIA!!
THERE MUST BE SOME KIND OF EXPLANATION...
I CAN SAY THIS MUCH, HOWEVER... ARACHNE IS VERY SKILLED AT USING WORDS TO LURE PEOPLE IN. SHE PREYS ON THEIR WEAKNESSES.
SHE TELLS THEM JUST WHAT THEY NEED TO HEAR...
...AND ONCE THEY'RE CAUGHT IN HER TRAP, SHE MAKES SURE THERE'S NO ESCAPE.

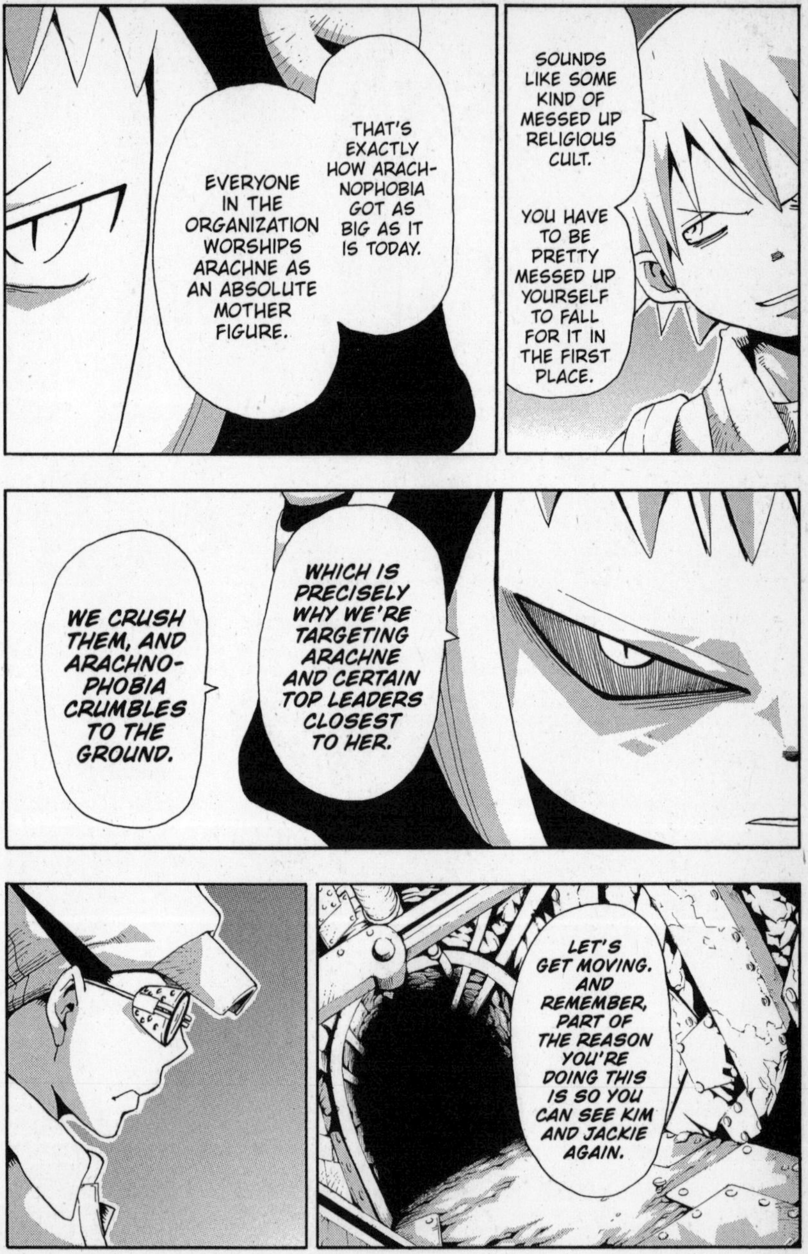
SOUNDS LIKE SOME KIND OF MESSED UP RELIGIOUS CULT.
YOU HAVE TO BE PRETTY MESSED UP YOURSELF TO FALL FOR IT IN THE FIRST PLACE.
THAT'S EXACTLY HOW ARACH-NOPHOBIA GOT AS BIG AS IT IS TODAY.
EVERYONE IN THE ORGANIZATION WORSHIPS ARACHNE AS AN ABSOLUTE MOTHER FIGURE.
WHICH IS PRECISELY WHY WE'RE TARGETING ARACHNE AND CERTAIN TOP LEADERS CLOSEST TO HER.
WE CRUSH THEM, AND ARACHNO-PHOBIA CRUMBLES TO THE GROUND.
LET'S GET MOVING. AND REMEMBER, PART OF THE REASON YOU'RE DOING THIS IS SO YOU CAN SEE KIM AND JACKIE AGAIN.

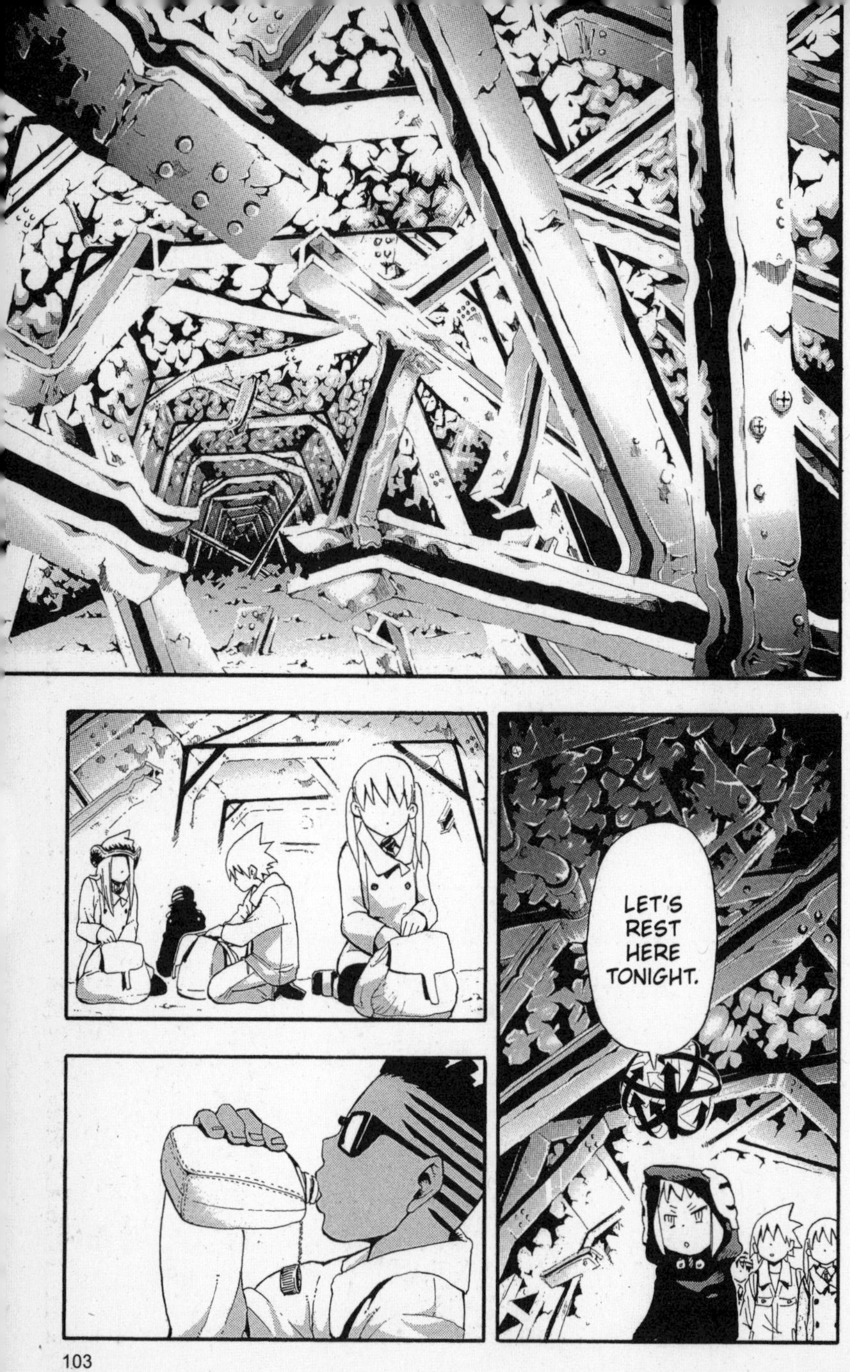
LET'S REST HERE TONIGHT.

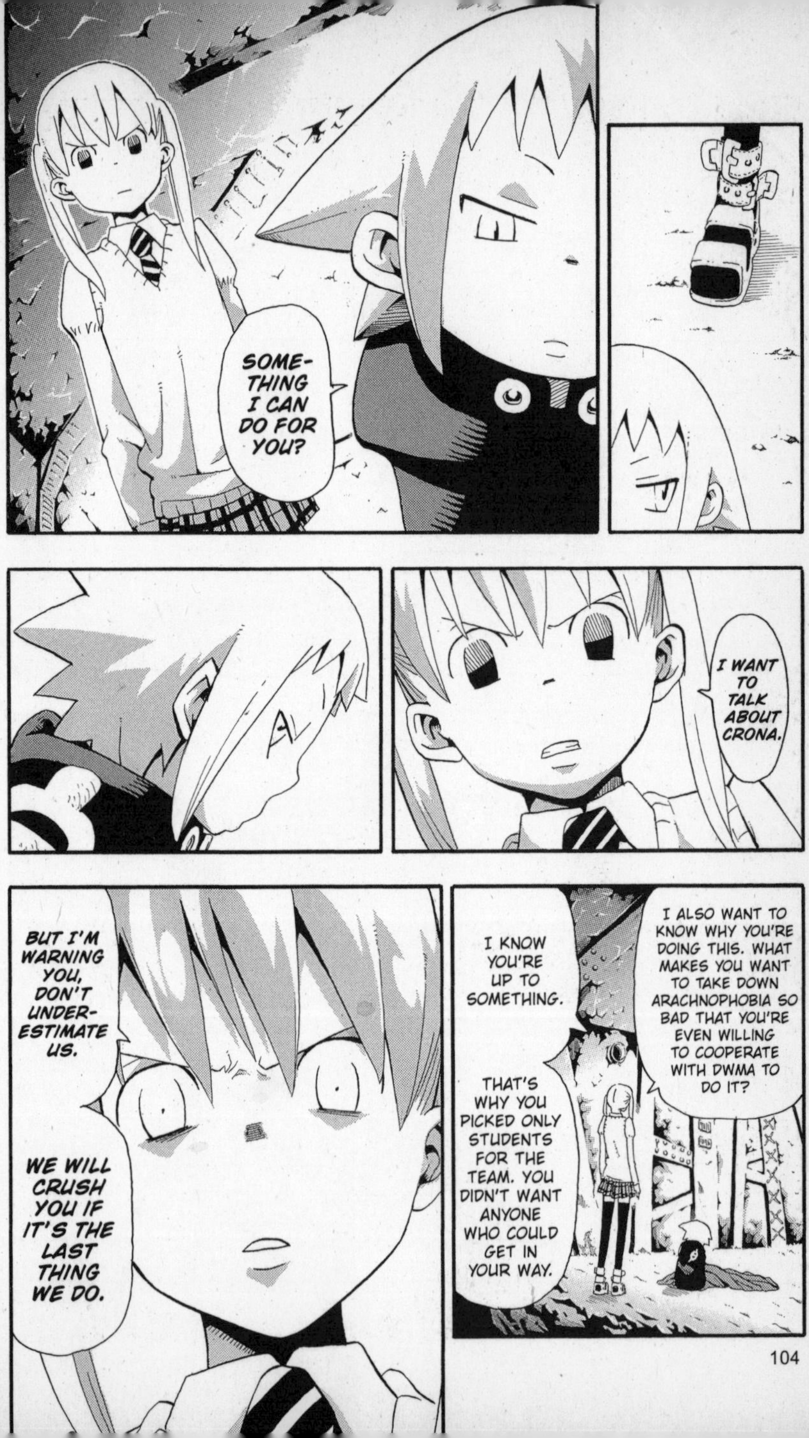
SOMETHING I CAN DO FOR YOU?
I WANT TO TALK ABOUT CRONA.
I KNOW YOU'RE UP TO SOMETHING.
THAT'S WHY YOU PICKED ONLY STUDENTS FOR THE TEAM. YOU DIDN'T WANT ANYONE WHO COULD GET IN YOUR WAY.
I ALSO WANT TO KNOW WHY YOU'RE DOING THIS. WHAT MAKES YOU WANT TO TAKE DOWN ARACHNOPHOBIA SO BAD THAT YOU'RE EVEN WILLING TO COOPERATE WITH DWMA TO DO IT?
BUT I'M WARNING YOU, DON'T UNDERESTIMATE US.
WE WILL CRUSH YOU IF IT'S THE LAST THING WE DO.

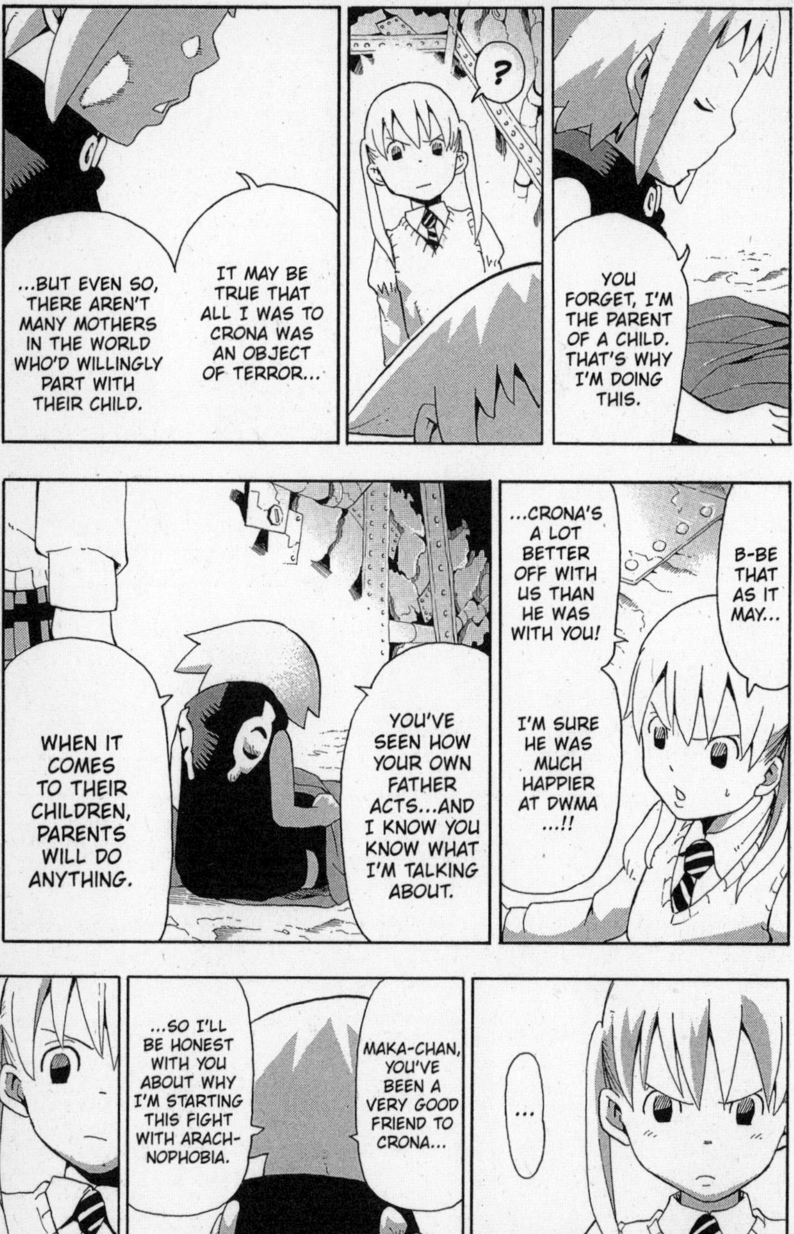
YOU FORGET, I'M THE PARENT OF A CHILD. THAT'S WHY I'M DOING THIS.
?
IT MAY BE TRUE THAT ALL I WAS TO CRONA WAS AN OBJECT OF TERROR...
...BUT EVEN SO, THERE AREN'T MANY MOTHERS IN THE WORLD WHO'D WILLINGLY PART WITH THEIR CHILD.
B-BE THAT AS IT MAY...
...CRONA'S A LOT BETTER OFF WITH US THAN HE WAS WITH YOU!
I'M SURE HE WAS MUCH HAPPIER AT DWMA ...!!
YOU'VE SEEN HOW YOUR OWN FATHER ACTS...AND I KNOW YOU KNOW WHAT I'M TALKING ABOUT.
WHEN IT COMES TO THEIR CHILDREN, PARENTS WILL DO ANYTHING.
...
MAKA-CHAN, YOU'VE BEEN A VERY GOOD FRIEND TO CRONA...
...SO I'LL BE HONEST WITH YOU ABOUT WHY I'M STARTING THIS FIGHT WITH ARACH-NOPHOBIA.

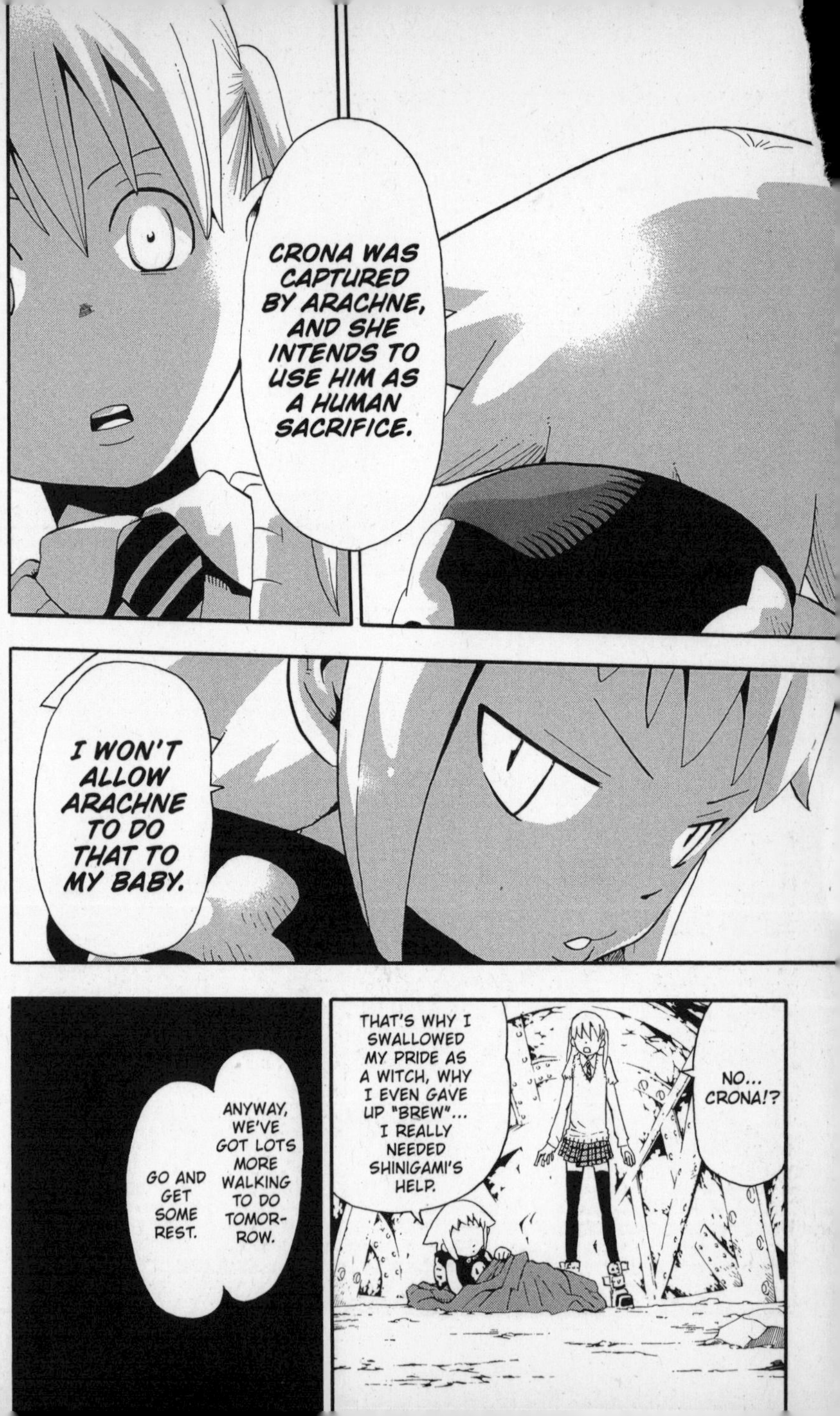
CRONA WAS CAPTURED BY ARACHNE, AND SHE INTENDS TO USE HIM AS A HUMAN SACRIFICE.
I WON'T ALLOW ARACHNE TO DO THAT TO MY BABY.
NO... CRONA!?
THAT'S WHY I SWALLOWED MY PRIDE AS A WITCH, WHY I EVEN GAVE UP "BREW"... I REALLY NEEDED SHINIGAMI'S HELP.
ANYWAY, WE'VE GOT LOTS MORE WALKING TO DO TOMOR-ROW.
GO AND GET SOME REST.

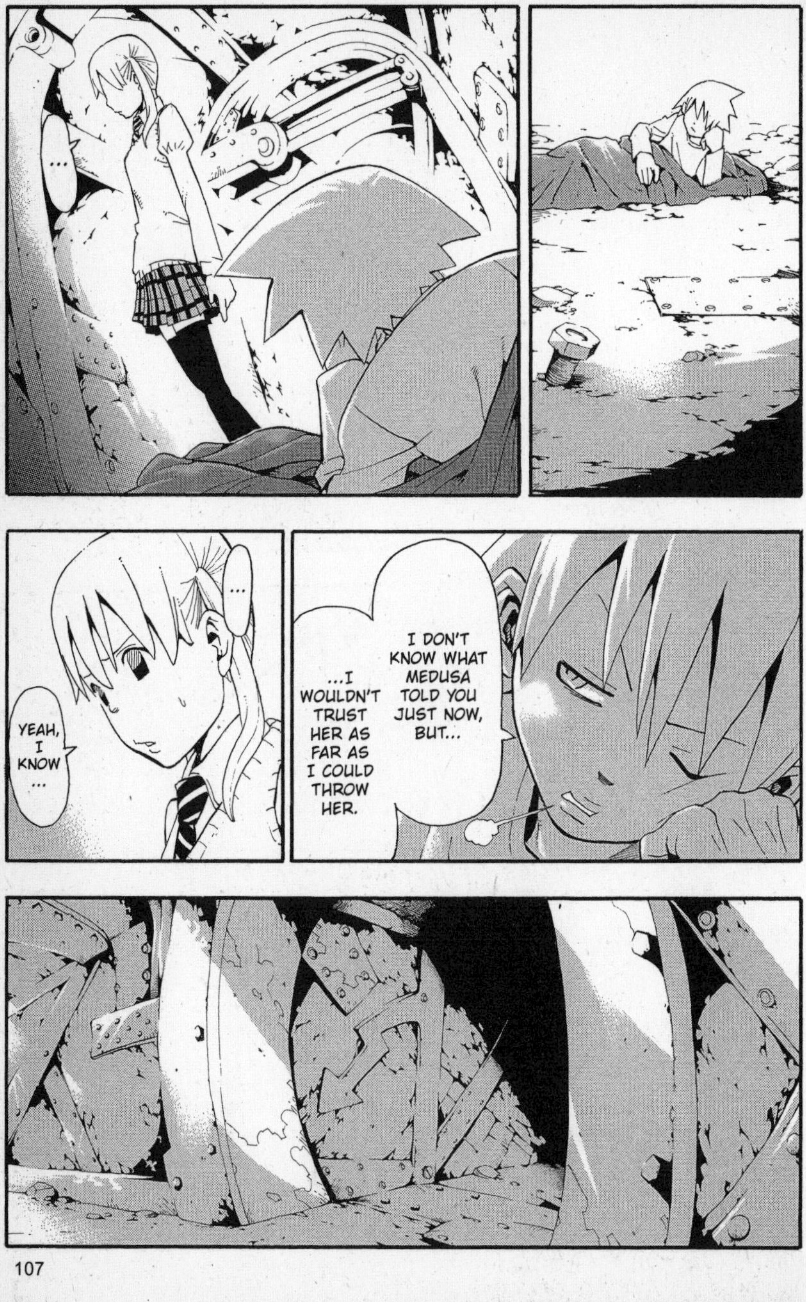
...
I DON'T KNOW WHAT MEDUSA TOLD YOU JUST NOW, BUT...
...I WOULDN'T TRUST HER AS FAR AS I COULD THROW HER.
...
YEAH, I KNOW ...

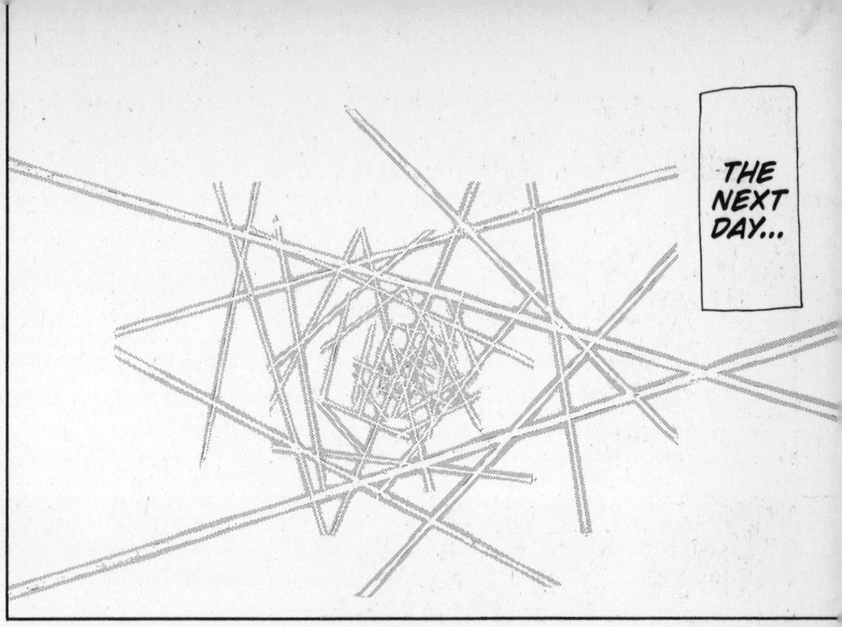
THE NEXT DAY...

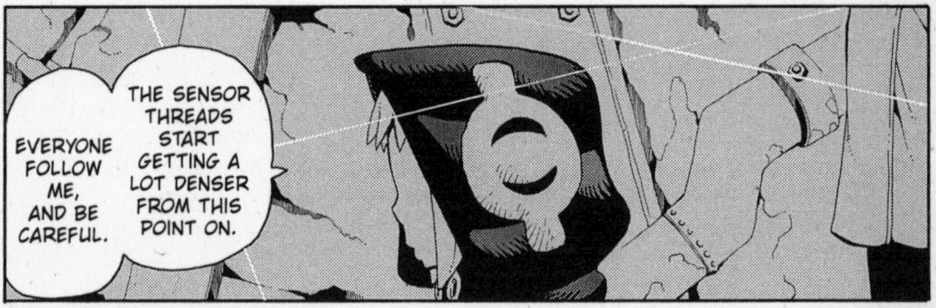
THE SENSOR THREADS START GETTING A LOT DENSER FROM THIS POINT ON.
EVERYONE FOLLOW ME, AND BE CAREFUL.

SFX: HAA (PANT) HAA

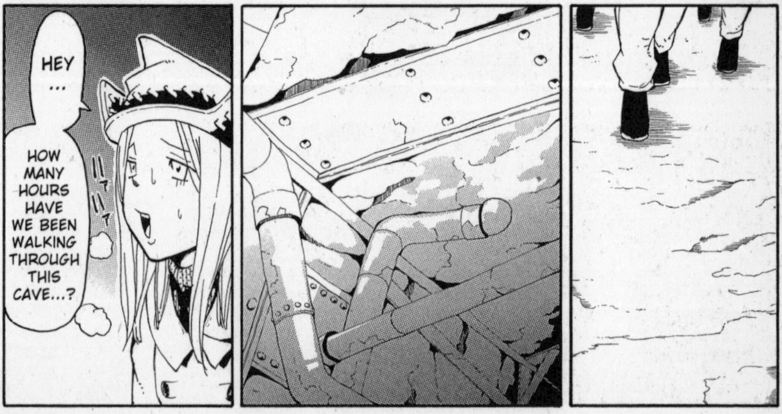
HEY...
HOW MANY HOURS HAVE WE BEEN WALKING THROUGH THIS CAVE...?

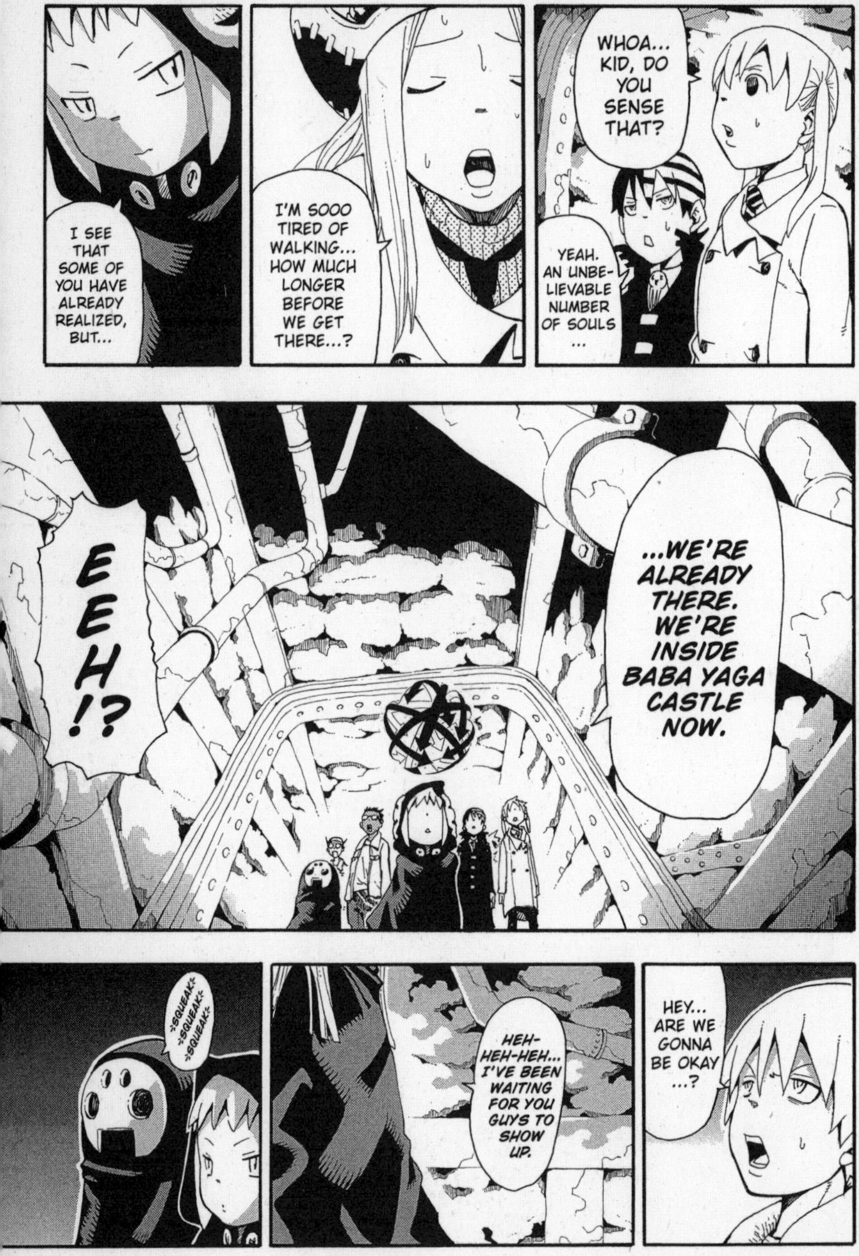
WHOA... KID, DO YOU SENSE THAT?
YEAH. AN UNBE-LIEVABLE NUMBER OF SOULS ...
I'M SOOO TIRED OF WALKING... HOW MUCH LONGER BEFORE WE GET THERE...?
I SEE THAT SOME OF YOU HAVE ALREADY REALIZED, BUT...
...WE'RE ALREADY THERE. WE'RE INSIDE BABA YAGA CASTLE NOW.
EEH!?
HEY... ARE WE GONNA BE OKAY ...?
HEH-HEH-HEH... I'VE BEEN WAITING FOR YOU GUYS TO SHOW UP.
SQUEAK SQUEAK SQUEAK

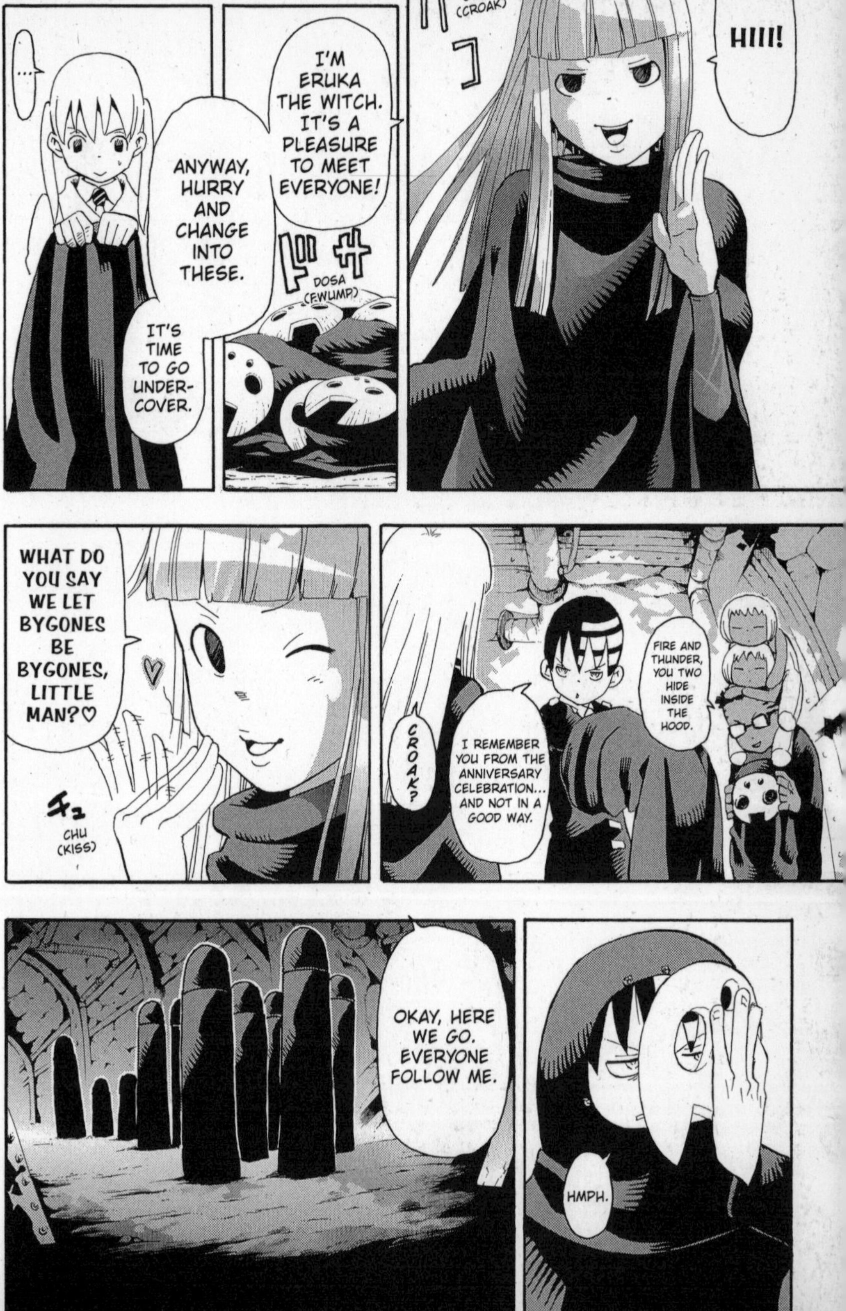
ゲコ
GEKO (CROAK)
HIII!
I'M ERUKA THE WITCH. IT'S A PLEASURE TO MEET EVERYONE!
ドサ
DOSA (FWUMP)
...
ANYWAY, HURRY AND CHANGE INTO THESE.
IT'S TIME TO GO UNDERCOVER.
FIRE AND THUNDER, YOU TWO HIDE INSIDE THE HOOD.
I REMEMBER YOU FROM THE ANNIVERSARY CELEBRATION... AND NOT IN A GOOD WAY.
CROAK?
WHAT DO YOU SAY WE LET BYGONES BE BYGONES, LITTLE MAN?♡
チュ
CHU (KISS)
HMPH.
OKAY, HERE WE GO. EVERYONE FOLLOW ME.

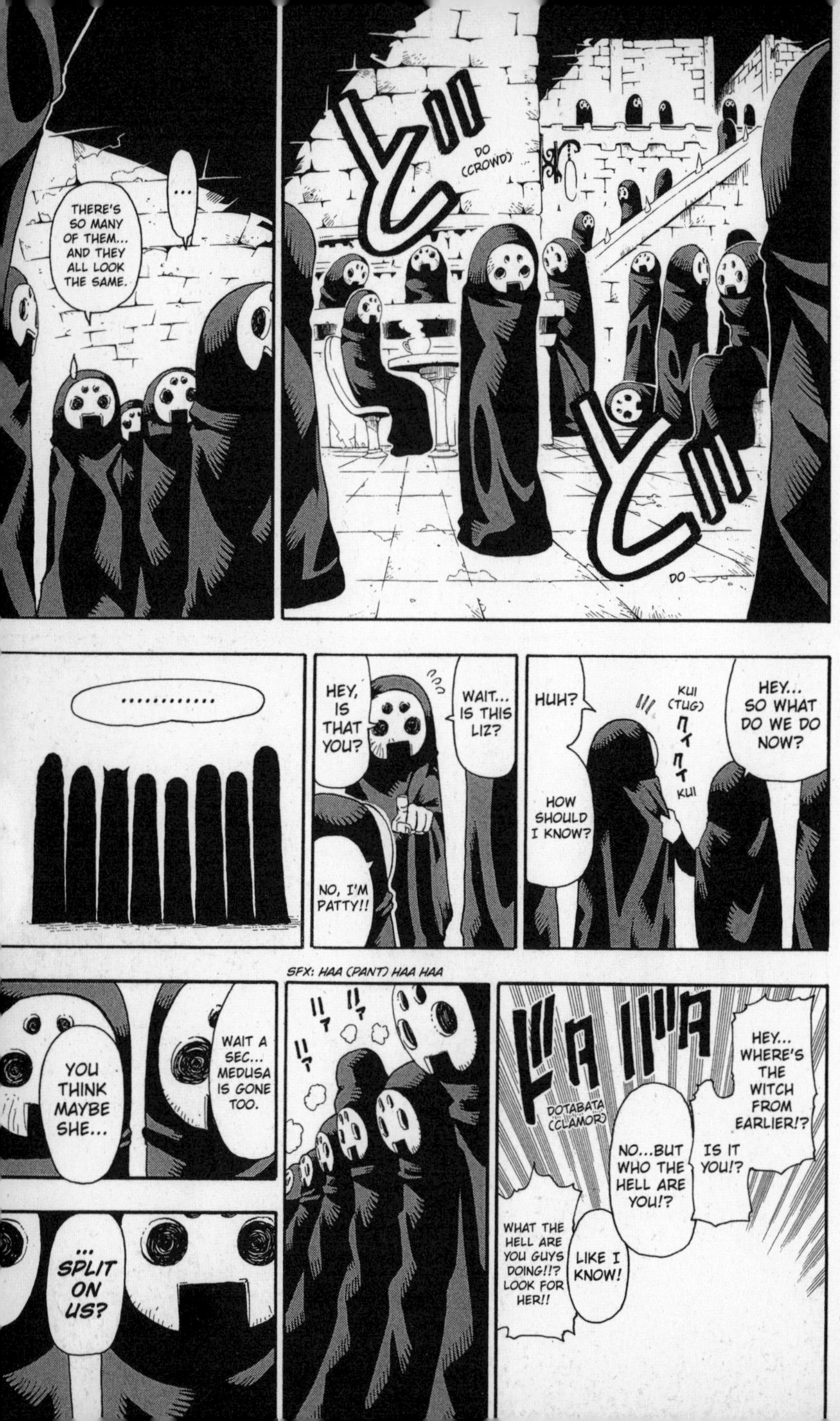
DO (CROWD)
DO
...
THERE'S SO MANY OF THEM... AND THEY ALL LOOK THE SAME.
HEY... SO WHAT DO WE DO NOW?
KUI (TUG)
KUI
HUH?
HOW SHOULD I KNOW?
WAIT... IS THIS LIZ?
HEY, IS THAT YOU?
NO, I'M PATTY!!
....
SFX: HAA (PANT) HAA HAA
HEY... WHERE'S THE WITCH FROM EARLIER!?
IS IT YOU!?
DOTABATA (CLAMOR)
NO...BUT WHO THE HELL ARE YOU!?
LIKE I KNOW!
WHAT THE HELL ARE YOU GUYS DOING!!? LOOK FOR HER!!
WAIT A SEC... MEDUSA IS GONE TOO.
YOU THINK MAYBE SHE...
...SPLIT ON US?

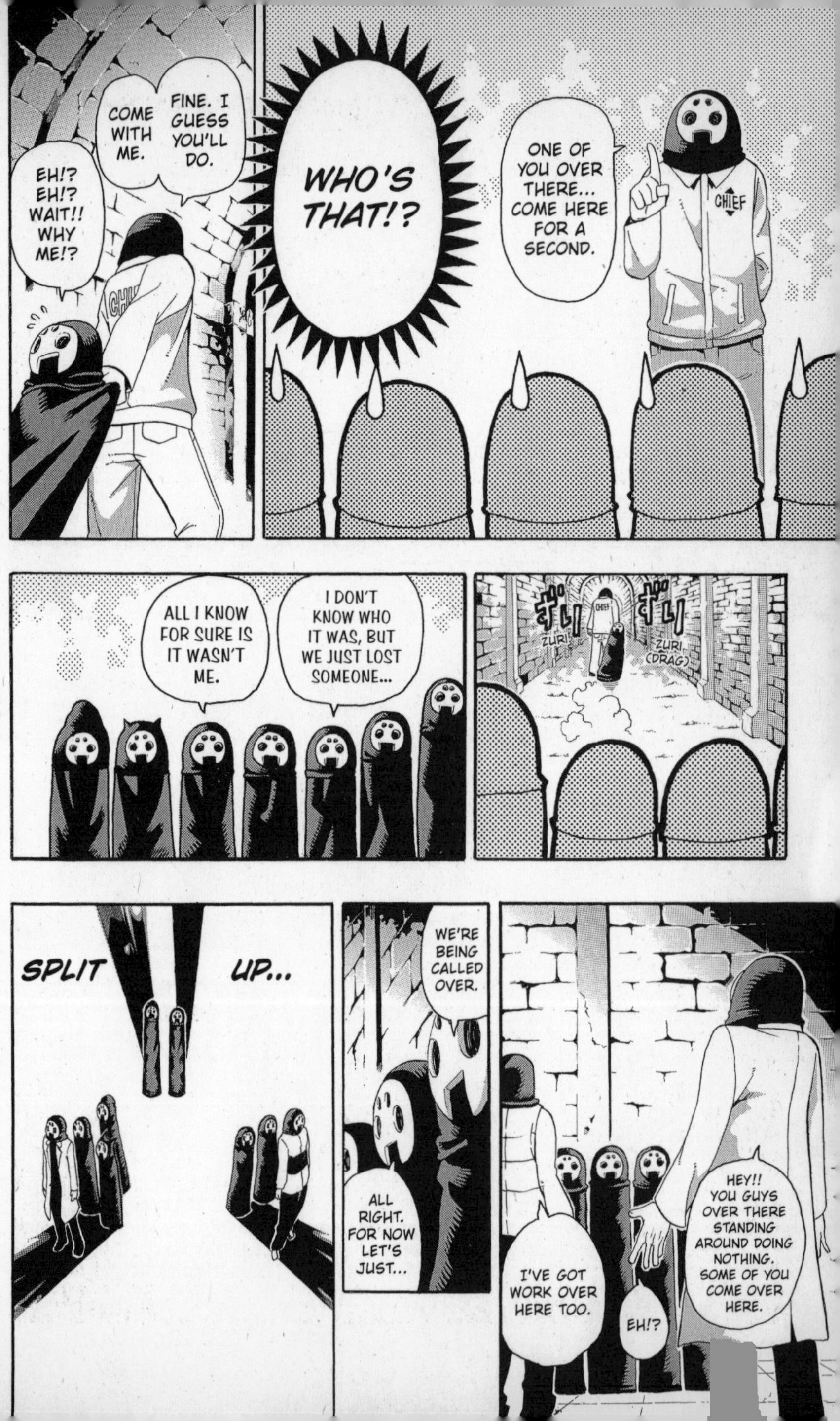
ONE OF YOU OVER THERE... COME HERE FOR A SECOND.
CHIEF
WHO'S THAT!?
FINE. I GUESS YOU'LL DO.
COME WITH ME.
EH!? EH!? WAIT!! WHY ME!?
ズリ ZURI
ズリ ZURI (DRAG)
I DON'T KNOW WHO IT WAS, BUT WE JUST LOST SOMEONE...
ALL I KNOW FOR SURE IS IT WASN'T ME.
HEY!! YOU GUYS OVER THERE STANDING AROUND DOING NOTHING. SOME OF YOU COME OVER HERE.
I'VE GOT WORK OVER HERE TOO.
EH!?
WE'RE BEING CALLED OVER.
ALL RIGHT. FOR NOW LET'S JUST...
SPLIT
UP...

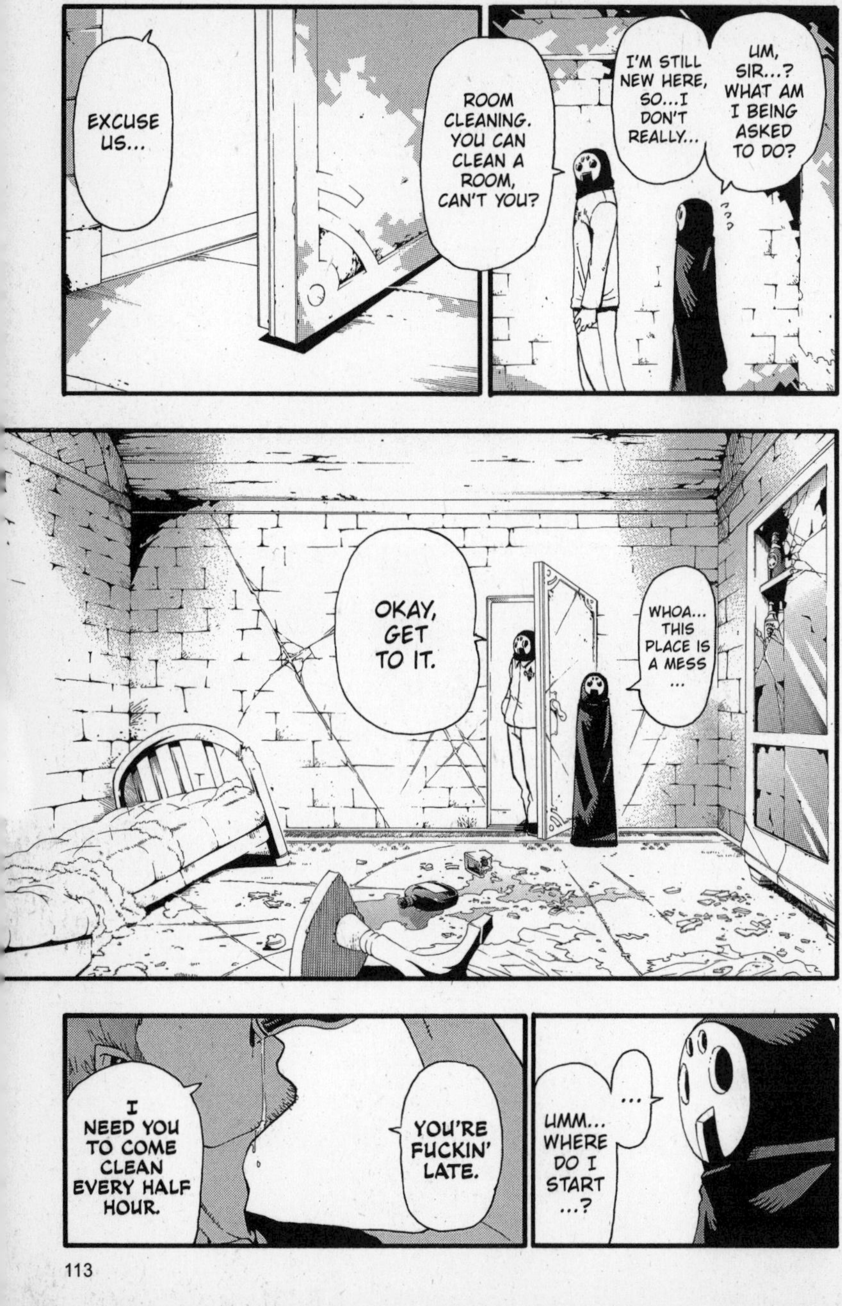
UM, SIR...? WHAT AM I BEING ASKED TO DO?
I'M STILL NEW HERE, SO...I DON'T REALLY...
ROOM CLEANING. YOU CAN CLEAN A ROOM, CAN'T YOU?
EXCUSE US...
WHOA... THIS PLACE IS A MESS ...
OKAY, GET TO IT.
...
UMM... WHERE DO I START ...?
YOU'RE FUCKIN' LATE.
I NEED YOU TO COME CLEAN EVERY HALF HOUR.

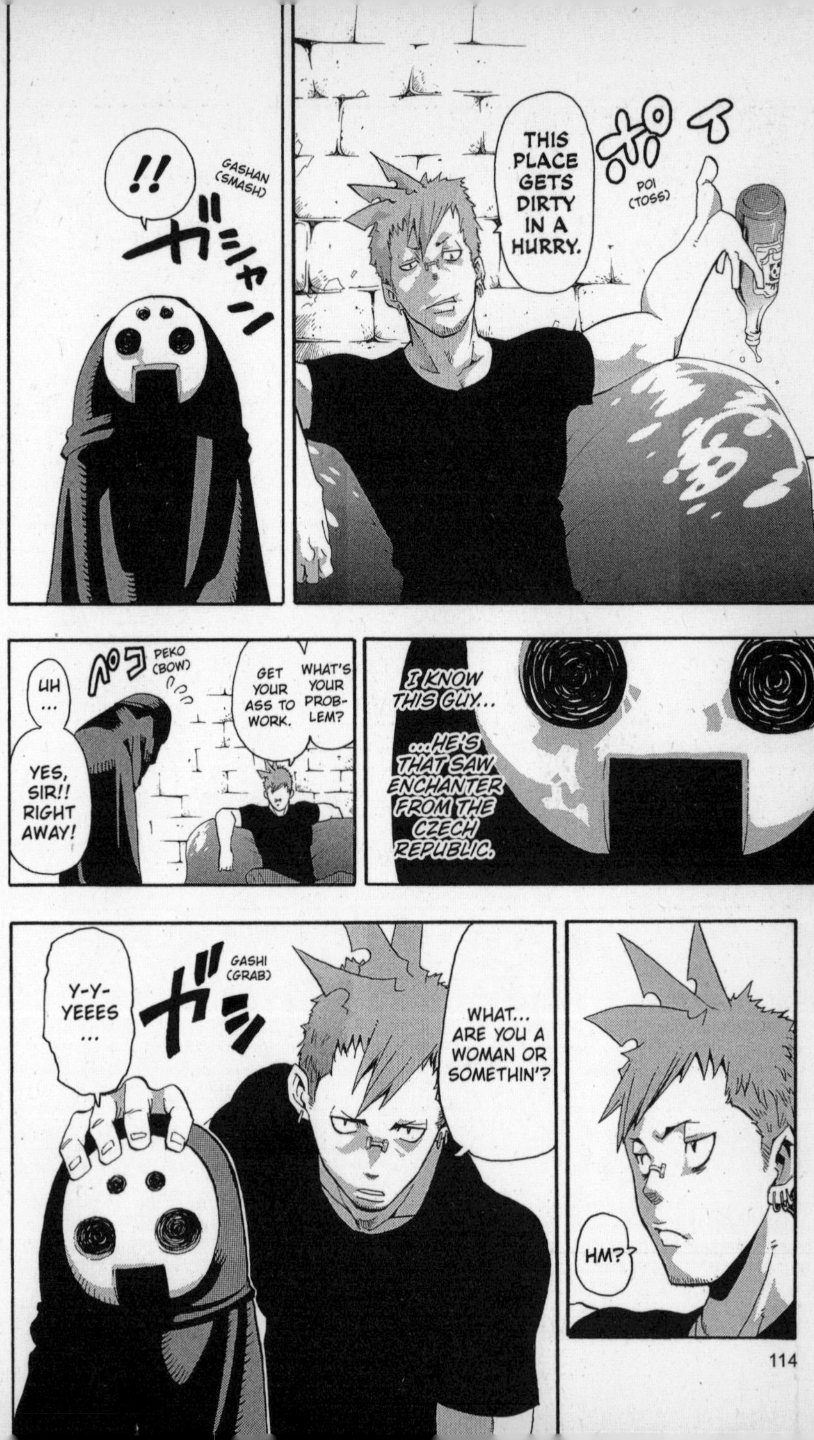
THIS PLACE GETS DIRTY IN A HURRY.
ポイ
POI (TOSS)
!!
ガシャン
GASHAN (SMASH)
I KNOW THIS GUY...
...HE'S THAT SAW ENCHANTER FROM THE CZECH REPUBLIC.
WHAT'S YOUR PROB-LEM?
GET YOUR ASS TO WORK.
ペコ
PEKO (BOW)
UH ...
YES, SIR!! RIGHT AWAY!
HM?
WHAT... ARE YOU A WOMAN OR SOMETHIN'?
ガシ
GASHI (GRAB)
Y-Y-YEEES ...

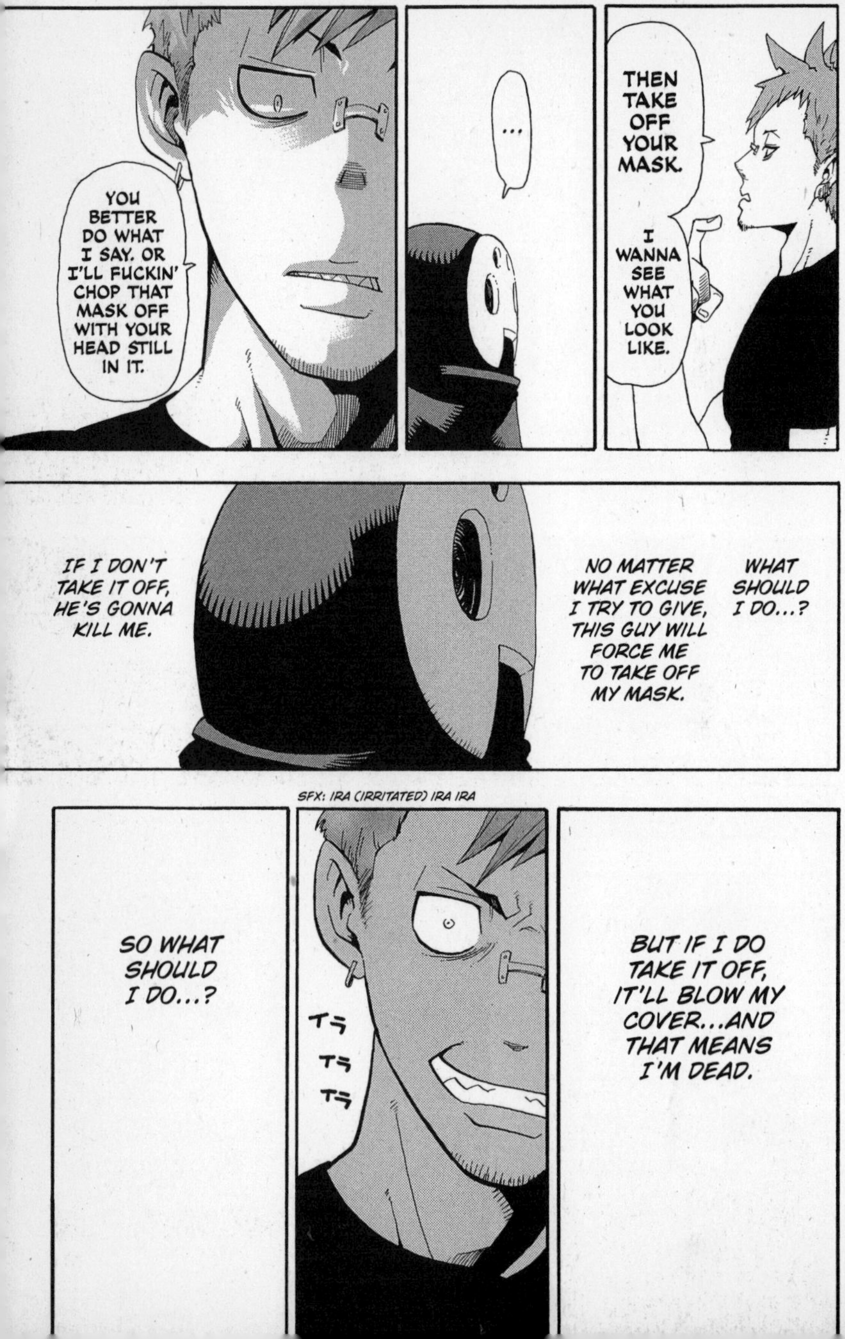
THEN TAKE OFF YOUR MASK.
I WANNA SEE WHAT YOU LOOK LIKE.
...
YOU BETTER DO WHAT I SAY. OR I'LL FUCKIN' CHOP THAT MASK OFF WITH YOUR HEAD STILL IN IT.
WHAT SHOULD I DO...?
NO MATTER WHAT EXCUSE I TRY TO GIVE, THIS GUY WILL FORCE ME TO TAKE OFF MY MASK.
IF I DON'T TAKE IT OFF, HE'S GONNA KILL ME.
SFX: IRA (IRRITATED) IRA IRA
BUT IF I DO TAKE IT OFF, IT'LL BLOW MY COVER...AND THAT MEANS I'M DEAD.
イラ
イラ
イラ
SO WHAT SHOULD I DO...?

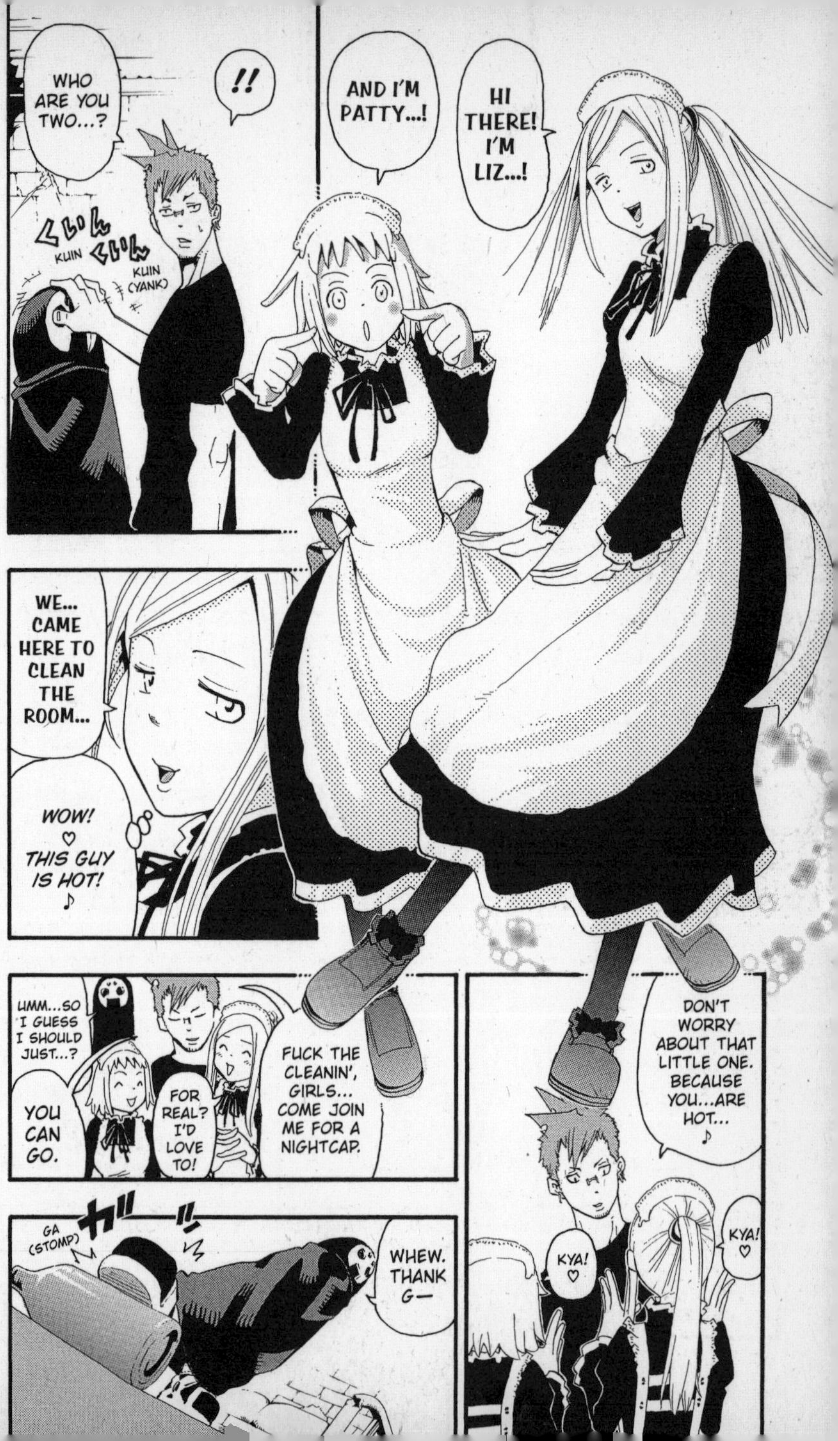
HI THERE! I'M LIZ...!
AND I'M PATTY...!
!!
WHO ARE YOU TWO...?
KUIN
KUIN (YANK)
WE... CAME HERE TO CLEAN THE ROOM...
WOW! ♡ THIS GUY IS HOT! ♪
DON'T WORRY ABOUT THAT LITTLE ONE. BECAUSE YOU...ARE HOT... ♪
KYA! ♡
KYA! ♡
FUCK THE CLEANIN', GIRLS... COME JOIN ME FOR A NIGHTCAP.
UMM...SO I GUESS I SHOULD JUST...?
FOR REAL? I'D LOVE TO!
YOU CAN GO.
WHEW. THANK G—
GA (STOMP)

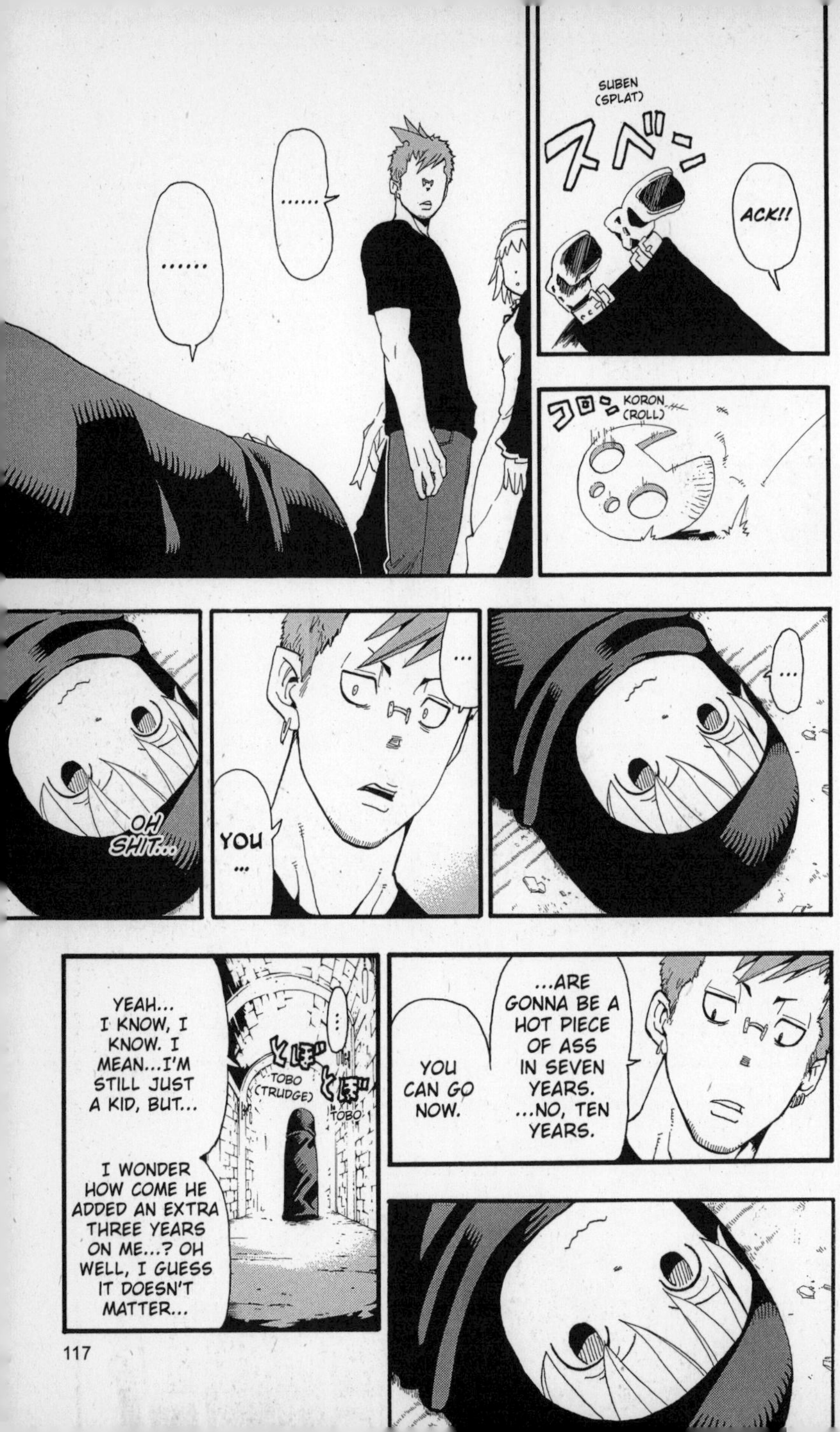
SUBEN (SPLAT)
ACK!!
KORON (ROLL)
......
......
...
...
YOU ...
OH SHIT...
...ARE GONNA BE A HOT PIECE OF ASS IN SEVEN YEARS. ...NO, TEN YEARS.
YOU CAN GO NOW.
...
TOBO (TRUDGE) TOBO
YEAH... I KNOW, I KNOW. I MEAN...I'M STILL JUST A KID, BUT...
I WONDER HOW COME HE ADDED AN EXTRA THREE YEARS ON ME...? OH WELL, I GUESS IT DOESN'T MATTER...

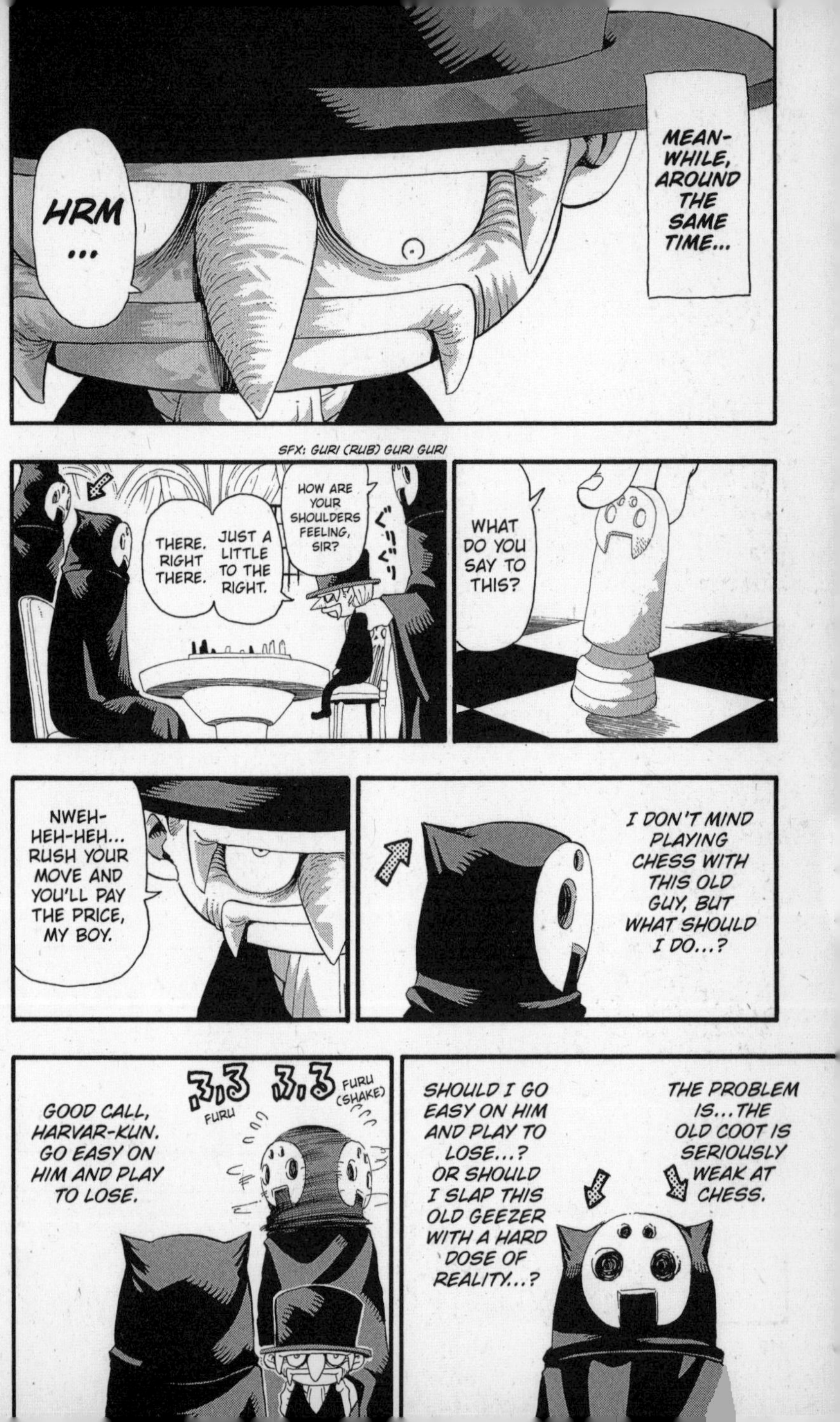
MEAN-WHILE, AROUND THE SAME TIME...
HRM ...
SFX: GURI (RUB) GURI GURI
WHAT DO YOU SAY TO THIS?
HOW ARE YOUR SHOULDERS FEELING, SIR?
JUST A LITTLE TO THE RIGHT.
THERE. RIGHT THERE.
I DON'T MIND PLAYING CHESS WITH THIS OLD GUY, BUT WHAT SHOULD I DO...?
NWEH-HEH-HEH... RUSH YOUR MOVE AND YOU'LL PAY THE PRICE, MY BOY.
THE PROBLEM IS...THE OLD COOT IS SERIOUSLY WEAK AT CHESS.
SHOULD I GO EASY ON HIM AND PLAY TO LOSE...? OR SHOULD I SLAP THIS OLD GEEZER WITH A HARD DOSE OF REALITY...?
FURU (SHAKE)
FURU
GOOD CALL, HARVAR-KUN. GO EASY ON HIM AND PLAY TO LOSE.

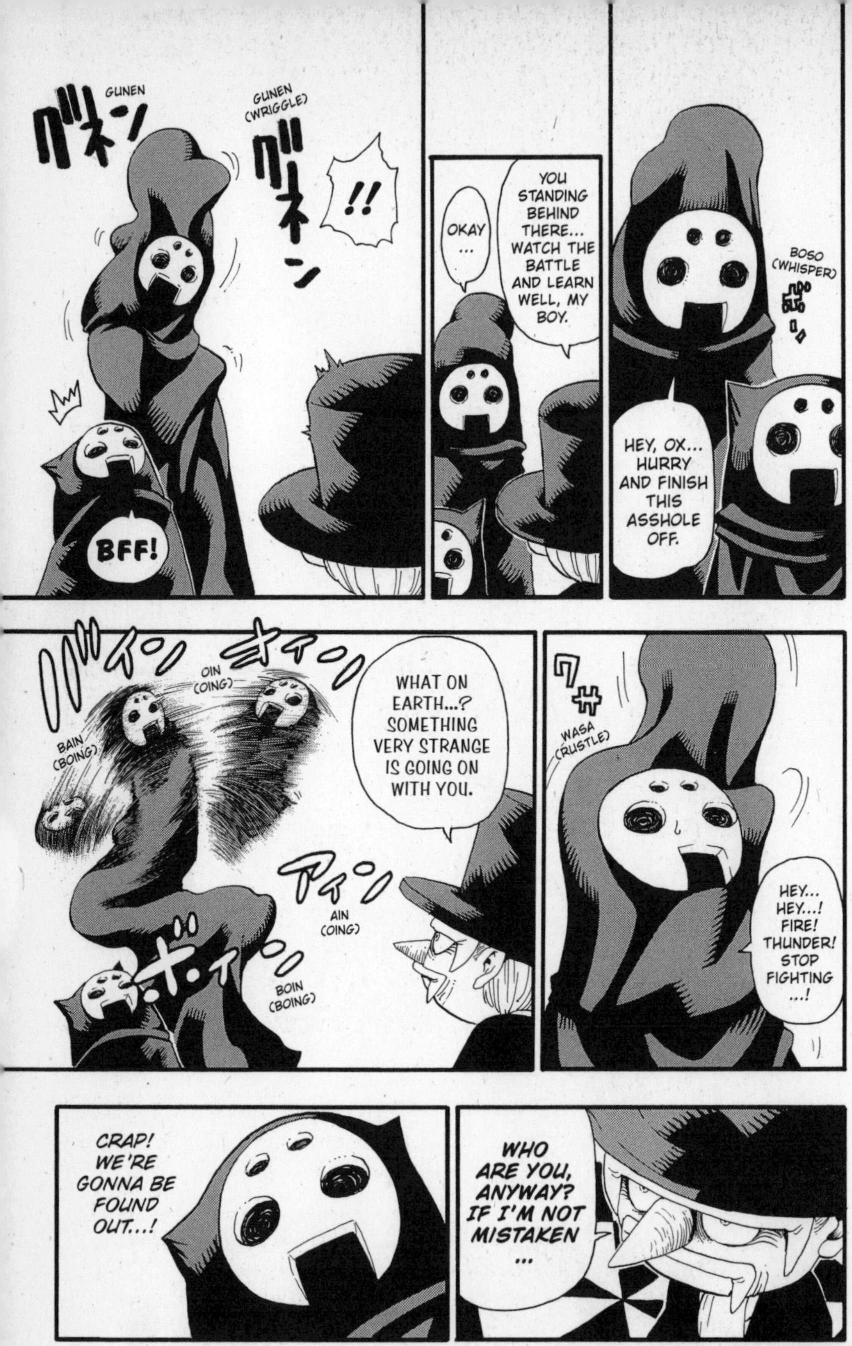
BOSO (WHISPER)
HEY, OX... HURRY AND FINISH THIS ASSHOLE OFF.
YOU STANDING BEHIND THERE... WATCH THE BATTLE AND LEARN WELL, MY BOY.
OKAY ...
GUNEN (WRIGGLE)
!!
GUNEN
BFF!
WASA (RUSTLE)
HEY... HEY...! FIRE! THUNDER! STOP FIGHTING ...!
WHAT ON EARTH...? SOMETHING VERY STRANGE IS GOING ON WITH YOU.
OIN (OING)
BAIN (BOING)
AIN (OING)
BOIN (BOING)
WHO ARE YOU, ANYWAY? IF I'M NOT MISTAKEN ...
CRAP! WE'RE GONNA BE FOUND OUT...!

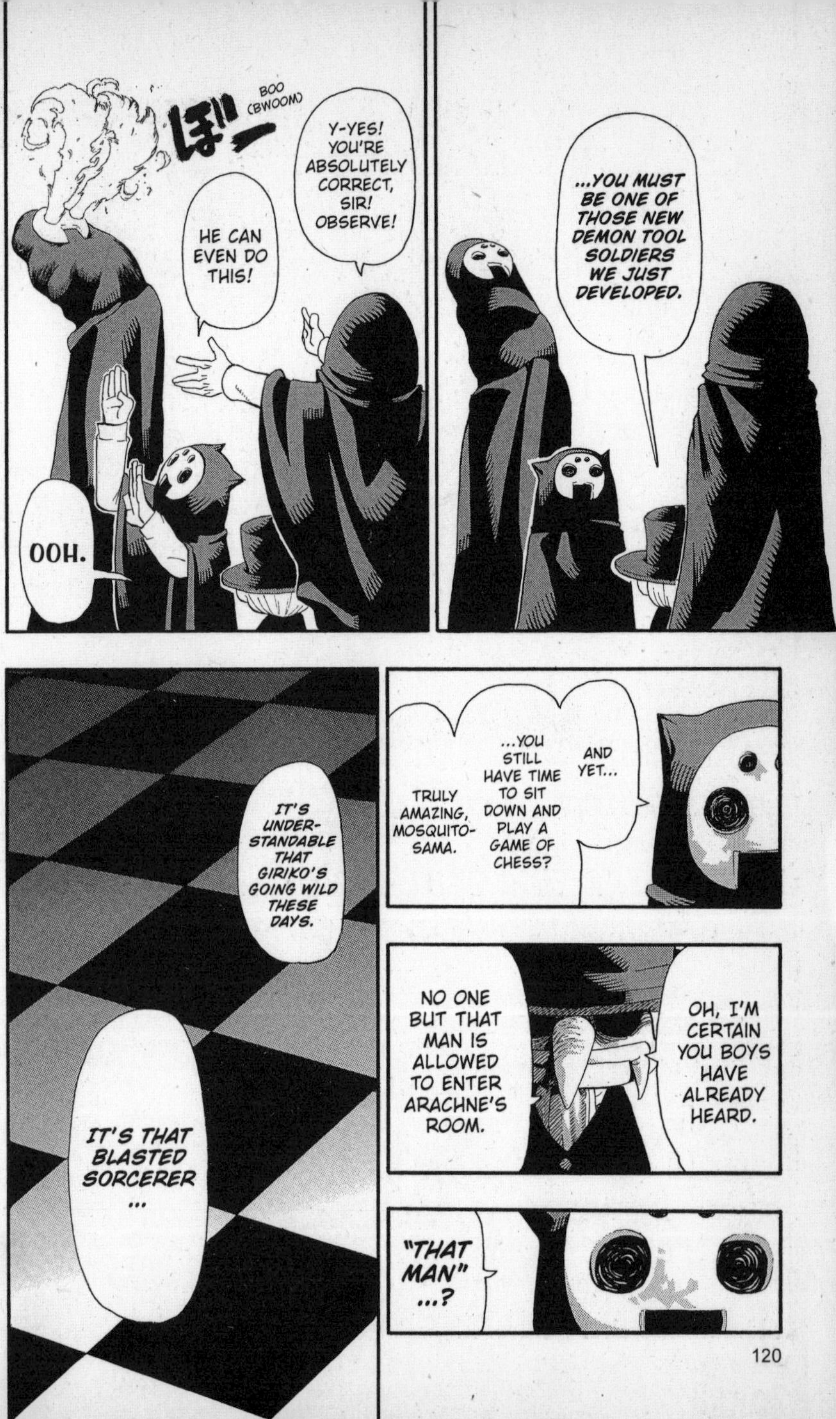
...YOU MUST BE ONE OF THOSE NEW DEMON TOOL SOLDIERS WE JUST DEVELOPED.
Y-YES! YOU'RE ABSOLUTELY CORRECT, SIR! OBSERVE!
HE CAN EVEN DO THIS!
ぼー BOO (BWOOM)
OOH.
TRULY AMAZING, MOSQUITO-SAMA. ...YOU STILL HAVE TIME TO SIT DOWN AND PLAY A GAME OF CHESS? AND YET...
OH, I'M CERTAIN YOU BOYS HAVE ALREADY HEARD.
NO ONE BUT THAT MAN IS ALLOWED TO ENTER ARACHNE'S ROOM.
"THAT MAN"...?
IT'S UNDER-STANDABLE THAT GIRIKO'S GOING WILD THESE DAYS.
IT'S THAT BLASTED SORCERER...

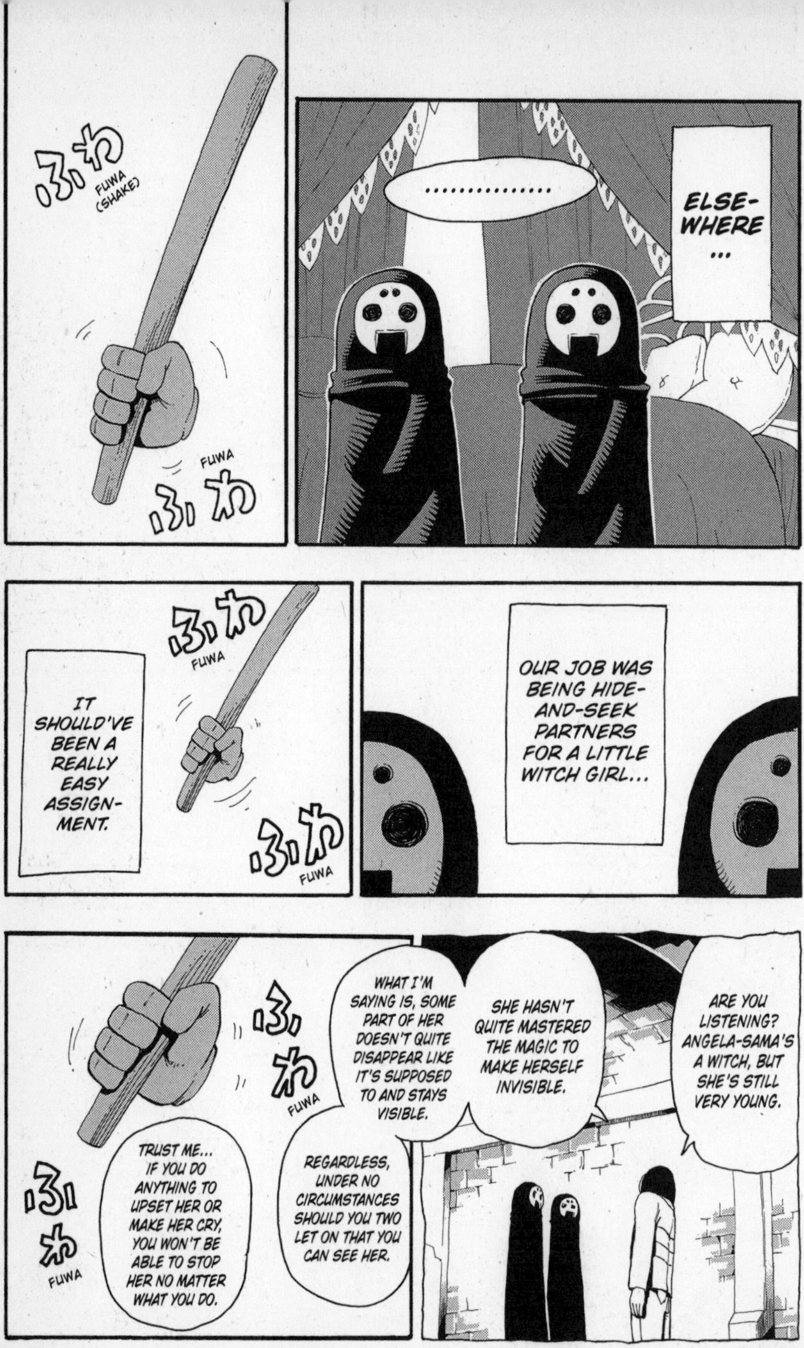
ELSE-WHERE...
....
ふわ FUWA (SHAKE)
ふわ FUWA
OUR JOB WAS BEING HIDE-AND-SEEK PARTNERS FOR A LITTLE WITCH GIRL...
IT SHOULD'VE BEEN A REALLY EASY ASSIGN-MENT.
ふわ FUWA
ふわ FUWA
ARE YOU LISTENING? ANGELA-SAMA'S A WITCH, BUT SHE'S STILL VERY YOUNG.
SHE HASN'T QUITE MASTERED THE MAGIC TO MAKE HERSELF INVISIBLE.
WHAT I'M SAYING IS, SOME PART OF HER DOESN'T QUITE DISAPPEAR LIKE IT'S SUPPOSED TO AND STAYS VISIBLE.
REGARDLESS, UNDER NO CIRCUMSTANCES SHOULD YOU TWO LET ON THAT YOU CAN SEE HER.
TRUST ME... IF YOU DO ANYTHING TO UPSET HER OR MAKE HER CRY, YOU WON'T BE ABLE TO STOP HER NO MATTER WHAT YOU DO.
ふわ FUWA
ふわ FUWA

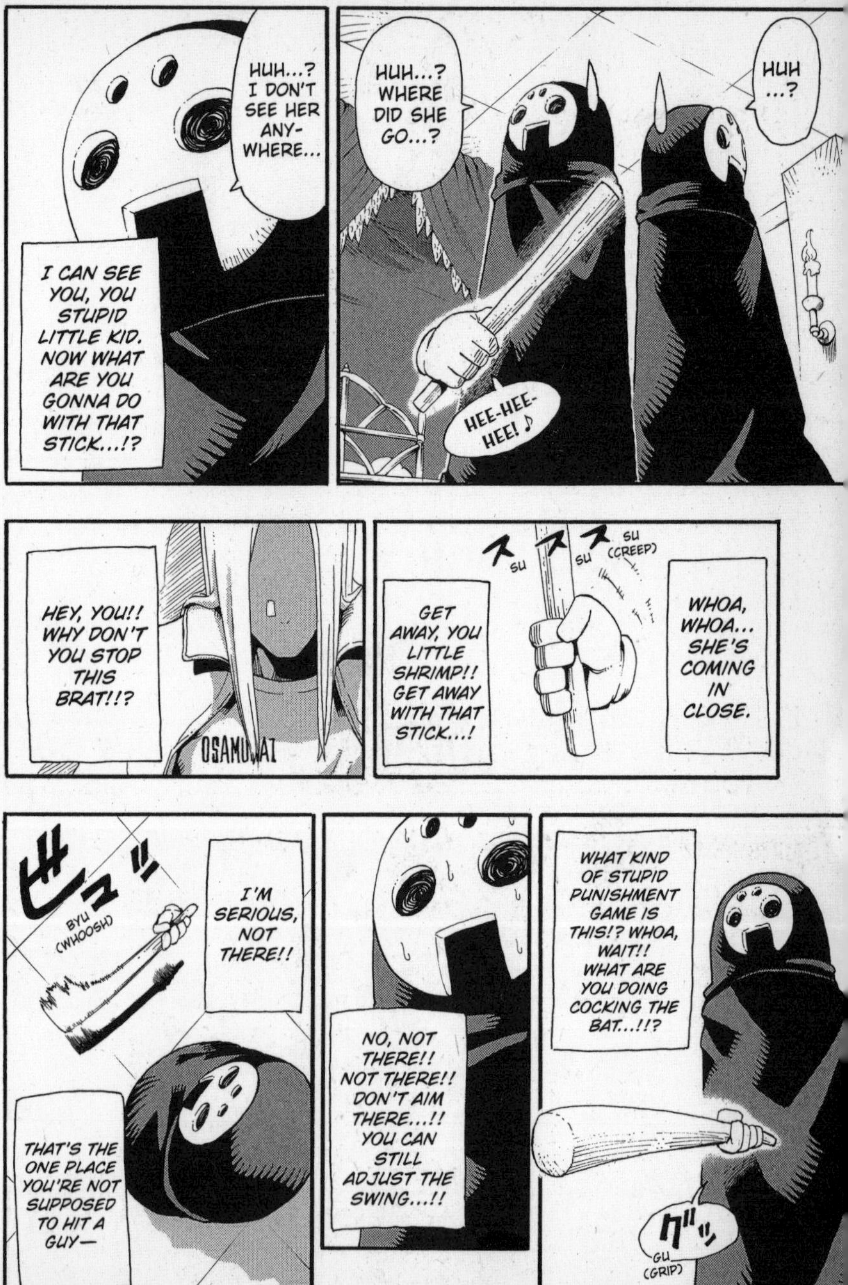
HUH ...?
HUH...? WHERE DID SHE GO...?
HEE-HEE-HEE! ♪
HUH...? I DON'T SEE HER ANYWHERE...
I CAN SEE YOU, YOU STUPID LITTLE KID. NOW WHAT ARE YOU GONNA DO WITH THAT STICK...!?
SU SU SU (CREEP)
WHOA, WHOA... SHE'S COMING IN CLOSE.
GET AWAY, YOU LITTLE SHRIMP!! GET AWAY WITH THAT STICK...!
HEY, YOU!! WHY DON'T YOU STOP THIS BRAT!!?
WHAT KIND OF STUPID PUNISHMENT GAME IS THIS!? WHOA, WAIT!! WHAT ARE YOU DOING COCKING THE BAT...!!?
GU (GRIP)
NO, NOT THERE!! NOT THERE!! DON'T AIM THERE...!! YOU CAN STILL ADJUST THE SWING...!!
BYU (WHOOSH)
I'M SERIOUS, NOT THERE!!
THAT'S THE ONE PLACE YOU'RE NOT SUPPOSED TO HIT A GUY—

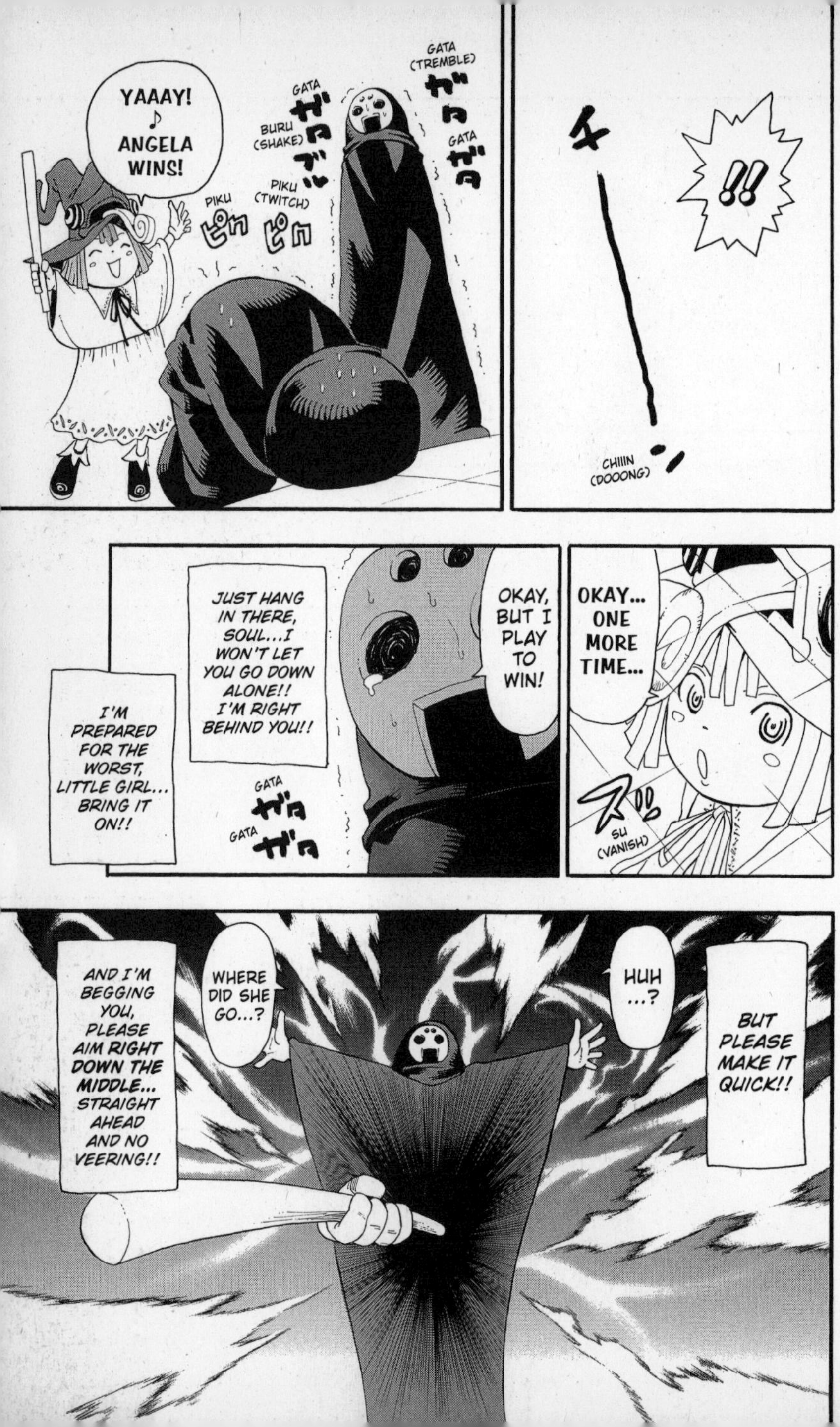
!!
CHIIIN (DOOONG)
GATA (TREMBLE)
GATA
GATA
BURU (SHAKE)
PIKU (TWITCH)
PIKU
YAAAY! ♪ ANGELA WINS!
OKAY... ONE MORE TIME...
SU (VANISH)
OKAY, BUT I PLAY TO WIN!
JUST HANG IN THERE, SOUL...I WON'T LET YOU GO DOWN ALONE!! I'M RIGHT BEHIND YOU!!
GATA
GATA
I'M PREPARED FOR THE WORST, LITTLE GIRL... BRING IT ON!!
BUT PLEASE MAKE IT QUICK!!
HUH ...?
WHERE DID SHE GO...?
AND I'M BEGGING YOU, PLEASE AIM RIGHT DOWN THE MIDDLE... STRAIGHT AHEAD AND NO VEERING!!

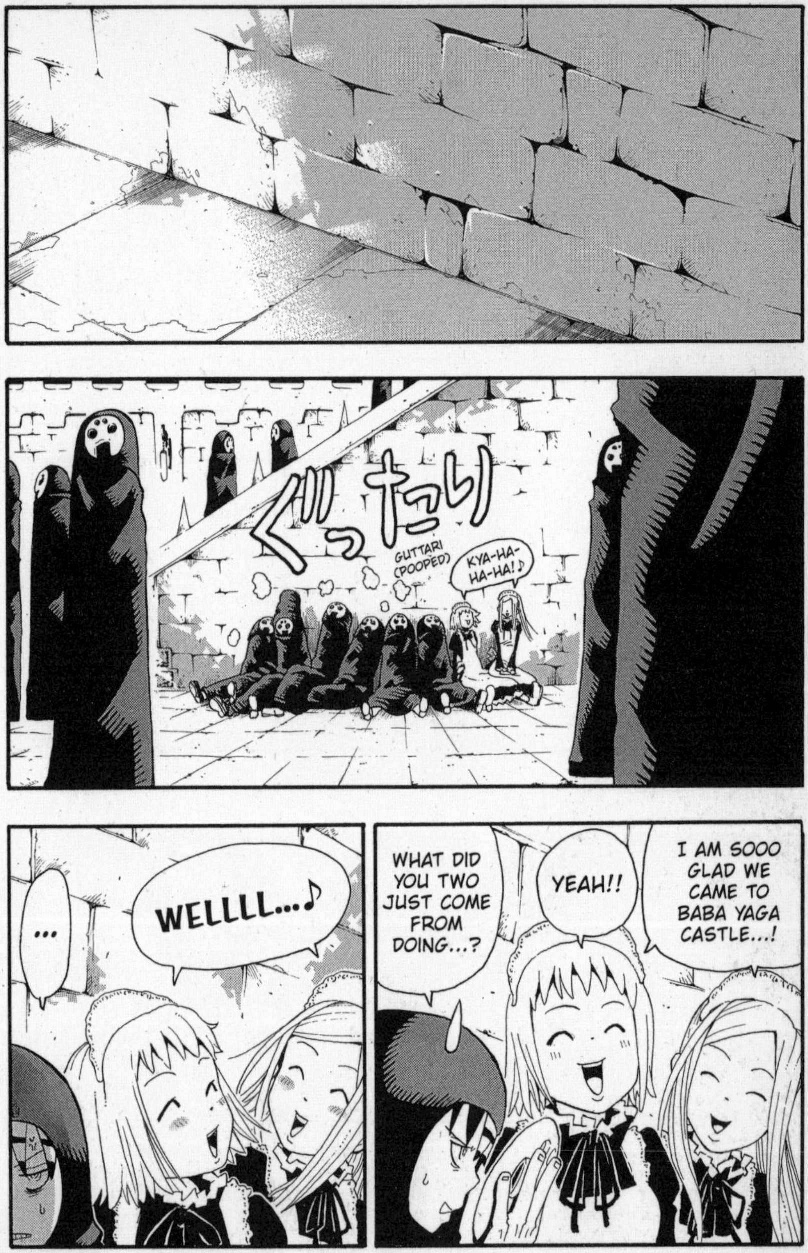
ぐったり
KYA-HA-HA-HA!♪
GUTTARI (POOPED)
I AM SOOO GLAD WE CAME TO BABA YAGA CASTLE...!
YEAH!!
WHAT DID YOU TWO JUST COME FROM DOING...?
WELLLL...♪
...

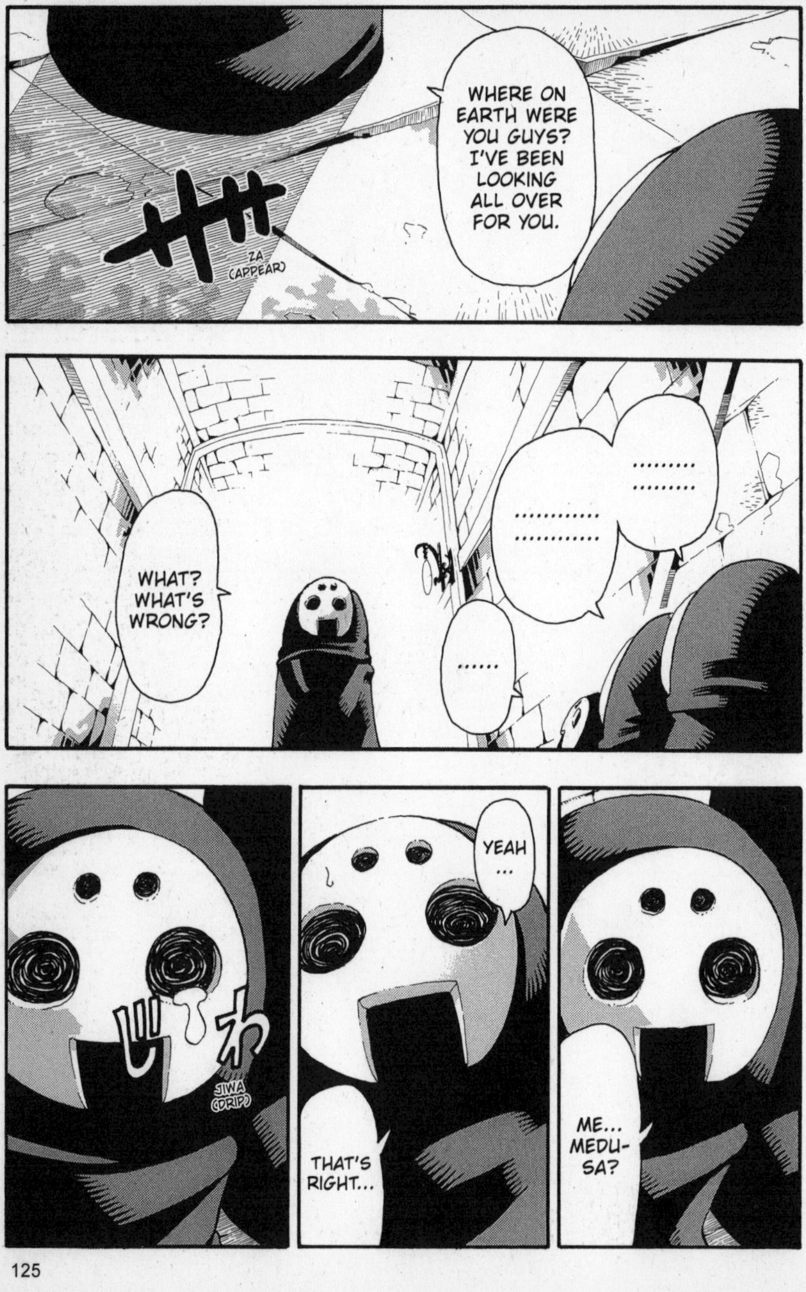
WHERE ON EARTH WERE YOU GUYS? I'VE BEEN LOOKING ALL OVER FOR YOU.
ZA (APPEAR)
....
....
......
WHAT? WHAT'S WRONG?
ME... MEDU-SA?
YEAH ...
THAT'S RIGHT...
じわ
JIWA (DRIP)

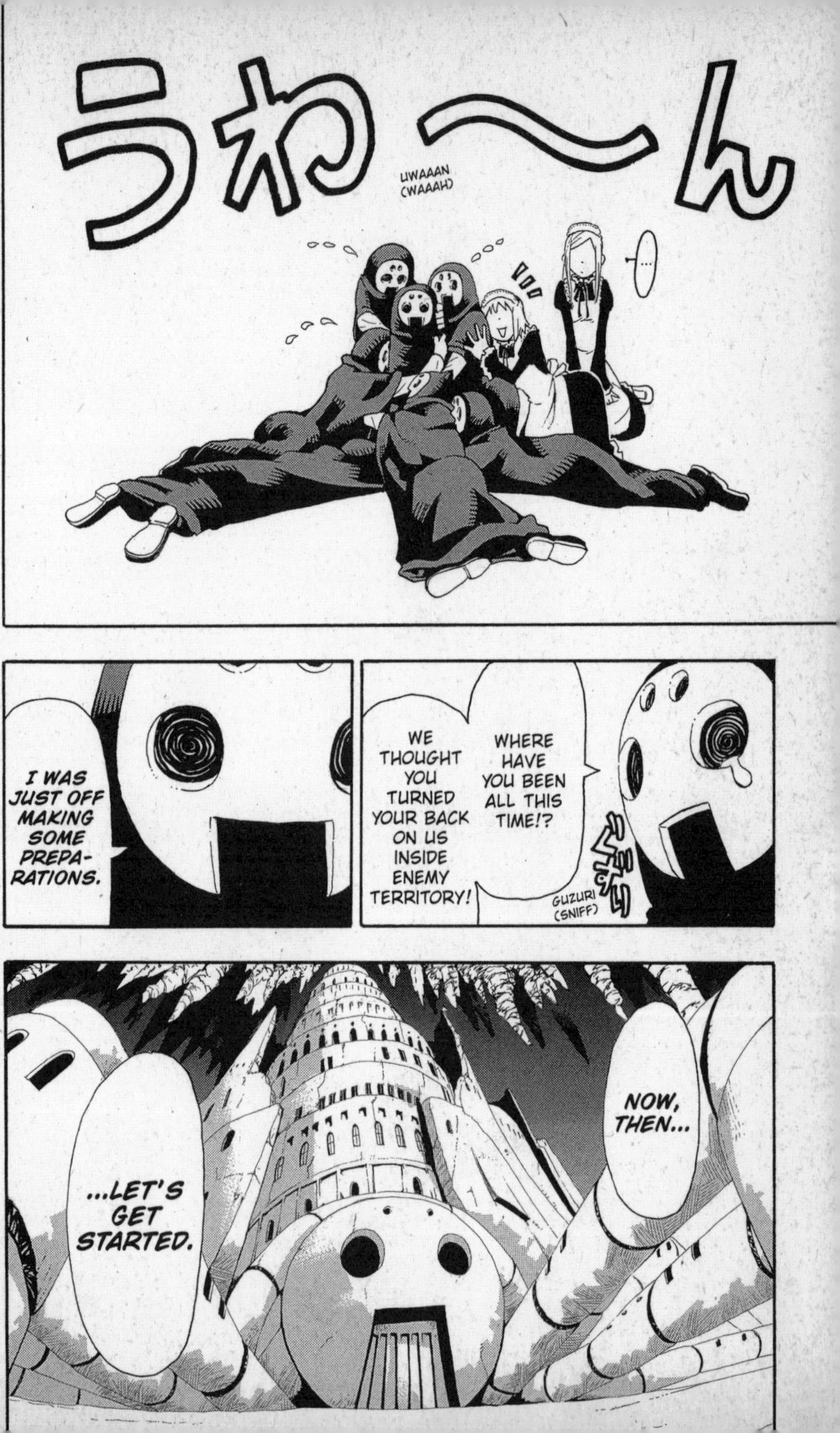
うわ〜ん
UWAAAN (WAAAH)
...
WHERE HAVE YOU BEEN ALL THIS TIME!?
WE THOUGHT YOU TURNED YOUR BACK ON US INSIDE ENEMY TERRITORY!
GUZURI (SNIFF)
I WAS JUST OFF MAKING SOME PREPA-RATIONS.
NOW, THEN...
...LET'S GET STARTED.

SOUL EATER

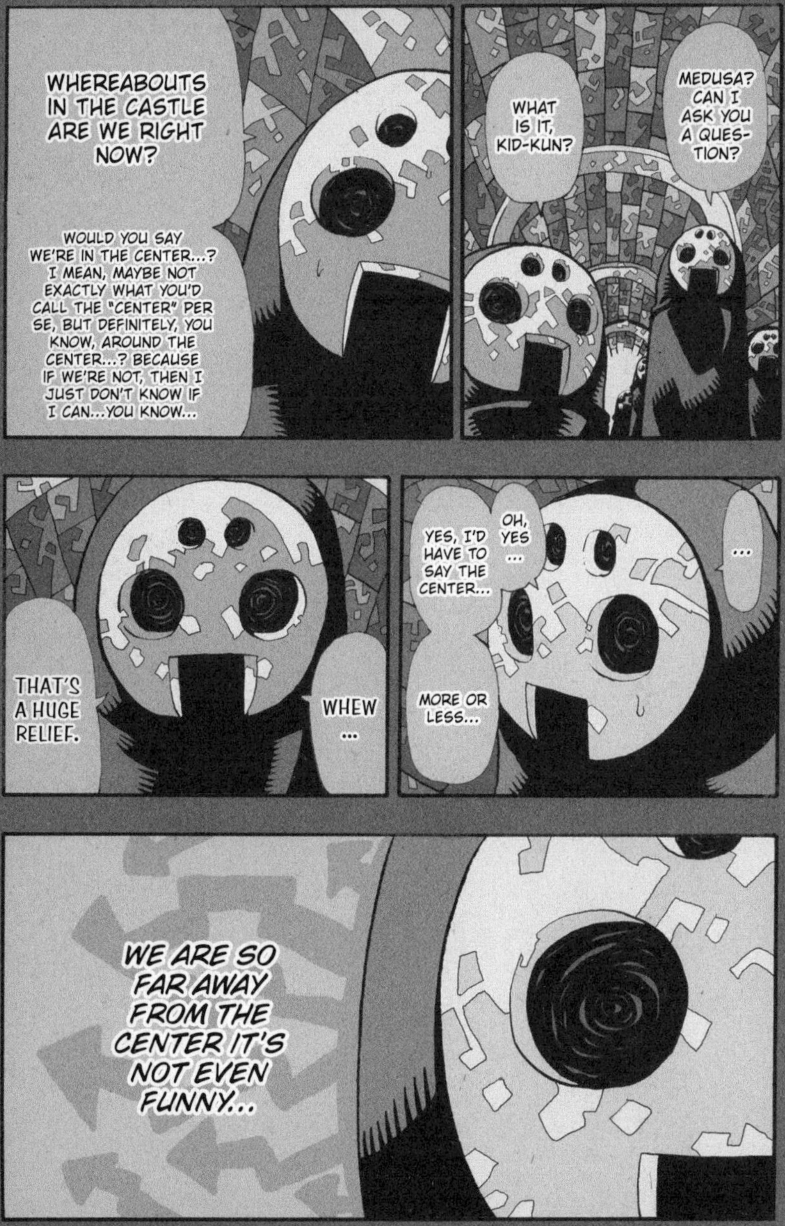
MEDUSA? CAN I ASK YOU A QUES-TION?
WHAT IS IT, KID-KUN?
WHEREABOUTS IN THE CASTLE ARE WE RIGHT NOW?
WOULD YOU SAY WE'RE IN THE CENTER...? I MEAN, MAYBE NOT EXACTLY WHAT YOU'D CALL THE "CENTER" PER SE, BUT DEFINITELY, YOU KNOW, AROUND THE CENTER...? BECAUSE IF WE'RE NOT, THEN I JUST DON'T KNOW IF I CAN...YOU KNOW...
...
OH, YES ...
YES, I'D HAVE TO SAY THE CENTER...
MORE OR LESS...
WHEW ...
THAT'S A HUGE RELIEF.
WE ARE SO FAR AWAY FROM THE CENTER IT'S NOT EVEN FUNNY...

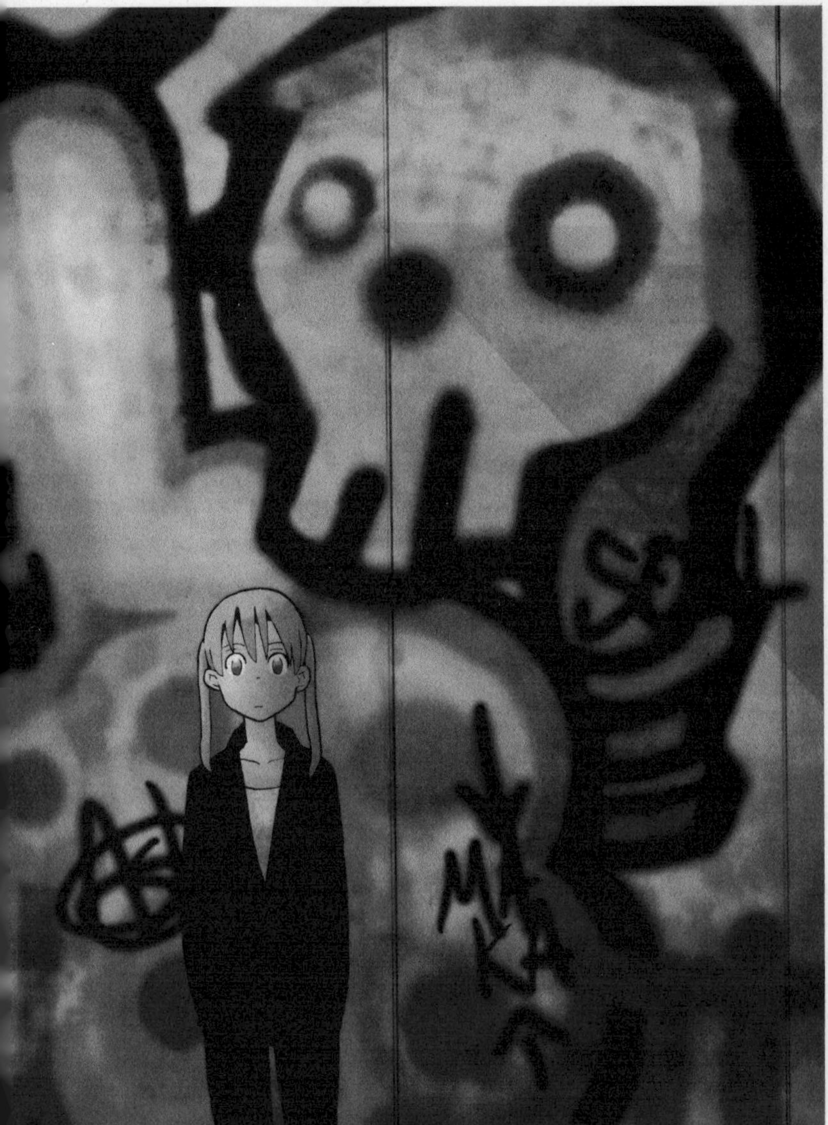

CHAPTER 48: OPERATION CAPTURE BABA YAGA CASTLE (PART 3)

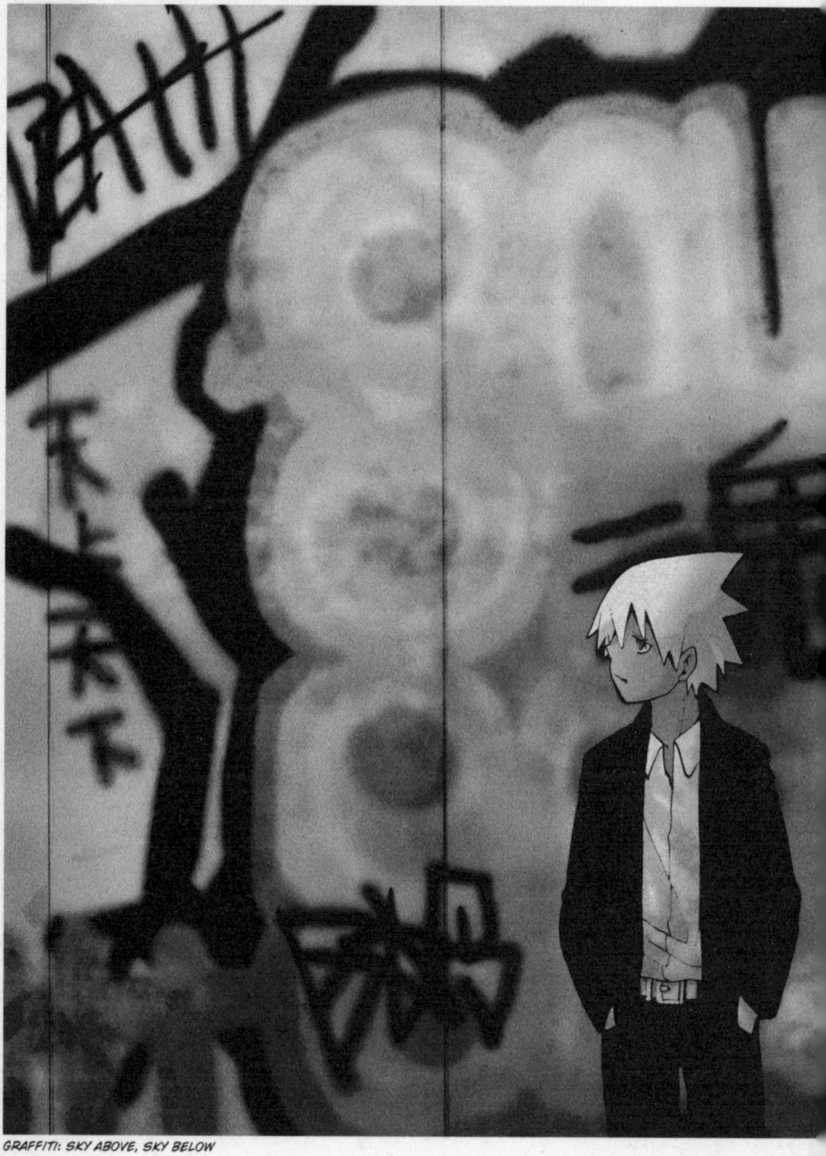

GRAFFITI: SKY ABOVE, SKY BELOW

SOUL EATER

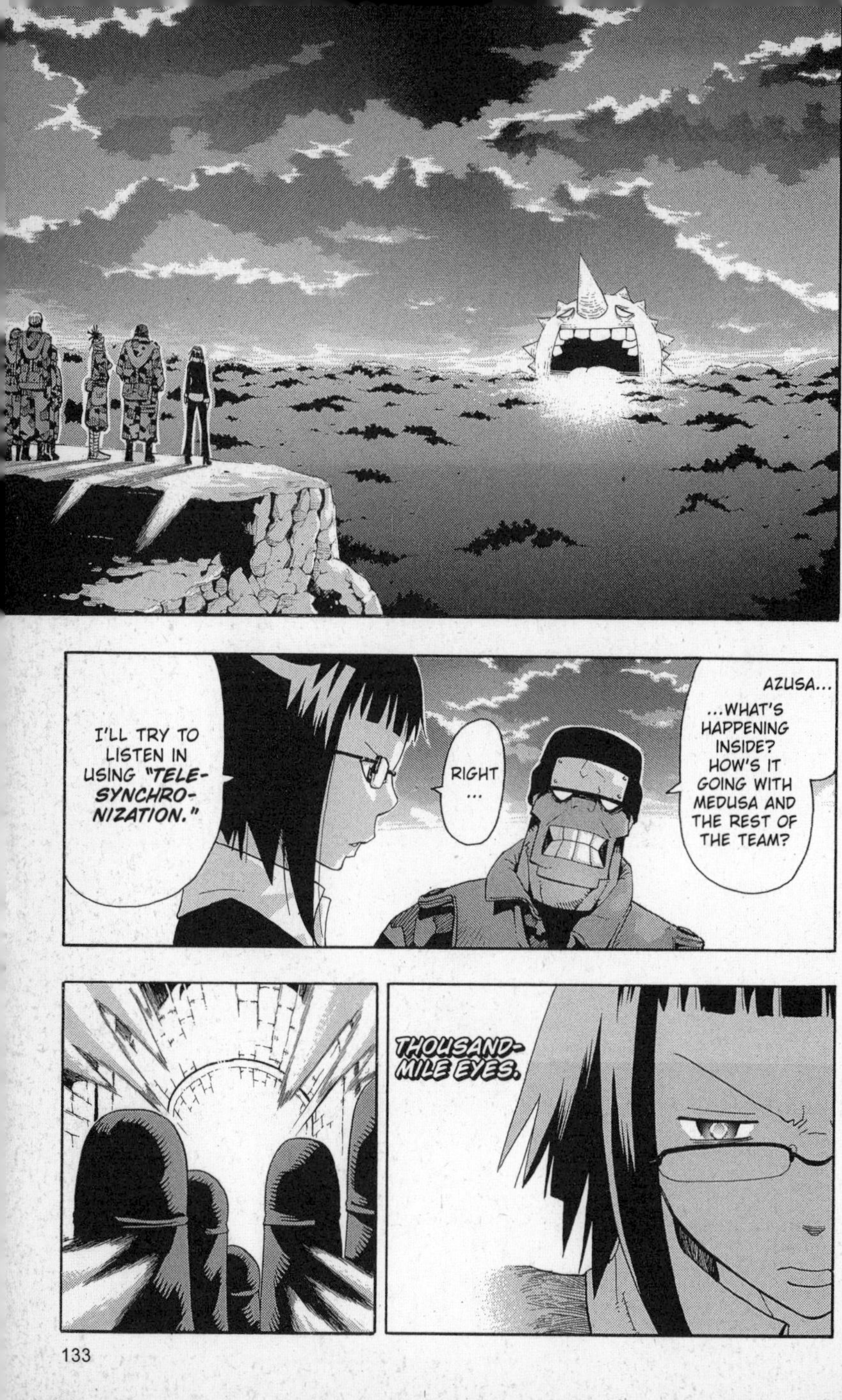
AZUSA... ...WHAT'S HAPPENING INSIDE? HOW'S IT GOING WITH MEDUSA AND THE REST OF THE TEAM?
RIGHT ...
I'LL TRY TO LISTEN IN USING "TELE-SYNCHRO-NIZATION."
THOUSAND-MILE EYES.

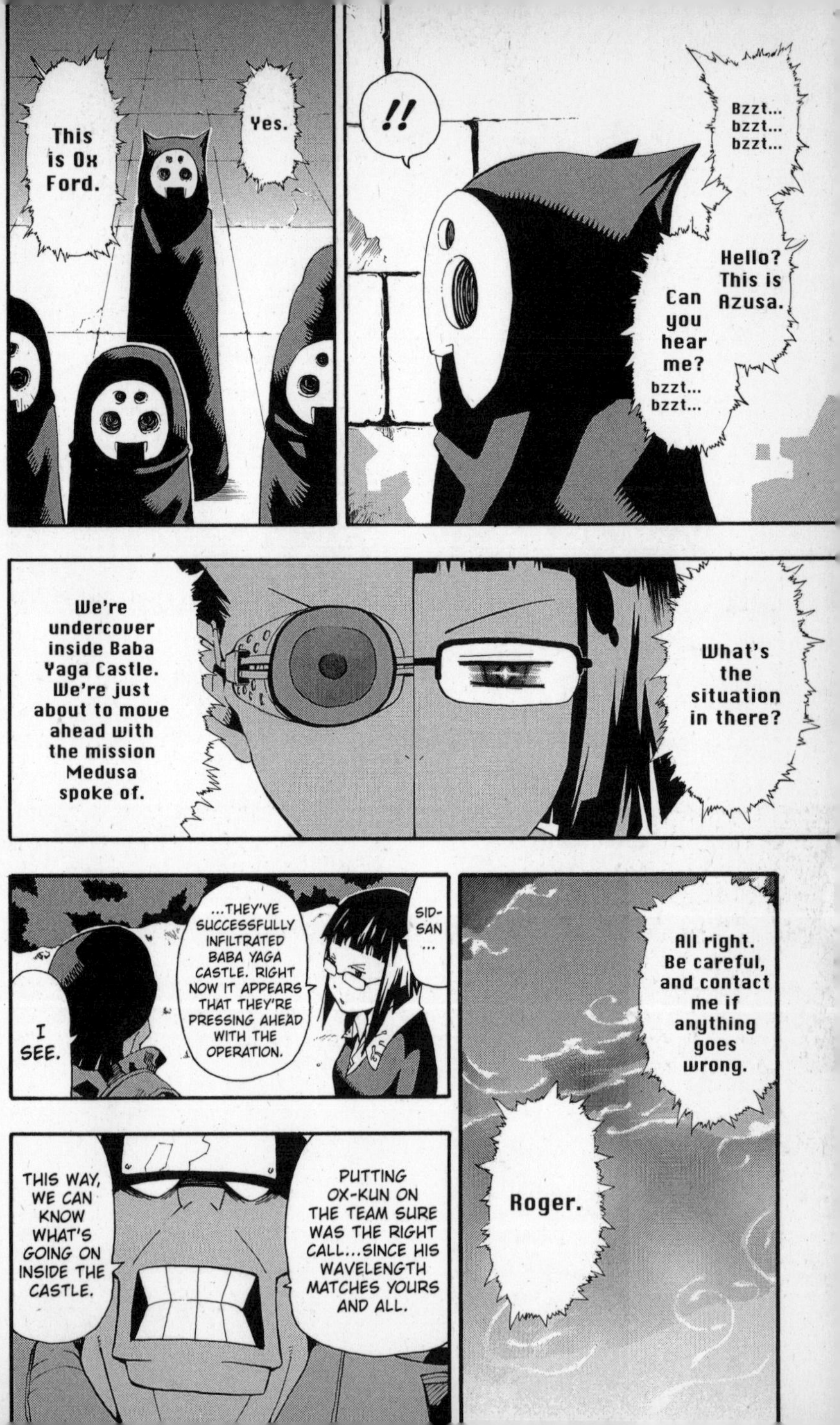
!!
Bzzt... bzzt... bzzt...
Hello? This is Azusa.
Can you hear me? bzzt... bzzt...
Yes.
This is Ox Ford.
What's the situation in there?
We're undercover inside Baba Yaga Castle. We're just about to move ahead with the mission Medusa spoke of.
All right. Be careful, and contact me if anything goes wrong.
Roger.
SID-SAN...
...THEY'VE SUCCESSFULLY INFILTRATED BABA YAGA CASTLE. RIGHT NOW IT APPEARS THAT THEY'RE PRESSING AHEAD WITH THE OPERATION.
I SEE.
PUTTING OX-KUN ON THE TEAM SURE WAS THE RIGHT CALL...SINCE HIS WAVELENGTH MATCHES YOURS AND ALL.
THIS WAY, WE CAN KNOW WHAT'S GOING ON INSIDE THE CASTLE.

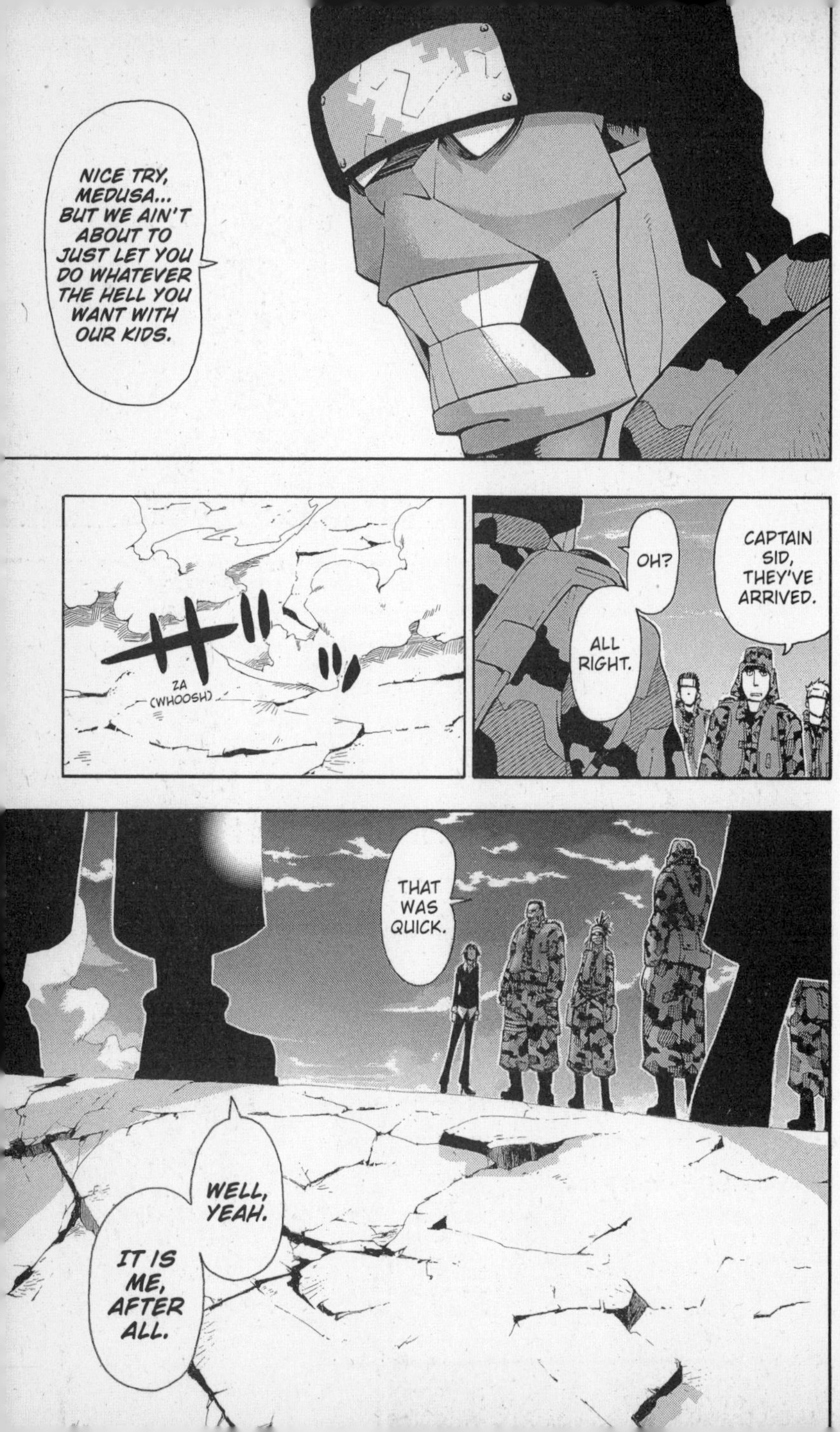
NICE TRY, MEDUSA... BUT WE AIN'T ABOUT TO JUST LET YOU DO WHATEVER THE HELL YOU WANT WITH OUR KIDS.
CAPTAIN SID, THEY'VE ARRIVED.
OH?
ALL RIGHT.
ZA (WHOOSH)
THAT WAS QUICK.
WELL, YEAH.
IT IS ME, AFTER ALL.

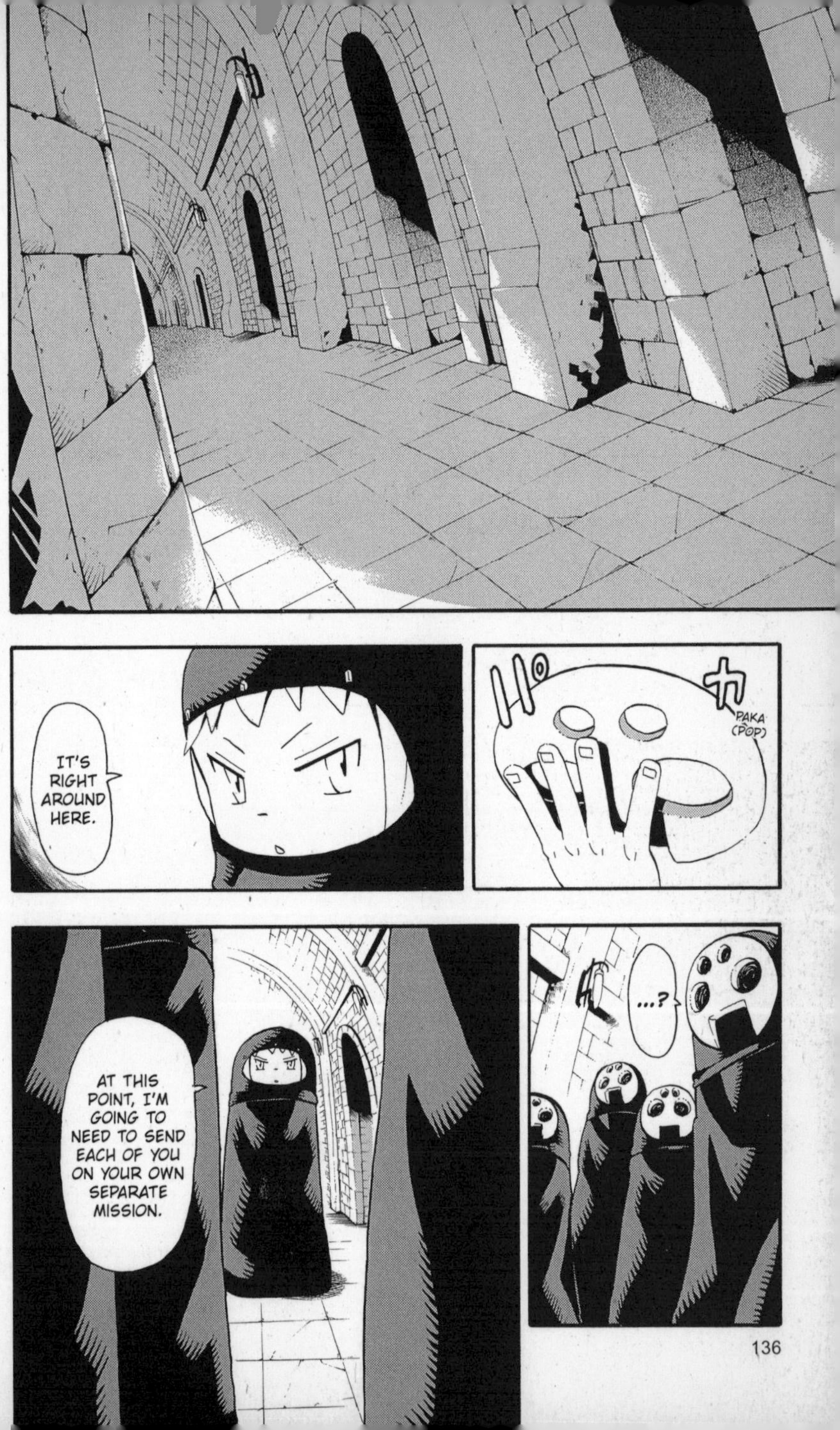

パカ
PAKA (POP)
IT'S RIGHT AROUND HERE.
...?
AT THIS POINT, I'M GOING TO NEED TO SEND EACH OF YOU ON YOUR OWN SEPARATE MISSION.

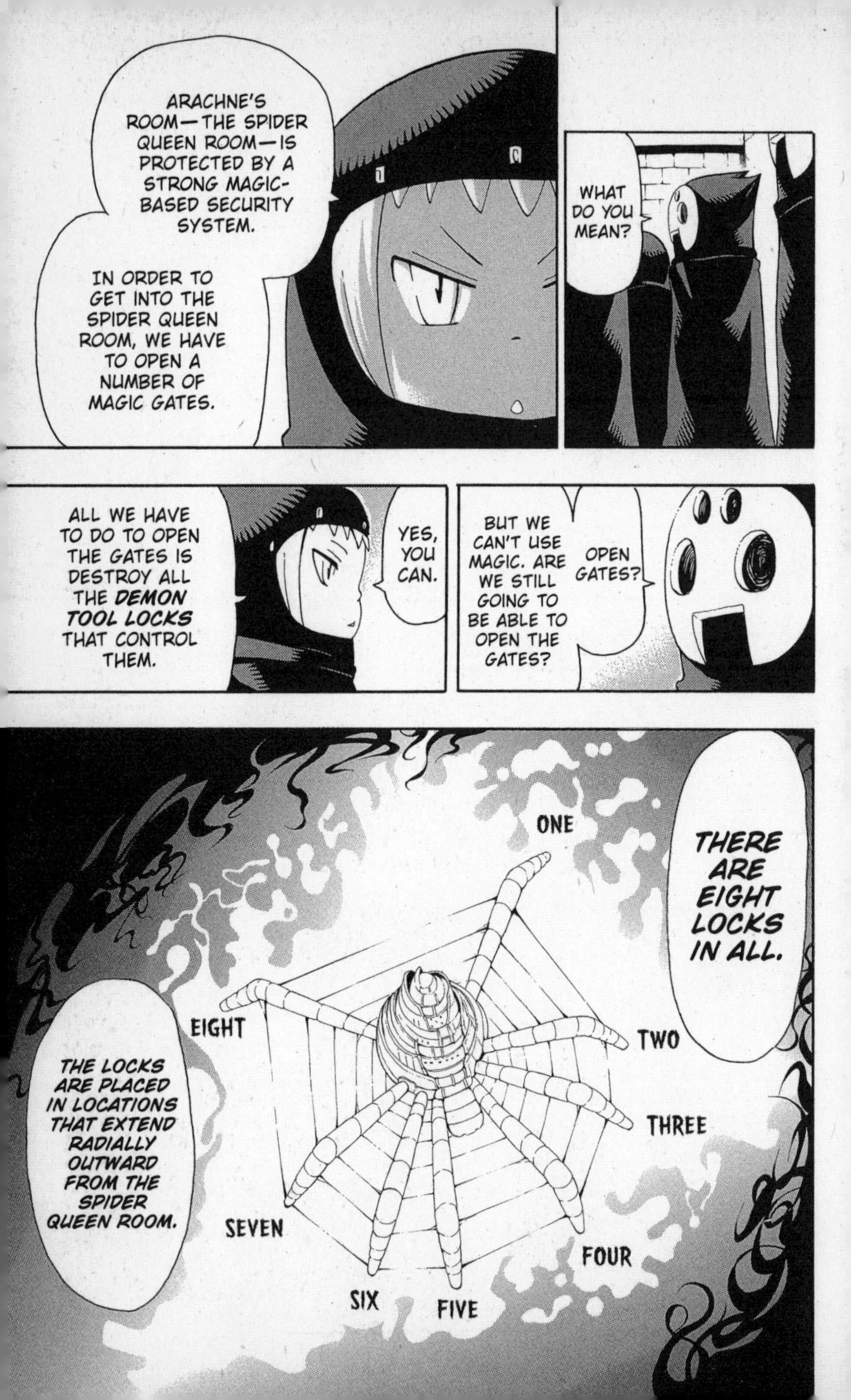
WHAT DO YOU MEAN?
ARACHNE'S ROOM—THE SPIDER QUEEN ROOM—IS PROTECTED BY A STRONG MAGIC-BASED SECURITY SYSTEM.
IN ORDER TO GET INTO THE SPIDER QUEEN ROOM, WE HAVE TO OPEN A NUMBER OF MAGIC GATES.
OPEN GATES?
BUT WE CAN'T USE MAGIC. ARE WE STILL GOING TO BE ABLE TO OPEN THE GATES?
YES, YOU CAN.
ALL WE HAVE TO DO TO OPEN THE GATES IS DESTROY ALL THE ***DEMON TOOL LOCKS*** THAT CONTROL THEM.
THERE ARE EIGHT LOCKS IN ALL.
ONE
TWO
THREE
FOUR
FIVE
SIX
SEVEN
EIGHT
THE LOCKS ARE PLACED IN LOCATIONS THAT EXTEND RADIALLY OUTWARD FROM THE SPIDER QUEEN ROOM.

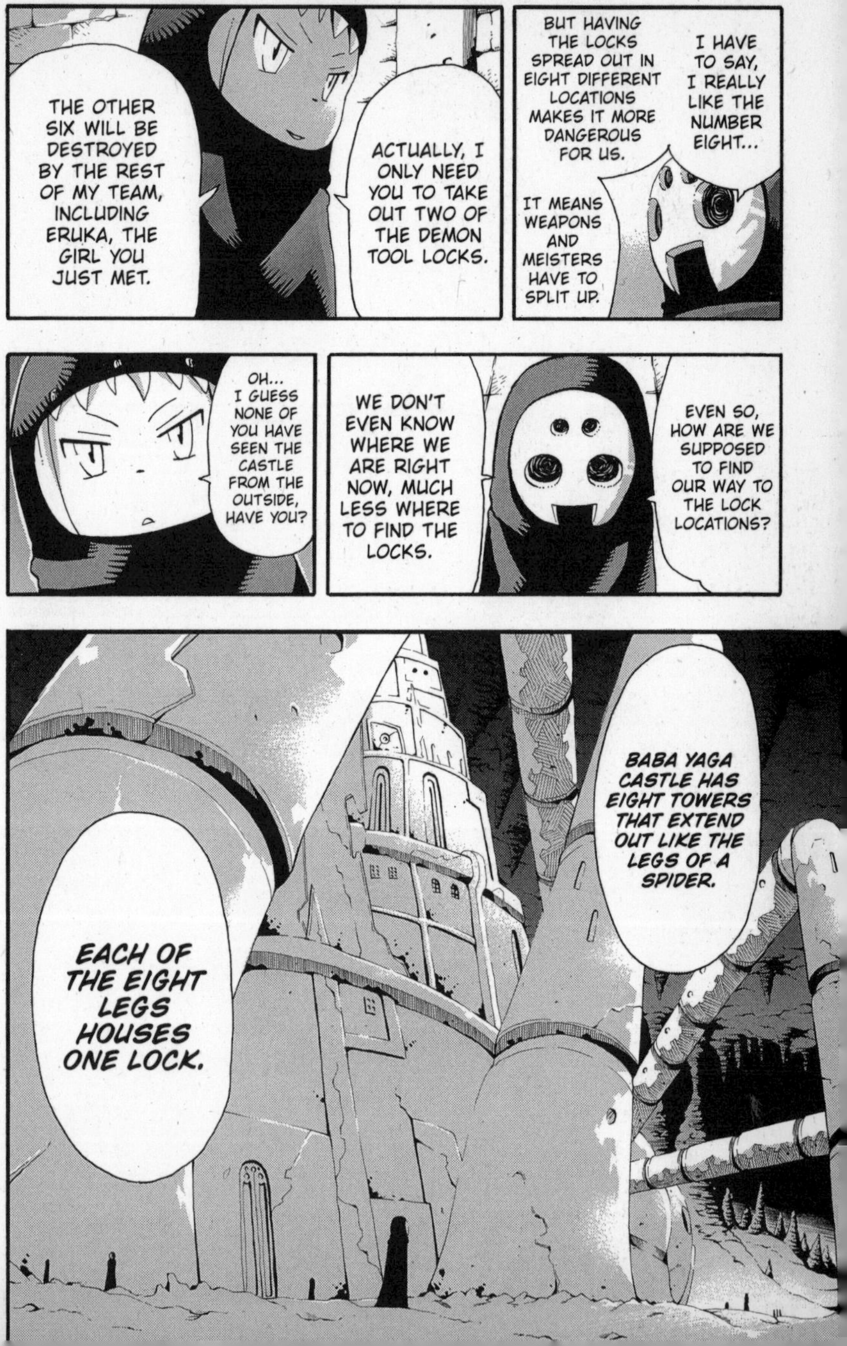
I HAVE TO SAY, I REALLY LIKE THE NUMBER EIGHT...
BUT HAVING THE LOCKS SPREAD OUT IN EIGHT DIFFERENT LOCATIONS MAKES IT MORE DANGEROUS FOR US.
IT MEANS WEAPONS AND MEISTERS HAVE TO SPLIT UP.
ACTUALLY, I ONLY NEED YOU TO TAKE OUT TWO OF THE DEMON TOOL LOCKS.
THE OTHER SIX WILL BE DESTROYED BY THE REST OF MY TEAM, INCLUDING ERUKA, THE GIRL YOU JUST MET.
EVEN SO, HOW ARE WE SUPPOSED TO FIND OUR WAY TO THE LOCK LOCATIONS?
WE DON'T EVEN KNOW WHERE WE ARE RIGHT NOW, MUCH LESS WHERE TO FIND THE LOCKS.
OH... I GUESS NONE OF YOU HAVE SEEN THE CASTLE FROM THE OUTSIDE, HAVE YOU?
BABA YAGA CASTLE HAS EIGHT TOWERS THAT EXTEND OUT LIKE THE LEGS OF A SPIDER.
EACH OF THE EIGHT LEGS HOUSES ONE LOCK.

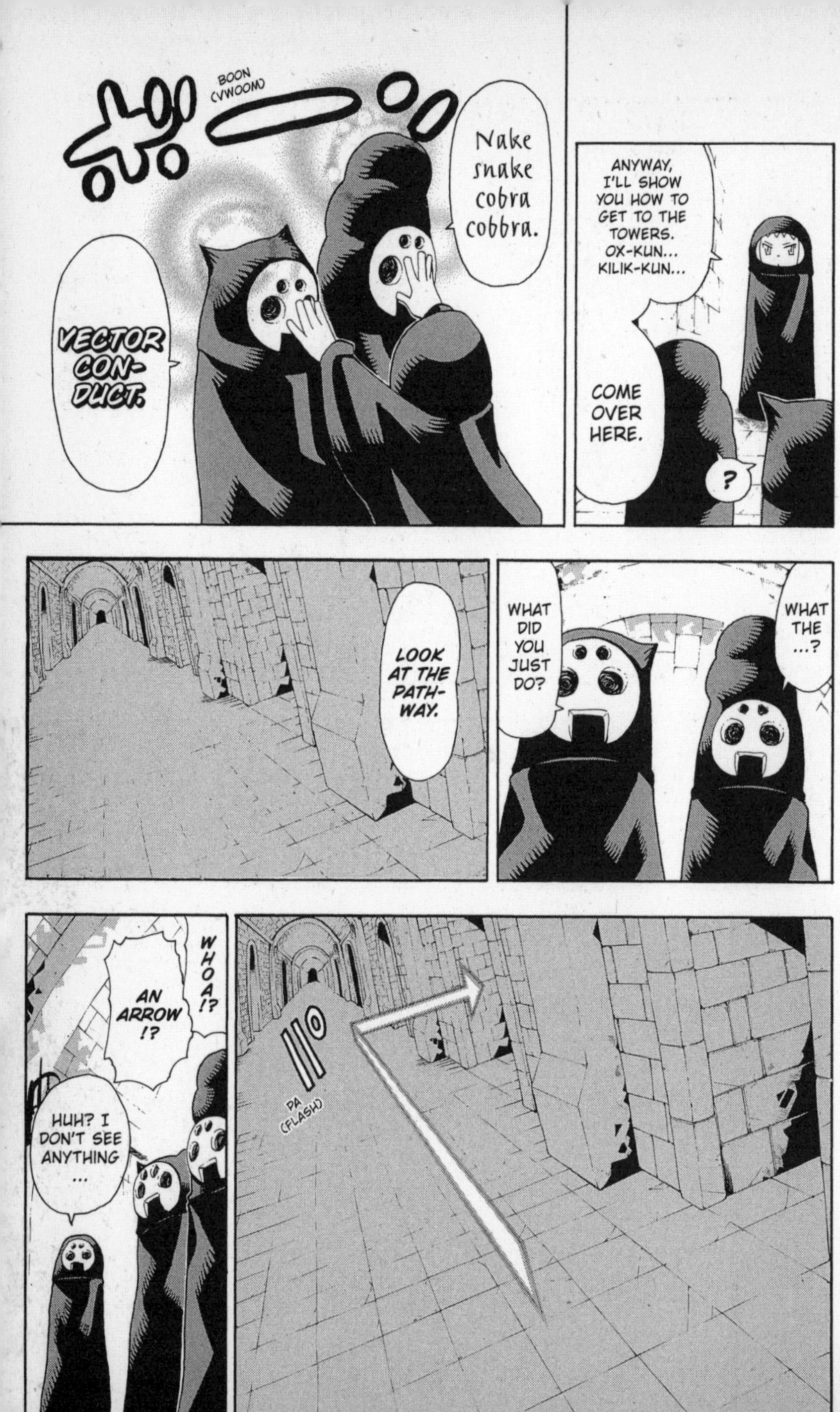
ANYWAY, I'LL SHOW YOU HOW TO GET TO THE TOWERS. OX-KUN... KILIK-KUN...
COME OVER HERE.
?
Nake snake cobra cobbra.
BOON (VWOOM)
VECTOR CON-DUCT.
WHAT THE ...?
WHAT DID YOU JUST DO?
LOOK AT THE PATH-WAY.
PA (FLASH)
WHOA!?
AN ARROW!?
HUH? I DON'T SEE ANYTHING ...

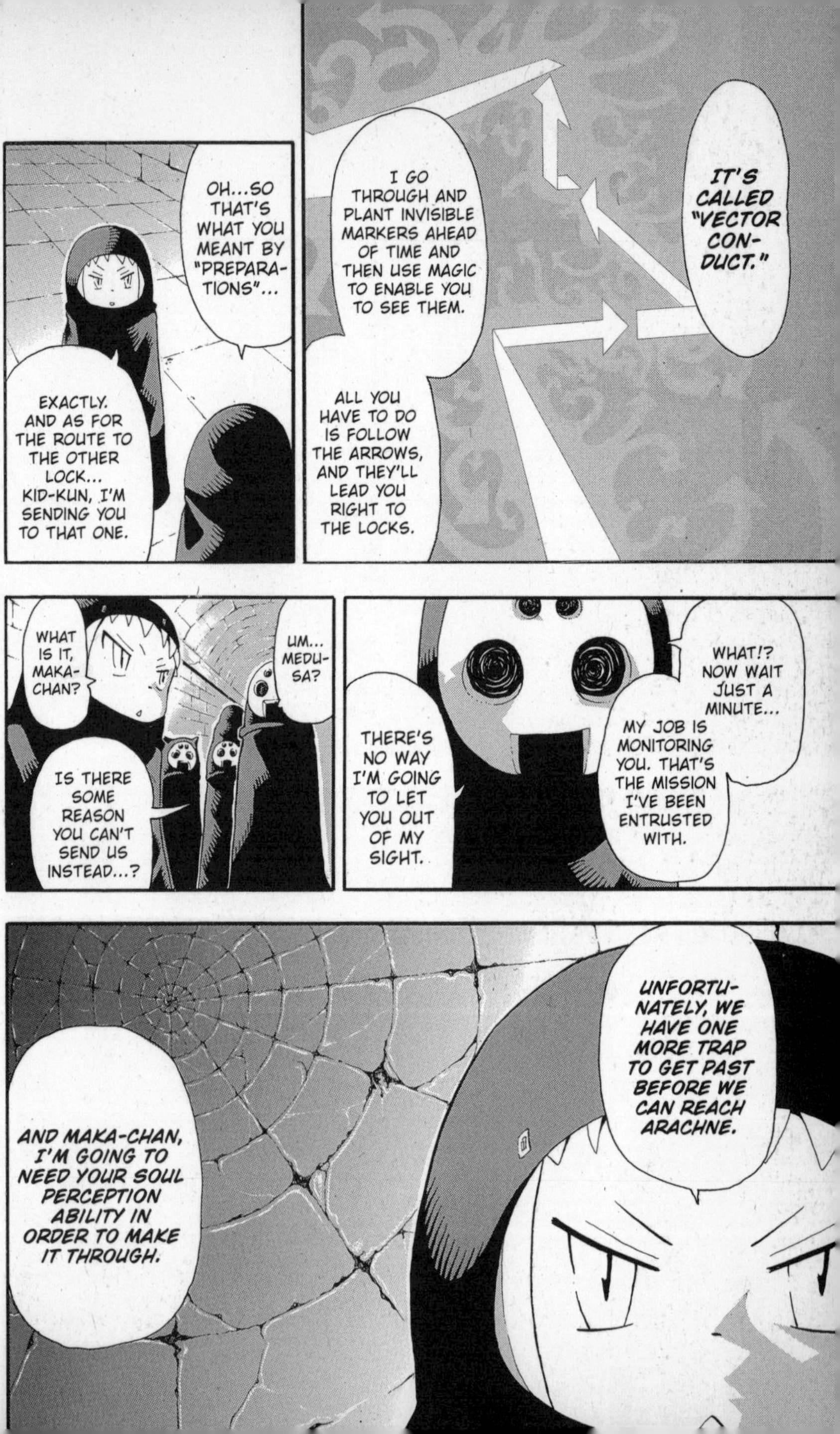
IT'S CALLED "VECTOR CONDUCT."
I GO THROUGH AND PLANT INVISIBLE MARKERS AHEAD OF TIME AND THEN USE MAGIC TO ENABLE YOU TO SEE THEM.
ALL YOU HAVE TO DO IS FOLLOW THE ARROWS, AND THEY'LL LEAD YOU RIGHT TO THE LOCKS.
OH...SO THAT'S WHAT YOU MEANT BY "PREPARATIONS"...
EXACTLY. AND AS FOR THE ROUTE TO THE OTHER LOCK... KID-KUN, I'M SENDING YOU TO THAT ONE.
WHAT!? NOW WAIT JUST A MINUTE...
MY JOB IS MONITORING YOU. THAT'S THE MISSION I'VE BEEN ENTRUSTED WITH.
THERE'S NO WAY I'M GOING TO LET YOU OUT OF MY SIGHT.
UM... MEDUSA?
WHAT IS IT, MAKA-CHAN?
IS THERE SOME REASON YOU CAN'T SEND US INSTEAD...?
UNFORTUNATELY, WE HAVE ONE MORE TRAP TO GET PAST BEFORE WE CAN REACH ARACHNE.
AND MAKA-CHAN, I'M GOING TO NEED YOUR SOUL PERCEPTION ABILITY IN ORDER TO MAKE IT THROUGH.

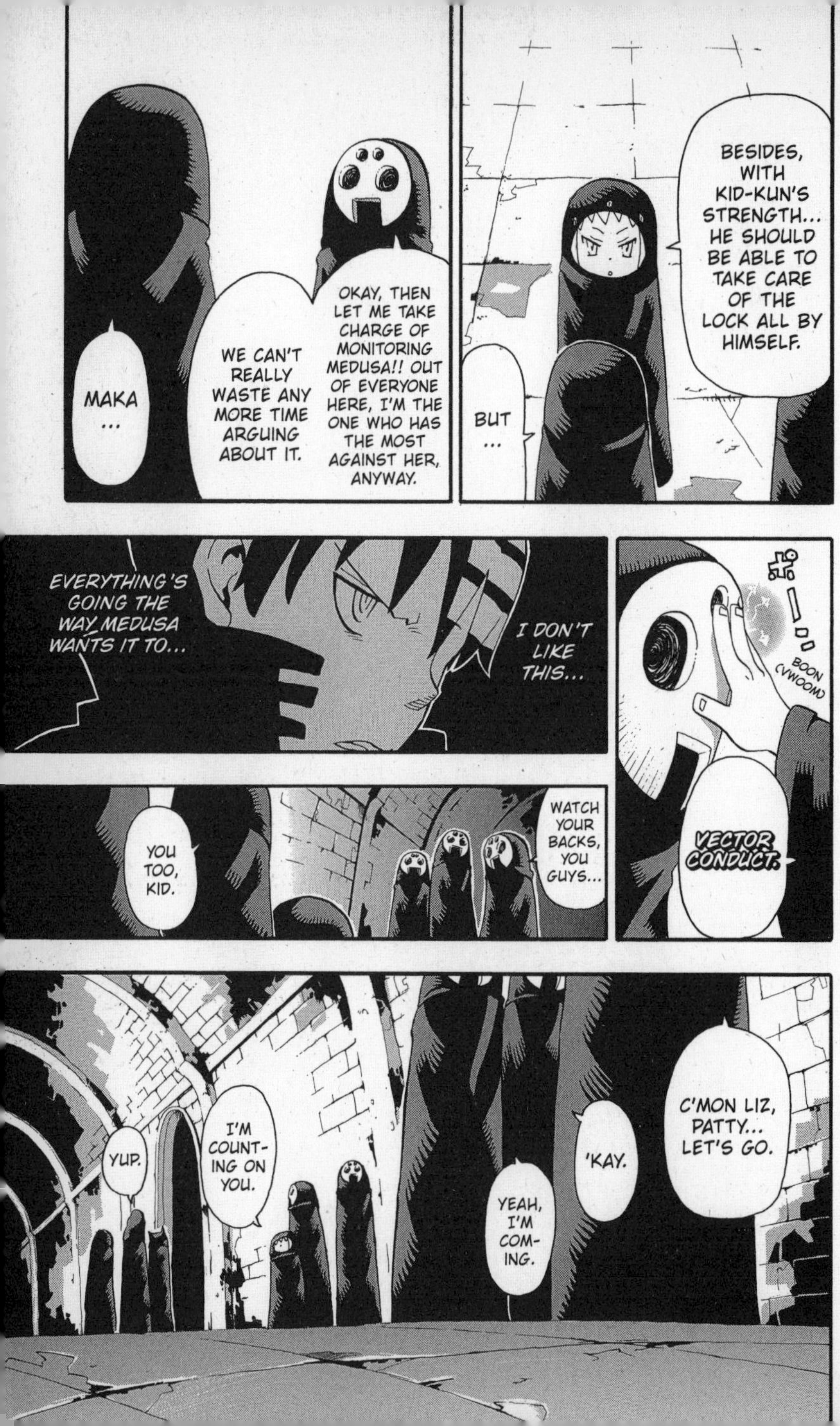
BESIDES, WITH KID-KUN'S STRENGTH... HE SHOULD BE ABLE TO TAKE CARE OF THE LOCK ALL BY HIMSELF.
BUT...
OKAY, THEN LET ME TAKE CHARGE OF MONITORING MEDUSA!! OUT OF EVERYONE HERE, I'M THE ONE WHO HAS THE MOST AGAINST HER, ANYWAY.
WE CAN'T REALLY WASTE ANY MORE TIME ARGUING ABOUT IT.
MAKA...
BOON (VWOOM)
VECTOR CONDUCT.
I DON'T LIKE THIS...
EVERYTHING'S GOING THE WAY MEDUSA WANTS IT TO...
WATCH YOUR BACKS, YOU GUYS...
YOU TOO, KID.
C'MON LIZ, PATTY... LET'S GO.
'KAY.
YEAH, I'M COMING.
I'M COUNTING ON YOU.
YUP.

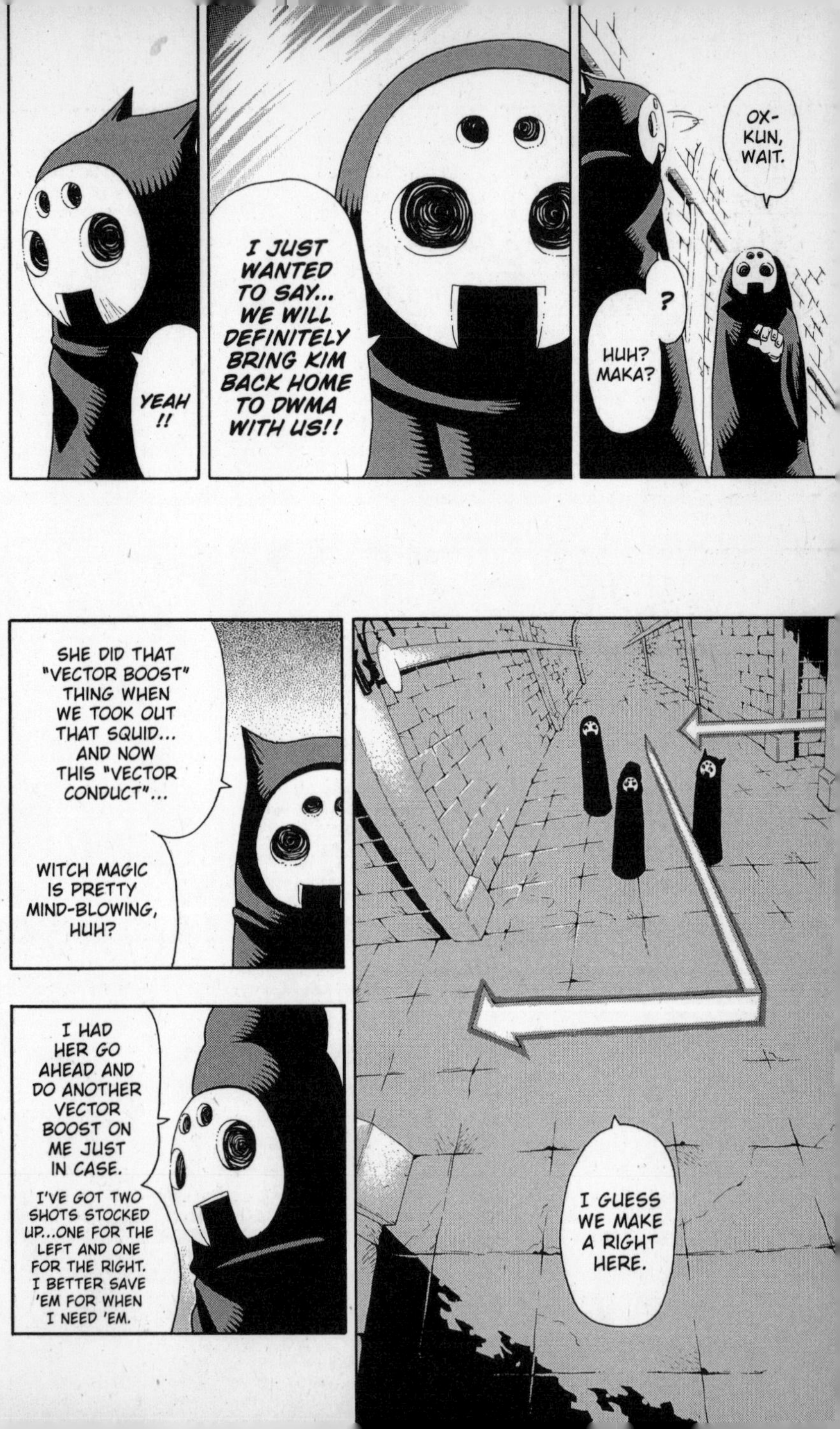
OX-KUN, WAIT.
?
HUH? MAKA?
I JUST WANTED TO SAY... WE WILL DEFINITELY BRING KIM BACK HOME TO DWMA WITH US!!
YEAH!!
I GUESS WE MAKE A RIGHT HERE.
SHE DID THAT "VECTOR BOOST" THING WHEN WE TOOK OUT THAT SQUID... AND NOW THIS "VECTOR CONDUCT"...
WITCH MAGIC IS PRETTY MIND-BLOWING, HUH?
I HAD HER GO AHEAD AND DO ANOTHER VECTOR BOOST ON ME JUST IN CASE.
I'VE GOT TWO SHOTS STOCKED UP...ONE FOR THE LEFT AND ONE FOR THE RIGHT. I BETTER SAVE 'EM FOR WHEN I NEED 'EM.

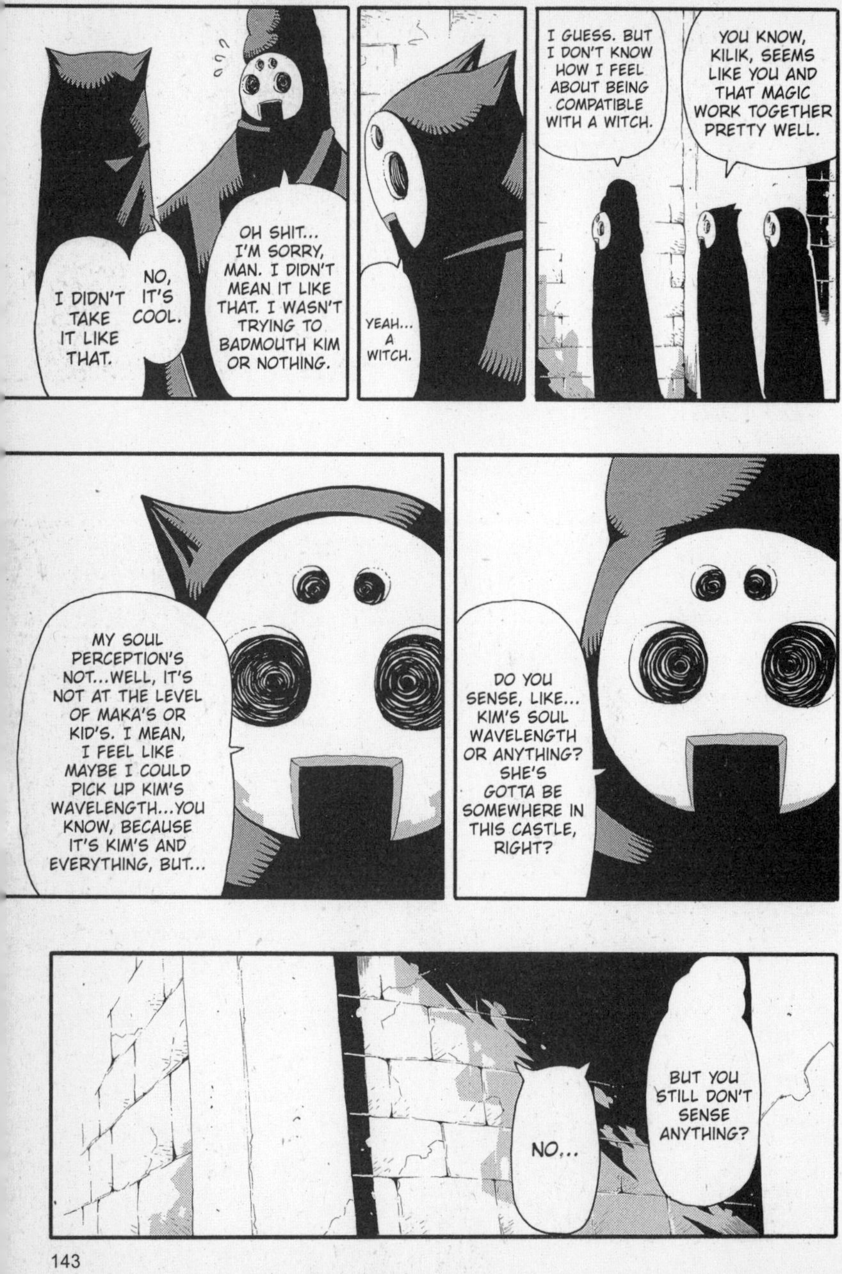
YOU KNOW, KILIK, SEEMS LIKE YOU AND THAT MAGIC WORK TOGETHER PRETTY WELL.
I GUESS. BUT I DON'T KNOW HOW I FEEL ABOUT BEING COMPATIBLE WITH A WITCH.
YEAH... A WITCH.
OH SHIT... I'M SORRY, MAN. I DIDN'T MEAN IT LIKE THAT. I WASN'T TRYING TO BADMOUTH KIM OR NOTHING.
NO, IT'S COOL.
I DIDN'T TAKE IT LIKE THAT.
DO YOU SENSE, LIKE... KIM'S SOUL WAVELENGTH OR ANYTHING? SHE'S GOTTA BE SOMEWHERE IN THIS CASTLE, RIGHT?
MY SOUL PERCEPTION'S NOT...WELL, IT'S NOT AT THE LEVEL OF MAKA'S OR KID'S. I MEAN, I FEEL LIKE MAYBE I COULD PICK UP KIM'S WAVELENGTH...YOU KNOW, BECAUSE IT'S KIM'S AND EVERYTHING, BUT...
BUT YOU STILL DON'T SENSE ANYTHING?
NO...

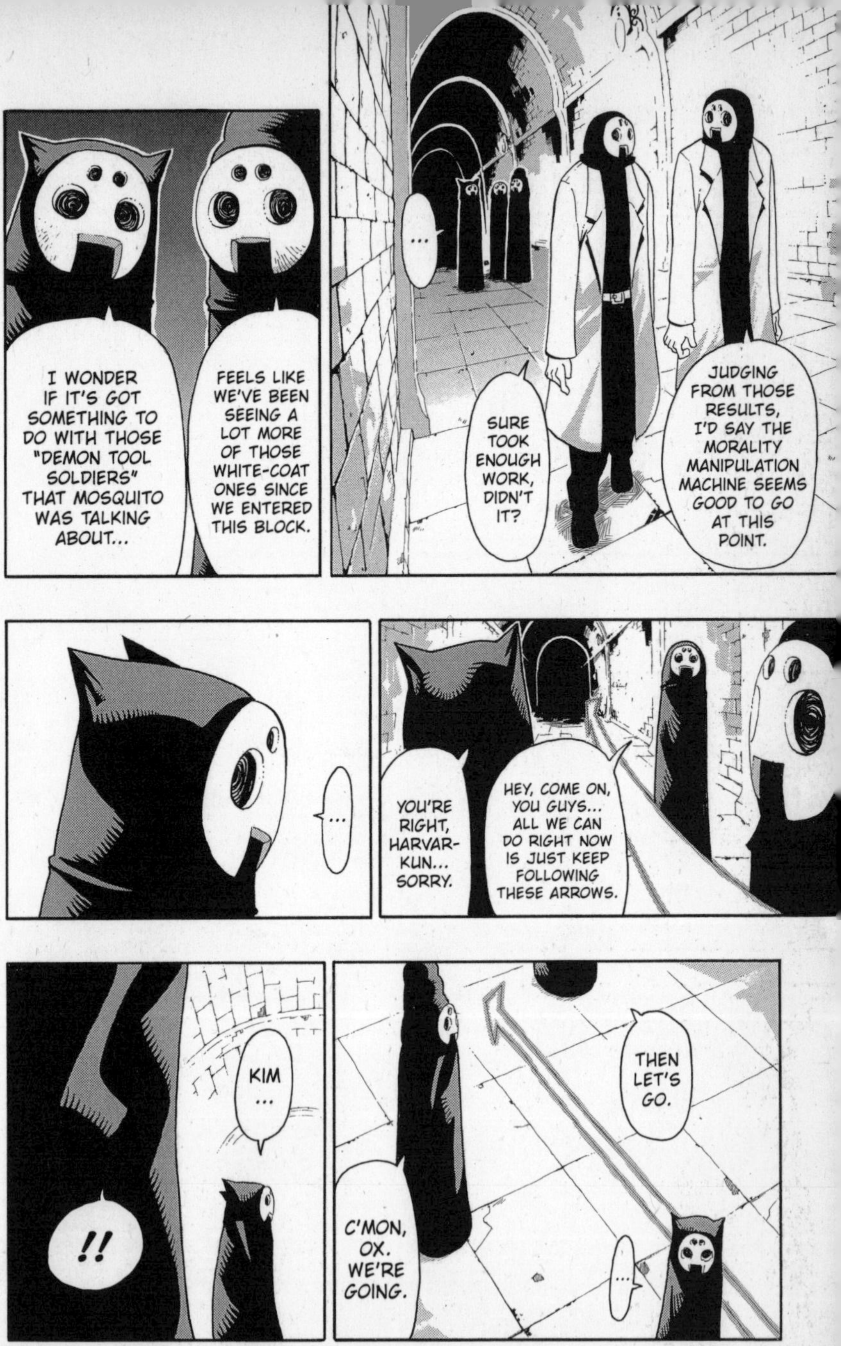
JUDGING FROM THOSE RESULTS, I'D SAY THE MORALITY MANIPULATION MACHINE SEEMS GOOD TO GO AT THIS POINT.
SURE TOOK ENOUGH WORK, DIDN'T IT?
...
FEELS LIKE WE'VE BEEN SEEING A LOT MORE OF THOSE WHITE-COAT ONES SINCE WE ENTERED THIS BLOCK.
I WONDER IF IT'S GOT SOMETHING TO DO WITH THOSE "DEMON TOOL SOLDIERS" THAT MOSQUITO WAS TALKING ABOUT...
HEY, COME ON, YOU GUYS... ALL WE CAN DO RIGHT NOW IS JUST KEEP FOLLOWING THESE ARROWS.
YOU'RE RIGHT, HARVAR-KUN... SORRY.
...
THEN LET'S GO.
C'MON, OX. WE'RE GOING.
...
KIM ...
!!

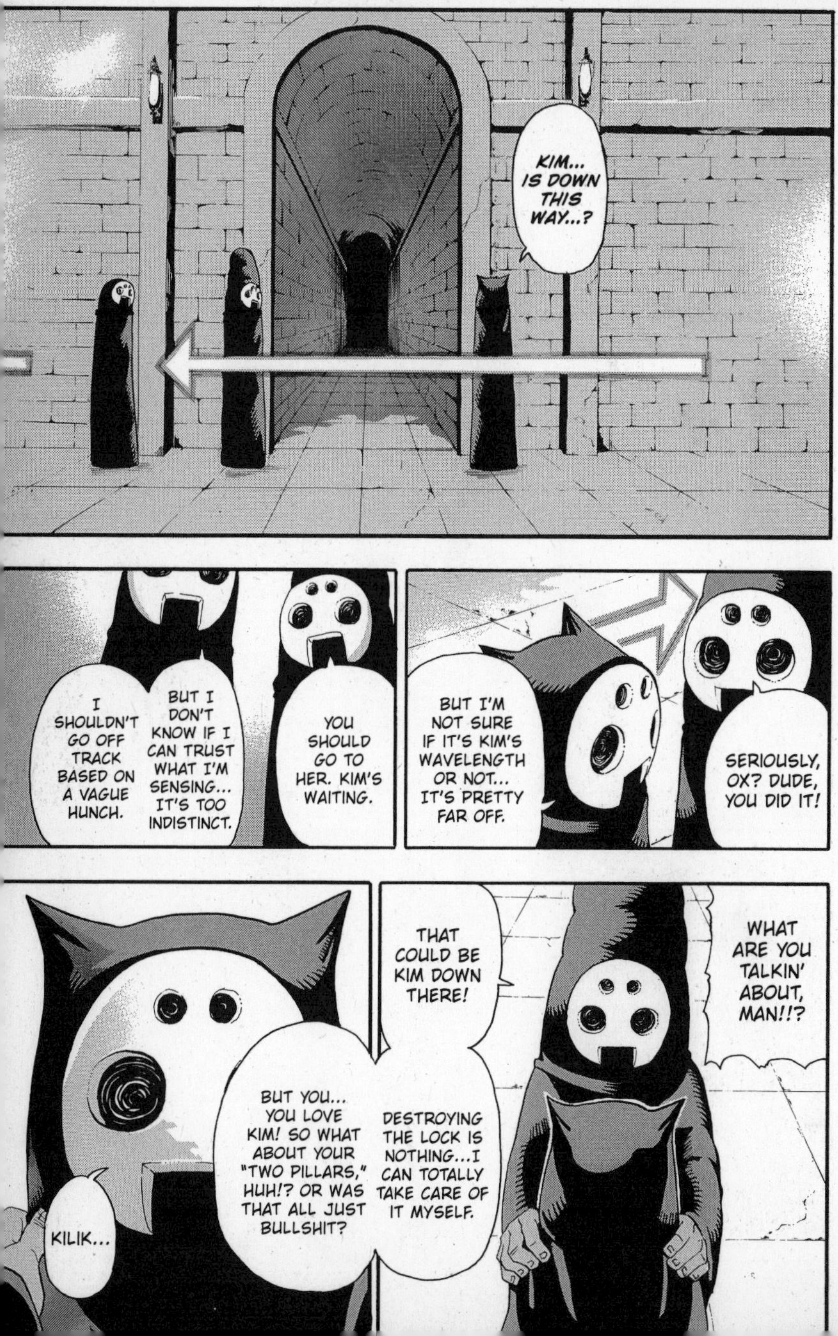
KIM... IS DOWN THIS WAY...?
SERIOUSLY, OX? DUDE, YOU DID IT!
BUT I'M NOT SURE IF IT'S KIM'S WAVELENGTH OR NOT... IT'S PRETTY FAR OFF.
YOU SHOULD GO TO HER. KIM'S WAITING.
BUT I DON'T KNOW IF I CAN TRUST WHAT I'M SENSING... IT'S TOO INDISTINCT.
I SHOULDN'T GO OFF TRACK BASED ON A VAGUE HUNCH.
WHAT ARE YOU TALKIN' ABOUT, MAN!!?
THAT COULD BE KIM DOWN THERE!
DESTROYING THE LOCK IS NOTHING...I CAN TOTALLY TAKE CARE OF IT MYSELF.
BUT YOU... YOU LOVE KIM! SO WHAT ABOUT YOUR "TWO PILLARS," HUH!? OR WAS THAT ALL JUST BULLSHIT?
KILIK...

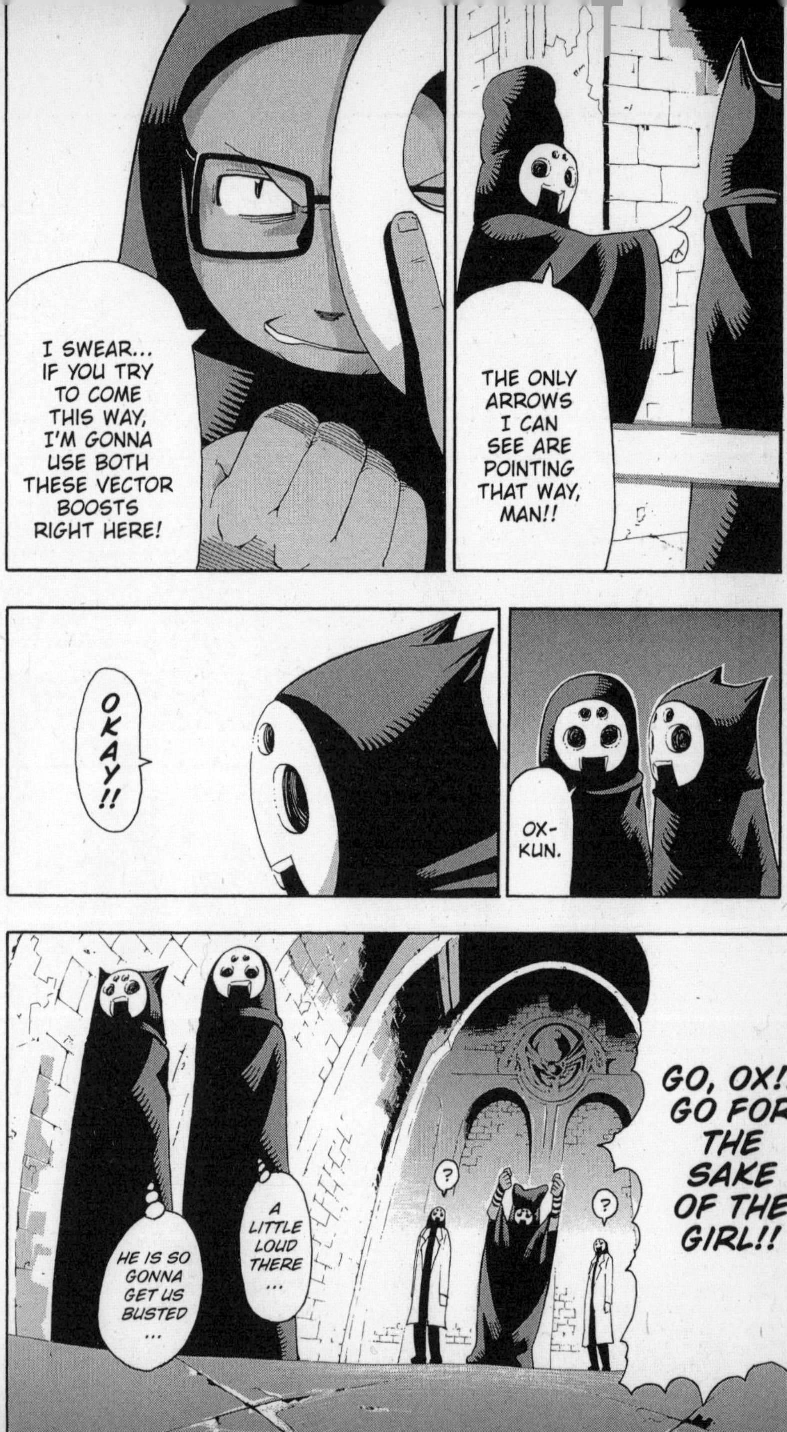

THE ONLY ARROWS I CAN SEE ARE POINTING THAT WAY, MAN!!
I SWEAR... IF YOU TRY TO COME THIS WAY, I'M GONNA USE BOTH THESE VECTOR BOOSTS RIGHT HERE!
OX-KUN.
OKAY!!
GO, OX!! GO FOR THE SAKE OF THE GIRL!!
?
?
A LITTLE LOUD THERE ...
HE IS SO GONNA GET US BUSTED ...

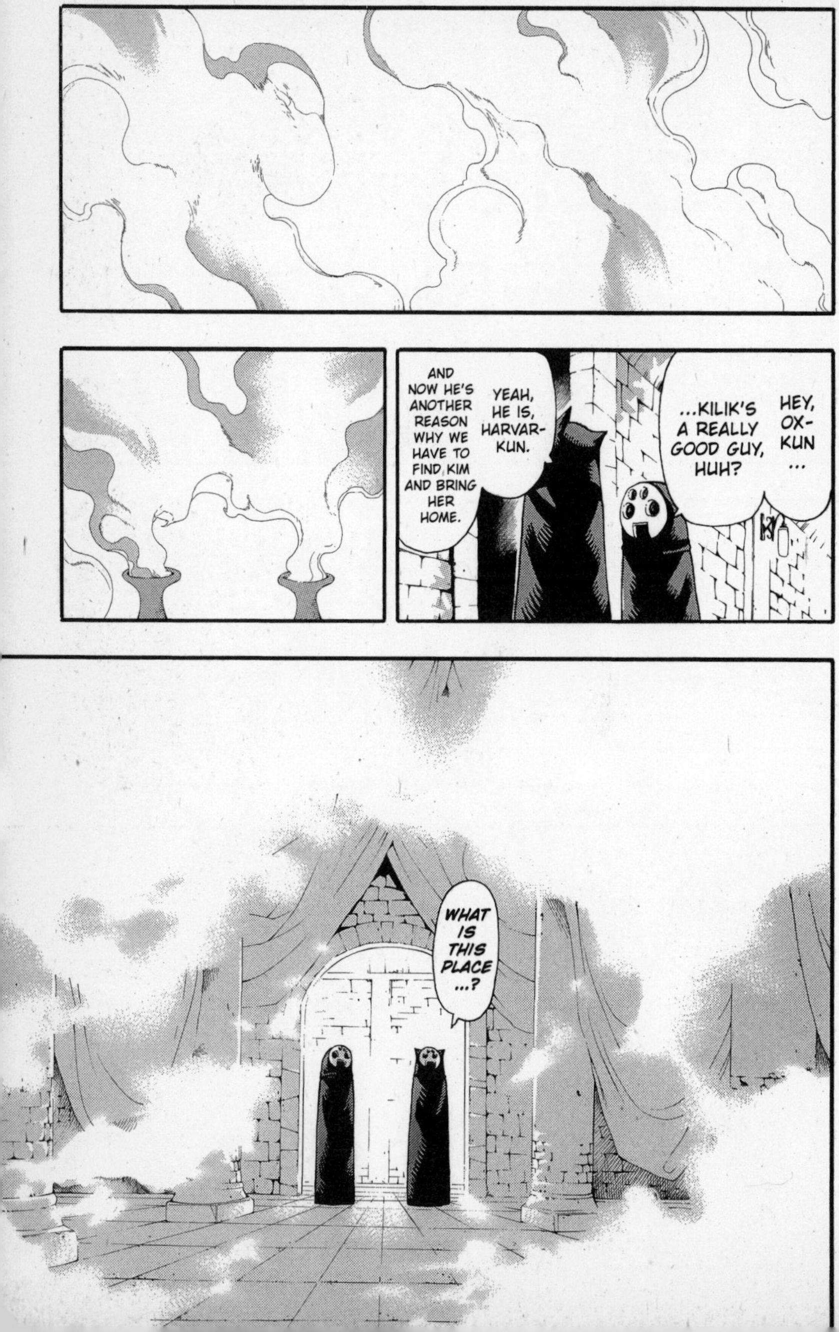
HEY, OX-KUN...
...KILIK'S A REALLY GOOD GUY, HUH?
YEAH, HE IS, HARVAR-KUN.
AND NOW HE'S ANOTHER REASON WHY WE HAVE TO FIND KIM AND BRING HER HOME.
WHAT IS THIS PLACE...?

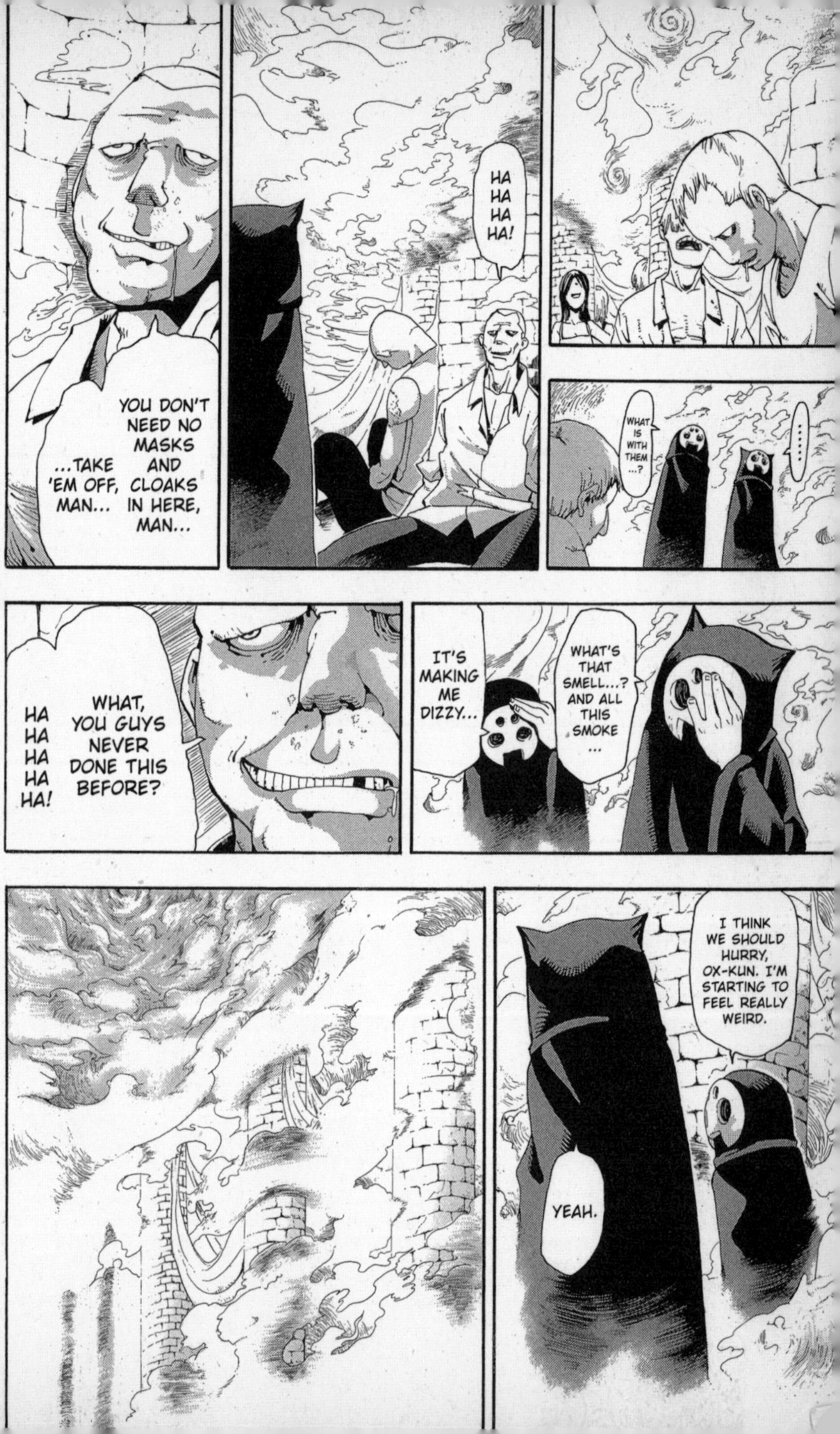
WHAT IS WITH THEM ...?
......
HA HA HA HA!
YOU DON'T NEED NO MASKS AND CLOAKS IN HERE, MAN...
...TAKE 'EM OFF, MAN...
WHAT'S THAT SMELL...? AND ALL THIS SMOKE ...
IT'S MAKING ME DIZZY...
WHAT, YOU GUYS NEVER DONE THIS BEFORE?
HA HA HA HA HA!
I THINK WE SHOULD HURRY, OX-KUN. I'M STARTING TO FEEL REALLY WEIRD.
YEAH.

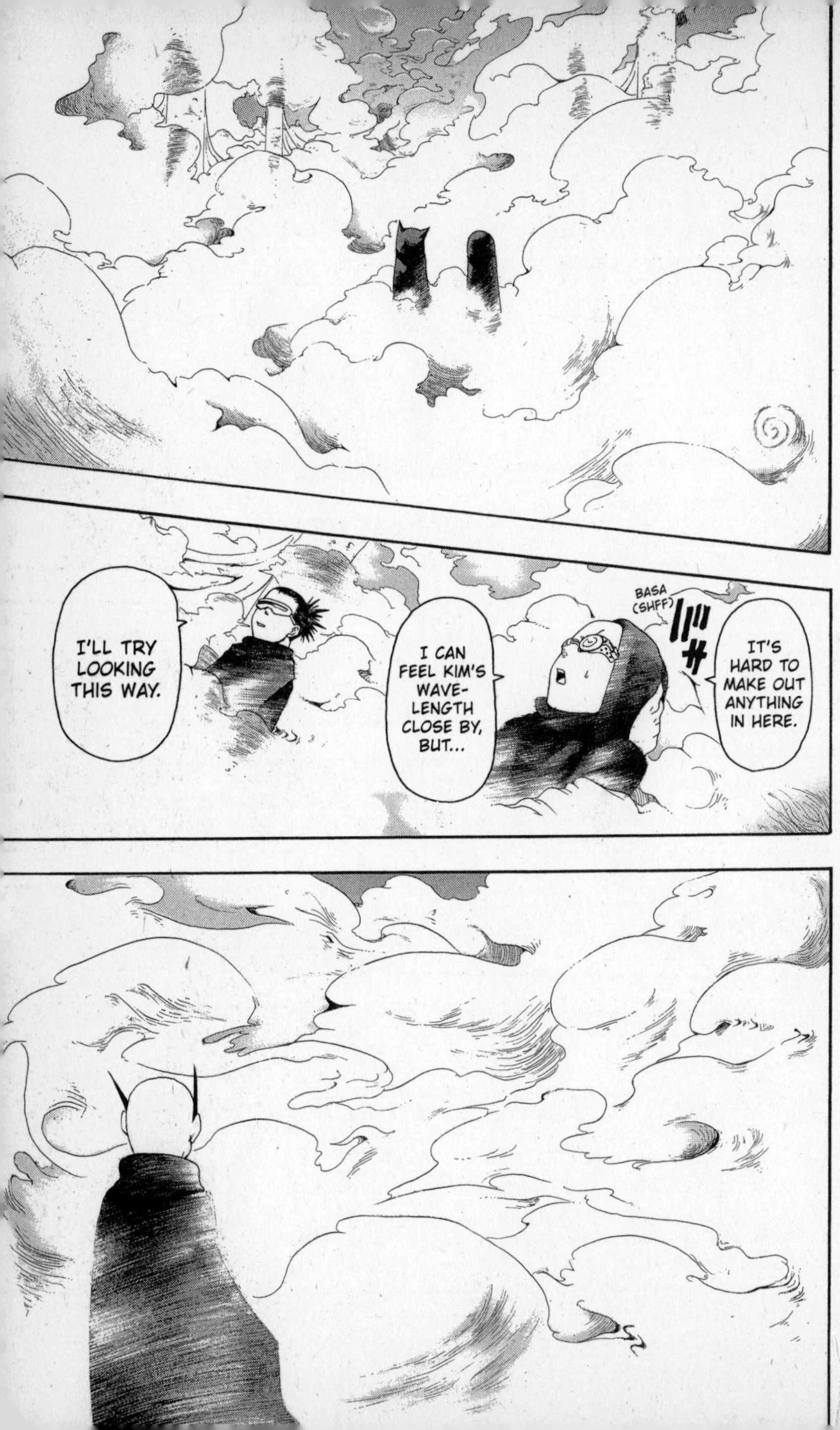
IT'S HARD TO MAKE OUT ANYTHING IN HERE.
BASA (SHFF)
I CAN FEEL KIM'S WAVE-LENGTH CLOSE BY, BUT...
I'LL TRY LOOKING THIS WAY.

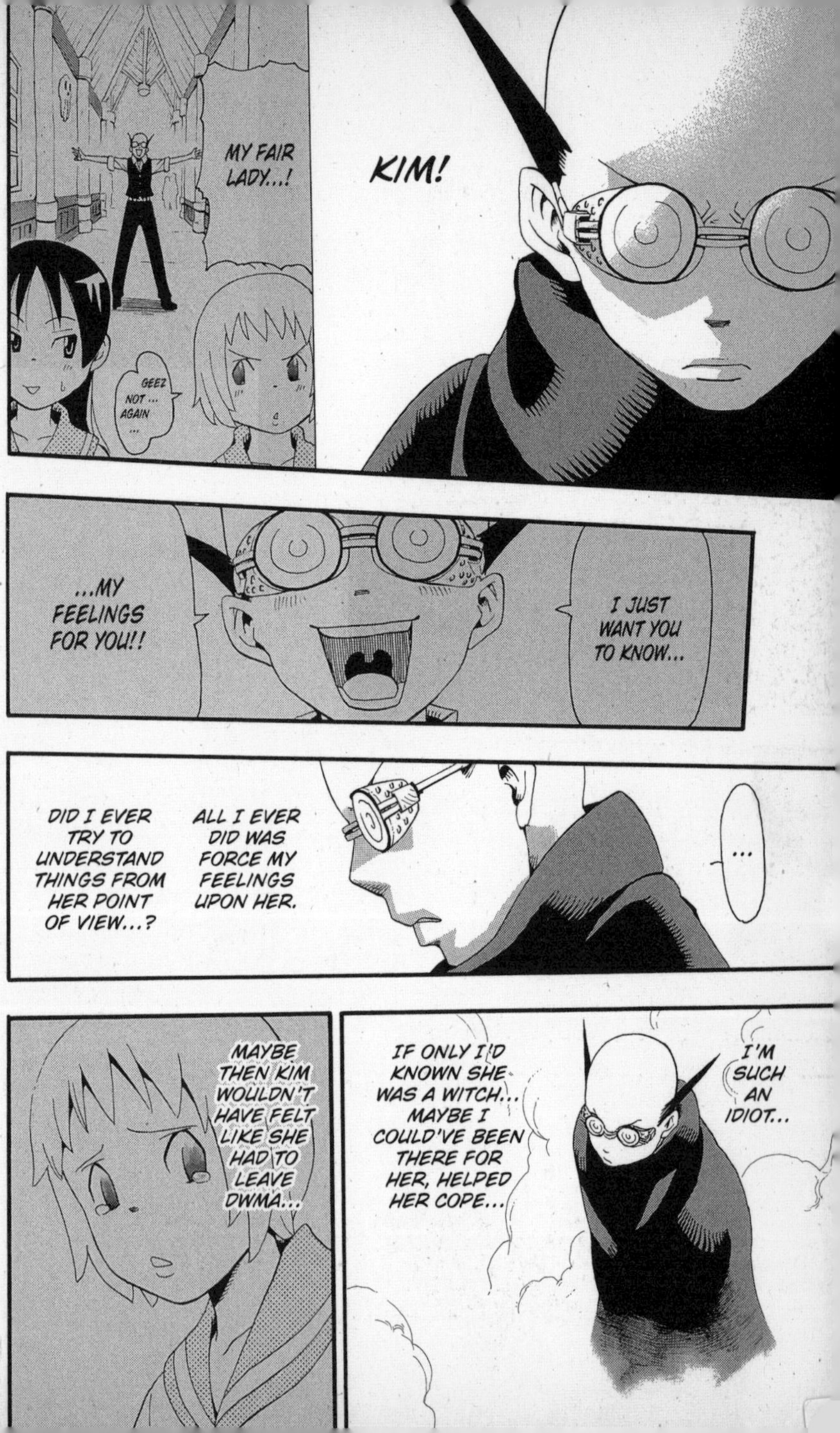
KIM!
MY FAIR LADY...!
GEEZ NOT ... AGAIN ...
I JUST WANT YOU TO KNOW...
...MY FEELINGS FOR YOU!!
...
ALL I EVER DID WAS FORCE MY FEELINGS UPON HER.
DID I EVER TRY TO UNDERSTAND THINGS FROM HER POINT OF VIEW...?
I'M SUCH AN IDIOT...
IF ONLY I'D KNOWN SHE WAS A WITCH... MAYBE I COULD'VE BEEN THERE FOR HER, HELPED HER COPE...
MAYBE THEN KIM WOULDN'T HAVE FELT LIKE SHE HAD TO LEAVE DWMA...

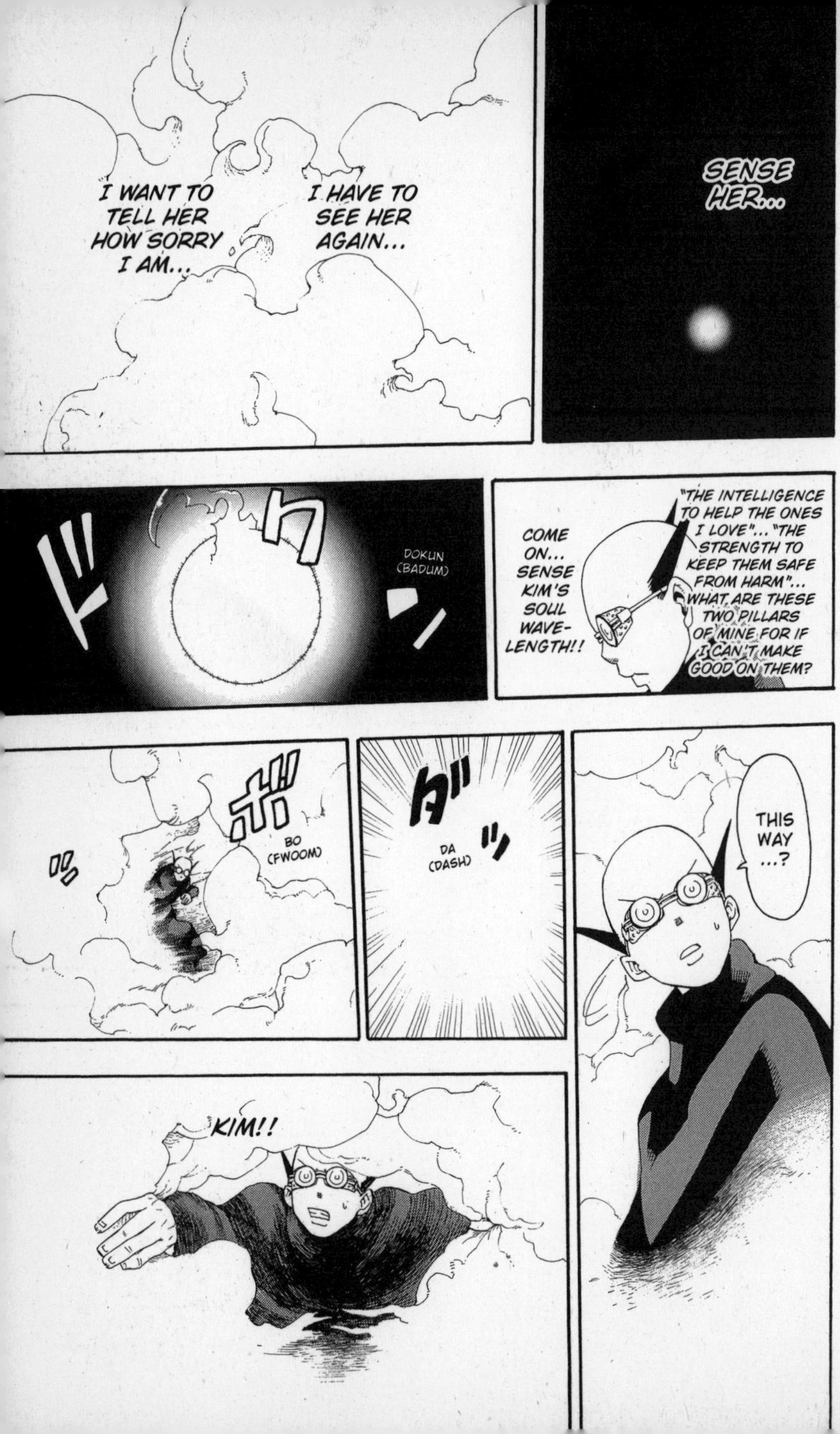
SENSE HER...
I HAVE TO SEE HER AGAIN...
I WANT TO TELL HER HOW SORRY I AM...
"THE INTELLIGENCE TO HELP THE ONES I LOVE"... "THE STRENGTH TO KEEP THEM SAFE FROM HARM"... WHAT ARE THESE TWO PILLARS OF MINE FOR IF I CAN'T MAKE GOOD ON THEM?
COME ON... SENSE KIM'S SOUL WAVE-LENGTH!!
ドクン
DOKUN (BADUM)
THIS WAY ...?
ダッ
DA (DASH)
ボッ
BO (FWOOM)
KIM!!

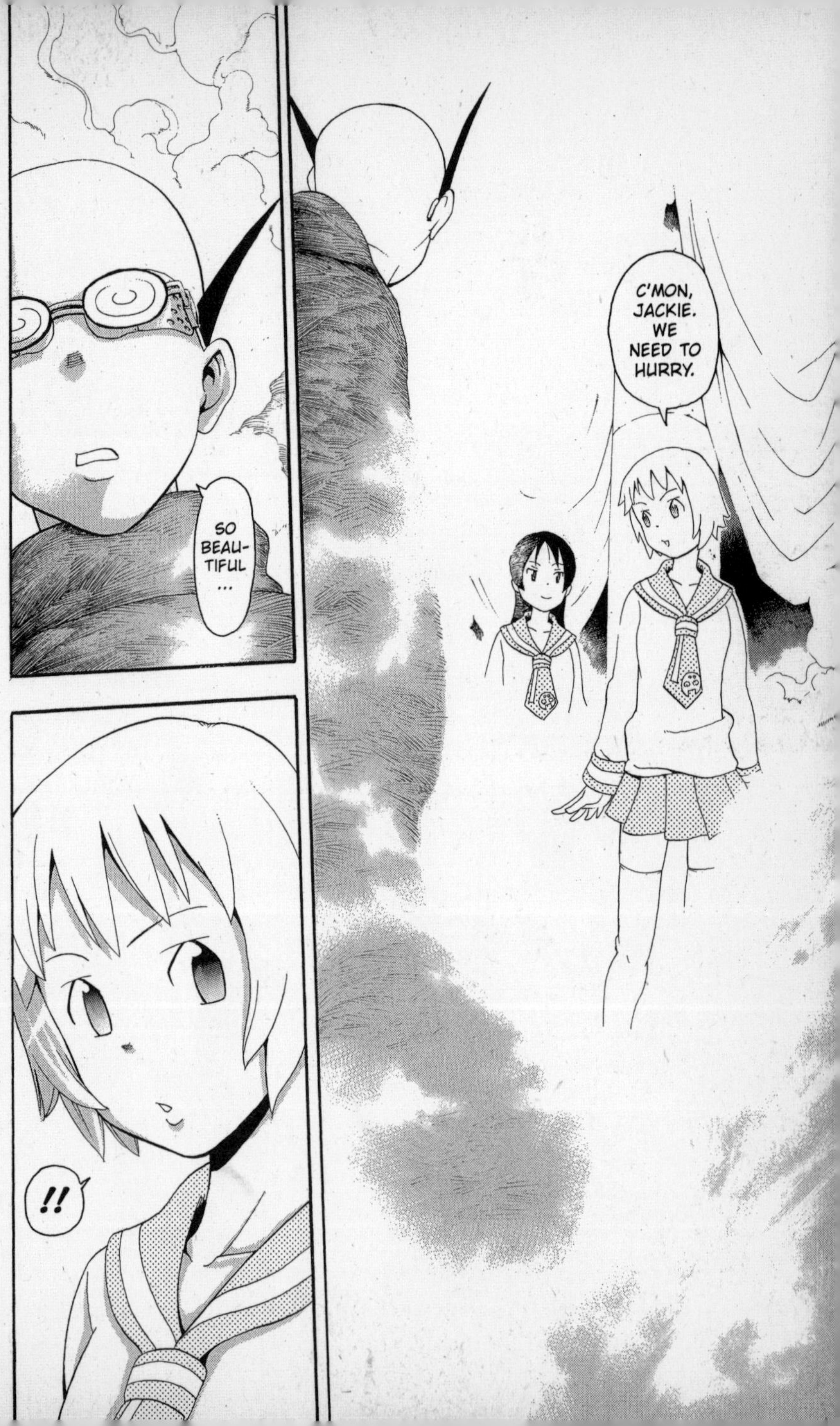
C'MON, JACKIE. WE NEED TO HURRY.
SO BEAU-TIFUL ...
!!

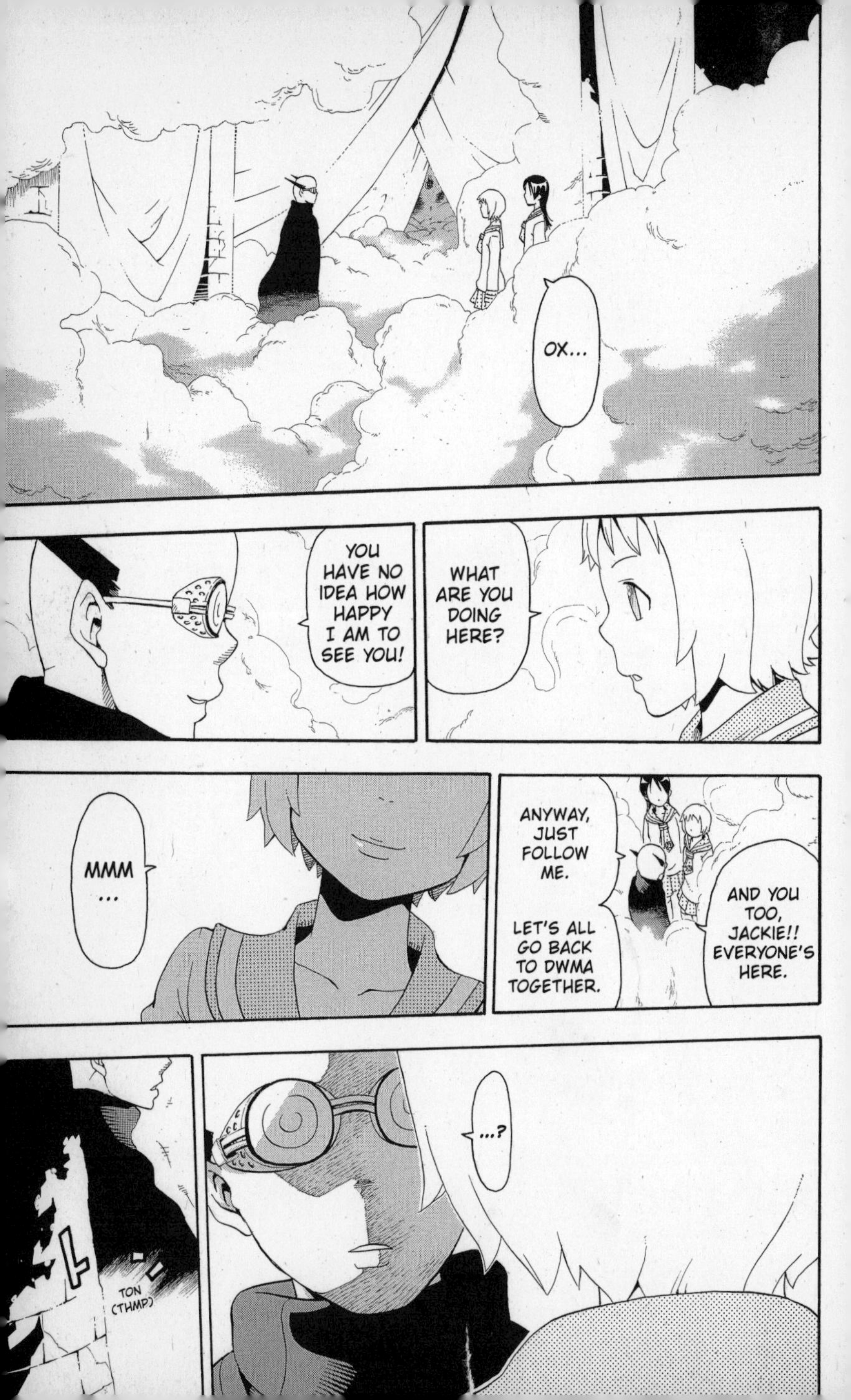
OX...
WHAT ARE YOU DOING HERE?
YOU HAVE NO IDEA HOW HAPPY I AM TO SEE YOU!
ANYWAY, JUST FOLLOW ME.
LET'S ALL GO BACK TO DWMA TOGETHER.
AND YOU TOO, JACKIE!! EVERYONE'S HERE.
MMM ...
...?
TON (THMP)

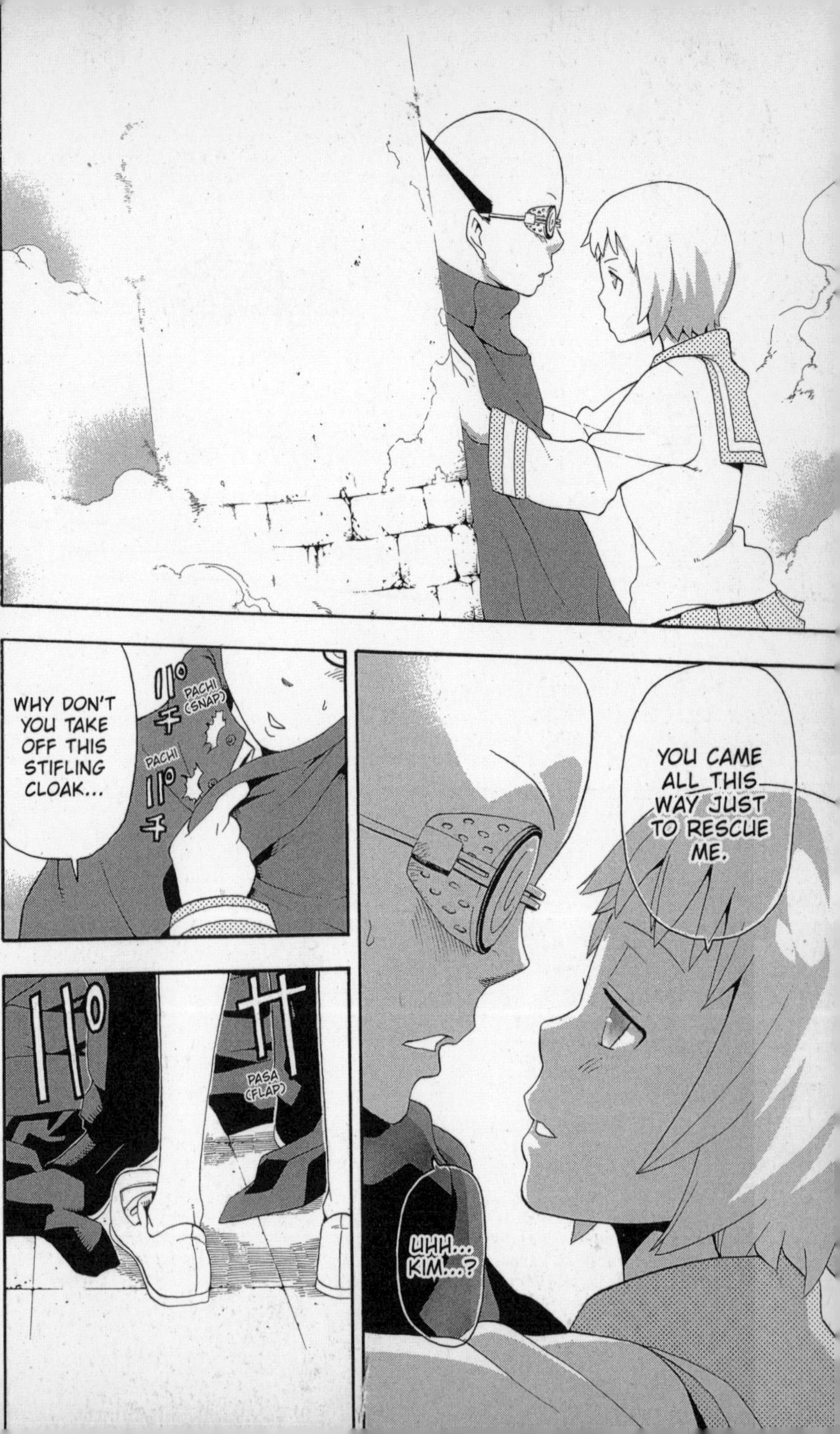
YOU CAME ALL THIS WAY JUST TO RESCUE ME.
UHH... KIM...?
WHY DON'T YOU TAKE OFF THIS STIFLING CLOAK...
PACHI (SNAP)
PACHI
PASA (FLAP)

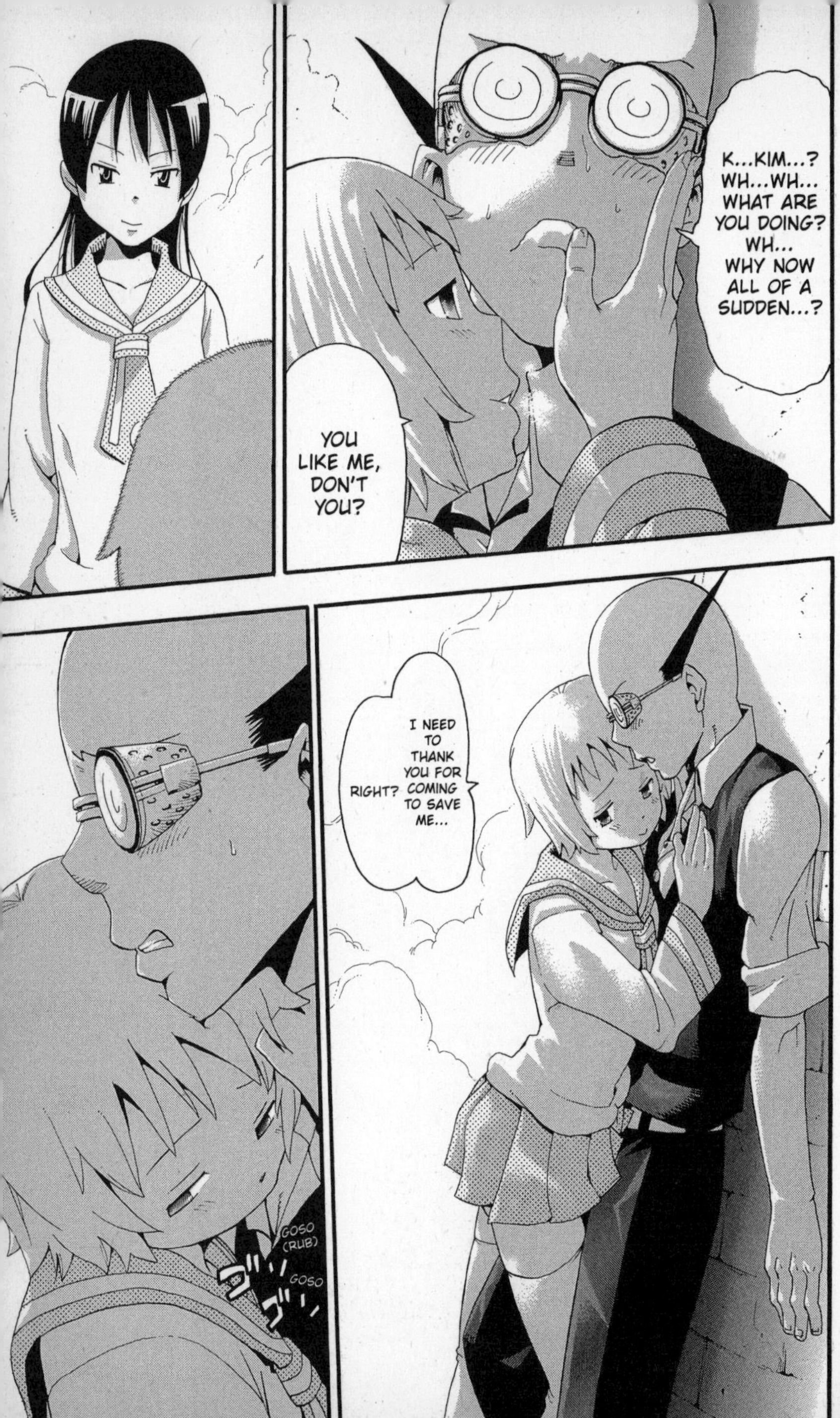
K...KIM...? WH...WH... WHAT ARE YOU DOING? WH... WHY NOW ALL OF A SUDDEN...?
YOU LIKE ME, DON'T YOU?
I NEED TO THANK YOU FOR COMING TO SAVE ME... RIGHT?
GOSO (RUB)
GOSO

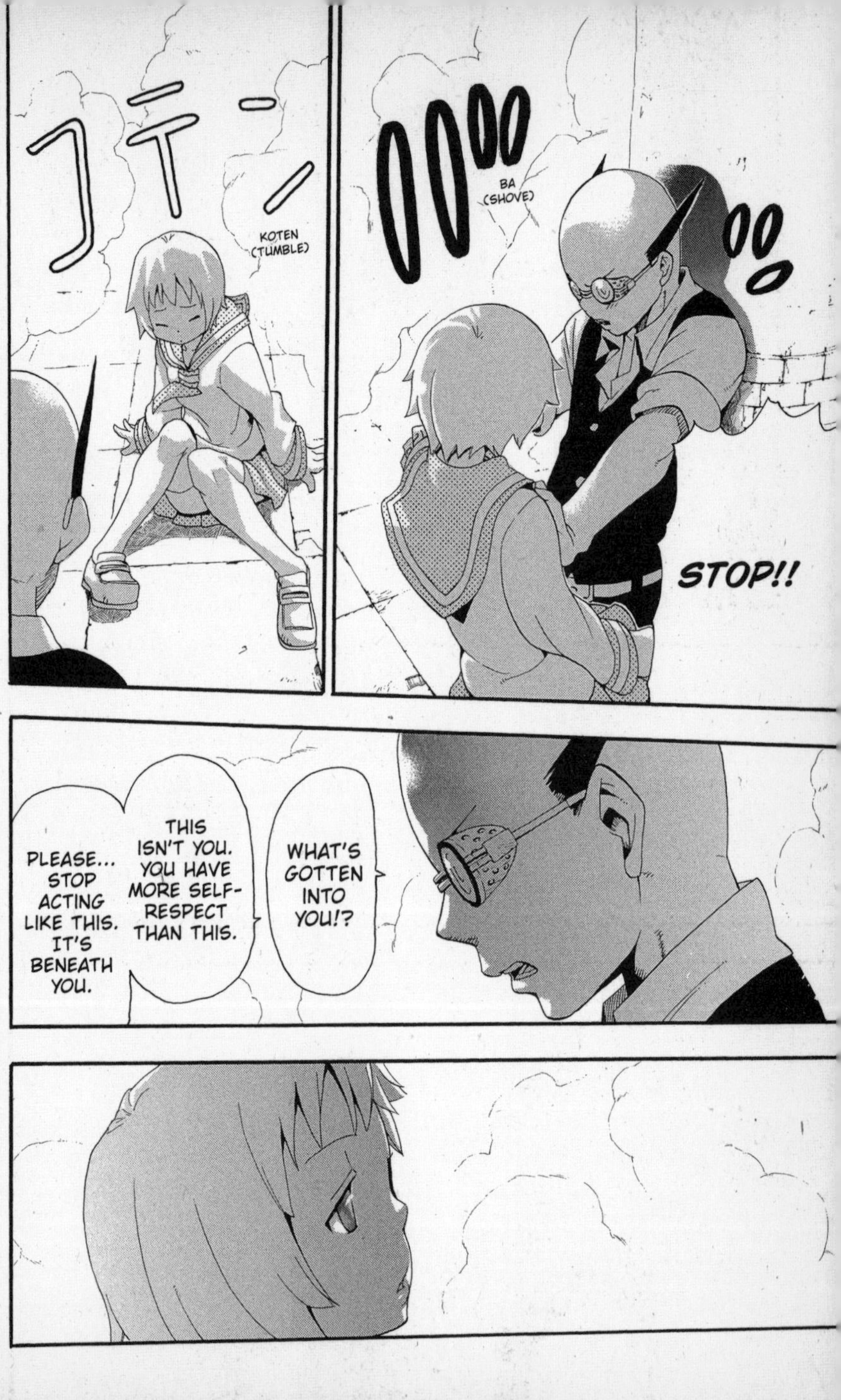
BA (SHOVE)
STOP!!
コテーン
KOTEN (TUMBLE)
WHAT'S GOTTEN INTO YOU!?
THIS ISN'T YOU. YOU HAVE MORE SELF-RESPECT THAN THIS.
PLEASE... STOP ACTING LIKE THIS. IT'S BENEATH YOU.

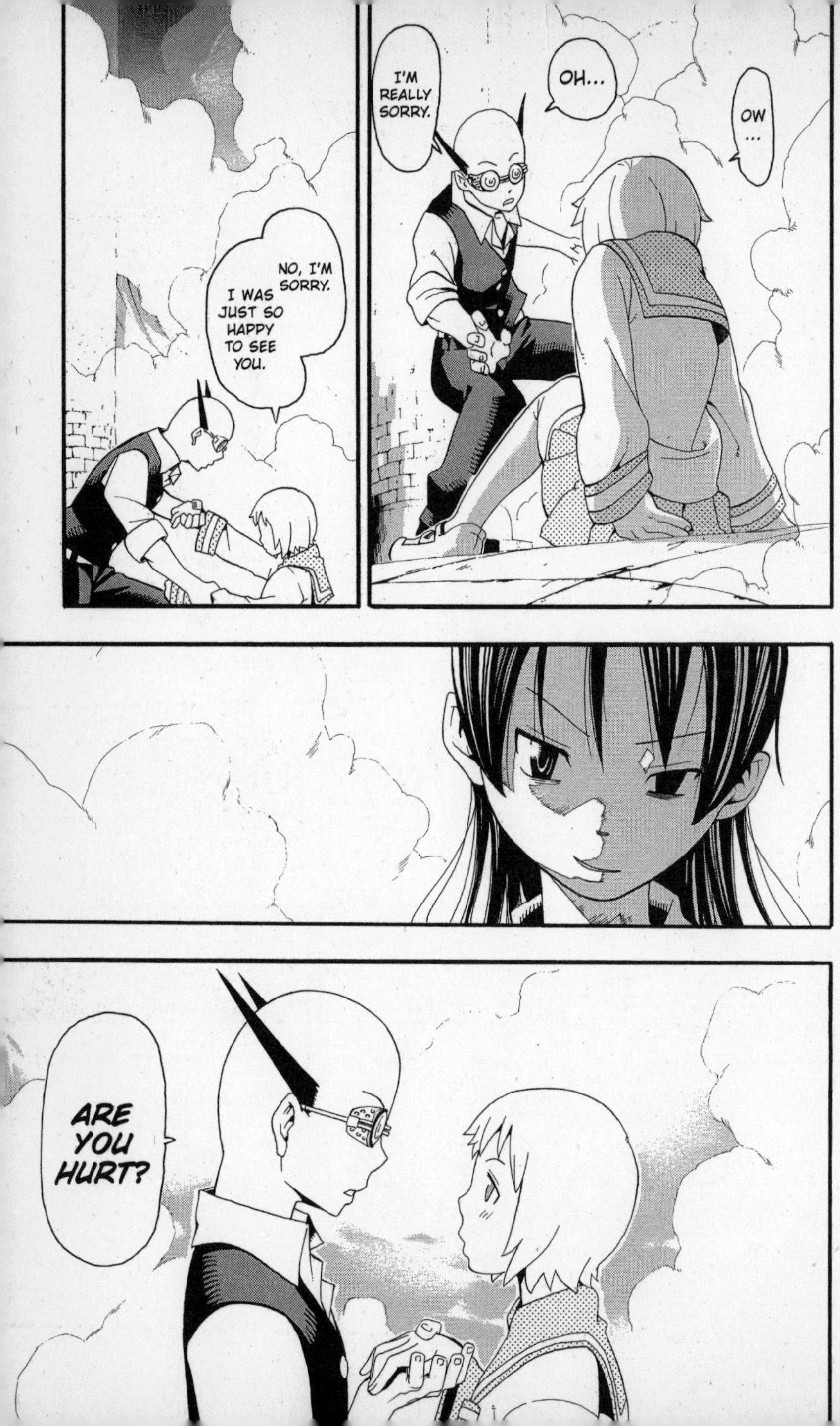
OW...
OH...
I'M REALLY SORRY.
NO, I'M SORRY. I WAS JUST SO HAPPY TO SEE YOU.
ARE YOU HURT?

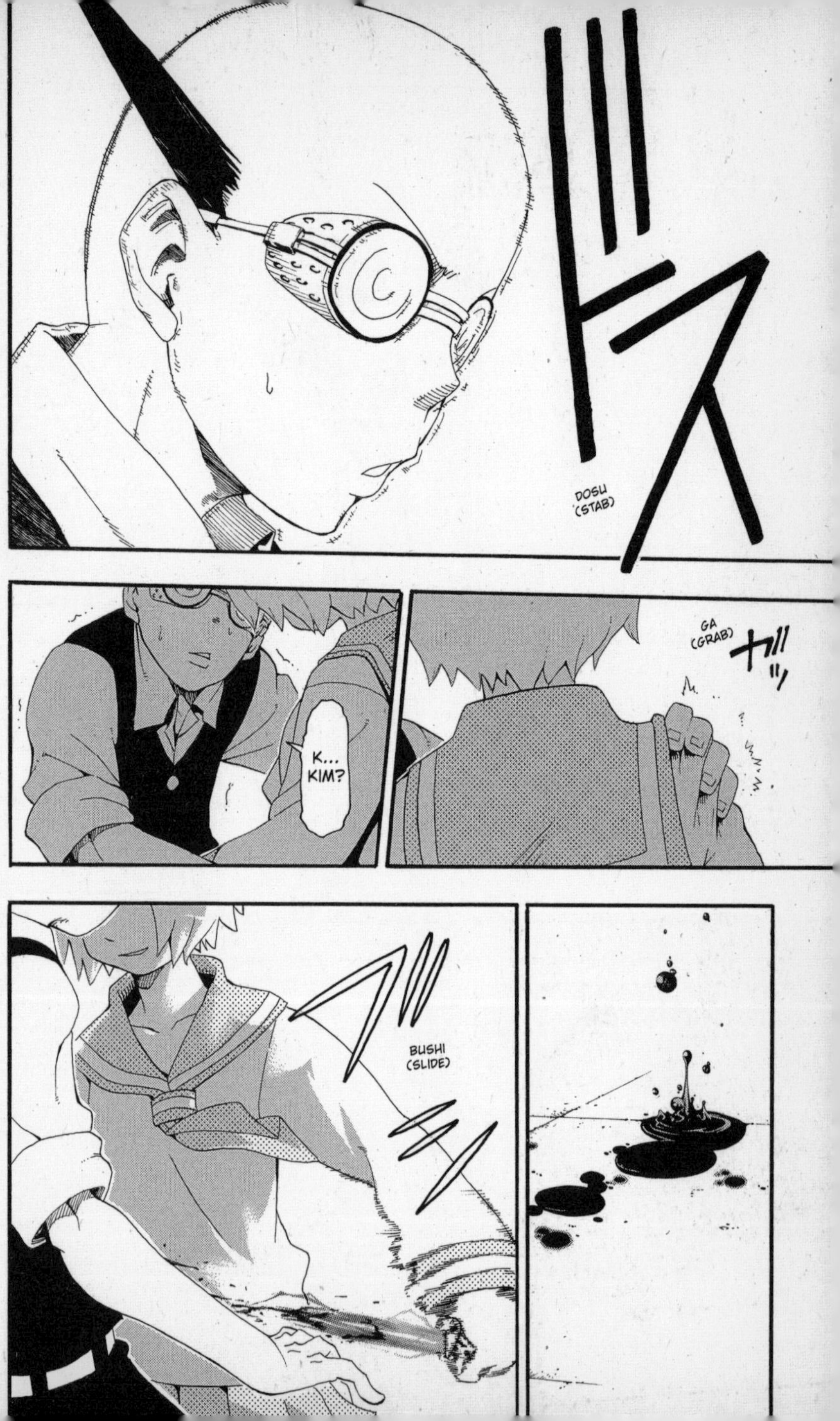
DOSU
(STAB)
GA
(GRAB)
K... KIM?
BUSHI
(SLIDE)

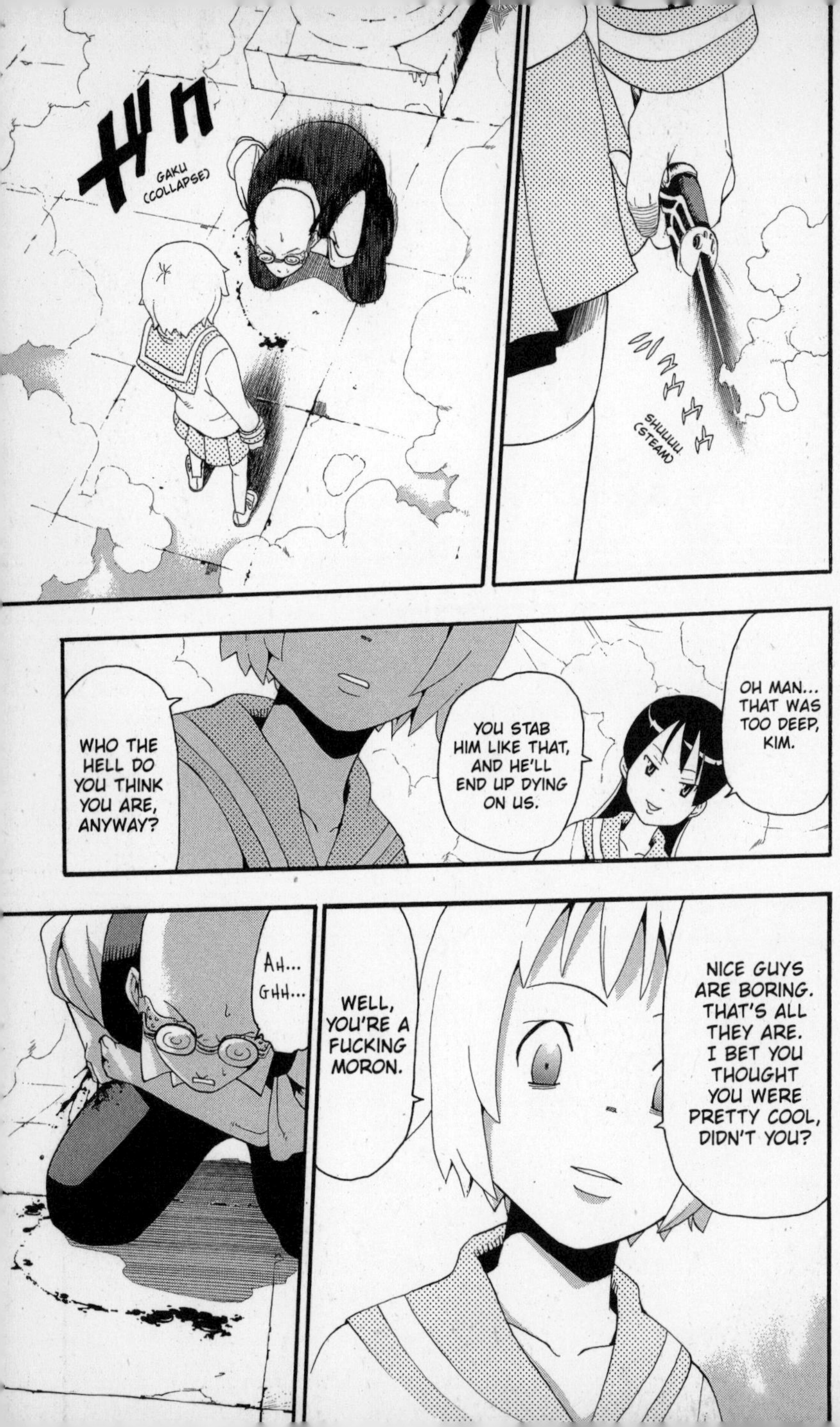
SHUUUU (STEAM)
GAKU (COLLAPSE)
OH MAN... THAT WAS TOO DEEP, KIM.
YOU STAB HIM LIKE THAT, AND HE'LL END UP DYING ON US.
WHO THE HELL DO YOU THINK YOU ARE, ANYWAY?
NICE GUYS ARE BORING. THAT'S ALL THEY ARE. I BET YOU THOUGHT YOU WERE PRETTY COOL, DIDN'T YOU?
WELL, YOU'RE A FUCKING MORON.
AH... GHH...

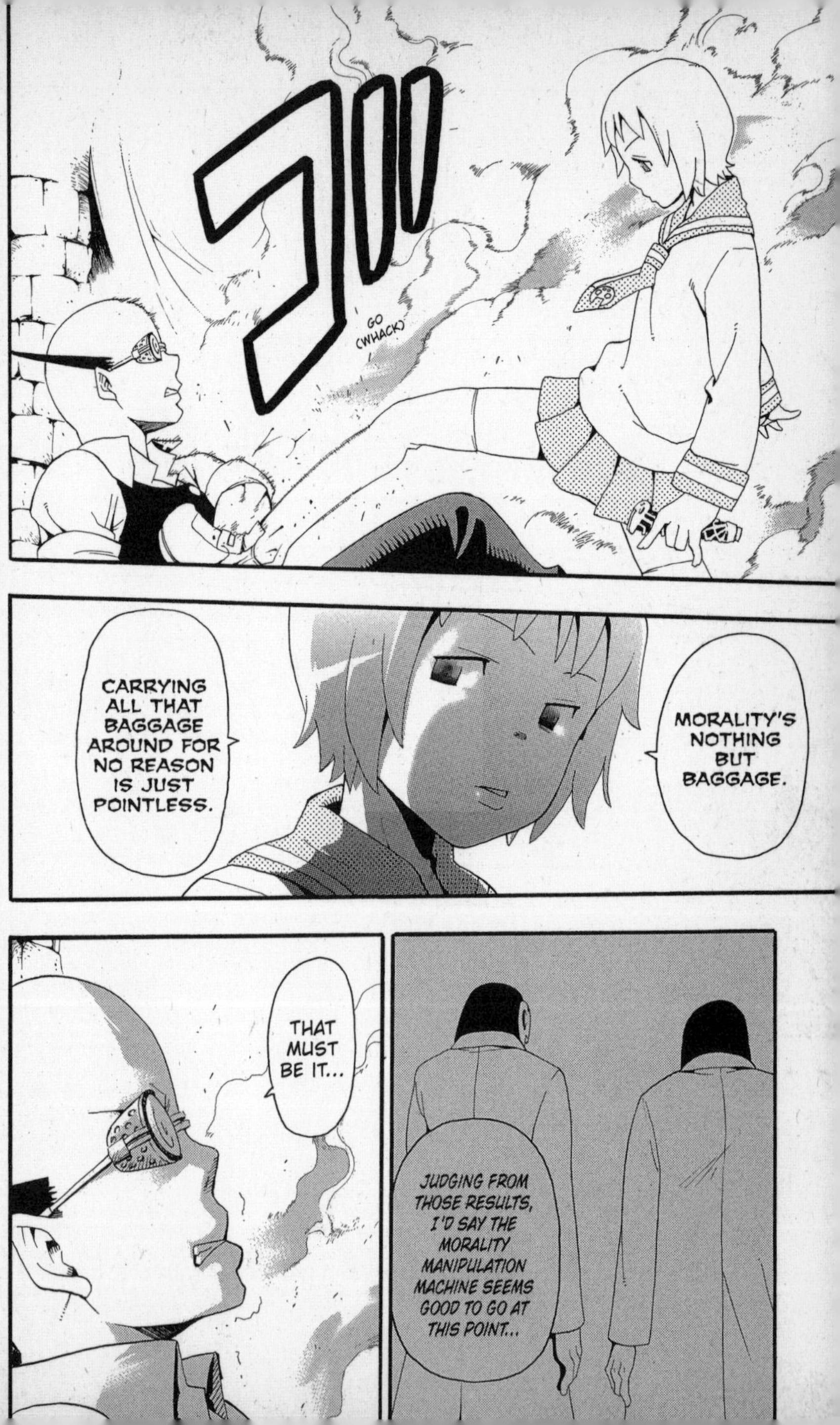
ゴッ
GO (WHACK)
MORALITY'S NOTHING BUT BAGGAGE.
CARRYING ALL THAT BAGGAGE AROUND FOR NO REASON IS JUST POINTLESS.
JUDGING FROM THOSE RESULTS, I'D SAY THE MORALITY MANIPULATION MACHINE SEEMS GOOD TO GO AT THIS POINT...
THAT MUST BE IT...

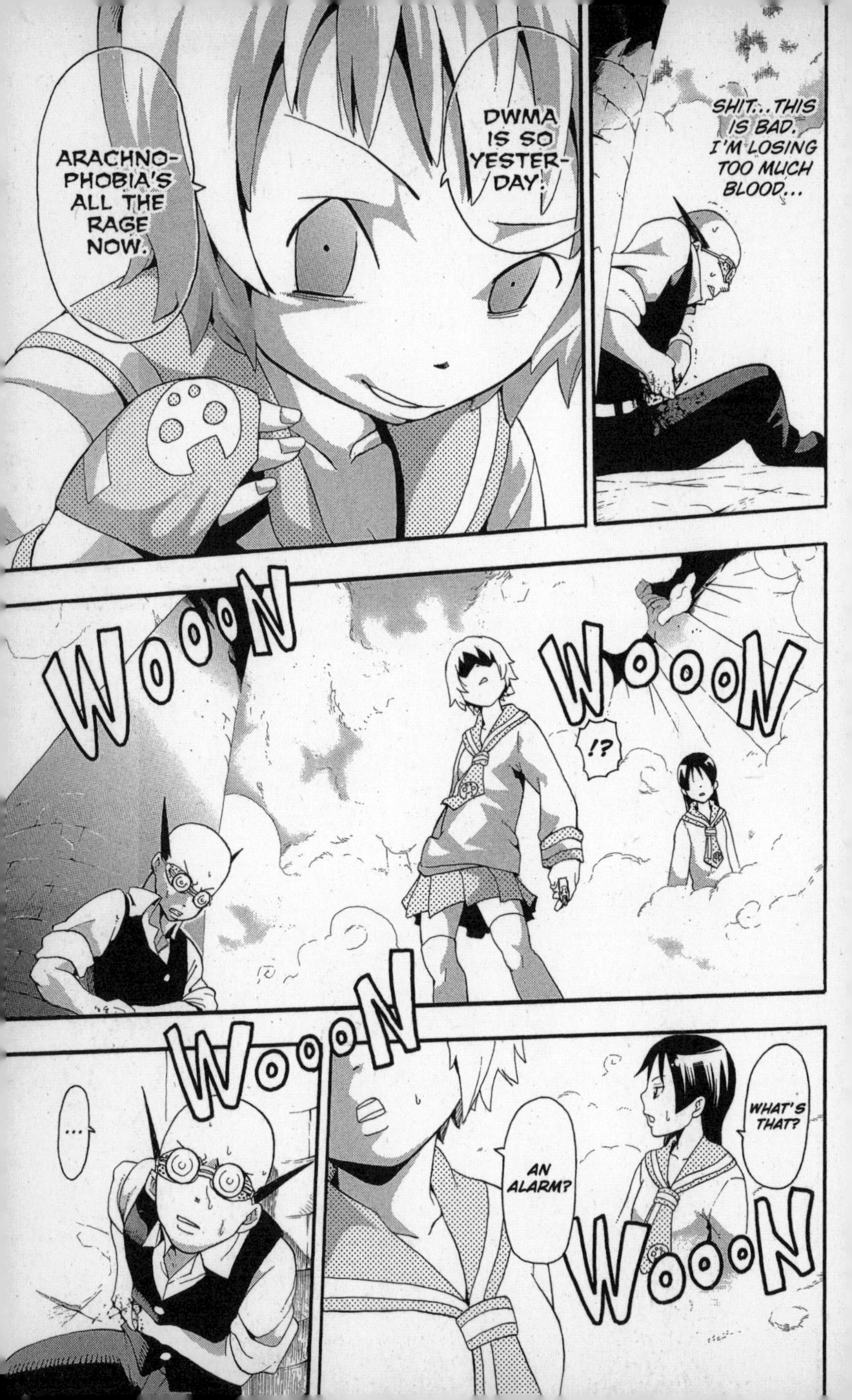

SHIT...THIS IS BAD. I'M LOSING TOO MUCH BLOOD...
DWMA IS SO YESTERDAY.
ARACHNOPHOBIA'S ALL THE RAGE NOW.
WOOON
!?
WOOON
WHAT'S THAT?
WOOON
AN ALARM?
WOOON
...

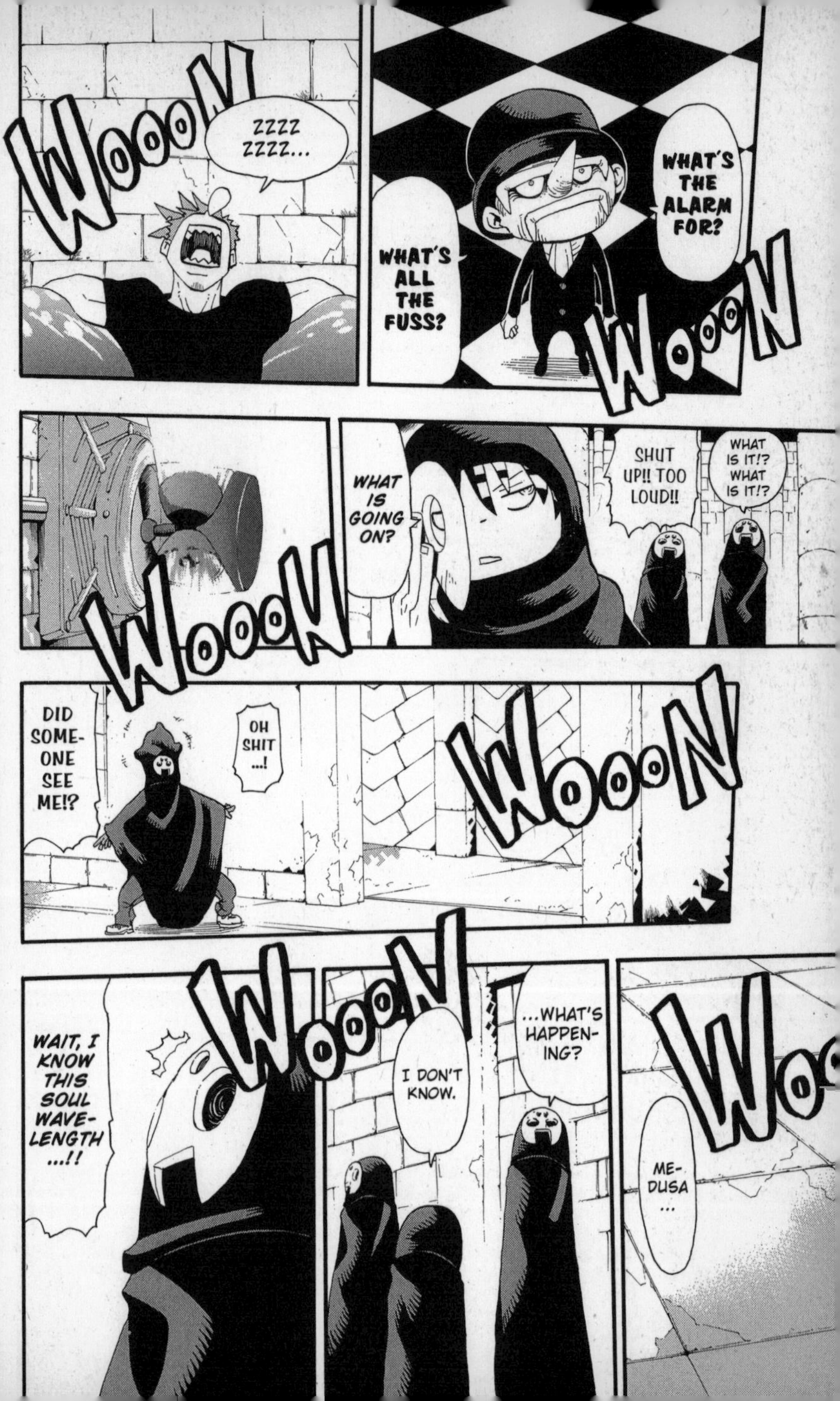
WHAT'S THE ALARM FOR?
WHAT'S ALL THE FUSS?
WOOON
WOOON
ZZZZ ZZZZ...
WHAT IS IT!? WHAT IS IT!?
SHUT UP!! TOO LOUD!!
WHAT IS GOING ON?
WOOON
WOOON
OH SHIT ...!
DID SOMEONE SEE ME!?
WOO
ME-DUSA ...
...WHAT'S HAPPENING?
I DON'T KNOW.
WOOON
WAIT, I KNOW THIS SOUL WAVELENGTH ...!!

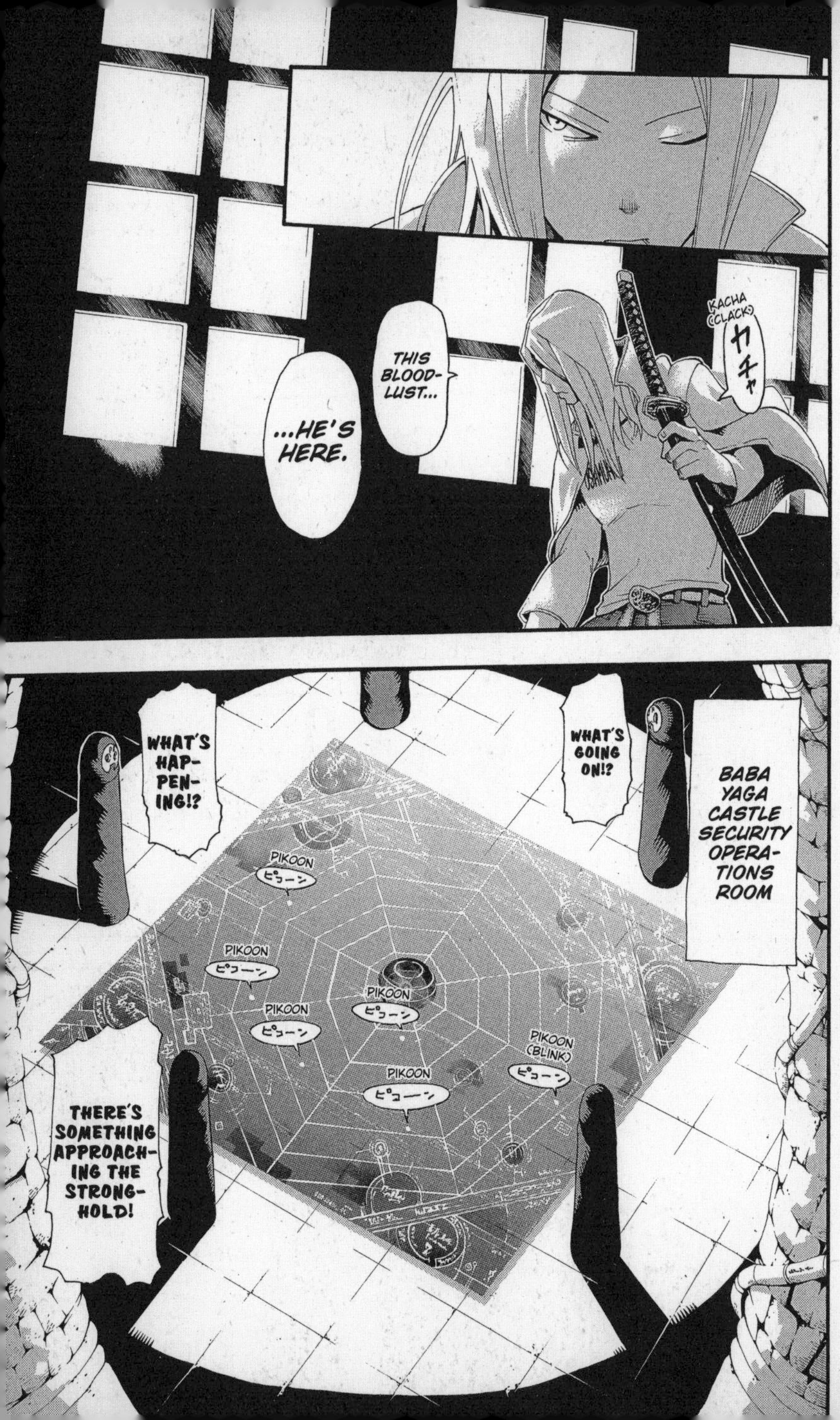
KACHA (CLACK)
カチャ
THIS BLOOD-LUST...
...HE'S HERE.
BABA YAGA CASTLE SECURITY OPERATIONS ROOM
WHAT'S GOING ON!?
WHAT'S HAPPENING!?
PIKOON (BLINK)
ピコーン
PIKOON
ピコーン
PIKOON
ピコーン
PIKOON
ピコーン
PIKOON
ピコーン
PIKOON
ピコーン
THERE'S SOMETHING APPROACHING THE STRONGHOLD!

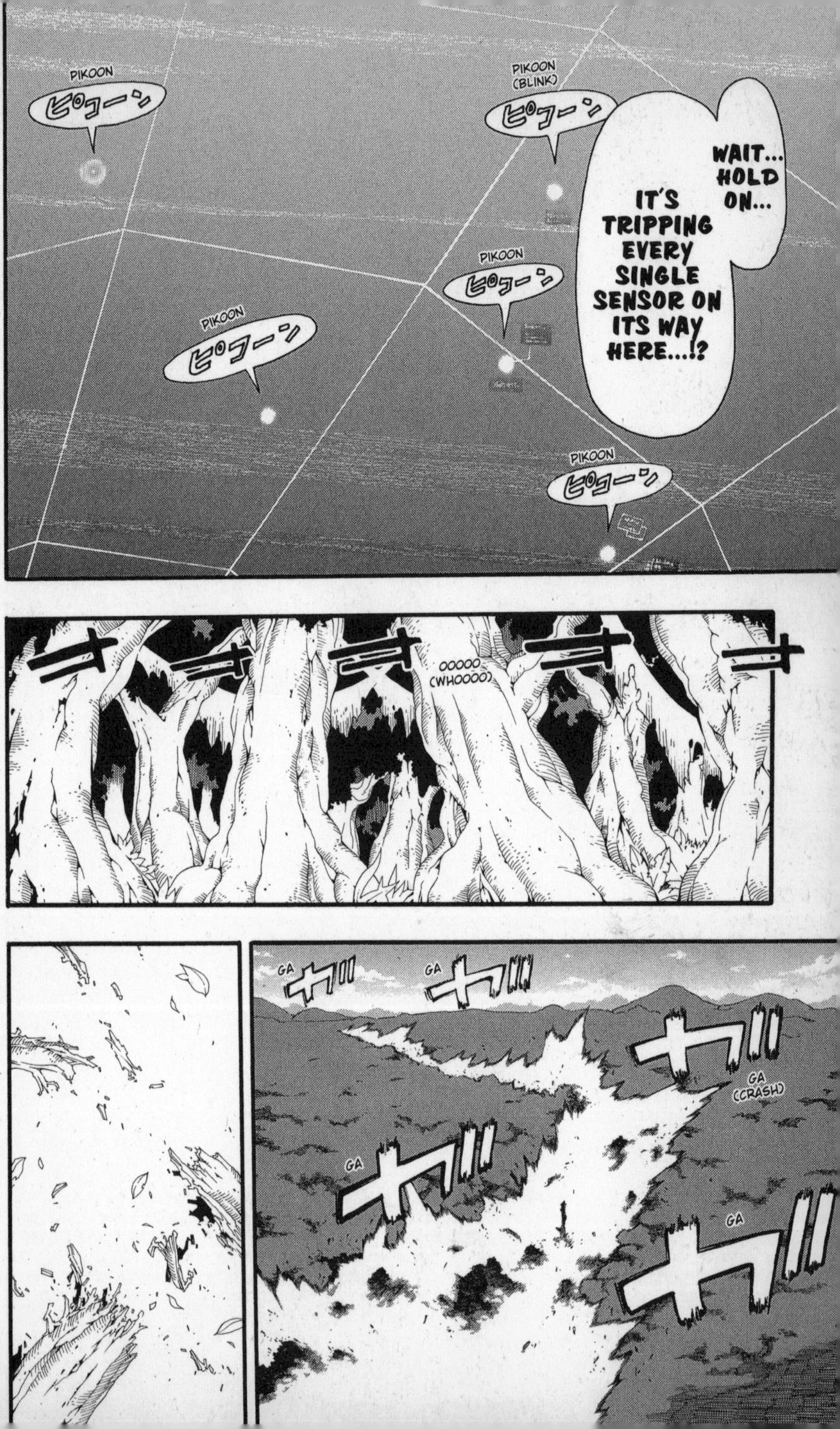

WAIT... HOLD ON...
IT'S TRIPPING EVERY SINGLE SENSOR ON ITS WAY HERE...!?
ピコーン
PIKOON (BLINK)
ピコーン
PIKOON
ピコーン
PIKOON
ピコーン
PIKOON
ピコーン
PIKOON
OOOOO (WHOOOO)
GA
GA
GA (CRASH)
GA
GA

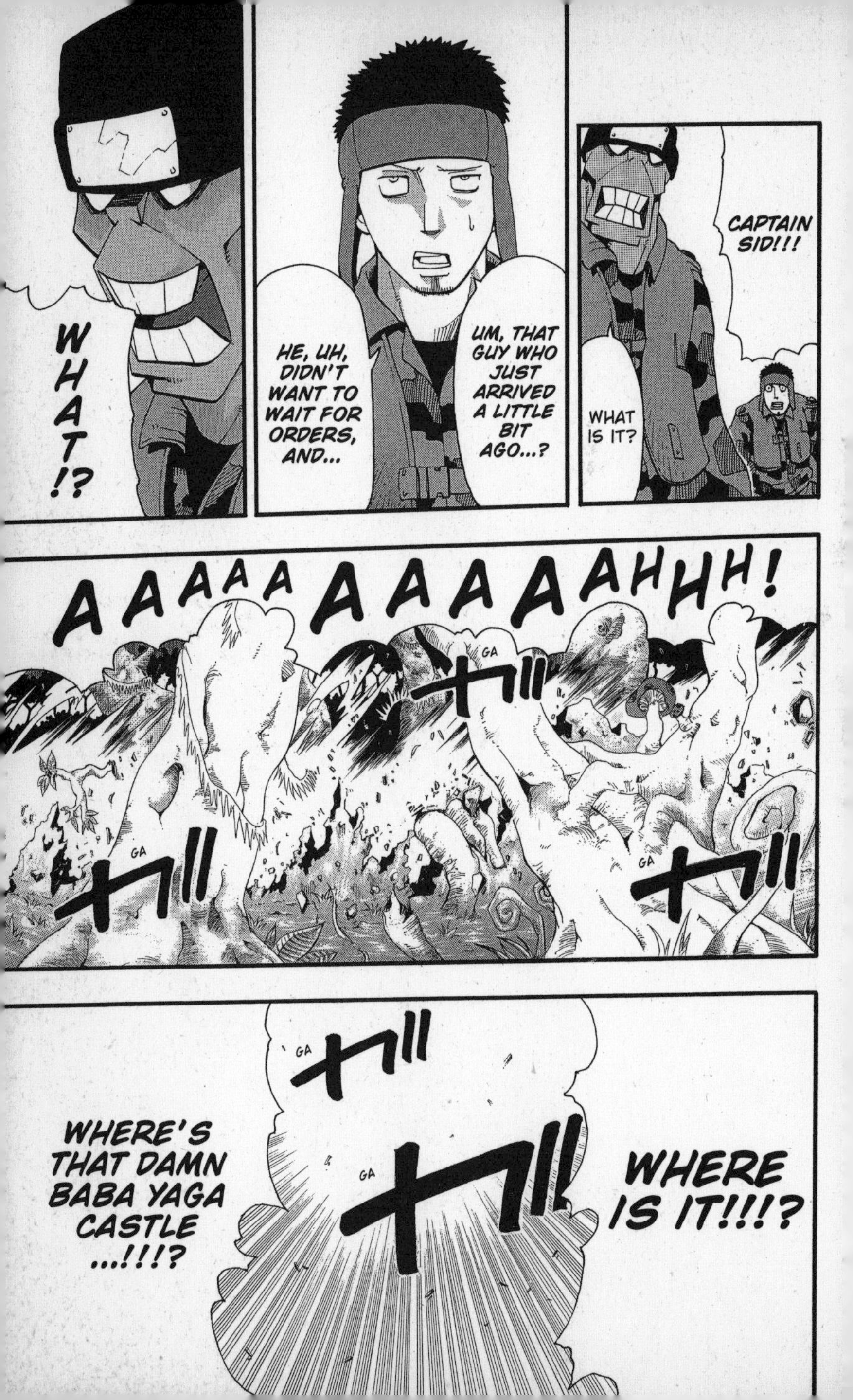
CAPTAIN SID!!!
WHAT IS IT?
UM, THAT GUY WHO JUST ARRIVED A LITTLE BIT AGO...?
HE, UH, DIDN'T WANT TO WAIT FOR ORDERS, AND...
WHAT!?
AAAAAAAAAHHH!
GA ガッ
GA ガッ
GA ガッ
GA ガッ
GA ガッ
WHERE IS IT!!!?
WHERE'S THAT DAMN BABA YAGA CASTLE ...!!!?

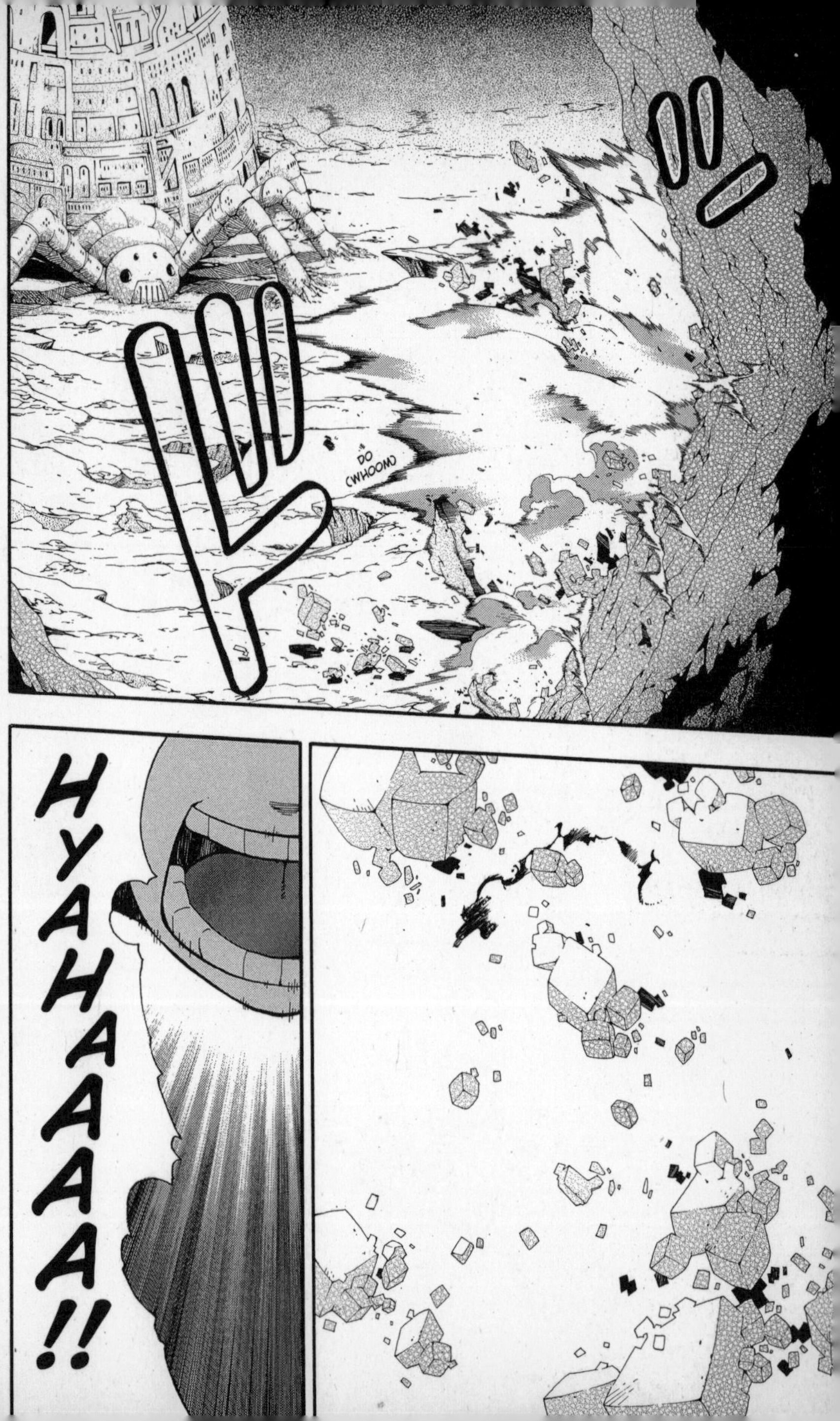
DO (WHOOM)
HYAHAAAAA!!

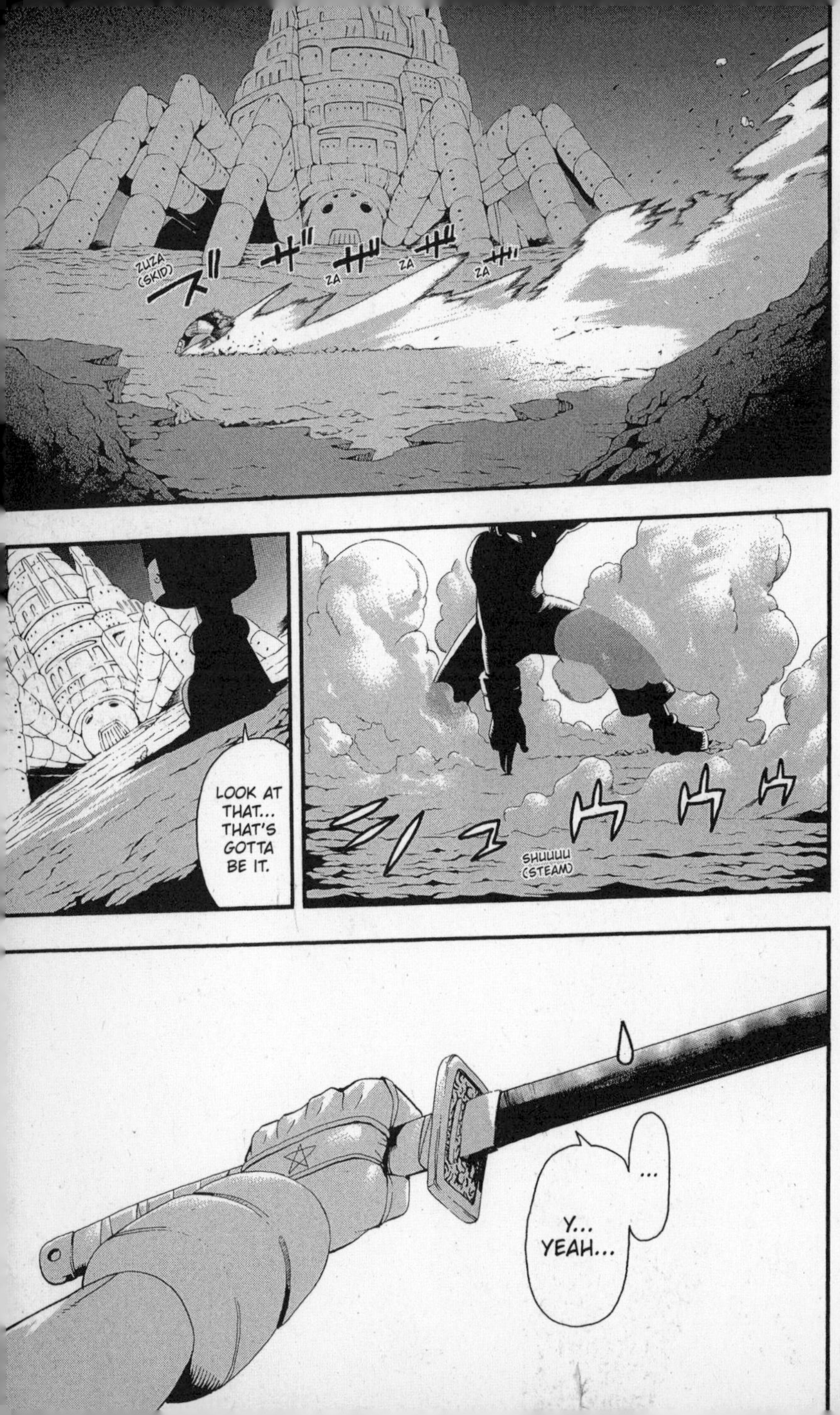
ZUZA (SKID)
ZA
ZA
ZA
SHUUUU (STEAM)
LOOK AT THAT... THAT'S GOTTA BE IT.
...
Y... YEAH...

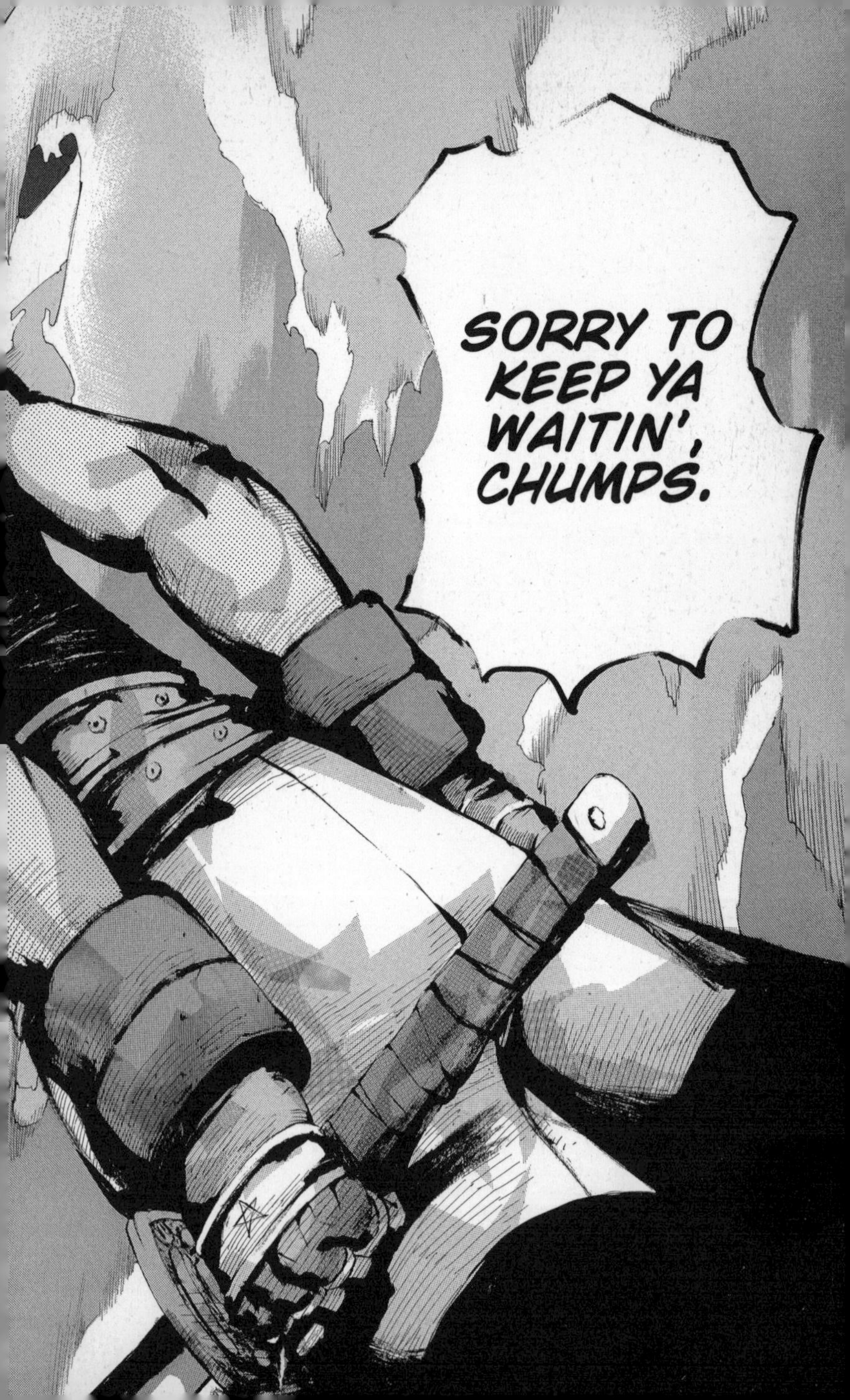
SORRY TO KEEP YA WAITIN', CHUMPS.

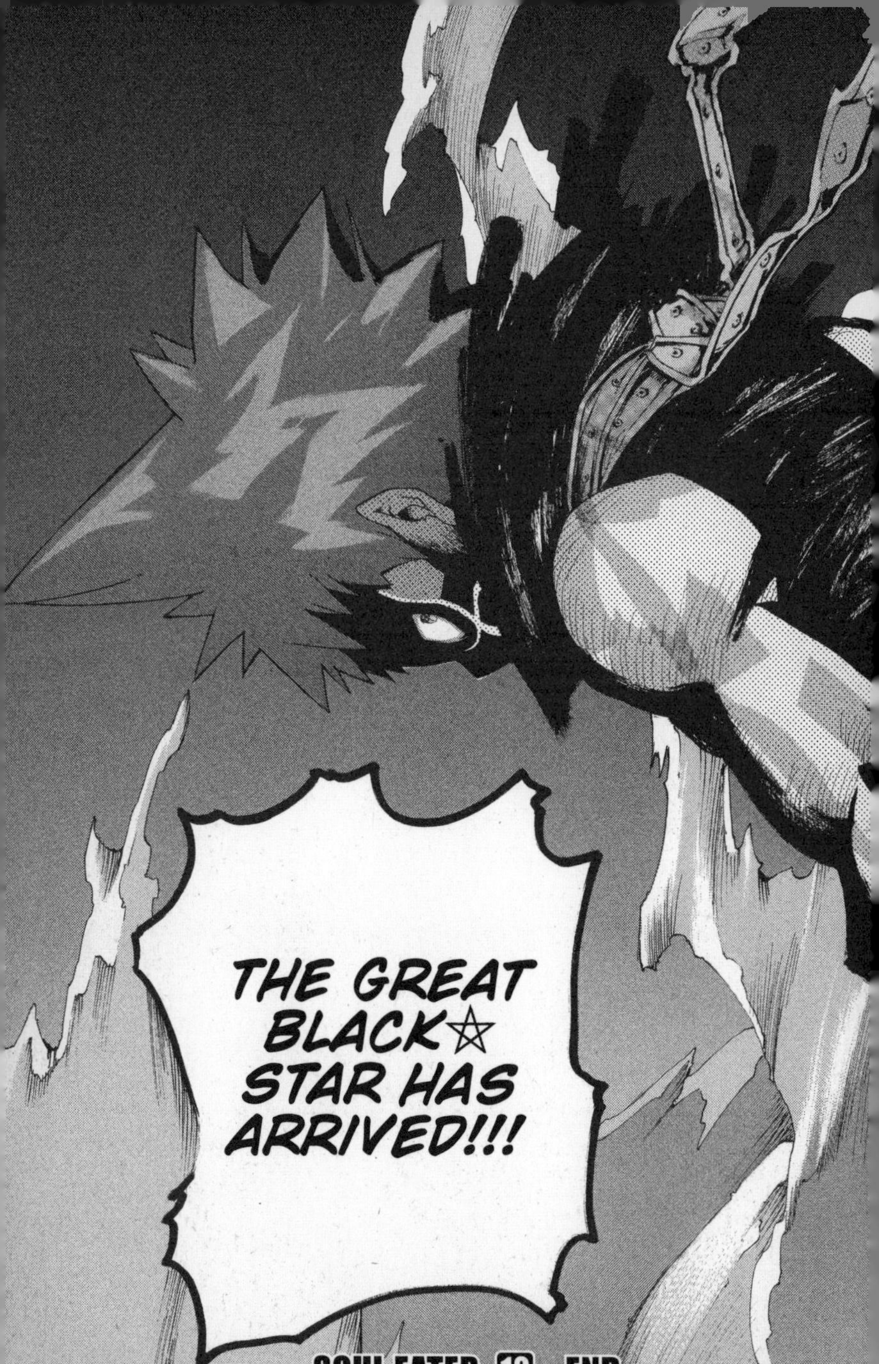
THE GREAT BLACK☆STAR HAS ARRIVED!!!

SOUL EATER 12 END

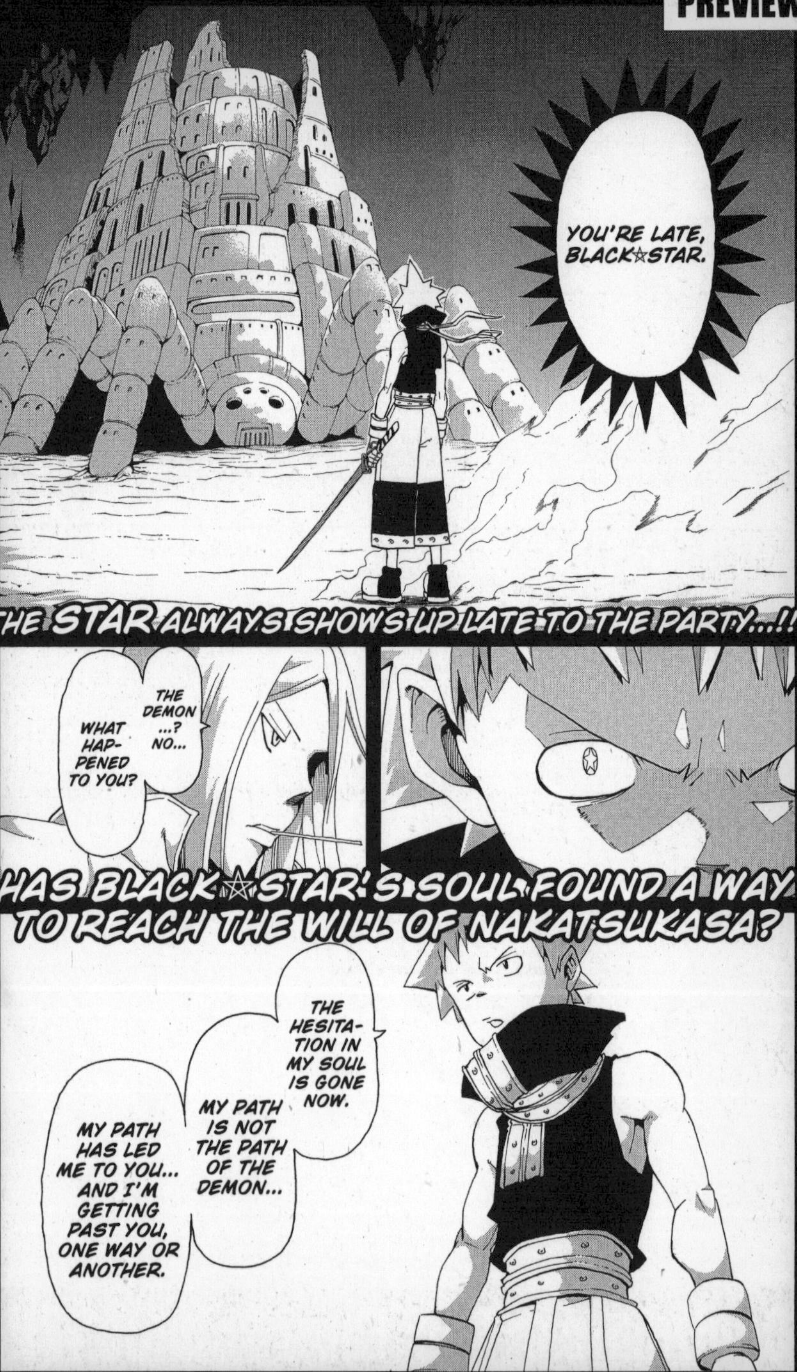
YOU'RE LATE, BLACK☆STAR.
HE STAR ALWAYS SHOWS UP LATE TO THE PARTY...!!!
THE DEMON ...? NO...
WHAT HAPPENED TO YOU?
HAS BLACK☆STAR'S SOUL FOUND A WAY TO REACH THE WILL OF NAKATSUKASA?
THE HESITATION IN MY SOUL IS GONE NOW.
MY PATH IS NOT THE PATH OF THE DEMON...
MY PATH HAS LED ME TO YOU... AND I'M GETTING PAST YOU, ONE WAY OR ANOTHER.

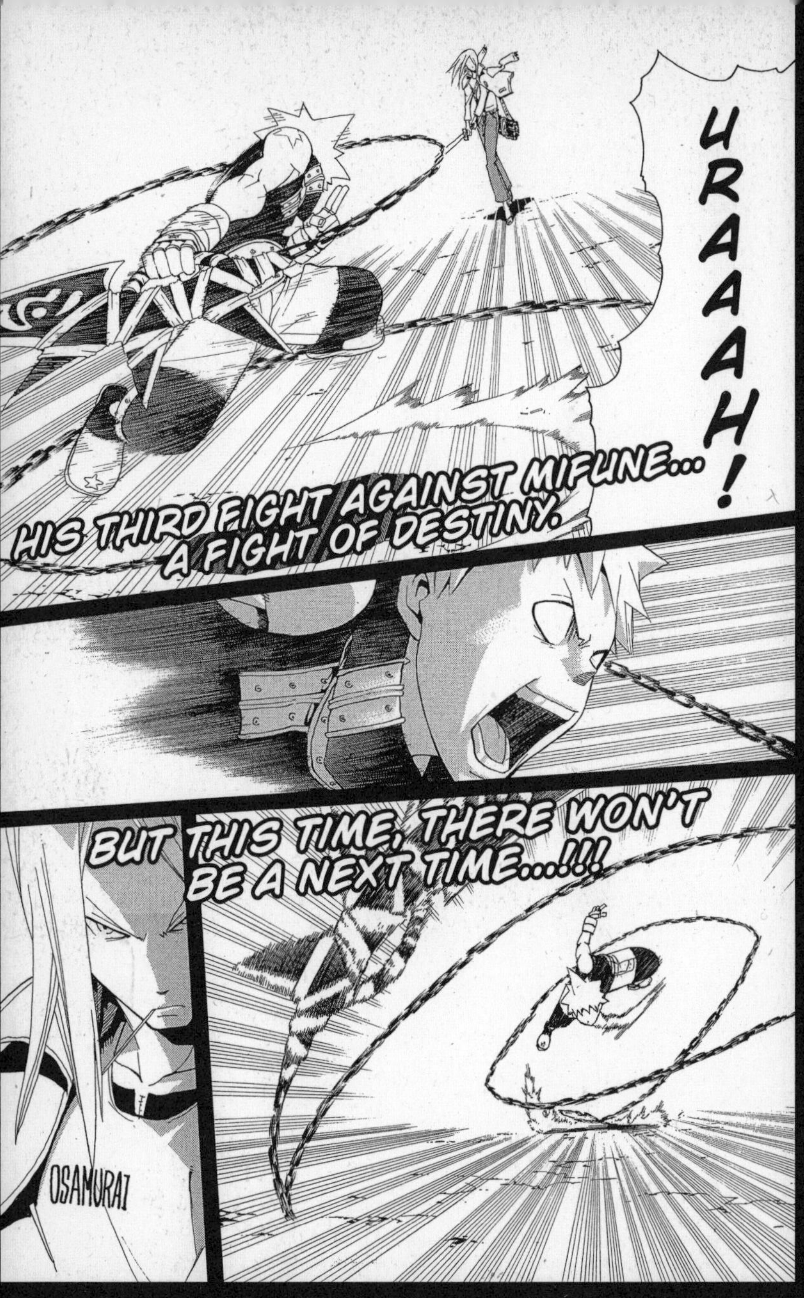
URAAAAH!
HIS THIRD FIGHT AGAINST MIFUNE... A FIGHT OF DESTINY.
BUT THIS TIME, THERE WON'T BE A NEXT TIME...!!!
OSAMURAI

Continued in Soul Eater Volume 13!!

SIGN: KAETTE KITA ATSUSHI-YA

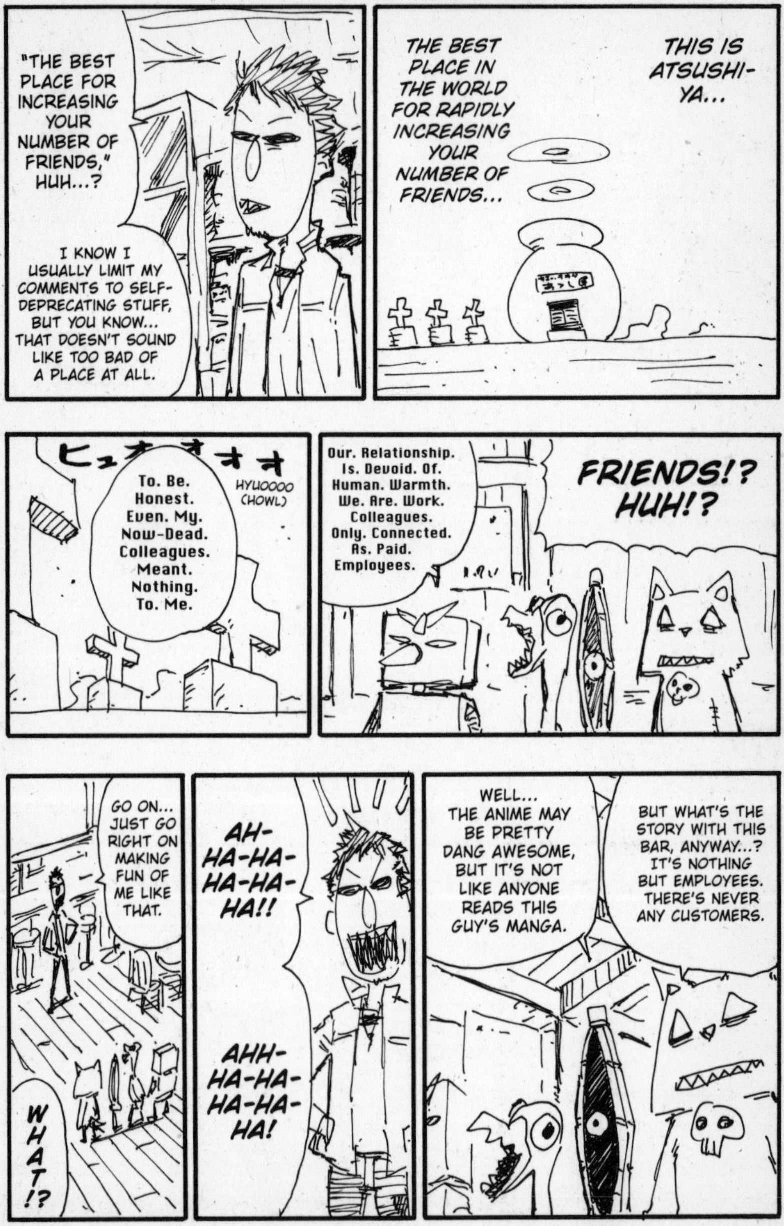
THIS IS ATSUSHI-YA...
THE BEST PLACE IN THE WORLD FOR RAPIDLY INCREASING YOUR NUMBER OF FRIENDS...
"THE BEST PLACE FOR INCREASING YOUR NUMBER OF FRIENDS," HUH...?
I KNOW I USUALLY LIMIT MY COMMENTS TO SELF-DEPRECATING STUFF, BUT YOU KNOW... THAT DOESN'T SOUND LIKE TOO BAD OF A PLACE AT ALL.
FRIENDS!? HUH!?
Our. Relationship. Is. Devoid. Of. Human. Warmth. We. Are. Work. Colleagues. Only. Connected. As. Paid. Employees.
ヒュオオオオ
HYUOOOO (HOWL)
To. Be. Honest. Even. My. Now-Dead. Colleagues. Meant. Nothing. To. Me.
BUT WHAT'S THE STORY WITH THIS BAR, ANYWAY...? IT'S NOTHING BUT EMPLOYEES. THERE'S NEVER ANY CUSTOMERS.
WELL... THE ANIME MAY BE PRETTY DANG AWESOME, BUT IT'S NOT LIKE ANYONE READS THIS GUY'S MANGA.
AH-HA-HA-HA-HA-HA!!
AHH-HA-HA-HA-HA-HA!
GO ON... JUST GO RIGHT ON MAKING FUN OF ME LIKE THAT.
WHAT!?

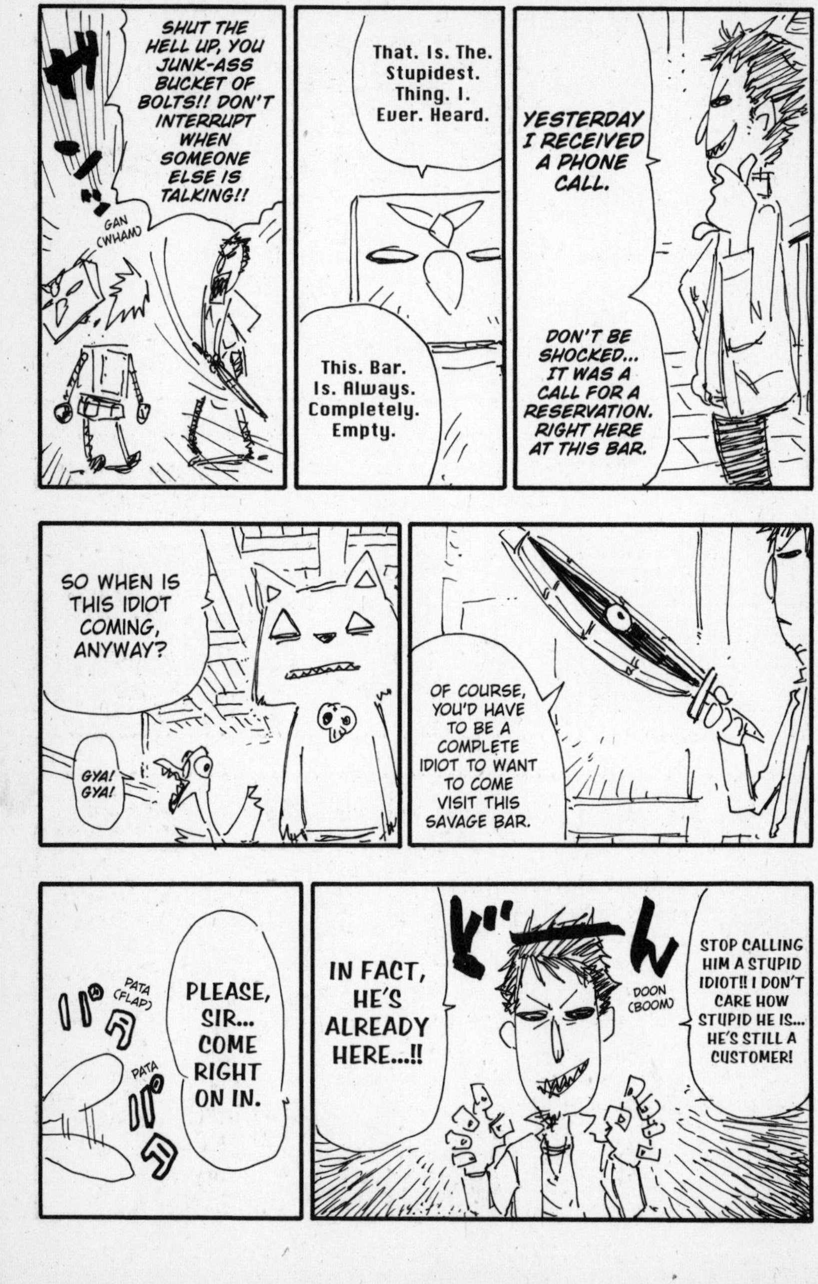
YESTERDAY I RECEIVED A PHONE CALL.
DON'T BE SHOCKED... IT WAS A CALL FOR A RESERVATION. RIGHT HERE AT THIS BAR.
That. Is. The. Stupidest. Thing. I. Ever. Heard.
This. Bar. Is. Always. Completely. Empty.
SHUT THE HELL UP, YOU JUNK-ASS BUCKET OF BOLTS!! DON'T INTERRUPT WHEN SOMEONE ELSE IS TALKING!!
GAN (WHAM)
OF COURSE, YOU'D HAVE TO BE A COMPLETE IDIOT TO WANT TO COME VISIT THIS SAVAGE BAR.
SO WHEN IS THIS IDIOT COMING, ANYWAY?
GYA! GYA!
STOP CALLING HIM A STUPID IDIOT!! I DON'T CARE HOW STUPID HE IS... HE'S STILL A CUSTOMER!
どーん
DOON (BOOM)
IN FACT, HE'S ALREADY HERE...!!
PLEASE, SIR... COME RIGHT ON IN.
PATA (FLAP)
PATA

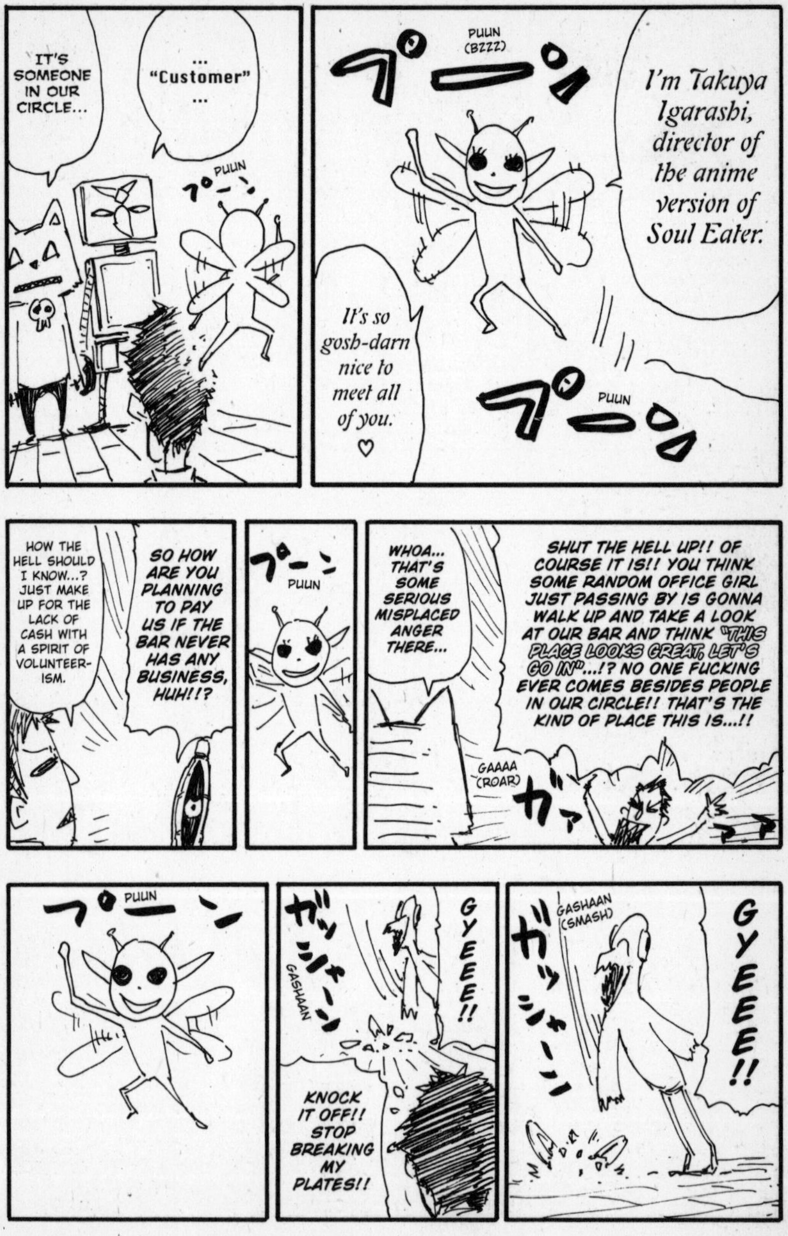
PUUN (BZZZ)
I'm Takuya Igarashi, director of the anime version of Soul Eater.
It's so gosh-darn nice to meet all of you. ♡
PUUN
... "Customer" ...
IT'S SOMEONE IN OUR CIRCLE...
PUUN
SHUT THE HELL UP!! OF COURSE IT IS!! YOU THINK SOME RANDOM OFFICE GIRL JUST PASSING BY IS GONNA WALK UP AND TAKE A LOOK AT OUR BAR AND THINK "THIS PLACE LOOKS GREAT, LET'S GO IN"...!? NO ONE FUCKING EVER COMES BESIDES PEOPLE IN OUR CIRCLE!! THAT'S THE KIND OF PLACE THIS IS...!!
WHOA... THAT'S SOME SERIOUS MISPLACED ANGER THERE...
GAAAA (ROAR)
PUUN
SO HOW ARE YOU PLANNING TO PAY US IF THE BAR NEVER HAS ANY BUSINESS, HUH!!?
HOW THE HELL SHOULD I KNOW...? JUST MAKE UP FOR THE LACK OF CASH WITH A SPIRIT OF VOLUNTEER-ISM.
GYEEEE!!
GASHAAN (SMASH)
GYEEE!!
GASHAAN
KNOCK IT OFF!! STOP BREAKING MY PLATES!!
PUUN

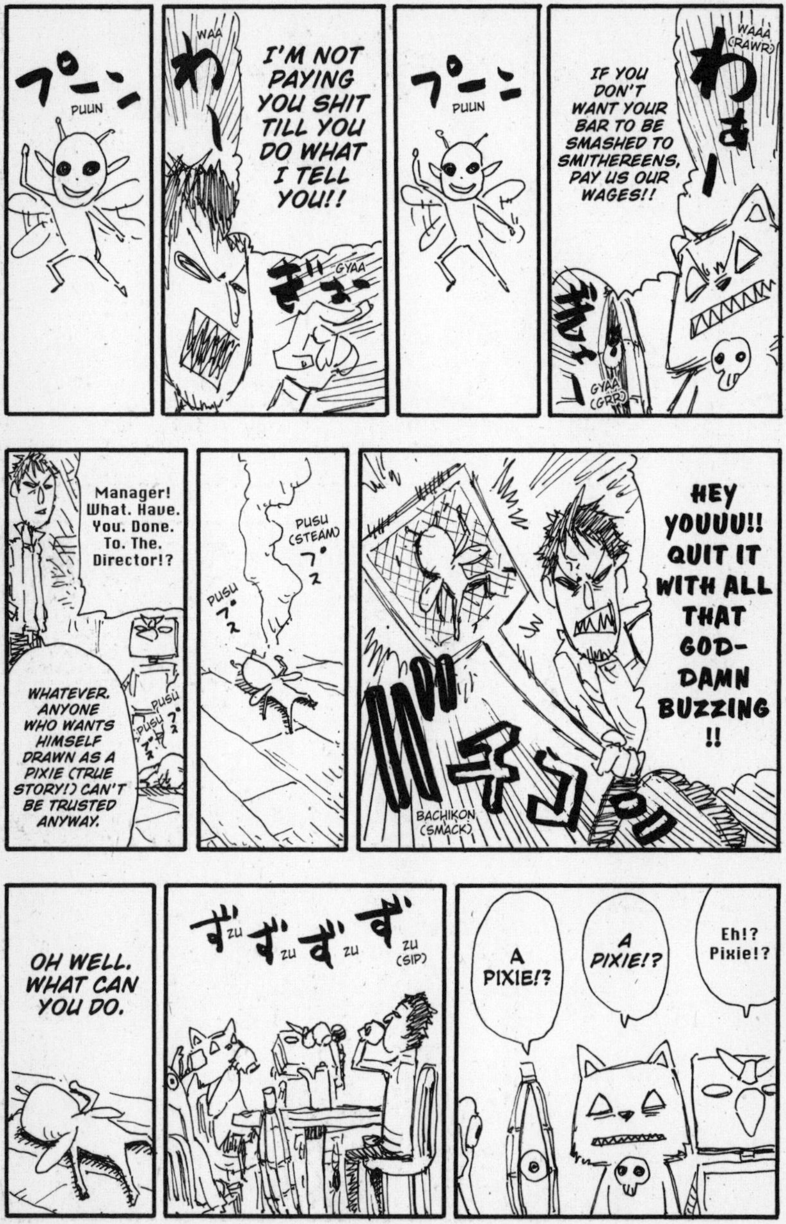
WAAA (RAWR)
IF YOU DON'T WANT YOUR BAR TO BE SMASHED TO SMITHEREENS, PAY US OUR WAGES!!
GYAA (GRR)
プーン
PUUN
WAA
I'M NOT PAYING YOU SHIT TILL YOU DO WHAT I TELL YOU!!
GYAA
プーン
PUUN
HEY YOUUU!! QUIT IT WITH ALL THAT GOD-DAMN BUZZING!!
BACHIKON (SMACK)
PUSU (STEAM)
PUSU
Manager! What. Have. You. Done. To. The. Director!?
PUSU
PUSU
WHATEVER. ANYONE WHO WANTS HIMSELF DRAWN AS A PIXIE (TRUE STORY!) CAN'T BE TRUSTED ANYWAY.
Eh!? Pixie!?
A PIXIE!?
A PIXIE!?
ZU ZU ZU ZU (SIP)
OH WELL. WHAT CAN YOU DO.

TAKATOSHI SHIOZAWA

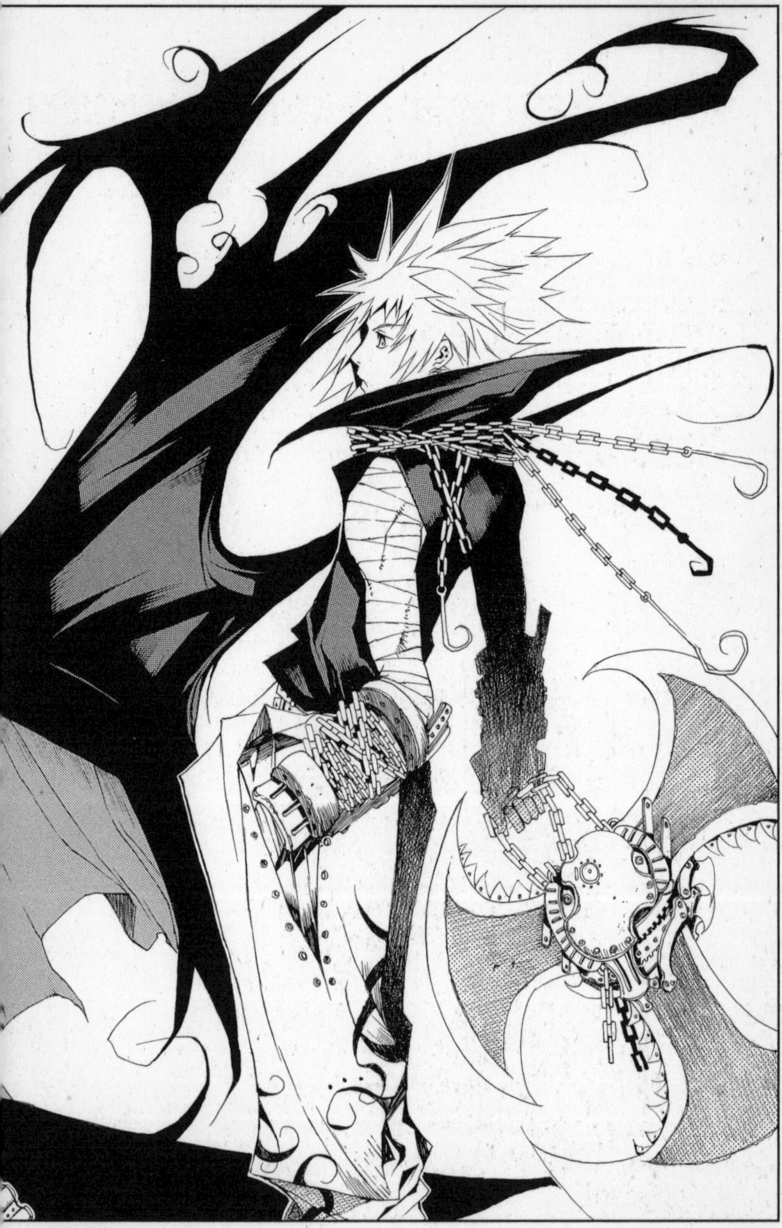

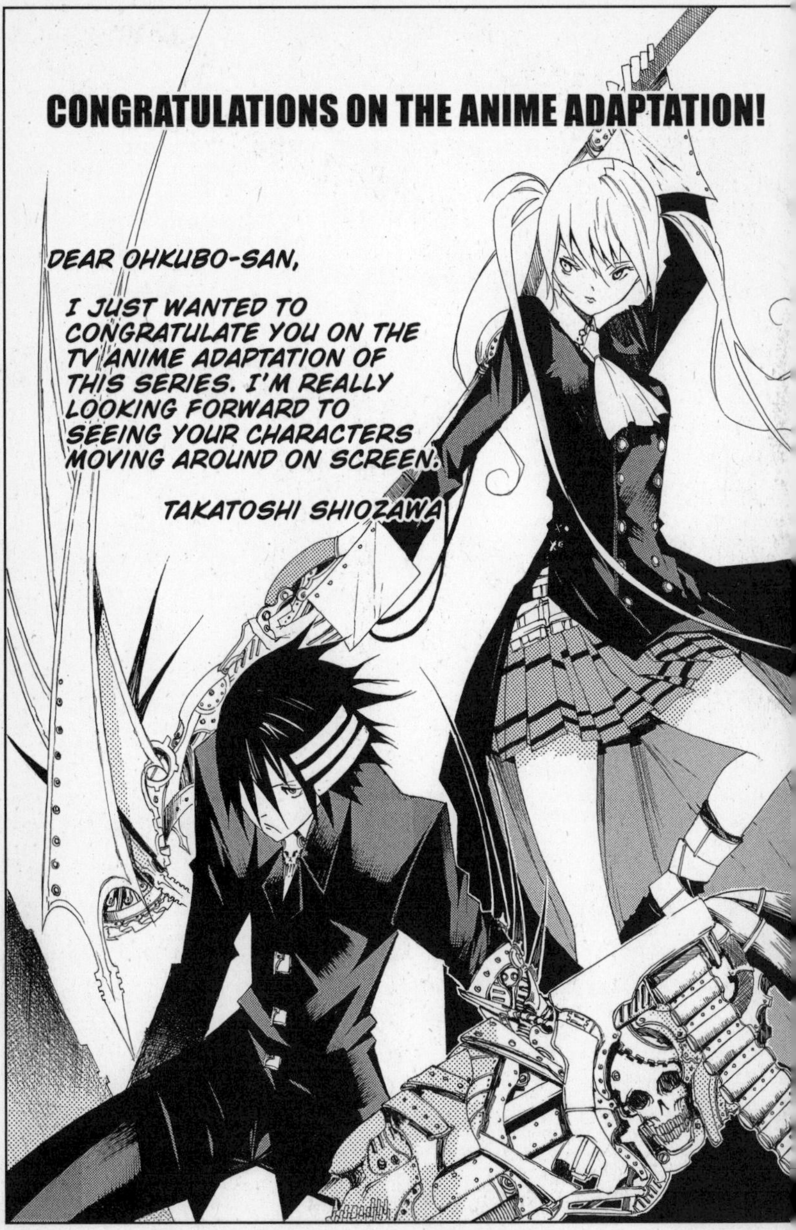
CONGRATULATIONS ON THE ANIME ADAPTATION!
DEAR OHKUBO-SAN,
I JUST WANTED TO CONGRATULATE YOU ON THE TV ANIME ADAPTATION OF THIS SERIES. I'M REALLY LOOKING FORWARD TO SEEING YOUR CHARACTERS MOVING AROUND ON SCREEN.
TAKATOSHI SHIOZAWA

YOSHIKI TONOGAI

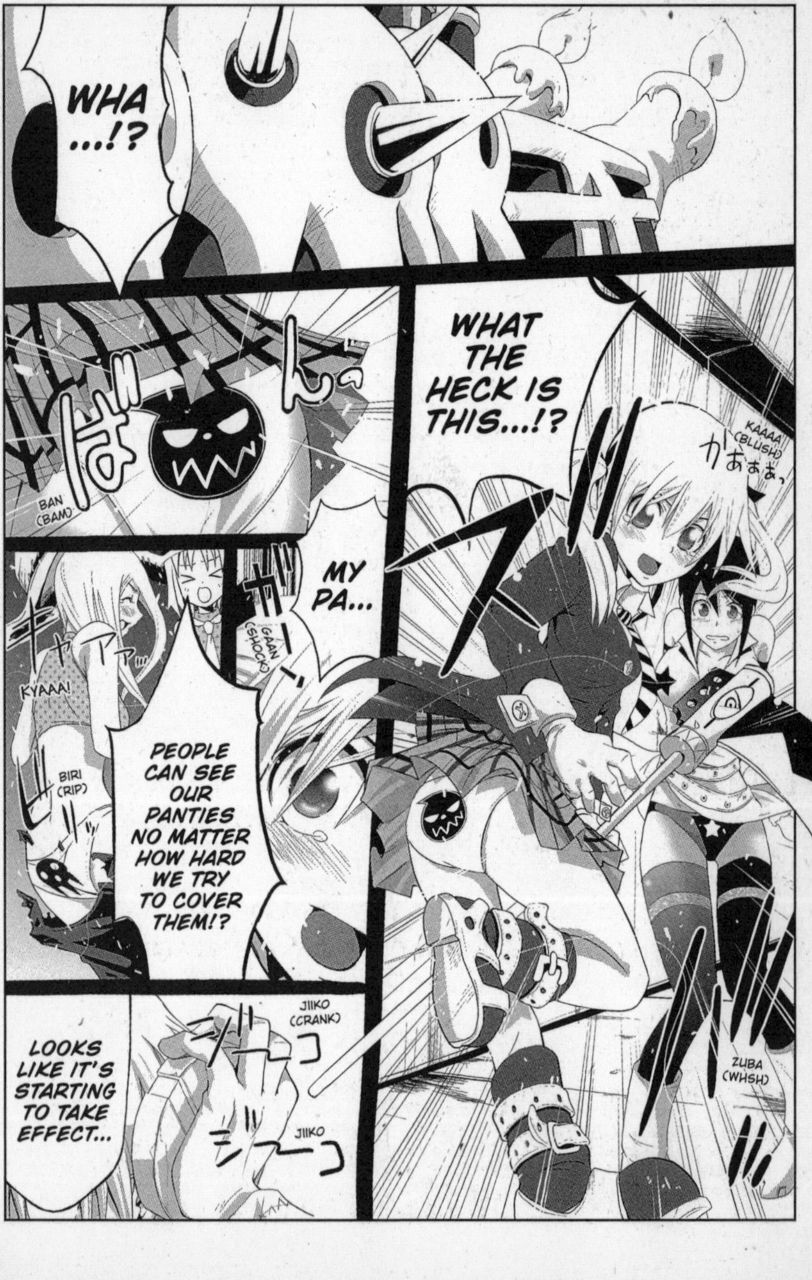
WHA ...!?
WHAT THE HECK IS THIS...!?
KAAAA (BLUSH)
ZUBA (WHSH)
BAN (BAM)
MY PA...
GAAN (SHOCK)
PEOPLE CAN SEE OUR PANTIES NO MATTER HOW HARD WE TRY TO COVER THEM!?
KYAAA!
BIRI (RIP)
JIIKO (CRANK)
LOOKS LIKE IT'S STARTING TO TAKE EFFECT...
JIIKO

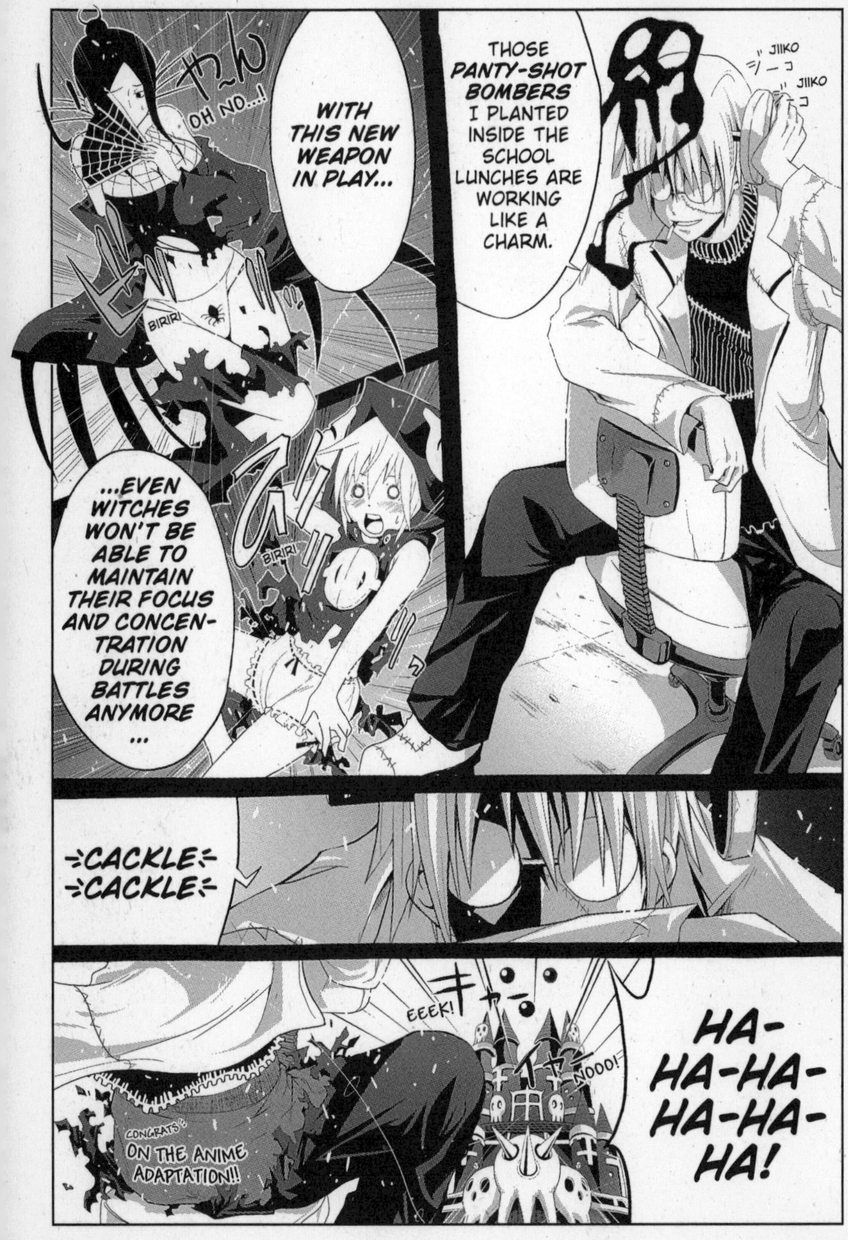
JIIKO
JIIKO
THOSE PANTY-SHOT BOMBERS I PLANTED INSIDE THE SCHOOL LUNCHES ARE WORKING LIKE A CHARM.
OH NO...!
BIRIRI
WITH THIS NEW WEAPON IN PLAY...
...EVEN WITCHES WON'T BE ABLE TO MAINTAIN THEIR FOCUS AND CONCENTRATION DURING BATTLES ANYMORE...
BIRIRI
CACKLE
CACKLE
HA-HA-HA-HA-HA-HA-HA!
EEEK!
NOOO!
CONGRATS ON THE ANIME ADAPTATION!!

TOMOYUKI MARU

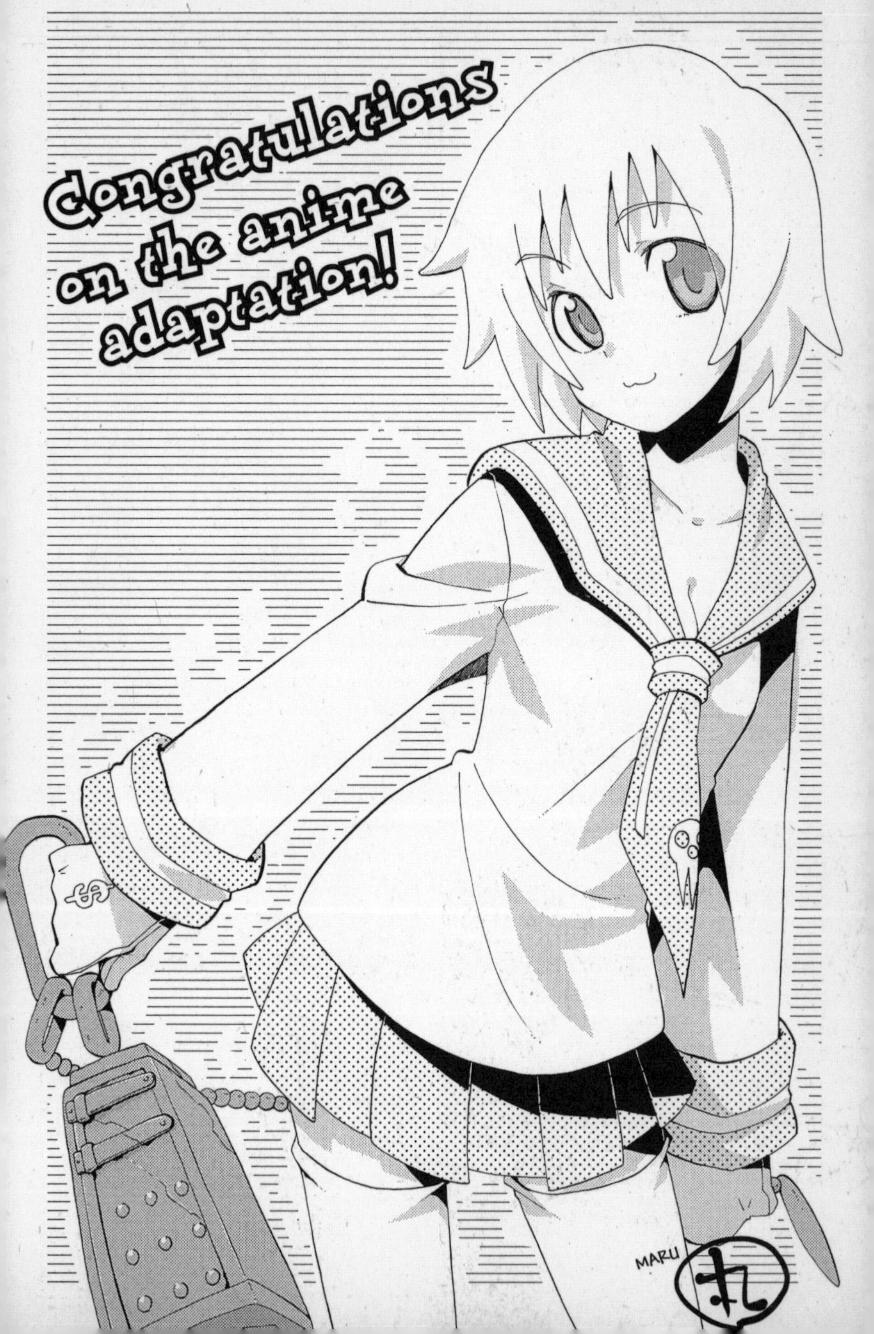
Congratulations on the anime adaptation!
MARU

CRAB: MARU

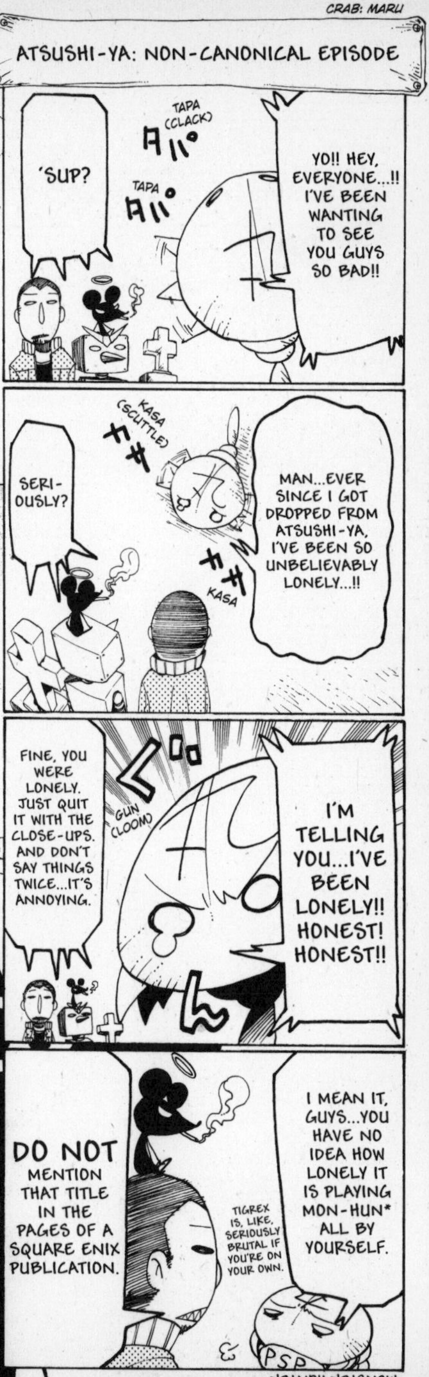
ATSUSHI-YA: NON-CANONICAL EPISODE
YO!! HEY, EVERYONE...!! I'VE BEEN WANTING TO SEE YOU GUYS SO BAD!!
TAPA (CLACK)
TAPA
'SUP?
MAN...EVER SINCE I GOT DROPPED FROM ATSUSHI-YA, I'VE BEEN SO UNBELIEVABLY LONELY...!!
KASA (SCUTTLE)
KASA
SERI-OUSLY?
I'M TELLING YOU...I'VE BEEN LONELY!! HONEST! HONEST!!
GUN (LOOM)
FINE, YOU WERE LONELY. JUST QUIT IT WITH THE CLOSE-UPS. AND DON'T SAY THINGS TWICE...IT'S ANNOYING.
I MEAN IT, GUYS...YOU HAVE NO IDEA HOW LONELY IT IS PLAYING MON-HUN* ALL BY YOURSELF.
TIGREX IS, LIKE, SERIOUSLY BRUTAL IF YOU'RE ON YOUR OWN.
DO NOT MENTION THAT TITLE IN THE PAGES OF A SQUARE ENIX PUBLICATION.
PSP

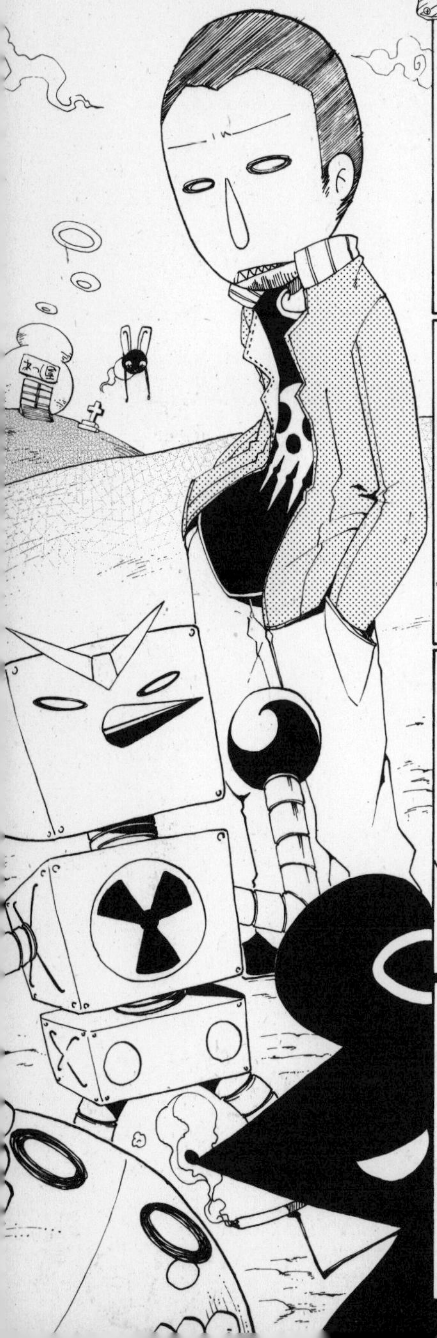

*MONSTER HUNTER

Translation Notes

Common Honorifics

no honorific: Indicates familiarity or closeness; if used without permission or reason, addressing someone in this manner would constitute an insult.

-san: The Japanese equivalent of Mr./Mrs./Miss. If a situation calls for politeness, this is the fail-safe honorific.

-sama: Conveys great respect; may also indicate that the social status of the speaker is lower than that of the addressee.

-kun: Used most often when referring to boys, this indicates affection or familiarity. Occasionally used by older men among their peers, but it may also be used by anyone referring to a person of lower standing.

-chan: An affectionate honorific indicating familiarity used mostly in reference to girls; also used in reference to cute persons or animals of either gender.

-senpai: A suffix used to address upperclassmen or more experienced coworkers.

-sensei: A respectful term for teachers, artists, or high-level professionals.

Page 41
When Shinigami-sama refers to the comedy technique of **repeating a joke**, he uses comedy lingo, referring to the gag as a *tendon*, which means repeating a comedy bit word-for-word for extra comedic effect. The name literally means "tempura (shrimp) over rice" but acquired this special meaning because it's typical to get two tempura shrimp in a single serving.

Page 123
Chin is a sound effect used for a ding or a ring, but in this case the sound word was chosen specifically to bring to mind the word *chin chin*, Japanese slang for "penis."

DING-DONG!
DEAD-DONG!

DON'T BE LATE FOR THE "NOT" CLASS AT DEATH WEAPON MEISTER ACADEMY!

OLDER TEEN
OT

SOUL EATER NOT!

ATSUSHI OHKUBO

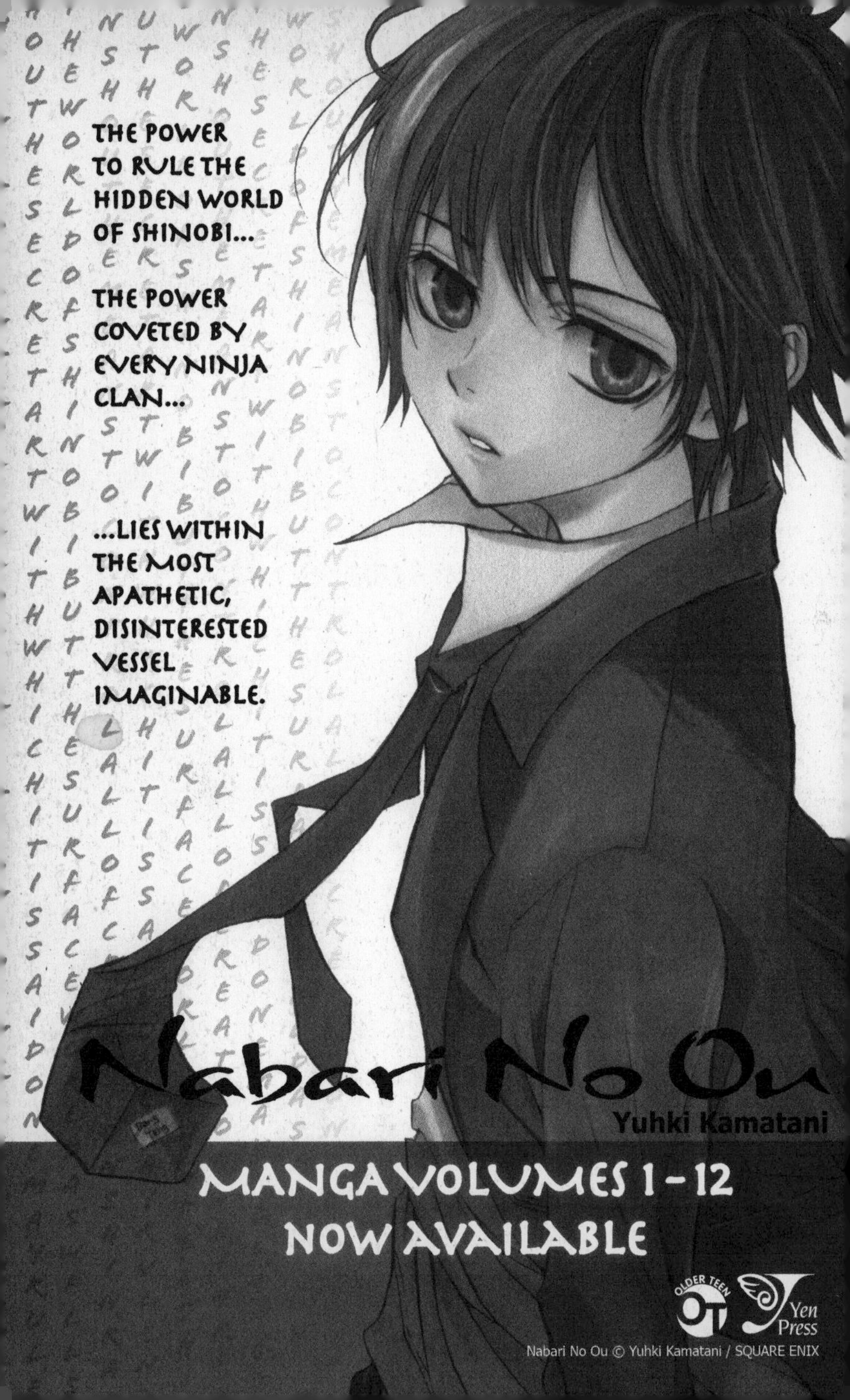
THE POWER TO RULE THE HIDDEN WORLD OF SHINOBI...
THE POWER COVETED BY EVERY NINJA CLAN...
...LIES WITHIN THE MOST APATHETIC, DISINTERESTED VESSEL IMAGINABLE.
Nabari No Ou
Yuhki Kamatani
MANGA VOLUMES 1–12
NOW AVAILABLE
OLDER TEEN OT
Yen Press
Nabari No Ou © Yuhki Kamatani / SQUARE ENIX

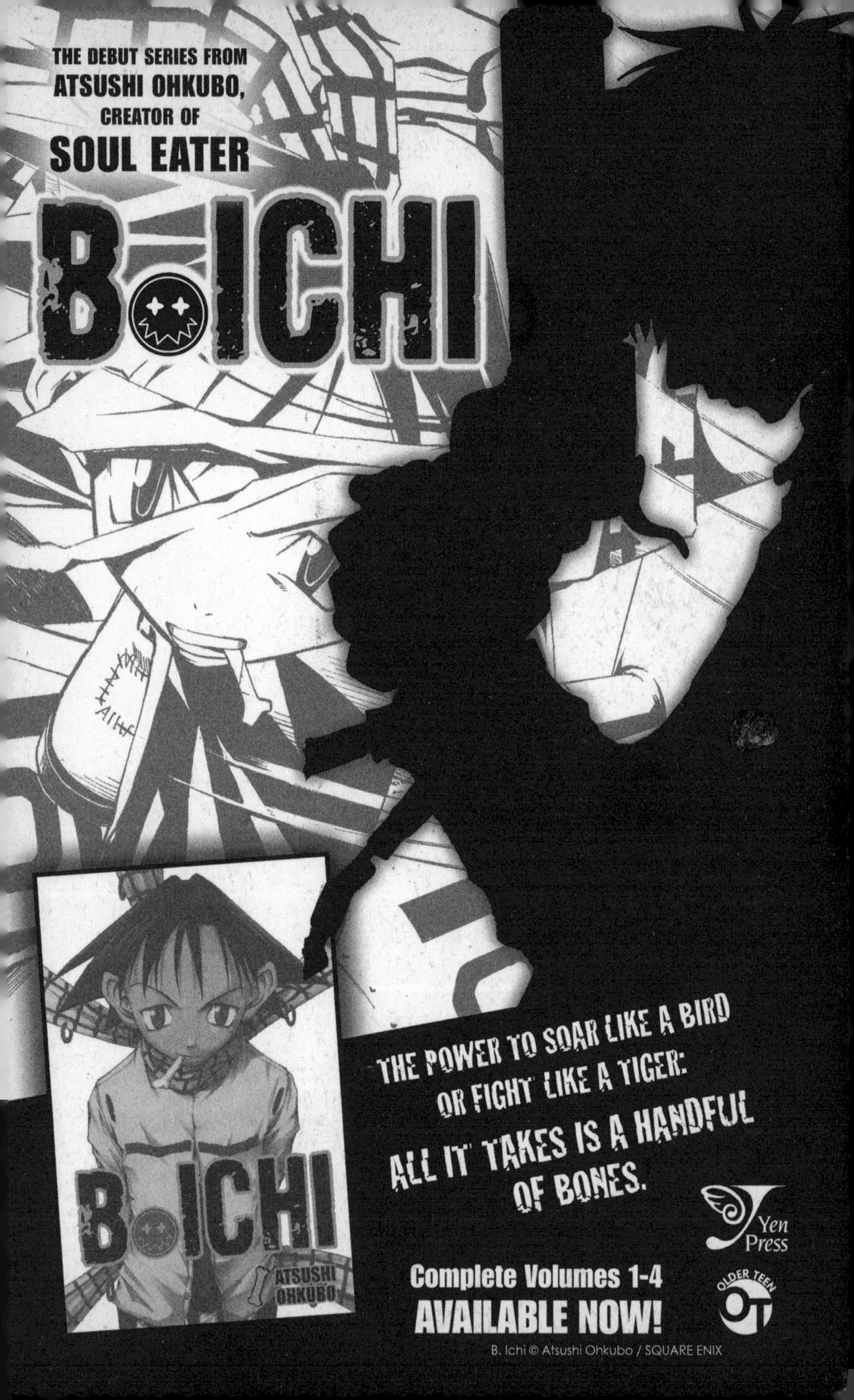
THE DEBUT SERIES FROM
ATSUSHI OHKUBO,
CREATOR OF
SOUL EATER
B. ICHI
B. ICHI
ATSUSHI OHKUBO
THE POWER TO SOAR LIKE A BIRD
OR FIGHT LIKE A TIGER:
ALL IT TAKES IS A HANDFUL
OF BONES.
Yen Press
Complete Volumes 1-4
AVAILABLE NOW!
OLDER TEEN
OT
B. Ichi © Atsushi Ohkubo / SQUARE ENIX

SOUL EATER ⑫

ATSUSHI OHKUBO

Translation: Jack Wiedrick

Lettering: Alexis Eckerman

SOUL EATER Vol. 12 © 2008 Atsushi Ohkubo / SQUARE ENIX. All rights reserved. First published in Japan in 2008 by SQUARE ENIX CO., LTD. English translation rights arranged with SQUARE ENIX CO., LTD. and Hachette Book Group through Tuttle-Mori Agency, Inc.

Translation © 2013 by SQUARE ENIX CO., LTD.

Yen Press
Hachette Book Group
237 Park Avenue, New York, NY 10017

HachetteBookGroup.com
YenPress.com

Yen Press is an imprint of Hachette Book Group, Inc. The Yen Press name and logo are trademarks of Hachette Book Group, Inc.

First Yen Press Edition: January 2013

ISBN: 978-0-316-07293-9

10 9 8 7 6 5 4 3 2 1

BVG

Printed in the United States of America